ANCIENT INDIAN TRADITION & MYTHOLOGY

Translated by

A BOARD OF SCHOLARS

Edited by

G.P. Bhatt

VOLUME 67

ANCIENT INDIAN TRADITION AND MYTHOLOGY

Mahāpurāṇas *Translated into English*

Gen. Ed. Dr. G.C. Tripathi

Founder Eds. Late J.L. Shastri and Late G.P. Bhatt

PUBLISHED VOLUMES

Vols. 1-4	ŚIVA PURĀṆA *Tr.* J.L. Shastri
Vols. 5-6	LIṄGA PURĀṆA *Tr.* J.L. Shastri
Vols. 7-11	BHĀGAVATA PURĀṆA *Tr.* G.V. Tagare
Vols. 12-14	GARUḌA PURĀṆA *Tr.* J.L. Shastri
Vols. 15-19	NĀRADA PURĀṆA *Tr.* G.V. Tagare
Vols. 20-21	KŪRMA PURĀṆA *Tr.* G.V. Tagare
Vols. 22-26	BRAHMĀṆḌA PURĀṆA *Tr.* G.V. Tagare
Vols. 27-30	AGNI PURĀṆA *Tr.* N. Gangadharan
Vols. 31-32	VARĀHA PURĀṆA *Tr.* S. Venkitasubramonia Iyer
Vols. 33-36	BRAHMA PURĀṆA *Tr.* J.L. Shastri
Vols. 37-38	VĀYU PURĀṆA *Tr.* G.V. Tagare
Vols. 39-48	PADMA PURĀṆA *Tr.* N.A. Deshpande
Vols. 49-71	SKANDA PURĀṆA *Ed.* G.P. Bhatt, *Tr. & Annot.* Shridhar Balooni & Pratosh Panda
Vols. 72-73	VĀMANA PURĀṆA *Tr. & Annot.* R.S. Shiva Ganesha Murthy
Vols. 74-76	GAṆEŚA PURĀṆA *Tr. & Annot.* Greg Bailey
Vols. 77-82	BRAHMAVAIVARTA PURĀṆA *Tr. & Annot.* G.P. Bhatt

PURĀṆAS UNDER PREPARATION

Viṣṇu Purāṇa • Harivaṁśa Purāṇa • Bhaviṣya Purāṇa • Matsya Purāṇa • Devī Bhāgavata Purāṇa • Kālika Purāṇa • Mārkaṇḍeya Purāṇa • Viṣṇudharmottara Purāṇa

THE SKANDA PURĀṆA

Part- XIX

Translated and annotated by

DR. G.V. TAGARE

MOTILAL BANARSIDASS PUBLISHERS
PRIVATE LIMITED • DELHI

Reprint : **Delhi, 2017**
First Edition : Delhi, 2003

ISBN: 978-81-208-1984-9

MOTILAL BANARSIDASS
41 U.A. Bungalow Road, Jawahar Nagar, Delhi 110 007
8 Mahalaxmi Chamber, 22 Bhulabhai Desai Road, Mumbai 400 026
120 Royapettah High Road, Mylapore, Chennai 600 004
236, 9th Main III Block, Jayanagar, Bengaluru 560 011
8 Camac Street, Kolkata 700 017
Ashok Rajpath, Patna 800 004
Chowk, Varanasi 221 001

UNESCO COLLECTION OF REPRESENTATIVE WORKS—*Indian Series*
This book has been accepted in the Indian Translation Series of the UNESCO Collection of Representative Works, jointly sponsored by the United Nations Educational, Scientific and Cultural Organization (UNESCO) and the Government of India

MLBD Cataloging-in-Publication Data
The Skanda Purana (Part XIX)
Translation and Annotated by
Dr. G.V. Tagare
Includes Notes
ISBN: 978-81-208-1984-9
I. Hinduism II. Purana III. Skanda
IV. Tagare, Dr. G.V.

Printed in India

by RP Jain at NAB Printing Unit,
A-44, Naraina Industrial Area, Phase I, New Delhi–110028
and published by JP Jain for Motilal Banarsidass Publishers (P) Ltd,
41 U.A. Bungalow Road, Jawahar Nagar, Delhi-110007

PUBLISHER'S NOTE

The purest gems lie hidden in the bottom of the ocean or in the depth of rocks. One has to dive into the ocean or delve into the rocks to find them out. Similarly, truth lies concealed in the language which with the passage of time has become obsolete. Man has to learn that language before he discovers that truth.

But he has neither the means nor the leisure to embark on that course. We have, therefore, planned to help him acquire knowledge by an easier course. We have started the series of Ancient Indian Tradition and Mythology in English Translation. Our goal is to universalize knowledge through the most popular international medium of expression. The publication of the Purāṇas in English Translation is a step towards that goal.

Acknowledgements

It is our pleasant duty to put on record our sincere thanks to Dr. R.N. Dandekar and the UNESCO authorities for their kind encouragement and valuable help in the publication of the volumes in this series.

CONTENTS

SKANDA-PURĀṆA
Book VII: PRABHĀSA KHAṆḌA
Section I: PRABHĀSA-KṢETRA-MĀHĀTMYA

Chapters

ABBREVIATIONS

Common and self-evident abbreviations such as Ch(s)—Chapter(s), p—page, pp—pages, v—verse, vv—verses, Ftn—Footnote, Hist. Ind. Philo.—History of Indian Philosophy are not included in this list.

AGP	S.M. Ali's *The Geography of Purāṇas*, PPH, New Delhi, 1973
AIHT	*Ancient Indian Historical Tradition*, F.E. Pargiter, Motilal Banarsidass (MLBD), Delhi
AITM	*Ancient Indian Tradition and Mythology Series*, MLBD, Delhi
AP	*Agni Purāṇa*, Guru Mandal Edition (GM), Calcutta, 1957
AV	*Atharva Veda*, Svādhyāya Maṇḍal, Aundh
Bdp	*Brahmāṇḍa Purāṇa*, MLBD, Delhi, 1973
BG	*Bhagavadgītā*
BhP	*Bhāgavata Purāṇa*, Bhagavat Vidyapeeth, Ahmedabad
Br	*Brāhmaṇa* (preceded by name such as *Śatapatha*)
BsP	*Bhaviṣya Purāṇa*, Vishnu Shastri Bapat, Wai
BVP	*Brahma Vaivarta Purāṇa*, GM, 1955-57
CC	*Caturvarga Cintāmaṇi* by Hemādri
CVS	*Caraṇa Vyūha Sūtra* by Śaunaka, Com. by Mahīdāsa
DB	*Devī Bhāgavata*, GM, 1960-61
De or GDAMI	*The Geographical Dictionary of Ancient and Medieval India*, N.L. De/Dey, Oriental Reprint, Delhi, 1971
DhS	*Dharma Sūtra* (preceded by the author's name such as Gautama)
GP	*Garuḍa Purāṇa*, ed. R.S. Bhattacharya, Chowkhamba, Varanasi, 1964
GS	*Gṛhya Sūtra* (preceded by the name of the author such as *Āpastamba*)
HD	*History of Dharma Śāstra*, P.V. Kane, G.O.S.
JP	*Purāṇa* (Journal of the Kashiraj Trust), Varanasi
KA	*Kauṭilya Arthaśāstra*
KP	*Kūrma Purāṇa*, Veṅkaṭeśvara Press Edn., Bombay; also Kashiraj Trust Edn., Varanasi, 1971
LP	*Liṅga Purāṇa*, GM, 1960; also MLBD, Delhi, 1981

Manu	*Manusmṛti*
Mbh	*Mahābhārata*, Gītā Press, Gorakhpur, VS 2014
MkP	*Mārkaṇḍeya Purāṇa*
MN	*Mahābhārata Nāmānukramaṇī*, Gītā Press, Gorakhpur, VS 2016
MtP	*Matsya Purāṇa*, GM, 1954
MW	M. Monier-Williams' *Sanskrit-English Dictionary*, MLBD, Delhi, 1976
NP	*Nāradīya* or *Nārada Purāṇa*, Veṅkaṭeśvara Press, Bombay
PdP	*Padma Purāṇa*, GM, 1957-59
PE	*Purāṇic Encyclopaedia*, V. Mani, English Version, MLBD, Delhi, 1975
PR or PRHRC	*Purāṇic Records on Hindu Rites and Customs*, R.C. Hazra, Calcutta, 1948
ṚV	*Ṛg Veda*, Svādhyāya Maṇḍal, Aundh
Śat Br	*Śatapatha Brāhmaṇa*
SC or SMC	*Smṛti Candrikā* by Devanna Bhaṭṭa
SkP	*Skanda Purāṇa*
SP	*Śiva Purāṇa*
VāP	*Vāyu Purāṇa*
VR	*Vālmīki Rāmāyaṇa*
VdP	*Viṣṇudharmottara Purāṇa*
VmP	*Vāmana Purāṇa*
VP	*Viṣṇu Purāṇa*
VrP	*Varāha Purāṇa*

SKANDA PURĀṆA

Book VII: PRABHĀSA KHAṆḌA[1]

Section I: PRABHĀSA-KṢETRA-MĀHĀTMYA

CHAPTER ONE

Queries of Sages

Obeisance to Śrī Gaṇeśa

Now begins the Prabhāsa Khaṇḍa. The first section is called:

PRABHĀSA-KṢETRA-MĀHĀTMYA (The greatness of the sacred place called Prabhāsa)

Om. Obeisance to the Supreme Soul *(Paramātman),* the highest and the most excellent Puruṣa.

Om. Obeisance to the gods Hari, Hara and Hiraṇyagarbha (Brahmā).

Obeisance to (Sages) Vyāsa, Vālmīki, Śuka and Parāśara.

1. The Lord (Śiva) is proclaimed and eulogized everywhere, the primordial PURUṢA and the eternal ancient being. The devotees of Śiva by whom the Lord of Umā, accompanied by Suras has been viewed on the earth by their own eyes, cross

---

1. This last Khaṇḍa of the Skanda Purāṇa (SkP) called Prabhāsa consists of four sections:

   (i) Prabhāsa-Kṣetra-Māhātmya of 365 chapters
   (ii) Vastrāpatha-Kṣetra-Māhātmya of 19 chapters
   (iii) Arbuda-Khaṇḍa of 63 chapters
   (iv) Dvārakā-Māhātmya of 44 chapters

   Prabhāsa is famous on two counts:

   (i) It is the sacred place famous for the Jyotirliṅga called Somanātha.
   (ii) It was the scene of the fratricidal battle among Yādavas and the spot of Kṛṣṇa's death which took place here in B.C. 3102 according to the consensus of Brāhmaṇical Purāṇas. The advent of Kali took place on that very day when Kṛṣṇa passed away (BhP XII. 2. 33) Also vide VāP 49.428-429: MtP 273.49, Viṣṇu P.III.74.241. Hindu calendars-(Pañcāṅgas) give this date as the *Yugādi* (beginning of Kaliyuga).

the extensive terrible ocean of worldly existence and become embellished with prosperity just as *Yajvans* (performers of sacrifices) proceed to heaven (Svarga) through excellent aerial chariots on account of those well-performed *Yajñas*.

2. Obeisance to the Supreme Being, the embodiment of pure consciousness and knowledge. His body is constituted of thirty-six categories[1] (from Parama Śiva down to the element earth). His soul is (consists of) pure, immortal nectar. He is the expanding Nāda (vibrating spiritual sound) and Bindu[2].

3. Despite the presence of Amṛta within the belly, all the Devas die. But despite the presence of poison (Halāhala) in his throat, Lord Śiva continued to be alive. May that Lord Śiva protect you all.

4. At the conclusion of the *Satra* (Sacrifice of a long duration) the great sages of Naimiṣa forest asked the blemish-free Sūta Romaharṣaṇa about the meritorious Purāṇa Saṁhitā:

5. "O highly intelligent Sūta, holy Lord Vyāsa, the foremost among the knowers of Brahman, has been perfectly served and propitiated by you for the sake of acquiring the Itihāsa and the Purāṇas.

6. Due to the exalted majesty and dignity of Dvaipāyana, and on account of his words all your hairs stood on ends through delight and you became known as Romaharṣaṇa.

7. It was to you that the Lord of the sages himself propounded the ancient legend, the Purāṇasaṁhitā.

8. When the Yajña pertaining to Svayaṁbhū (Brahmā) was being elaborately performed, on the *Sutyāha*(the day when Soma Juice is extracted), Hari, the Supreme person manifested himself by a part of himself in your form, for propounding the Purāṇasaṁhitā.

---

1. According to Śaivism there are 36 Tattvas, viz. Śiva, Śakti, Sadāśiva, Īśvara, Śuddha Vidyā, Māyā, Kalā, Vidyā, Rāga, Kāla, Niyati, Puruṣa, Prakṛti, Buddhi (Intelligence), Ahaṁkāra (Ego), Manas (Mind), ears (power of hearing), also powers of touch, of taste, of vision, of smelling, of speech, feet (power of locomotion), hands, anus, penis, five objects of senses and five elements, viz. earth, water, fire, wind and ether or firmament.

   The order varies with different texts. Vaiṣṇavism has accepted a similar list of 35 Tattvas. It is noteworthy that both -isms have accepted the Tattvas of the Sāṅkhya system in toto.

2. According to Śaivism it is not the Big Bang which created the world. They say a subtle vibrating *sound* (Nāda) manifested a *Bindu* which expanded into this universe.

9. The Brāhmī Yātrā (religious pilgrimage pertaining to Brahmā) has already been heard by us, in the context of Prabhāsa-Kṣetra-Māhātmya (the greatness of the sacred place called Prabhāsa[1]) in the Purāṇa propounded by Skanda.

10. Now, O holy Sir, O Purāṇa specialist, it behoves you to expound the Yātrā pertaining to Viṣṇu and Rudra along with all the themes thereof."

11. On hearing the words of the sages, Sūta, the most excellent one among those conversant with Purāṇas, bowed down his head to Vyāsa, the son of Satyavatī and said:

Romaharṣaṇa said:

12-16. After bowing down to the Supreme Soul, the Almighty Lord, I shall propound the story with two *Vidhās* (modes of narration) and two *Śarīras* (bodies, i.e. units). Śrīvatsa marks his chest. He is the source of origin of the worlds. He is Hari with OM as his form. He is incomprehensible and unmeasurable. He is the Lord-preceptor. He is free from impurities. His resort is free from impurities. He is *Haṁsa* (pure spiritual being), *Śuciṣad* (abiding in the purest essence). He pervades the entire firmament. He is Śiva, the bestower of all things, *Udāsīna* (indifferent), free from worldly ties and physical extension. He is unsullied. He is the vacuity (*Śūnya*). He is of the form of *Bindu* (point whence the universe evolves). He is worthy of being meditated upon. He is one without (beyond) meditation. They say that he is and he is not, that he is far-off and also very close. He is the greatest refulgence worthy of being comprehended through the mind. He is called Puruṣa who is identical with *Jagat* (Universe). He is seated in the lotus of the heart. He is in the form of fiery splendour. He is devoid of *Indriyas* (sense-organs).

17. The story is couched in the celestial language. It has the Veda for its basis. It has five Sandhis (divisions, joints such as *Mukha, Pratimukha* etc.). It is embellished with six ornaments (figures of speech).

18. It possesses seven *Sādhanas* (means of achieving objectives). It is coloured (brightened) with the eight *Rasas* and

1. This Probably refers to some other Purāṇa like *Nārada*.

Guṇas. Further, the nine Guṇas can be seen spread over throughout. It is free from ten defects.

19. It is embellished with Vibhāṣās (alternatives). Similarly it is completely converging into a single purpose. It is pleasing to the mind. It has the five Kāraṇas (purposes). It is approved by the four Karaṇas (means of achieving objects).

20. It is further divided into two aspects. It bestows successive waves of knowledge (consciousness). Listen ye all to the meritorious story narrated by Vyāsa. It is destructive of all sins.

21. On hearing it even a man of evil actions attains the greatest goal. He will be relieved of the three types of miseries. He shall be freed from all distressing worries.

22. Never should one narrate this meritorious story to a *Nāstika* (atheist). It should be propounded to a twice-born one who is quiescent and faithful.

23. It should be known that only he is entitled to hear (or read) this scripture and none else, for whom the consecratory rites beginning with *Niṣeka* (impregnation by dropping the semen within the womb) and ending with obsequial rites at the cremation ground, are enjoined with relevant Mantras.

24. The purity of a Brāhmaṇa is the purity in all the four sides (his father and mother, wife's father and mother). To this scripture approved by the Vedas, all men of good conduct are entitled.

25-26. Just as Maheśvara, the Lord of Devas, is the most excellent one among Suras, just as Gaṅgā is the greatest of all rivers, just as Brāhmaṇa is the greatest of all castes, just as Oṁkāra is the foremost among all *Akṣaras* (syllables), just as mother is the greatest among those worthy of adoration, just as father is the greatest (most respectable) of all elders, so also the Purāṇa narrated by Skanda is the most important of all scriptural texts.

27.[1] The *Skanda Purāṇa* was formerly narrated by the Pinākabearing Lord (Śiva) in front of Pārvatī, in the presence of Brahmā and others on a peak of Kailāsa.

28. It was then narrated by Pārvatī to Ṣaṇmukha (Skanda), by him to the Gaṇa Nandin and to Kumāra by Nandin and by him to the intelligent Vyāsa.

---

1. Verses 27-29 relate the transmission of this Purāṇa from Śiva to Romaharṣaṇa, the Sūta.

29. It was narrated to me by Vyāsa and I shall propound it to you all.

30. You are all endowed with good mental attitude. You are all great sages. Hence I am sincerely eager to propound the *Skanda Saṁhitā* to you.

CHAPTER TWO

Merit in Gifting Purāṇa Texts[1]

The sages said:

1. Describe the characteristic features of *Kathā* (story) and its good merits and demerits in detail. How shouid one assess the disticnctive characteristics of the composition of sages and those of ordinary persons? How should it be understood, O highly intelligent one? We wish to hear.

Sūta said:

2. Now I shall succinctly describe the due order of the Purāṇas, their characteristic features, number and the differences mentioned.

3. Formerly the Grandfather of *Amaras* (Devas) performed a severe penance. Then the Vedas along with the six Aṅgas, *Padas* (words) and *Kramas* (special manners in the recitation of Vedic passages) manifested themselves.

4-5a. Then the entire range of the Purāṇas containing all the sacred texts and extending to a hundred crores (of verses) manifested themselves. The Purāṇa constituted of eternal sounds and words is meritorious. They (the Purāṇas) came out of the mouth of Brahmā.

5b-7.[2] They are: (1) Brahmapurāṇa, (2) Viṣṇu Purāṇa,

---

1. This religious incentive to gift Purāṇa manuscripts has resulted in the preservation and spread of these ancient texts.
2. This list of Mahāpurāṇas includes both Śiva and Vāyu Purāṇas which are otherwise disjunctively mentioned. The inclusion of both led to the exclusion of Padma Purāṇa which is always included as a Mahāpurāṇa elsewhere.

(3) Śiva Purāṇa, (4) Bhāgavata Purāṇa, (5) Bhaviṣya Purāṇa, (6) Nāradīya Purāṇa, (7) Mārkaṇḍeya Purāṇa, (8) Āgneya Purāṇa, (9) Brahmavaivarta Purāṇa, (10) Liṅga Purāṇa, (11) Varāha Purāṇa, (12) Skanda Purāṇa, (13) Vāmana Purāṇa, (14) Kūrma Purāṇa, (15) Matsya Purāṇa, (16) Garuḍa Purāṇa, (17) Vāyavīya Purāṇa, and then (Padma Purāṇa) is called the eighteenth Purāṇa that is destructive of all sins.

8-9. Formerly there was only one Brahmāṇḍa (?Purāṇa) consisting of a hundred crores (of verses). In every Yuga, Vedavyāsa, the direct partial incarnation of Nārāyaṇa, divides it into eighteen Purāṇas and propounds it to the world.

10. Others, Upapurāṇas[1], also were narrated by that sage. I shall mention them briefly to you. May they be listened to and understood.

[List of Upapurāṇas]

11-15. The first one is that narrated by *Sanatkumāra*. Thereafter is the *Narasiṁha*. The third one is indicated as *Skanda* (or *Nanda)* which is recounted by Kumāra (Skanda). The fourth one is called *Śivadharma* directly proclaimed by Nandīśa. Then the wonderful one narrated by Durvāsas. Thereafter what is narrated by *Nārada*. Then *Kāpila* and *Mānava*. Then what is narrated by Uśanas. Then *Brahmāṇḍa*.[2] The next one is *Varuṇa*. Then the other one called *Kālikā*. Then *Māheśvara, Sāṁba* and *Saura* having the collection of all topics. What is narrated by Parāśara is great. Then *Mārīca*. Then what is called *Bhārgava*. These are the Upapurāṇas mentioned, O excellent Brāhmaṇas.

The sages said:

16. O Sūta, kindly mention the number of the Purāṇas in detail and due order, O Sūta, O knower of distinct features of Dāna and Dharma.

---

1. Traditionally 18 Upapurāṇas are mentioned and their relation with a particular Mahāpurāṇa is (many times wrongly) presumed. The lists of Upapurāṇas in Devībhāgavata, Kūrma Purāṇa etc. differ *inter se.* Hazra records a list of 100 Upapurāṇas *(Studies in Upapurāṇas)*. Some Mahāpurāṇas e.g. Matsya (53.59-62,) mention Upapurāṇas like Narasiṁha, Nandī, Āditya and Sāmba. Some Upapurāṇas have the same names as the Mahāpurāṇas as found in the list here in this text.

   It is a complex problem as many of the Upapurāṇas are unpublished.
2. This is different from the Mahāpurāṇa called Brahmāṇḍa.

Sūta said :

17. That immanent soul of the universe narrated to Manu this alone. The ancient Puruṣa mentioned this in this Purāṇa. Understand what he said:

18. Brahmāṇḍa Purāṇa is the most ancient of all scriptural texts. Thereafter the Vedas came out of his mouth.

19. There was only one Purāṇa in that Kalpāntara. It was the means of achieving the three aims (i.e. Virtue, Wealth and Love). It is meritorious and extended to a hundred crore (of verses).

20-23. When all the worlds were completely burned, at the time of Pralaya, Kṛṣṇa, in the form of the infinite one, collected together the four Vedas along with their Aṅgas, the Purāṇas, the detailed texts of Nyāya, Mīmāṁsās and Dharmaśāstra and retained them within himself. At the beginning of the next Kalpa, he, assuming the form of a fish in the vast ocean, told the entire tract of lores to Brahmā, endowed with divine vision. Brahmā endowed with the knowledge and vision of the three divisions of time (past, present and future) narrated it to all sages. Thereafter, all the scriptures and Purāṇas became current.

24. Then in due course, Hari in the form of Vyāsa, will summarize and propagate the eighteen Purāṇas.

25. Always in every Dvāpara Yuga, the Purāṇas extended to four hundred thousand (verses). Kṛṣṇa expounds them in eighteen different forms (texts) on the earth.

26. Even today, in the celestial world, it extends to a hundred crores (of verses). The essence thereof is summarized into four hundred thousand (verses) (in this world).

[Mahāpurāṇas: Extent, Contents]

27. Now these are the eighteen Purāṇas, O excellent sages. I shall mention their names and the number (of verses)[1] too.

---

1. P.V. Kane in HD,V.ii. pp.831-832 gives a comparative Table of number of verses in each Purāṇa as stated in Mahāpurāṇas.The tabular statement shows that there is no consensus in this matter.Thus according to MtP and VāP and SkP here Brahma Purāṇa has 10,000 verses, also according to Nārada P. 92.31, Agni P. 272.1 gives 25,000 as the number of verses in Brahma P. Presumably the authors of these Purāṇas had different versions of Brahma P. before them.

28. The entire thing mentioned earlier to Marīci by Brahmā is called *Brahma Purāṇa.* It contains ten thousand (verses).

29. He who copies it in writing and makes a gift of it along with *Jaladhenu* on the Full-Moon day in the month of Vaiśākha is honoured in the world of Brahmā.

30. When this universe was a golden lotus, the incidents therein were collected together and that Purāṇa is called *Padma Purāṇa* by learned men.

31. The *Padma Purāṇa* contains fifty-five thousand verses. He who makes a gift of it along with a golden lotus and gingelly seeds in the month of Jyeṣṭha, obtains the merit of a horse-sacrifice.

32. Based on the incidents of the Vārāhakalpa[1], the Lord, greater than the greatest, recounted all the virtues and holy rites. They know that Purāṇa as *Vaiṣṇava (Viṣṇu) Purāṇa.*

33. This Purāṇa is beautified through the activities of Viṣṇu. This is proclaimed as the Purāṇa consisting of twenty-three thousand verses.

34. He who makes a gift of it along with *Ghṛtadhenu* on the bright full-moon day in Āṣāḍha attains the region of Viṣṇu.

35. Vāyu recounted the holy rites and virtues in the context of Śrutakalpa as the background. This Purāṇa is *Vāyavīya Purāṇa.* It contains *Rudramāhātmya* also.

36. It consists of twenty-four thousand verses and many events are recounted in it. Virtue, wealth, love and salvation are dealt with along with the good conduct of the well-behaved.

37. He who makes a gift of it on the Full-Moon day in the month of Śrāvaṇa along with *Guḍadhenu* and curd to a Brāhmaṇa burdened with a large family, shall become a purified soul and he will live in Śivaloka for the period of a Kalpa.

38. He is reborn as a man once again. He will be a Brāhmaṇa, the most excellent one among those conversant with the Vedas. He will be an expert in the Vedic lore and the principles and

---

1. This Purāṇa indicates that different Mahāpurāṇas describe events that took place in different Kalpas. Thus *Vaiṣṇava* or *Viṣṇu Purāṇa* refers to Vārāha Kalpa, *Vāyu* P. to Śruta Kalpa, *Bhāgavata* P. to Sārasvata Kalpa.

meanings thereof and be the foremost among scholars of the themes and principles of writing glosses.

39. That Purāṇa is called *Bhāgavata* where Dharma is described on the basis of Gāyatrī.[1] The killing of the demon Vṛtra is also contained in it.

40. It also contains the events about men and Devaṣ who live in the Sārasvata Kalpa. It is holy and there is meritorious description of marriages too.

41. He who copies it and makes a gift of it on the Full-Moon day in the month of Bhādrapada along with a gold replica of a lion attains the greatest goal.

42. It is glorified as a Purāṇa containing eighteen thousand verses.

43. That is *Nāradīya Purāṇa* in which Nārada expounds Dharma as current in Bṛhatkalpa. It consists of twenty-five thousand verses.

44. He who copies it and makes a gift of it on the Full-Moon day in the month of Āśvina along with a cow attains the highest Siddhi in this world and in the next. He obtains all his cherished desires. No doubt need be entertained in this respect.

45. That which contains discussion about Dharma and Adharma with reference to (and in consultation with) birds[2] is called the *Mārkaṇḍeya Purāṇa*. It contains nine thousand verses.

46. He who copies it and makes a gift of it along with a gold replica of an elephant on the full-moon day of the month of Kārttika, attains the merit of the Pauṇḍarīka Yajña.

47. What is narrated to Vasiṣṭha by Agni taking into account (and with reference to) the events of Īśānakalpa is called *Āgneya Purāṇa*.

48. He who copeis it and makes a gift of it along with a golden lotus and *Tiladhenu* (cow made of gingelly seeds) in the

---

1. It appears that the author of this Purāṇa has not seen or read the *Bhāgavata* P. or had a very different version containing no reference to Kṛṣṇa's life.The ruse of claiming Sārasvata Kalpa for such glaring differences comes in handy to the author.
2. This reference to birds is given in the *Nārada Purāṇa* which also gives the list of contents of this Purāṇa.

month of Mārgaśīrṣa in accordance with the injunctions, obtains the merit of all Kratus. It (the Purāṇa) contains sixteen thousand verses.

49-50. In the context of the events of Aghorakalpa, the Four-faced Lord of the universe explained to Manu the characteristics of all the Bhūtas (living beings, elements, spirits) on the basis of the greatness of Āditya. It is called *Bhaviṣya Purāṇa* because mostly future events are described. It contains fourteen thousand five hundred verses.

51. He who is free from jealousy and makes a gift of the Purāṇa on the full-moon day in the month of Pauṣa along with a pot of jaggery, shall obtain the merit of Agniṣṭoma.

52-53. With reference to the events of the Rathantara Kalpa, the story of Brahma-Varāha along with the greatness of Kṛṣṇa was narrated by Sāvarṇi to Nārada. It is called *Brahmavaivarta Purāṇa*. It contains eighteen thousand verses. He who makes a gift of *Brahmavaivarta Purāṇa* to an excellent Brāhmaṇa on the full-moon day in the month of Māgha, is honoured in the world of Brahmā.

54-55. Lord Maheśvara staying in the middle of a fiery Liṅga expounds (the Puruṣārthas) Virtue, Wealth, Love and Salvation in the context of Āgneya Kalpa. It is called *Liṅga Purāṇa* by Brahmā himself.

56. It contains eleven thousand verses. He who makes a gift of it on the full-moon day in the month of Phālguna along with *Tiladhenu* attains identity with Śiva.

57. With reference to the greatness of Mahāvarāha Viṣṇu expounds (virtue etc.) to the Earth. It is called *Varāhapurāṇa.*

58. O excellent sages, it is in the context of Dhanya (a blessed one), the son of Manu. That Purāṇa contains twenty-five thousand verses.

59. A devotee should make a gold replica of Garuḍa and give it along with *Tiladhenu* to a Brāhmaṇa of a large family. He attains the region of Viṣṇu with the favour of Varāha.

60-61. It is with reference to the religious practices of (the followers) of Maheśvara and with special reference to the Six-faced Lord. It describes in details the events which happened in Tatpuruṣa Kalpa. That Purāṇa called *Skanda* is said to consist of eighty-one thousand one hundred verses. It is thus recited among mortals (people).

62. He who copies it and makes a gift of it along with a trident made of gold when the Sun enters Capricorn, attains the region of Śiva.

63. With reference to the greatness of Trivikrama as the basis, the Four-faced Lord expounds the three aims of life. It is glorified as *Vāmana Purāṇa*.

64. This Purāṇa contains ten thousand verses. It is a Śaiva Purāṇa consisting of (the events of) Kaurmakalpa.

65. He who makes a gift of it on the autumnal equinox along with gold and garments, covered with a silk cloth and accompanied by a cow, attains the region of Viṣṇu.

66-68. In Rasātala, in the presence of Indra and sages, Janārdana, in the form of a Tortoise expounded the greatness of (the Puruṣārthas, viz.) Virtue, Wealth, Love and Liberation, in the Lakṣmīkalpa in the context of the interlude of Indradyumna. It (*Kūrma Purāṇa*) consists of seventeen thousand verses. He who makes the gift of the *Kūrma Purāṇa* along with a gold replica of tortoise, shall obtain the merit of gifting a thousandcows.

69-70. For the propagation of the Vedas at the beginning of a Kalpa, Janārdana assumed the form of a Fish and expounded to Manu the events of seven Kalpas in the course of the description of Narasiṁha. O sage of holy rites, know this as the *Matsya Purāṇa*. It contains fourteen thousand verses.

71. If anyone makes the gift (of this *Purāṇa*) covered with a silk cloth on the day of equinox along with a gold replica of a fish and a cow, it is as though the entire earth has been gifted by him.

72. In Garuḍa Kalpa, Garuḍa came out of *Viśvāṇḍa* (Cosmic Egg). Kṛṣṇa expounded this Purāṇa on that as the basis. It is called *Garuḍa Purāṇa*.

73. It is recited in (i.e. consists of) nineteen thousand verses. He who makes a gift of it along with a gold replica of a swan in the latter *Ayana* (i.e. Southern transit) [If *pare* is taken to mean "the great", then the *Ayana* will be the Northern] one achieves the principal Siddhi and a stay in Śiva Loka.

74. Brahmā again expounded the greatness of the Cosmic Egg. That is *Brahmāṇḍa Purāṇa* containing twelve thousand two hundred verses.

75. A detailed description of the future Kalpas is found therein. That *Brahmāṇḍa Purāṇa* is narrated by Brahmā.

76-77a. A man who makes the gift of that Purāṇa along with two woollen cloths, attains the merit of a thousand Rājasūyas. If the gift is accompanied by a gold replica of a cow, it bestows the region of Brahmā.

77b-78. Thus (the whole range of Purāṇas) was spoken by Vyāsa of miraculous deeds in four hundred thousand verses briefly in Dvāpara, O Brāhmaṇas, for the sake of the benefit of all the worlds.

79. The same tract of literature called Purāṇa among the celestial beings extends to a hundred crores.

[Upapurāṇas: Extent and Contents]

Now I shall narrate the different Upapurāṇas that have been established in the world.

80. The description of Narasiṁha has been included in *Padma Purāṇa.* It contains eighteen thousand verses. It is called *Nārasiṁha* (Upa) *Purāṇa.*

81. (The text) wherein the greatness (of the Lord) has been described by Kārttikeya to Nandin has become well-known in the world as *Nandi Purāṇa,* O excellent Brāhmaṇas.

82. O Brāhmaṇas of holy Vratas, that Upapurāṇa of Sāṁba is famous in the world and the story therein pertains to Sāṁba.

83. Thus the *Āditya* Upapurāṇa is mentioned there itself. It is seen as separate from the eighteen Upapurāṇas, O excellent Brāhmaṇas, know that it has been taken out of these.

84. There are five Aṅgas (limbs or sections) of the Purāṇa. They are: *Sarga* (creation), *Pratisarga* (subsidiary creation), *Vaṁśa* (the royal lineage), *Manvantaras* (the periods of the rule of Manus), *Vaṁśānuvaṁśa Carita* (the description of the dynasties of Sages etc.). Thus a Purāṇa has five characteristics.

85. Another interpretation : the five characteristics are the description of the greatness of Brahmā, Viṣṇu, Arka (the Sun god) and Rudra and the annihilation of the universe. All these five are seen in a Purāṇa.

86. In all the Purāṇas virtue, wealth, love and salvation as well as the benefit contained in them have been explained.

87. In the Sāttvika Kalpas the greatness of Hari is supreme. They know that the greatness of Brahmā reigns supreme in the Rājasa Kalpas.

88. Similarly the greatness of Śiva is to be found in the

Tāmasa Kalpas. In a Purāṇa of a mixed nature, the greatness of Sarasvatī and Pitṛs is narrated.

89. Among the eighteen Purāṇas, Lord Viṣṇu is extolled in four (Purāṇas), Brahmā and Ravi each in two and Lord Śiva in the remaining ones.

90. O excellent Brāhmaṇas, I think that Purāṇa is steady (unchangeable) like the Vedas. All the Vedas are established in the Purāṇas. There is no doubt about it.

91. The Veda is afraid of the men of insufficient knowledge of the lore and feels: "Oh! This man will move and dislodge me." It (Veda) has been rendered firm and steady formerly by means of Itihāsas and Purāṇas.

92. What is not seen in the Vedas, O Brāhmaṇas, what is not seen in the Smṛtis and what is not seen in both of them is being sung about in the Purāṇas.

93. A Brāhmaṇa who knows all the four Vedas along with their Aṅgas and the Upaniṣads, but who does not know the Purāṇa is not learned.

94. After composing the eighteen Purāṇas, the son of Satyavatī (Vyāsa) wrote the narrative (epic) of Bhārata rendering it strengthened through the topics of the Vedas.

95-97. It was propounded by the noble soul by means a hundred thousand verses at the end of Dvāpara.

Brahmā composed the story of Rāma in a hundred crores of verses. He spoke (transmitted) it unto Nārada and through him to Vālmīki and Vālmīki narrated the excellent story of Rāma that enables one to achieve virtue, wealth and love in this world in one-fourth of a Lakṣa of verses i.e. in twenty- five thousand verses.

98. Thus these twenty-five thousand verses are glorified as meritorious. Learned men understood everything about the ancient Kalpas from the Purāṇa.

99-100. In accordance with the demands of the age *(Kāla)* the Itihāsas and Purāṇas differ, O leading Brāhmaṇas. Different versions of the Purāṇas, *Skanda, Brahmāṇḍa* and *Liṅga* are current in the Vāraha Kalpa. Indeed Brahmāṇḍa is different in eighteen ways.

101. Therefore, the Purāṇas came to be eighteen in the world. The splendid *Liṅga Purāṇa* was divided into eleven different sections in Dvāpara.

[Khaṇḍas of the Skanda Purāṇa]

102. 'The intelligent Vedavyāsa has divided the *Skanda Purāṇa* into seven Khaṇḍas. The number of verses in the *Skanda* is eighty-one thousand one hundred.

103. The first Book or Khaṇḍa is called *Māheśvara Khaṇḍa*. It contains the greatness of Skanda. The second one is remembered as *Vaiṣṇava Khaṇḍa*.

104. The third one is mentioned as *Brahma Khaṇḍa*. It briefly expounds the creation (of the universe). The fourth one is cited as one containing the greatness of Kāśī (*Kāśī Khaṇḍa*).

105. The fifth one is glorified as describing the greatness of Revā along with that of Ujjayinī. The sixth one is *Nāgara Kalpa* (Khaṇḍa). It indicates the greatness of the Tīrthas.

106. O Brāhmaṇas, this seventh book is remembered as *Prābhāsika* (Khaṇḍa). Each of these Books is glorified as containing twelve thousand verses (approximately).

107. In this *Prābhāsika Khaṇḍa* all the details of holy spots, greatness of the Tīrthas and greatness of Śaṅkara are explained.

108. Of course the greatness of the other Devas too is mentioned.

Thus, O Brāhmaṇas, the different Purāṇas are succinctly told.

109. One who reads this enumeration of the eighteen Purāṇas at the time of the offering of *Havyas* and *Kavyas* goes to the abode of Hari.

110. This is indeed the storehouse of renown. This is a favourite of the Pitṛs. This gives satisfaction to the Devas always, like nectar. This destroys great sins of men.

CHAPTER THREE

Queries Made by Devī

The sages said:

1-3. The regular creation and the counter-creation (or subsidiary creation) have been mentioned by Your Holiness. So also the story of the main dynasties and races (of sages) (Genealogies of kings and sages), the order or sequence of the

Purāṇas, the extent of Manvantaras, the magnitude of the cosmic egg and the nature of the circle of the luminaries have been described factually.

Now we wish to hear from you the details of the Tīrthas. O Sūtaja, It behoves you to describe entirely and factually all the auspicious and evil-destroying Tīrthas on the earth.

Sūta said:

4-5. This same question was formerly asked by the Goddess on the excellent peak of Kailāsa that possesses different kinds of gems. It is variegated due to various kinds of minerals. It is full of all types of trees and creepers. It shines with all sorts of flowers. Yakṣas, Vidyādharas and groups of celestial damsels frequent it.

6-9. There were present there the following: Brahmā, Viṣṇu, Skanda, Nandin, the leading Gaṇas, the Moon, the Sun along with the Planets, the Galaxies of Stars, the group of Stars round the Pole-star, Vāyu, Varuṇa, Kubera the bestower of wealth, Īśāna, Agni, Indra, Yama, Nirṛti, the Rivers, all the Oceans, Mountains, Serpents, Brāhmī and other Mothers, sages, ascetics, the Tīrthas in their personified forms, the holy places and shrines as well as Dānavas, Asuras, Daityas, Piśācas, Bhūtas (evil spirits) and Rākṣasas.

10. There was a divine throne there, a hundred Yojanas (a Yojana=12 Kms) in extent. Its refulgence was like that of ten million Suns. It was adorned with jewels and pearls.

11. It was decorated with lotuses and lilies. It was resorted to by Siddhas and Kinnaras. By means of millions of its white umbrellas, it covered up all the regions and quarters.

12. In the center thereof, there was a *Sarvatobhadra* (temple-like structure with doors on all sides) with ornamental gates. It was surrounded by thousands, ten thousands, hundred thousands and millions of Rudras.

13. It was covered with peaks and ramparts shining with crystal-clear pearls. There were sentries like Nandīśvara, Mahākāla and others.

14. It was adorned with excellent banners producing resonant sounds with tiny tinkling bells. There were awnings and pieces of umbrella-like stretches with pearl strings hanging down.

15. Its beauty was enhanced by means of mirrors having

the lustre of hanging bells and chowries. Big pots had been placed at the entrances and were decorated with tender sprouts and jewels.

16. Experts in the science of ornamental decorations had embellished it with shining powders of jewels. There were Svastika-shaped fittings embellished with creeper-like designs above the Liṅga-like fittings.

17. In the assembly hall there were hundreds of thrones and refulgent altars. Groups of Rudras and Rudra-girls were seated there.

18. It was adorned with white lotuses with hundred thousands of petals. Flowers had been scattered all round and the Apsarās had occupied all those places.

19-20. Saffron waters were sprinkled. The place was fumigated with incense sticks. The entire area resounded with the sounds of the notes of flutes, lutes, Gomukhas and Mṛdaṅga drums, mouth organs, the sounds of conchs and Bherī drums, Dundubhi (war drums) etc. The roaring groups of Gaṇas filled the place (as if) with the sounds of rumbling clouds.

21. There was the sound of the prayers of the Gaṇas along with chanting of Sāman. They were handsome to look at and their voice was at its highest pitch. Now and then, gruff sounds came out of them laconically in the midst of their songs.

22. All the quarters were filled with sounds of bellowing of bulls, neighing and trumpeting of horses and elephants and tinkling of girdles and anklets.

23-24. The palatial abode of Śaṅkara was glorious with all rich equipments. It was resonant here and there with the notes and sounds of flutes, lutes and Mṛdaṅgas.

In the eastern wing (of the hall) was the personified form of Ṛgveda with the lustre of sapphire embellished with divine ornaments and smeared with divine unguents. It was refulgent with self-luminosity.

25. Yajurveda who resembled the lustre of pure crystal was present in the northern wing. He had a huge body with large arms and he wore divine earrings.

26. The eternal Sāmaveda was present in the western wing. He was glorious in red robes having the lustre of ruby.

27-28a. Atharvaveda wore a garland. He appeared with the embellishments of Gīta (Music) and ornaments.

He was as dark-complexioned as collyrium. His eyes were reddish-brown and the neck red. The hairs were greenish and the body was huge.

28b-30a. God Brahmā was himself present there along with these: Itihāsas, all the Purāṇas, the six Aṅgas, Upaniṣads, Chandas, Mīmāṁsā, Āraṇyakas, Svāhākāra, Vaṣaṭkāra and the (their) esoteric secrets.

30b-32. Lord Śiva shone there with the eternal glorious refulgence of ten million moons. In a respectful way, he was attended upon by Suras who worship the Mantras in the form of Śaktis endowed with supreme Yogic powers, by means of thousand-petalled lotuses. He was adored by Rudras and Gaṇas. He was respectfully bowed to by Brahmā, Viṣṇu and Indra who served him with moving of fans and waving of chowries.

33. His (Śiva's) soul is perfectly contented with nectarine (spiritual) knowledge. This excellent Dvija (Twice-born one i.e. Parama Haṁsa) who shines in the lotus-like hearts of Yogins enlightens them with rich Yogic powers and supernatural achievements.

34. There stays the Moon-crested Lord, the destroyer of the darkness of ignorance, embellished with thirty-six Tattvas, giving happiness to all.

35. The goddess with the refulgence of heated gold is seated on his lap. He is adored by the groups of Yoginīs and the Suras and Kinnaras who are the aspirant devotees.

36. She is endowed with all excellent characteristic features and embellished with all kinds of ornaments. She is the perpetual bestower of Yogic powers and of the worldly prosperity and salvation.

37-38. Pārvatī is the root of origin of all spiritual felicity with wonder. She looked at the face of the Lord whose eyes were bedimmed with tears of joy displaying the state of enjoyment of bliss. Smilingly Goddess Satī of charming eyes, spoke these sweet words with the palms joined together in veneration:

The Devī said:

39. O Lord of the worlds, you have been sought by me, with the anxiousness for living in the course of hundreds and thousands of crores of lives.

40. O Lord of the worlds, though I have occupied half of your person with a desire to meditate on your countenance, O Lord, I have however not achieved the perfect realization of it.

[Devī's prayer:]

41. O Lord of Devas, of infinite forms, obeisance to you. Obeisance to you who are the secret of the Vedas, Obeisance to one who is eulogized by the Vedas.

42. Obeisance to you who loves to stay in cremation ground perpetually. Obeisance to the Lord moving about in the sky. Obeisance to the secret of the Jyeṣṭha Sāman. Obeisance to the Lord fond of Śatarudra prayer.

43. Obeisance to the Lord who adopted bull as his emblem, to the Lord who holds the Yajur-veda. Obeisance to the Lord wearing the garland wreathed out of crores of Cosmic Eggs, to the Lord identical with the sky (or the soul of the sky).

44. Obeisance to the Lord with the neck appearing variegated with jewels. Obeisance to the one who has achieved all objectives. Obeisance to the one who is the real form of the Vedas, to the one who likes the spiritual achievement of the twice-born.

45. Obeisance to the one in the form of transformation of man and woman. Obeisance to the one wearing the crescent moon. Obeisance to Agni with Homa, to Āditya and Varuṇa.

46. Obeisance to Pṛthivī and also to the Space, to the Wind, to the Dīkṣita (the initiated one). Obeisance to *Saṁyoga* (Contact) and to *Viyoga* (Separation), to *Dhātṛ* (Creator), *Kartṛ* (Doer), *Apahārin* or destroyer.

47. Obeisance to the Lord with the brilliant trident in the hand, to the one who holds the *Brahma-Daṇḍa* (the staff of Brahmā). Obeisance to the Lord of Lords. Obeisance to the Lord of the great.

48. Obeisance to Kālāgnirudra (Rudra, the Fire of destruction), the inhabitant of the seven worlds. You are the ultimate goal of all the living beings. Obeisance to the Lord of goblins.

49. O holy Lord Rudra, obeisance to you. O holy Lord Śiva, obeisance to you. Obeisance to you, the greater than the greatest. O Lord, O one greater than the greatest, obeisance to you.

50. O Lord, you have been pained by me due to the fickleness of my tongue. O Maheśāna, that should be pardoned. Obeisance to you, O Lord endowed with the divine knowledge.

Īśvara said:

51. O goddess, you are on my lap. Why should your eyes be turbid with tears ? What is it that is yet incomplete in regard to you. I shall make it full.

52. Mention the boon. Welfare unto you. By this prayer (I am pleased), O lady of holy vows. I will give you (everything) undoubtedly. O Maheśvarī, share off your sorrow.

53. O goddess, you are one with Kāla and one without Kalā. O goddess of Devas, I do not see anything without you in the whole universe consisting of mobile and immobile beings whether gross or subtle.

54. O Gaurī, I am abiding in your heart. You are stationed in my heart. I am your brother, son, kinsman and husband.

55. You are my sister, wife, daughter, kinswoman and daughter-in-law. I am the performer of Yajña and the Lord of Yajña. You are Śraddhā (faith) and also the Dakṣiṇā.

56. I am Oṁkāra and Vaṣaṭkāra. I am Sāman, Ṛk and Yajus. I am Agni, Hotṛ and Yajamāna.

57. I am Adhvaryu, Udgātṛ and Brahmā. I am the knower of Brahman. O Devī, you are Araṇi (the stick from which sacrificial fire is produced by attrition). You are glorified as Patnī (wife of the performer of a sacrifice).

58. O lady of excellent hips, you are Svāhā and Svadhā. Everything is established in you. I am the desired great Yajña duly performed. You are said to be Pūrvayajña (the earlier Yajña).

59. O fair lady, I am Puruṣa. You are mentioned as Prakṛti. I am Viṣṇu of great vigour and exploits. You are Lakṣmī, the promoter of the welfare of the worlds.

60. I am the highly refulgent Indra. You are the great goddess Prācī (the East). I am stabilized as omniformed through the forms of Prajāpatis.

61. You have become established in the different forms of their spouses. O great goddess, I am *Divasa* (day) and you are mentioned as *Rajanī* (night).

62. I am *Nimeṣa* (Moment) and *Muhūrta* (period of

forty-eight minutes). You are Kalā and Siddhi (achievement). I am the highly refulgent Sun. You are glorified as Sandhyā (Twilight).

63. I am the sower of seed, the most excellent one. O lady of excellent countenance, you are the *Kṣetra* (field). I am the Plakṣa tree. You are mentioned as *Vanaspati.*

64. O eternal one, I have assumed the form of Śeṣa, adorned with a jewel on the hood. O Viśālākṣī (goddess of large eyes), you are Revatī with the eyes of inebriated graceful charms.

65. I am salvation, the release from all sorrows. O goddess, you are the greatest goal. O fair lady, I am the Lord of Waters. O goddess, you are the most excellent one of the rivers.

66. O fair lady, I am the submarine fire. You are glorified as the coruscant splendour. I am Prajāpati and the Doer. You are Prajā (subject) and the Prakṛti.

67. I am the Lord of the serpents staying in the nether regions. You are the Nāgī and I am the king of Nāgas adorned with a thousand hoods.

68. I am the excellent *Niśākara* (the Moon). You are the excellent *Rajanīkarī* (cause of night). I am Kāma, the bestower of love, O goddess. You are Rati and Smṛti (memory).

69. O fair lady, I am Durvāsas. You are *Kṣamā* (forgiveness) acting impartially. I am *Tapas* (penance) performed with delusion and covetousness. You are remembered as the thirst (desire) overwhelmed by dark traits.

70. I am Bull with a big hump. You are the saintly Yogamātā (Mother of Yogic feats). I am the unmanifest Vāyu (Wind). You are the movement that animates the mind.

71. I am the releaser in the case of covetousness. O lady of renown, you are Nirmamā (free from the feelings of mineness or possession). I am circumspection in regard to all tasks. You are the lotus-eyed Nīti (Judicious policy).

72. I am food and its enjoyer. You are mentioned as *Oṣadhī* (medicinal herb). I am Agni and smoke. You are the heat and flame.

73. I am the Saṁvartaka (occurring at the time of ultimate annihilation) cloud. You are the many-sided downpour. I am in the form of the sages. You are glorified as the wives of those sages.

74. O lady of excellent countenance, I am the creator of

the worldly existence and you are the creation. I am semen, bone and hairs. You are marrow and strength.

75. O highly blessed lady, I am *Parjanya* (cloud). O great goddess, you are *Vṛṣṭi* (downpour of rain). O goddess, I am *Saṁvatsara* (year). You are glorified as *Ṛtu* (season).

76. O goddess, I am Kṛtayuga. You are mentioned as Tretā. I am the glorious Dvāpara. O great goddess, you are Kali.

77. O fair lady, I am *Ākāśa* (Sky). You are mentioned as *Pṛthvī* (Earth). I am one of unmanifest form. You are mentioned as one of manifest form.

78. O beautiful lady, I am the bestower of boons. You are mentioned as *Mantra.* I am the seer and the hearer. You are the seen and the act of hearing.

79. I am the speaker and the *Ramayitṛ* (one who delights). O great goddess, you are what is spoken. I am the listener and the singer. You are the music and song.

80. I am the *Ghrātṛ* (one who smells) and the scent. You are the act (or organ) of smelling. I am *Sparśayitṛ* (one who touches) and the creator. You are the *Sparśya* (that which is to be touched) and the *Sṛṣṭa* (what is created).

81. There is no doubt, O goddess, that you and I constitute this visible range of living beings. O goddess of Devas, I am your creator. You do create the entire universe.

82. O goddess of Devas, this universe is woven together in every direction (period?) by you and me once, ten times, hundred times, thousand times.

83. O large-eyed lady, you and I are always established as controllers in all the living beings. We are in close contact with all supernatural powers.

84. O goddess of excellent countenance, I divert myself with you in all sports. You are certainly *Dhṛti* (fortitude, that which holds), you are Lakṣmī (glory) that sustains and holds, my beloved and my Prakṛti.

85. You are *Rati* (pleasure), *Smṛti* (mensory), *Kāmacārī* (moving as you like) and one who is always present in my limbs. O goddess, why speak much? You are greater than my own vital airs.

86. O goddess of the Devas, choose your boon, whatever is present in your mind. I am pleased and I shall give the same to you even if it be very difficult to get.

The Devī said:

87. O Lord of the universe, I am blessed. I am one who has performed meritorious deeds. Penance has been performed by me very well inasmuch as I have been looked upon by you with a pleased eye.

88. O Lord, if you are pleased with me, if you wish to grant me a boon, then, O Lord of Devas, tell me now the details of all holy spots.

89. Whatsoever holy spots, conducive to welfare and destructive of sins, are spread all over the earth, O Lord of Devas, it behoves you to narrate them entirely.

Īśvara said:

90. O goddess, listen, I shall expound to you the greatness of the Tīrthas. It is excellent and destructive of all sins of men. It is meritorious and honoured by the celestial sages.

91. O goddess of Suras, visit to a Tīrthas is excellent. So also is ablution performed therein. Excellent sages always praise the listening to (the glory) thereof.

92. The following are the Tīrthas on the earth: Naimiṣa, Puṣkara in the sky, Kedāra, Prayāga, Vipāśā (Bias) and Urmilā (all on the earth),

93. Karṇaveṇā (probably Kṛṣṇāveṇī), Mahādevī, Candrabhāgā (Chinab), Sarasvatī, the confluence of Gaṅgā and the ocean, and the splendid Vārāṇasī.

94. Ardha Tīrtha (Semi-Tīrtha), Gaṅgā Dvāra, the Mahā Tīrtha, is a place of (plenty of) snow and the auspicious Māyāpurī (Hardwar, U. P.).

95. Śatabhadrā is highly blessed and esteemed. Sindhu is a great river. So also is Airāvatī (Rāvī—De), Kapilā (Narmadā, near its source) and the great Nada i.e. Śoṇa.

96. Kauśikī (Kosī) is a vast storehouse of waters. Similarly Godāvarī is splendid. Devakhāta, Gayā and Dvārāvatī (Dwarka, Gujarat) are splendid.

97. Prabhāsa is a great Tīrtha that is destructive of all sins.

98. If a person visits these and similar other Tīrthas that abound on the surface of the earth, O goddess of Devas, he is never reborn.

99. There are three and a half crores of Tīrthas on the earth. They are holy and destructive of all sins.

100. O great goddess, they should be visited for the purpose of augmenting one's own piety. O goddess of Suras, if it is difficult to go to all these auspicious (Tīrthas), they can all be resorted to mentally by (devotees) with concentration and purity of mind.

The Devī said:

101. O holy Lord, all the living beings are overwhelmed by all sorts of harassments and tortures. Their span of life is short and they are fettered down. They are faced with delusions regarding holy shrines.

102. If this is the case even in Tretā as well as Dvāpara, then it is still more so in the terrible age of Kali. Hence for the sake of their welfare, do glorify that (one) Tīrtha which accords, when visited, the benefit of all the Tīrthas.

103. On being told thus by Pārvatī, Lord Parameśvara laughed joyously and spoke these sweet words :

Īśvara said :

104. You alone are the moving vital airs of the entire universe. You are the source of origin of the universe even as the Araṇi (attrition stick) is that of the fire. O goddess, I cannot bear to be separated from you even for a Muhūrta (short while).

105. O Pārvatī, there is no difference between Śiva and Śakti[1]. O splendid great goddess, there is nothing that you do not know.

106. I am nowhere without you, O goddess and you without me. Our relation is like that of the Moon and moonlight or of fire and warmth.

107. O beloved one, there is no difference between you and me. O goddess of Suras, I shall state everything factually as it is (exists).

108. This is the secret of secrets and it should be guarded carefully. It should not be imparted to an atheist nor to one engrossed in sinful activities.

109. It should be imparted to one endowed with devotion, one's own disciple or son. O my beloved, the essence of all essences has already been narrated by me.

---

1. '*śakti-śaktimator abhedaḥ*' is the fundamental tenet of Śaivism.

110. The well-known Tīrthopaniṣads as well as the Liṅgopaniṣads and the Yogopaniṣads have been narrated to you before.

Pārvatī said:

111. Those who desire the greatest region do not attain it despite all pain and strain. Men of atheistic predilections are seen roaming through *Yonis* (births after births in different wombs).

112. They resort to Tīrthas and observe Vratas but they do not have faith and belief. O Śaṅkara, the entire universe has already been deluded through false knowledge.

113. What do you gain, O most excellent one among Suras, by creating this universal delusion?

114. O Lord of Devas, if I be your beloved, do mention to me the essence of the essential thing, that which is pleasing to your own vital airs.

115. On being requested thus by the goddess Śrīkaṇṭha, the leader of Suras, laughed loudly and spoke these words of profound import:

Īśvara said:

116. Listen attentively now to what I have been asked in regard to its fruitlessness. I shall mention everything as it is factually.

117. O beautiful lady among Suras, earlier three and a half crores of Tīrthas in the Cosmic Egg consisting of mobile and immobile beings, have been described to you.

118. The well-guarded Prabhāsa Tīrtha is among them, O lady of excellent holy vows.

119. O great goddess, the excellent holy spot of Prabhāsa has been thus extolled, but those who are deluded by sins and those who are devoid of religious purificators, rites and cultural refinement in Kali Age (do not benefit) even if they visit this Kṣetra.

120. They are of Rājasa and Tāmasa traits. Their minds have been assailed by sins.These men are engrossed in (acquiring) wealth and womenfolk of others. They also indulge in injuring others.

121. They undergo great excitement and worry. They become distressed everywhere. They are deluded but they think

very high of themselves. They are fascinated with improper and false knowledge. They are base men who do not hesitate to perform rites in the Tīrthas even when they are contrary to the injunctions regarding the Varṇas and the Āśramas.

122. They undertake pilgrimage with hypocrisy and deceit. O lady of excellent complexion, they do not get any benefit even if they die in a holy Tīrtha.

123. It is for this purpose, O goddess of excellent hips, that these diverse Tīrthas and Liṅgas have been concealed and guarded by me. O goddess of Devas, they do not bestow Siddhis in Kali Age on those who perform sinful activities.

124-125. O goddess of great renown, I shall now mention for the benefit of those good men among Brāhmaṇas, Kṣatriyas, Vaiśyas and Śūdras who have conquered the sense-organs, anger and covetousness, who are devoid of hypocrisy and jealousy and who are sanctified by devotion to me and who resort to the Tīrtha and perform holy rites.

126. The holy spot well-known as Prabhāsa is honoured by all the three worlds. Those who are deluded by my Māyā do not know that holy spot (its real nature).

127. If I, the great Being, have been adored with single-minded devotion in the course of many births, those people know that great Prabhāsa Kṣetra that is destructive of sins.

128. There is no doubt, O goddess, that the holy place of Prabhāsa has been fully comprehended by those who are sanctified through devotion to me and who resort to holy vows and rites pertaining to me.

129. Those who observe Yamas and Niyamas, those who are devoid of egotism (are to be benefitted). For the sake of those people, I shall clarify the question to which answer is very difficult to get. This ancient truth has been already revealed to Brahmā, Viṣṇu, Indra and the Devas by me.

130-131. Now I shall tell you, O lady of excellent countenance. Pay heed to it. O beautiful lady among Suras, among all the Tīrthas all over the earth the excellent Prabhāsa kṣetra is the dearest one to me. In that holy spot, I was worshipped by Soma (Moon). After granting him all the boons, I stayed here always in seclusion.

132. Therefore, the holy place that was kept secret, O goddess, has been revealed to you. There from me engrossed in Yoga, the divine Liṅga emerged.

133. It has divine refulgence. It is adorned by a fiery ring (around it). It is quiescent and has been there as mere focus point of concentration. It is very difficult to be perceived by men.

134. For the purpose of creation of the universe the three Śaktis viz. *Icchā* (Volition), *Jñāna* (Knowledge) and *Kriyā* (Activity) have originated from that Liṅga.

135. This universe consisting of mobile and immobile beings gets dissolved in that Liṅga. Further the whole thing appears originating from it.[1]

136. It has originated secretly. No one knows that great thing. By practice throughout the different births, it becomes known to men on the earth.

137. The holy place is called Prābhāsika. There is no doubt about this that I am the Kṣetrajña (the Soul, Knower thereof). In this holy spot I am named Someśa, O lady of excellent countenance.

138. Those who are born in this holy place are born from the parts of mine. This Liṅga was known to them even in the earlier Kalpa as Bhairava (Liṅga).

139. O goddess, this Liṅga is rarely accessible even in the other Yugas. In the sinful, terrible Kali Yuga, it is all the moreso.

140. O Pārvatī, I shall give another example in that connection.

141. In the excessively terrible Kali Yuga, men are prone to indulge in arguements and disputation. Those great sinners abiding by heresy will all say thus :

142-143. "All these things have been done falsely. It is glorified by fools. Where is the holy spot? What is its power? Where are the deities? Everything is false and glorified by deluded ones."

144. Thus the foolish ones will say. Others will laugh. The non-believers, the people destined to fall into hell, get their minds overwhelmed by sins. At the advent of Kali Age, they will never gain Siddhi.

145. Those who habitually censure Śiva and die in the Tīrtha, appear as persons born in all the lower strata of beings.

---

1. This is the definition of Liṅga. The word is derived from '$\sqrt{\text{lī}}$' to dissolve and '$\sqrt{\text{gam}}$' to go out, create.

146. It is on account of this, O goddess, that there are persons in great misery. Due to the great evil power of the Yuga, they are seen as persons devoid of truthfulness and purity.

147. This is the reason why holy spots are kept guarded and concealed. Thus everything has been mentioned to you, as to how Siddhi has become very difficult to achieve.

148. O goddess of Suras, Tīrthas are glorified in every age. Among them, O goddess, Prabhāsa Kṣetra alone is very dear to me.

149. Thus, O fair lady, the sin-destroying secret has been divulged—the very seed in the form of the holy spot. O great goddess, what else do you wish to ask?

150. Those who listen to the great power of holy spots, the narration that destroys great sins, will attain, by my power, the heavenly region, the abode of meritorious persons.

CHAPTER FOUR

The Extent of Prabhāsa Kṣetra

Sūta said:

1. When the efficaciousness was narrated by Śaṅkara thus, O leading sages, goddess Satī kept her palms joined together in reverence and asked again:

The Devī said:

2-3. O Lord of Devas, O Lord of the worlds, O Lord identical with the sacred places and holy rivers, do narrate in detail to me the greatness of Prabhāsa Kṣetra. How will you get pleased with men of confounded and wicked nature in the holy spot? Wherefore do Japa, Dāna, Homa, Yajña and Tapas performed there become rites of everlasting benefit?

4. O Śaṅkara, do tell me how the sin accumulated earlier in the course of thousands of births gets dissolved.

5. If Prabhāsa is considered the most excellent of all the Tīrthas, of what avail are the numerous other Tīrthas?

6. If the Tīrtha is confined to one holy spot the mind will

be free from doubts. When there is the multiplicity of Tīrthas the minds of men begin to waver.

7. Hence, O Lord of Suras, leave aside the entire mess of Tīrthas, and their details, and mention the greatness of Prabhāsa alone.

8. O Lord, it behoves you to narrate everything such as the extent of the holy spot, its boundary and its essential features etc. My curiousity is intense.

Īśvara said:

9. O goddess, listen. I shall describe the most excellent of all Kṣetras. The Prabhāsa Kṣetra is the dearest Kṣetra unto me.

10. The greatest Siddhi is achieved at Prabhāsa. One attains the greatest goal at Prabhāsa. O fair lady, it is the place where I am permanently stationed.

11. I shall mention its extent along with all the boundaries. The holy spot comprises three distinct sections which I shall mention in due order.

12. They are the *Kṣetra*, the *Pīṭha* and the *Garbhagṛha* (sanctum sanctorum) of Prabhāsa which I mention. The efficacy of each of the three is crore times more than the preceding one.

13. The *Kṣetra* is mentioned at the outset. It extends to twelve Yojanas (1 Yojana =12 Kms.). It is well-known. The Pīṭha of the Kṣetra measures five Yojanas.

14. The *Garbhagṛha* is in the form of a pericarp very dear to me. It extends to a *Gavyūti* (six kms.). I shall tell you about the frontiers of the Kṣetra in due order. O goddess, listen.

15. In length and breadth the frontiers are fixed at the beginning, middle and end. *Taptodakasvāmī* is to the east and *Mādhava* is to the west.

16. The ocean is to the south and the river Bhadrā is on the north. The *Kṣetra* with these boundaries extends to twelve Yojanas.

17. This is the Prābhāsika Kṣetra destructive of all sins. The *Pīṭhikā* is mentioned as stationed in the middle and it extends to five Yojanas.

18-19. The *Pīṭha* is mentioned as extending to five Yojanas lengthwise and breadthwise. It is beyond Nyaṅkumanya and to the east of Vajriṇī. It is to the south of Māheśvarī and to the north of the ocean. Now listen to the description of the *Garbhagṛha.*

20. Kauraveśvarī extends from south to north upto the ocean. Āśvamedhika extends from east to west upto Gomukha. This is what is called *Garbhagṛha* and it is dearer to me than Kailāsa.

21-22. Whatever Tīrtha is in between these two, O goddess of Devas, on the earth all the tanks, wells and lakes and all the shrines of the deities, the lakes and the rivers, the puddles and the whirlpools—all these are holy. All of them are destructive of all the sins.

23. By taking his holy bath anywhere (in the area) a man is honoured in the heavenly world.

The first part of the *Kṣetra* is in the highly sacred Māheśvara (pertaining to Śiva).

24. The second part pertains to Viṣṇu and the third one is Brahmā's part. A crore Tīrthas are well-established in the part pertaining to Brahmā.

25. O lady of excellent complexion, there are a crore Tīrthas in the part of Viṣṇu. It is said that there are one and a half crores in the middle part pertaining to Rudra.

26. Thus, O goddess, that holy spot has been described as having three divinities. O splendid lady, this holy spot is the greatest secret of all secrets and very dear to me.

27. Thus the assignment of the regions for the three and a half crores of Kṣetras (Tīrthas) has been explained.

The Yātrā (religious procession) should be understood as threefold. Listen to it, O lady of excellent countenance.

28. The first Yātrā is Raudrī (pertaining to Rudra). The second one is Vaiṣṇavī (concerning Viṣṇu). The third is reckoned as Brāhmī. It is destructive of all sins.

29. It is mentioned, O lady of excellent countenance, that the *Icchāśakti* (power of volition) is in the part pertaining to Brahmā. The *Kriyāśakti* (power of action) is glorified in the second part pertaining to Viṣṇu.

30-31a. O lady of excellent countenance, the *Jñānaśakti* (the power of cognition) is in the third part pertaining to Rudra.

Even a sinful man, a rogue or a person of the worst character shall become rid of all sins if he stays in the middle part.

31b-33. My great interest centres round Prabhāsa after leaving aside Himavān, mountain Gandhamādana, Kailāsa, Niṣadha, the lustrous Merupṛṣṭha, the charming Triśikhara (three-peaked one), the great mountain Mānasa, the beautiful parks of the Devas, the Nandana garden, the beautiful regions of heaven and all the Tīrthas and shrines.

34. O goddess, if a person stays there with restrained soul and concentration of mind, he shall be considered on a par with the one living with air alone as diet, even if he takes food thrice a day.

35. Despite being shaken by obstacles, if a man does not leave Prabhāsa, he actually frees himself from old age and death and the transient cycle of births and deaths.

36. O goddess, Yogic power may be obtained perhaps in the course of hundreds of births. But salvation cannot be obtained even after a thousand births.

37. But, O great goddess, those who continue to stay in Prabhāsa with determination shall undoubtedly attain liberation in the course of a single birth.

38-39. If the Brāhmaṇas of praise-worthy holy vows permanently residing in Prabhāsa perform the Japa of Śatarudriya together with Mṛtyuñjaya Mantra, in the very presence of Kālāgnirudra and resort to the southern quarter, they will get perfect knowledge within six months.

40. Śiva is extolled in the Veda under his name as well as synonyms. But the form of his soul is glorified as *Śatarudriya.*

41. O goddess, Smṛtis say that the Vedas and the Mantras are repeated in every Kalpa but Śatarudriya is not.

42. Those who resort to Prabhāsa Kṣetra and worship by means of this Mantra me alone who am worthy of being adored, are liberated souls. There is no doubt about it.

43. A man may stay there with or without (the repetition of) the Mantras, but the goal that he attains cannot be attained through Yajñas and Dānas.

44. In this holy spot, Maheśvara abides directly as the self-born deity. Crores of Rudras are established in Prabhāsa.

45. They are stationed in the south of Someśa, meditating on Oṁkāra.

46. O lady of excellent holy vows, all the Tīrthas, present

in the Cosmic Egg will flow on to Someśvara on the fourteenth day of Vaiśākha.

47. The mind, intellect and ego, Kāma and Krodha as well as others always guard Someśa, the destroyer of sins.

48. The goal that has been indicated as accessible in the case of men residing in the Prabhāsa Kṣetra is not (obtained) in Kurukṣetra, Gaṅgādvāra and Tripuṣkara.

49. Animals of lower species also that have their abodes in Prabhāsa and die in due course (there) attain the greatest goal.

50-53. That Tīrtha of the Lord of Devas is a penance grove that (should) be kept as a closely guarded secret.

There the Devas including Brahmā with Nārāyaṇa as the leader, Yogins and Sāṅkhyas and my devotees adore the eternal Lord having me as the greatest refuge at Prabhāsa.

Recluses of controlled souls have to go about for eight months. A few roam about for four months and stay behind for eight months. In the case of those who have entered Prabhāsa, they have no (need of) religious tour (Vihāra). Yoga and Mokṣa (salvation) which are rare are attained by men here.

54. Hence one should not leave Prabhāsa and go to another penance grove. Those who do not resort to Prabhāsa are deluded and overcome by darkness of ignorance.

55-56. They are repeatedly born amidst faeces, urine and semen (i.e. in the wombs of mothers). These ten, viz. *Kāma*(love), *Krodha* (anger), *Lobha* (covetousness), *Daṁbha* (hypocrisy), *Staṁbha* (arrogance), *Matsara* (rivalry), *Nidrā* (sleep), *Tandrā* (lethargy), *Ālasya* (sloth) and *Paiśunya* (backbiting, depravity), always protect Someśa, the leader of the Tīrthas.

57. No sinner dying in Prabhāsa falls into a hell, if a man resolutely stays there as long as he lives (during his life time) (He attains this benefit).

58-59. The great benefit that is obtained by Śaivas, Pāśupatas (devotees of Śiva, Paśupati), by Sannyāsins known as Tridaṇḍins, Ekadaṇḍins and such other Sannyāsins, performers of Fire-worship (Agnihotrins), can be attained by means of performance of pilgrimage to Śrī Someśvara.

60. He who adores Someśa is on a par with the best among those who worship a Liṅga and who perform a penance.

61. Whatever is to be known in Yoga, Sāṅkhya, Pañcarātra Siddhānta and other scriptures has been well-established in Prabhāsa.

62. The entire universe consisting of the mobile and immobile beings is stationed in the Liṅga. Hence the Lord has always to be assiduously adored in the Liṅga.

63. It is my supreme form that is stationed by the name Śrīsomeśa. Through it alone I am engrossed in propitiating my own Ātman (soul) through the Ātman.

64. Who roaming through thousands of births is able to attain liberation without the adoration of Someśa?

65. Whatever inauspicious and evil act has been committed through the petty intellect of a human being shall get entirely destroyed through the adoration of Someśvara.

66. The sin that has been committed by creatures in the course of crores of births, gets perished by the adoration of Śrī Someśvara.

67. All the Tīrthas resorted to by those who get rid of their sins, themselves enter Prabhāsa for their own purification.

68. He who is called Kālāgnirudra by the expounders of the Vedas, has become established in Prabhāsa by the name Bhairava.

69. O goddess of Suras, I have assumed the form of Bhairava, settled in the centre of the holy spot, and thus destroy the entire evil (acts) of the people.

70. I have wandered all over the world of mobile and immobile beings. Still I am steady and established. Hence I am well-established at Prabhāsa by the name Bhairava.

71. In the Meghavāhana Kalpa, Agni performed penance for a period of four Yugas according to the reckoning of divine years. At that place a Liṅga originated.

72. O beautiful lady of Suras, he is one whose prowess has been extolled by the words of the Vedas, *agnimīḍe* etc. (I praise Agni—RV. L.1-17). The Liṅga was addressed by all the Devas by the name of Kālāgnirudra.

73. O goddess of Devas, Agni, Īśāna and Kālāgnirudra, these three names are oft-repeated. O lady of excellent countenance, since the Kalpas and Brahmās are innumerable, the names (of the Lord) in every Kalpa cannot be mentioned.

74. Thus it is a very great secret, O lady of excellent countenance. It has to be kept strictly concealed. But due to your great affection for me and the excess of devotion, it has been glorified by me to you.

75-79. The entire universe is established in Karmakāṇḍa (mass of rituals), which includes Yajña, Dāna, Tapas, Homa, Self-study of the Vedic texts, offering libations to ancestors, fasts, holy vows, the whole range of the hundreds of Cāndrāyaṇas, Ṣaḍrātras, Trirātras, visiting pilgrim centres etc. By means of these holy rites, people of the various stages of life such as celibate students, householder, Vānaprastha, etc. devoted to the holy rites laid down in the Vedas should ordinarily hope to earn merits. So also is the case of other people engaged in the auspicious rites of the layman. But, O goddess, unless one adores Someśa the leader of the Liṅgas, none can attain that great region. They cannot even espy it. It is extremely difficult to attain.

80-83. If the Lord of the universe, Bhairava Someśa is worshipped, all those attain salvation, those who die in Prabhāsa, O fair lady. They may be animals and birds of the lowest species, even ants, worms, insects, locusts etc. under water, the mobile and immobile beings, men, beasts, women, boys, girls, old men and women, eunuchs, dogs, donkeys, crows, Cāṇḍālas, Śūdras, Puṣkasas, other people of base births, fools, scholars, all despicable persons etc.

84. O auspicious lady, all those creatures that die in Prabhāsa are burnt by the fire of Kālānala Rudra, by the Kālarāja fire.

85. O goddess, my holy spot Prabhāsa is difficult of access to sinners. O lady honoured by people, a sinful soul does not get the opportunity to die there.

86. In the southern side, Vighneśa has been installed by me. Daṇḍapāṇi protects this holy spot in the northern side.

87. Other Lords of Gaṇas also, subject to my behest, guard this holy spot, O goddess of Devas. Listen to their names:

88-90. Mahābala, Caṇḍīśa, Ghaṇṭākarṇa, Gomukha, Vināyaka, Mahānāda, Kākavaktra, Śubhekṣaṇa, Ekākṣa, Dundubhi, Caṇḍa, Tālajaṅgha, Bhūmidaṇḍa, the fierce Śaṅkukarṇa, Vaidhṛti, Tālacaṇḍa, Mahātejas, Vikaṭāsya, Hayānana, Hastivaktra, Śvānavaktra and Biḍālavadana. There are others with faces resembling those of lions, tigers etc. including Vīrabhadra.

91. Keeping Vināyaka at their head, they guard the Lord of Devas, Kapardin. They number eleven crores and thirteen million.

92-93. An *Arbuda* (one hundred million) of the Gaṇas have occupied the Prabhāsa Kṣetra. They are very fierce. They stand at every door with tridents and *Mudgaras* in their hands. They guard Prabhāsa Kṣetra, the abode of the Lord of Devas. They see to it that no one enters it with evil intention.

94. The Gaṇa named Aṭṭahāsa is surrounded by a hundred crores of Gaṇas in the eastern doorway. He protects Prabhāsa there.

95. Kālākṣa is terrible and fierce. He is surrounded by eighteen crores of Gaṇas. The Gaṇa named Ghaṇṭākarṇa has occupied the southern gate.

96. The Gaṇa named Viṣṭara has occupied the western doorway. Daṇḍapāṇi is stationed in the northern doorway of the abode of the Lord of Devas.

97. He looks after the Yogakṣema (acquisition and preservation i.e. maintenance) of all purified souls in Prabhāsa. Bhīṣaṇākṣa is in the north-east and Chāgavaktraka is in the south-east.

98-99. Caṇḍanāda is in the south-west and Bhairavānana is in the north-west.

Nandin, Mahākāla, Daṇḍapāṇi and Vināyaka are the bodyguards stationed in the middle, surrounded by a hundred crore Gaṇas. Thus innumerable leading Gaṇas guard everywhere.

100. That holy spot of the Crescent-moon-crested Lord is not approachable to those persons whose minds are overwhelmed by the outcome of the evils of Kali Age.

101-102. Prabhāsa is resorted to by Gandharvas, Kinnaras, Yakṣas, Apsarās and serpents and Siddhas who remain invisible. They adore Someśa, the Lord of Devas, the destroyer of sins. Siddhas of the seven worlds and those who reside in Pātāla circumambulate Someśa Kālabhairava.

103-106. All theTīrthas and holy shrines of the earth circumambulate Lord Someśvara and eulogize the Liṅga there. The Tīrthas are Lākuli, Bhāvabhūti, Āṣāḍhi, Daṇḍa, Puṣkara, Naimiṣa, Amareśa, another Bhairava, Madhyama, Kāla, Kedāra, Kaṇavīraka, Haricandra, Śaileśa, Vastrāntikeśvara, Aṭṭahāsa, Mahendra, Śrīśaila and Gayā.

107. Brahmā, Janārdana, and the other Devas stationed in

the universe come near the Agni Liṅga at the time of dusk and eulogize.

108. Sixty crores of thousands and sixty crores of hundreds of these go to Someśvara on the fourteenth day in the dark half of the month of Māgha.

109-110. At that time a devotee should offer the *Ghṛtakaṁbala* to Someśa, i.e. they are to collect together all these: Ghee, *Rasa* (juice), gingelly seeds, milk, water rendered fragrant with camphor and Kāśmīra (saffron).

111. This has to be done on the Śivarātri day. This is a secret and it is my favourite. It is impossible to reckon the merit that accrues when this is done.

112. If one desires one's siddhi, O goddess, one should adore at the outset Bhūtavināyaka himself in the southern side.

113. Of all *Ūṣaras* (arid regions) the Prabhāsa Kṣetra is the greatest *Ūṣara* (arid land). It is the most excellent of all Pīṭhas and Kṣetras. Of all *Sandehas* this is the greatest of *Sandeha* (?).

114. There are hundred crores of Yogins. They have great interest only in Prabhāsa Kṣetra and nowhere else.

115-116. O beautiful woman of Suras, the splendid Kalā named Umā, about whom I have already mentioned, is established on the north-east of the Liṅga. O goddess, she is called Satī and she was the daughter of Dakṣa formerly.

117. Being angry with Dakṣa, the greatest Kalā abandoned her body and was reborn in the abode of Himavān. She became well-known by the name Umā.

118. Therefore, O goddess, they remained there along with you. They are remembered as the bestowers of boons. Nine crores of Cāmuṇḍās are stationed in that holy spot.

119. If a devotee adores you there on the eighth day in the bright half of the month of Caitra, he will not meet with poverty in the course of twenty-one rebirths.

120. If the *Amā* (New-Moon) united with Monday is attainable at any time, a devotee should visit Someśvara. Thereby he attains the benefit of a crore of Yajñas.

121. This holy spot is something to be treated as a great secret. It is destructive of all sins, since it is the place where eleven crores of Rudras are collectively present.

122. Twelve Dineśas (Ādityas, Sun-gods) and eight Vasus arrive here. There are innumerable prominent Gaṇas, Gandharvas, Yakṣas and Rākṣasas.

123-126. Umā too who is eulogized by all the Devas is present very near at the side. There is Nandin, the leader of Gaṇas of the Trident-bearing Lord of Devas. There are other leading Gaṇas who stand by the side of Mahākāla. There are the rivers Gaṅgā, Yamunā, Sarasvatī and other sacred ones, Nadas and Hradas. There are oceans, mountains, wells and trees. All the mobile and immobile beings have arrived at Prabhāsa. Other Gaṇas too are stationed there at Prabhāsa.

127. All have not been mentioned by me. At random I have mentioned a few here and there. If one desires the benefit of the sacred place, O goddess of Devas, one should worship the third Vināyaka there with great devotion.

128. Thus, O beautiful lady, at the entrance to the Agni Tīrtha there are stationed twelve, eight and twenty-four crores of rivers.

129. If the (sin of) *Nirmālya Laṅghana* (i.e. over-stepping flowers and other leavings of adoration of God) has been committed unknowingly, the entire sin is washed off on visiting the Agni Tīrtha.

130. Of what avail is talking too much, O goddess? This holy spot is highly refulgent. It is impossible to describe it adequately to you even in the course of hundreds of crores of Kalpas.

131. Prabhāsa Kṣetra is the greatest of all the Tīrthas in the various quarters and of all the deities in the atmosphere, or on the earth. So also, O goddess, Someśvara is the greatest deity.

132. All the types of living beings such as the oviparous, viviparous, sweat-born ones and plants (coming out breaking through the ground) attain salvation if they meet with death at Prabhāsa. There is no doubt about it.

133. Thus the wonderful story of the Lord of Devas has been narrated. O goddess, the incomprehensible deeds of Śaṅkara have been narrated to you. He who reads, listens to this and eulogizes the Lord, all these people will attain salvation, destroying into smitherens the sins of Kali.

CHAPTER FIVE

Sages and Devas Residing in Prabhāsa Kṣetra

Sūta said:

1. O leading Brāhmaṇas, when this was narrated by the noble-souled Śaṅkara, the goddess became extremely delighted in her mind and asked again:

The Devī said:

2. For the sake of the welfare of all living beings, O Lord of Devas, O Lord of the universe, do tell me in detail the greatness of the Prabhāsa Kṣetra.

Īśvara said:

3. O renowned one, I shall give you another example as to why, O great goddess, this holy spot, a favourite of mine, has been created.

4. The great goal (region) that Yogins who are devoid of any attachment attain by constant meditation, is attained by those who give up their life at that holy place Prabhāsa.

5. Mārkaṇḍeya also, the great ascetic whose span of life extends to many Kalpas, always worships Lord Virūpākṣa at Prabhāsa.

6. Though he wanders over all the Tīrthas, he never leaves Prabhāsa. Durvāsas of excessive splendour endeavours to propitiate the Liṅga. O goddess, he does not forsake that holy place of the Moon-crested Lord even for a moment.

7-10. Similarly, Bharadvāja, Sage Marīci, Uddālaka, Kratu, Vasiṣṭha, Kaśyapa, Bhṛgu, Dakṣa, Sāvarṇi, Yama, Aṅgiras, Śuka, Vibhāṇḍaka, Ṛṣyaśṛṅga, Gobhila, Gautama, Ṛcīka, Agastya, the great Śaunaka, Nārada, Jamadagni, Viśvāmitra, Lomaśa and many other sages as well as celestial sages never leave the great holy spot. They endeavour to propitiate the Liṅga.

11. I stay there itself eager (in watching their) propitiation. I never leave that great Kṣetra, O lady of excellent countenance. It is the truth, nothing but the truth.

12. O goddess of Devas, all the Tīrthas on the earth have been seen by me. A Kṣetra on a par with Prabhāsa was neverseen.

13. O goddess, sixty thousand devotees with Yājñavalkya at the head, stay at Candrabhāgā. They perform Japa of the Rudra Mantras.

14. Forty thousand sages of absolute celibacy perform the *Japa* of *Śatarudriya* on the banks of Devikā (a local rivulet).

15-17. Fifty crores of the sages of perfect celibacy have resorted to the Umāpati Liṅga stationed there itself. Formerly, the Japa of the Rudra Mantras was performed by them a crore times there itself.

A hundred thousand great Siddhas who stay in that holy place of mine worship the Moon-crested Lord of Devas.

18. By visiting Candrabhūṣaṇa there, one gets entirely that benefit which has been mentioned by great sages in the Vedāntas.

19. O splendid lady, more than a crore of sages are staying at Agni Tīrtha. It is remembered that a hundred thousand have settled in Rudreśvara. So also in Kapardīśa.

20. A thousand sages of extraordinary celibacy are stationed in Ratneśvara. In the highly meritorious Arkasthala, O splendid lady, more than a crore are stationed.

21. Sixty thousand are stationed there in Siddheśvara. Those who are stationed in Mārkaṇḍa number seven thousand.

22-23. Innumerable sages are remembered as stationed in Sarasvatī and Brahma Kuṇḍa. Ten thousand *Arbudas* and three crores of sages stay at the place where there is Prācī Sarasvatī. It was there that Śaṅkara's sin of Brāhmaṇa-slaughter perished in a moment.

24. His (Śaṅkara's) body became golden and the skull fell down from his hand. After knowing this Śaṅkin performed a great penance there.

25. Lord Śrī Śaṅkara became pleased and blessed him with the boon of staying in the Liṅga. By having ablution in Prācī and worshipping the Liṅga one acquires merit of a crore of Yajñas.

26. If a ball of rice is offered on a New-Moon day, the benefit is a hundred times more than that at Gayā. One who offers balls of rice there on the *Bhūta day* (i.e. fourteenth lunar day) shall redeem a crore of the members of his family.

27. If men take a plunge here for quelling the dirt (of sins) they will earn the merit of gifting ten cows.

28-29. The merit of a Śrāddha performed in accordance with the injunctions of the scriptures will accrue to those also who play about in the waters with the feet in water. By viewing it too all will attain merit. By touching they get twice the merit. The Liṅgas beginning with Śūlabheda should be considered to give the merit of a horse-sacrifice.

30. Thus the Lord of the universe who is pleased is certainly stationed in the forests of Prācī. Even those who think mentally (of visiting etc.) are benefitted. Still more so in the case of those who perform *Snāna* and *Dāna.*

31. Nīlalohita, Śaṅkara, the Lord of the worlds is pleased with them. Thirty crores of Gaṇas guard Prācī all round.

32. A great sinner, one of evil conduct, a person of great misdeeds may by a happy chance meet with death in Prācī. He will attain Śiva.

33. The offering of *Dadhikaṁbala* (adoration of Śiva with cover of curds) should be made there by excellent Brāhmaṇas. It is said to certainly suppress sins. It is the most efficacious of all essential things.

34. Now I shall explain the great efficacy of Hiraṇī. The Sun-god was installed there and penance was performed by Durvāsas.

35-37. There too, there are a crore of sages of perfect celibacy.

O goddess of Devas, the deity who has power more than that of twenty-four Tattvas stands there accompanied by a crore of Bhṛgus.

If a single person is fed in Brahmasthāna, one gets the same benefit as by feeding a crore of Brāhmaṇas elsewhere. O great goddess, this I am aware of and hence I stay there extremely pleased.

38-39. I am surrounded by a crore of celestial sages and Devas.

In Kali Age, Tīrthas stay there latent (merged underneath) in the holy spot of great beauty where Someśvara is stationed. I have, O goddess, two Gaṇas there—Vibhrama and Saṁbhrama.

40. These two make the minds of the people residing in the Kṣetra excited and deluded due to ignorance. They are disunited and are in a dilemma.

41. There are then the Vināyakas, *Upasargas* (troubles) and ten other defects. They guard the Kṣetra from evil-minded sinners.

42. If the residents of the Kṣetra visit the deity Daṇḍapāṇi with devotion, they are excellent men and they will not meet with obstacles.

43-44. O splendid lady, those who die at Prabhāsa, whether Brāhmaṇas, Kṣatriyas, Vaiśyas, Śūdras, or of mixed castes, whether they have desires or not, they become identical with Śiva. All of them will have the crescent-moon for the coronet. They will have eyes in the forehead. They will be bull-bannered. Those men are born (or become) so in the splendid divine Śivapura of mine.

45. A Brāhmaṇa staying there with mental concentration and purity, may be taking food thrice a day. But he is on a par with one who subsists on air only.

46-47. O my beloved, the good qualities of Meru can be narrated. So also the good qualities of the continents. The good qualities of all the oceans can be enumerated. But, O goddess of Devas, one cannot enumerate the good qualities of the primordial Lord Maheśa, the great Lord, in hundreds of crores of years.

CHAPTER SIX

Greatness of Someśvara

The Devī said:

1-3. The extremely miraculous greatness has been narrated to me. This is unprecedented, O Lord of the chiefs of Devas. Never has it been heard by me before.

Of all the Liṅgas in the Cosmic Egg which have been extolled by you to me, how is it that Someśa has become extremely pre-eminent?

O great Lord, O Lord of Suras, is it the power of the holy place ? Hence, O Lord of Suras, narrate it factually to me.

Īśvara said:

4. O lady of excellent countenance, hereafter I shall narrate in detail the greatest secret, the greatness of Someśa and Prabhāsa Kṣetra.

5-6. Of all the Tīrthas, it is the greatest Tīrtha; of all the *Vratas* it is the greatest *Vrata;* of all the *Jāpyas* (Mantras to be muttered) it is the greatest *Jāpya;* it is the most excellent one of all meditations; it is the greatest Yoga among all Yogas; it is the greatest secret. I shall expound it to you. O my beloved, listen to it with concentrated attention.

7. Someśa is the greatest holy shrine. The Liṅga has five faces. I never leave it. It is the truth. The truth has been mentioned by me.

8. Whatever is the greatest, the most permanent, everlasting and immutable, do know it to be Someśa. Do not get confused in mind.

9-10. Know that Liṅga in Prabhāsa as one that is above fear, free from impurities, eternal, independent, not having (needing) another support, unsullied, devoid of ramifications, free from attachment and devoid of torments. It is well-established at Prabhāsa. It is the final beatitude, incomprehensible, pleasing to the mind and devoid of ailments.

11. That is the eternal, the cause of the universe, the destroyer of (Dakṣa's) sacrifice, Lord with faces everywhere (in all directions), the auspicious subtle (principle) identical with all, the primordial deity.

12. It is comprehensible only through self-realization. It is devoid of mental worries. It is devoid of birth and death. It is pure and absolute both within and without.

13. It is the object of self-realization. It is beyond the ken of eulogy. It is partless, the soul devoid of impurities. It is the manifest illumination of perfect knowledge.

14. Know that the Liṅga at Prabhāsa is of such a nature, O beautiful goddess. It is devoid of space-lessness. It is sound that is perceptible when all (other worldly) sounds cease.

15. It is unsullied and free from impurities. It is the Lord, the Lord of Devas. It is the soul of Suras. It is beyond reasoning. It is beyond the perview of imagination.

16. It is the object of mental view. It is stationed both

within and without. Know it to be Praṇava in the form of Liṅga at Prabhāsa.

17. The great soul is stable (unmoved by any pulsation or variation), beyond all perception of bliss. It is the pure and perfect knowledge on the path of survey of the world(?).

18. It is stationed on the path of special spiritual knowledge(?). It is designated by its innumerable forms. It can be comprehended through the concept of its own existence(?). It is beyond existence and characterization.

19. It is devoid of (beyond) development, display etc. of words. It is Śiva free from identity with the worldly units. It is stationed under the survey of knowledge and the knowable? It is devoid of fallacious reasoning.

20. It is present in the Śabda in the mystic (Yogic) Cakra named *Anāhata*. It originates from the groups of *Śabda* (sound) etc(?). Know Someśvara to be thus. It is in the form of a Liṅga in Prabhāsa.

21. It is quiescent. It is present in *Śabdabrahman*. Its place (resort) is beyond the ken of words. It is the object of that which surpasses everything. It is present in the path of meditation of all(?).

22. It is beginningless. It is divine and unswerving. It is the object of that which is beyond all valid testimony. It exists both above and below. It is stationed in the body and so is called Jīva.

23. (In Yogic meditation) it is stationed at the end of twelve *Aṅgulas* which is the extreme reach of the breadth both within (the heart) and outside (when exhaled). It is present at the rise (beginning) and end of Prāṇa and Apāna (inhalation and exhalation). It is identical with the soul (power) of sense- organs yet it is imperceptible (beyond the grasp of senses). It is blemishless and all-pervading.

24. It is beyond *Svara* (vowels) etc. and *Vyañjana* (consonant). It is beyond letters of alphabet etc. It is not the object of oral expression. It is in the form of half of Ahaṁkāra (?).

25. It is beyond the reach of logical argumentation or imagination. It cannot be expressed orally. It is devoid of time and act of reckoning. It is devoid of sound and movement. It is gentle. It is beyond the body, greater than the greatest.

26. It is beyond the grasp of (five) elements (or living beings). It is beyond existence and non-existence. It is extremely

subtle and incomprehensible. It originates from the five pentads etc.

27. It is immeasurable. It has infinite names (or it is designated as infinite). It is everlasting. It can assume any form it likes. It is the source of origin of all living beings. It originates like a sprout from seed.

28. It is pervasive. It has all desired names. It is imperishable and extremely great. It is present in the setup of the subtle and the gross. It is both manifest and unmanifest. It is eternal.

29. It is devoid of great periods of time called Kalpa and ends of Kalpas. It is great without beginning and end. It is the great element. It has a huge body. It is auspicious and *Nirvāṇabhairava* (terrific though quiescent).

30. Understand Sadāśiva thus in the form of the Liṅga at Prabhāsa. He is devoid of yogic activity. He is the conqueror of *Mṛtyu* (death) and has no beginning.

31. He is devoid of all torments. He is Śiva who pervades everything all round. He is unmanifest and eternal, more than the greatest. He is absolutely one without any duality.

32. It is not overwhelmed by another refulgence for the residents of Prabhāsa Kṣetra. He has excessive self-luminosity and refulgence. He is Hara who surpasses the splendour of all.

33. He is Lord Īśāna worthy of being the refuge. He is Oṁkāra in the form of Śiva. He is Mahādeva, the Lord of Devas. He is five-faced and bull-emblemed.

34. He is free from impurities. He is beyond the ken of the mind. He can be comprehended through *Bhāva* (emotion, devotion). He is incomparable. He is always quiescent. He is the trident-armed Virūpākṣa (Three-eyed Lord) having matted hairs.

35. He is stationed in the middle of the lotus (the Yogic plexus) of the heart. He is void-formed and unsullied. Understand Sadāśiva thus in the form of the Liṅga at Prabhāsa.

36. That Lord who is greater than the greatest is glorified by the name of Haṁsa and by the name of Nāda. He is stationed in this holy spot, O goddess of excellent holy vows.

37. This primordial form, the divine form of the Ātman has been comprehended by me through the power of Yoga and

this divine (form of the) soul has been narrated to you, O goddess.

38. He is stationed in the Ṛgveda in the forenoon. He is stationed in the Yajus in the midday. He is stationed in the Sāman in the afternoon. He is stationed in the Atharvan at the beginning of night.

39. I know this great Puruṣa of the brilliance of the sun beyond darkness. Death will not overtake if one knows it. There is no other pathway for the people.

40. Thus the great power of Someśaliṅga has been partially narrated to you. The deity cannot be extolled even by one endowed with many thousands of mouths in the course of many (innumerable) years.

41. A Brāhmaṇa, a Kṣatriya, a Vaiśya and even a Śūdra will become rid of all sins if he reads this. He shall attain all desires.

CHAPTER SEVEN

The Appearance (Origin) of Somanātha

Sūta said:

1-4. After hearing the excellent greatness there, the goddess asked Śaṅkara once again with words coming (profusely) through the throat due to eagerness and delight:

The Devī said:

O Lord of Devas, O Lord of the worlds, O conferor of blessings unto the devotees, obeisance to you, O Maheśvara, richly endowed with all knowledge.

Obeisance to the noble-souled one, to the slayer of the Tripuras, to the suppressor of Tāraka. Obeisance to you who bestowed the ocean of milk on the child (viz. Upamanyu) of the leading sage endowed with perfect concentration and mental purity.

Obeisance to you, the creator of all the worlds. O Lord identical with all everywhere! Obeisance, to the creator of all. Obeisance to *Bhava* (the origin of all). Obeisance to *Abhava* (having no birth). Obeisance to you, the eternal one, to you who are omnipresent.

Īśvara said:

5. O goddess, what do you ask? Everything has been narrated by me. If still you have any doubts, you may ask, O beautiful lady.

The Devī said:

6. When did that name Someśvara come into existence? At what time did it take place? What name did it have first? What will be the name of the Liṅga now?

7. O Lord, he whose power is such, has not been described by you before. The greatness of the other deities of the Tīrtha has been described by you. Nothing like the greatness of Śrīsomeśa has been expounded.

Īśvara said:

8. I was in existence even formerly in the form of Sparśa Liṅga. O goddess, none of the men here knew me in my real form.

9. In the great Kalpa when the *Pratisañcara* (re-absorption into the origin) of Brahmā took place the name of the Liṅga too originated. This shall be different and occur again and again.

10. Six Brahmās have passed away. The present Prajāpati who is well-known as Śatānanda is the seventh one, O goddess.

11. When this Brahmā became eight year old, O goddess of Devas, from that time onwards I became well-known as Someśa.

12. O Pārvatī, listen to those names that occurred in the periods that elapsed after the sleep and dissolution of Brahmās.

13. When the first grandfather Brahmā called Viriñci existed, the name Mṛtyuñjaya of Somanātha was glorified in that period.

14. When the second (incumbent) Brahmā well-known by the name Padmabhū became Brahmā, the Liṅga (Somanātha) was called Kālarudrāgni, O auspicious lady.

15. When the third one well-known as Svayaṁbhū became Brahmā, the name of the Lord was glorified as Amṛteśa.

16. When the fourth one well-known as Parameṣṭhin became Brahmā, O auspicious lady, the name of the Lord was remembered as Anāmaya.

17. When the fifth one remembered as Surajyeṣṭha became Brahmā, O Aṁbikā, the name of the Lord was mentioned as Kṛttivāsa.

18. When the sixth one well-known (by the name) Hemagarbha became Brahmā, the Lord was glorified as Bhairavanātha.

19. The present Brahmā is remembered as Śatānanda and the name of the Lord now is Somanātha.

20. Hereafter when the future Brahmā will be known as Caturvaktra, the name of the Lord shall be Prāṇanātha.

21. In the case of Brahmā of the past and those of the future, the respective name continues till the other one is eight years old. With reference to the difference of Sandhyā and Sandhyāṁśa (Twilight of Yugas and part of twilight between Yugas) they are Viṣṇu, Ananta and Sanātana.

22. Thus the names of the Lord have been described briefly by me. They cannot be expounded in detail because of the greatness of time (required for it).

The Devī said:

23. Wonderful indeed, O Lord of the chiefs of Devas, is what has been said by you. How is it that the names mentioned before have escaped my memory?

24. Mention the reason hereof in detail, O Lord of the worlds, with a desire to bless me as well as for the sake of the welfare of all living beings.

Īśvara said:

25. Since, O my beloved, O great goddess, you take incarnation in every Kalpa due to the power of Prakṛti, you do not have the recollection.

26. In the Āvaraṇas (coverings) constituted by the Tattvas, you have been established as the first. O lady of excellent countenance, along with me you incarnate in the middle of the (Cosmic) Eggs.

27. You manifest yourself again and again for the sake of blessing the worlds. In the first Kalpa (you were) Jaganmātā. In the second (you were) Jagadyoni.

28. In the third (Kalpa) you were (known by the) name Śāmbhavī and in the fourth Viśvarūpiṇī. In the fifth you were named Nandinī and in the sixth Gaṇāṁbikā.

29. Vibhūti (is your name) in the seventh Kalpa and Subhūti in the eighth. Ānandā in the ninth Kalpa and Vāmalocanā in the tenth.

30. (You were called) Varārohā in the eleventh and Sumaṅgalā in the twelfth. You are cited as Mahāmāyā in the thirteenth Kalpa.

31. You were glorified by the name Anantā in the fourteenth Kalpa, Bhūtamātā in the fifteenth and were remembered as Uttamā in the sixteenth.

32. Then in the seventeenth Kalpa (i.e. Pitṛkalpa) you became well-known as the highly lustrous daughter of Dakṣa, known by the name Satī.

33. Due to the insult at the hands of Dakṣa you forsook your body. Formerly you stationed yourself as Umā filling the digit of the moon.

34. Then, when the Vārāha Kalpa began, O beautiful lady of Suras, you were propitiated by Himavān and made his daughter.

35. Then, O goddess, you performed a wonderful penance very difficult to be performed and obtained me once again as your husband. You are now called Pārvatī.

36. I have my abode in Kailāsa, O lady of excellent countenance. O goddess of Devas, I thus sport with you till the end of the Kalpa.

37. This happens four times. Then for the sake of the killing of Mahiṣa, you were born as Kṛṣṇapiṅgalā (black-and tawny-coloured) in Dvāpara along with Viṣṇu.

38. You were born on the earth in nine crores of different ways with various names such as Kātyāyanī, Durgā etc.

39. O beautiful lady, your Kalpa names mentioned before have been enumerated by me beyond the thirteenth Kalpa.

40. O beautiful ladys the past, present and the future names— all of them—should be known thus till Brahma Kalpa.

The Devī said:

41-44. O Tripurāntaka (Destroyer of Tripuras), the name Somanātha has been cited by you before. How is it considered permanent ? Since the moons are many in view of their names and births (that name cannot be steady and permanent). At the end of seventy-one Caturyugas when a Manvantara is complete, the Moon, the Sun and the Devas are destroyed again and again. So also the seven sages, Suras, Śakra, Manu and the kings, his sons. They are simultaneously created and dissolved as before. Now, O Lord, it behoves you to clarify this duly and exactly.

Īśvara said:

45. A pertinent question has been asked by you, O goddess. It is a secret that is destructive of sins. I shall fully explain to you what has not been narrated to anyone before.

46-47. Now there is the Brahmā here well-known as Śatānanda. When he is eight years old, the first Manu (is born). He shall be the first. In his Manvantara Rohiṇīpati (i.e. Moon) is born at the outset from the bowels of the ocean along with Lakṣmī, Kaustubha etc.

48. The Liṅga named Kālabhairava was propitiated by him with great penance lasting for fourteen (Catur) Yugas.

49. On seeing his wonderful penance, O beautiful lady, I became pleased. That Niśākara (Moon) was told by me, "Choose your boon."

50. At that time, O goddess, O auspicious lady, he eulogized with devotion and said:

Candra said:

51. O Lord of the Devas, if you are pleased, if I am eligible for a boon, O Lord, let your name be Somanātha throughout the life-span of Brahmā.

52. May this deity alone be the family deity for all the other Śītaraśmis (Moons) who, are to be born in the other Manvantaras too.

53. O Lord, may they all be stationed in this holy spot and propitiate (You) throughout their life-span. May this continue till the dissolution of Brahmā.

54. May your name Somanātha become famous in the Brahmāṇḍa consisting of mobile and immobile beings. O Lord

of Devas, O one of luminous Liṅga, I pay obeisance to you.

Īśvara said:

55. After saying "Let this be so" I got merged into the Liṅga. Thus, O goddess, the reason has been explained to you entirely.

56. Since this was asked by you earlier, it has been explained leaving no doubt, though it is brief. Only a sample of the qualities of Śrīsomeśa has been narrated to you. The details thereof are incomprehensible (innumerable) like jewels in the sea.

57. It is confounding to those who are not his devotees but is conducive to the augmentation of the intellect of his devotees. Deluded persons do not perceive my real form as they are confused.

The Devī said:

58. O Śaṅkara, O Lord of Suras, the greatness of the luminous Liṅga is of such a nature. Where in that holy spot does that Liṅga stand installed?

Īśvara said:

59. O goddess, listen with care. Try to comprehend after listening. This Prabhāsa Kṣetra is the greatest holy spot and it is my favourite.

60. It is the place of stay of Devas too. It extends to twelve Yojanas (12x12 = 144 Kms.) The Pīṭha is glorified as measuring five Yojanas.

61. My abode is in the middle thereof, O goddess. It extends to a Gavyūti (3 Kms.), O goddess. That which is called Devikāmukha is on the north of the ocean.

62. It is to the east of the Vajriṇī (a local river) and extends as far as the river Nyaṅkumatī. The width is four (Yojanas) and the length is five Yojanas.

63. Thus the Kṣetrapīṭha is explained. Hereafter listen to the *Garbhagṛha*. It extends from the ocean in the south to Kauravī in the north and from Gomukha in the east upto Aśvamedhakā in the west.

64. This is my abode, O goddess, which I never forsake. The Liṅga is stationed in its middle as it has already been explained to you.

65-66. Near the ocean, in the western quarter, three hundred *Dhanvantaras* (the distance of three hundred Dhanus i.e. 1200 Hastas) to the west of Kṛtasmara stands the Liṅga of great prowess. It is the self-manifested Lord Śaṅkara, the Supreme Lord who stands installed there.

67-69. O goddess, in between these, near Someśa, in the fourteenth section, two hundred Dhanus (400 Hastas) in extent is my *Karṇikā* (pericarp) in the form of a circle. It is my favourite, O Pārvatī, living beings, worms, insects, locusts etc. the beings of superior and middling types as well that die in due course of time, get rid of their sins and go to my world.

70. The northern or southern transit of the time of death need not be taken into account. In regard to those who die in the middle of the Kṣetra all the times are auspicious.

71. For the purpose of the welfare of all living beings, O great goddess, the primordial Nātha (Lord) Śarva brought the *Ādyatattvas* (the primordial principles) and illuminated the Kṣetra of great refulgence where men can achieve Siddhis.

72-73. One who is wise, O goddess of Devas, may be assailed by hundreds of obstacles but, O goddess of Suras, he shall take a solemn vow (to stay behind) as long as he lives. Due to the greatness of that holy spot and of Sthāṇu of miraculous activities, he goes to the greatest region by reaching which one does not feel pain or misery.

74. Ordinarily one suffers repentance after committing thousands of sins. But he gets relieved from them in Prabhāsa. He does not go to the city of Antaka (god of death).

75. After realizing that Kali Age was terrible, cruel and insensitive to sufferings of beings, O goddess of Devas, Vighnanāyaka had been appointed there for the sake of protection.

76-78. By the side of Kālāgnirudra, Vighnanāyaka whose valour is on a par with that of Rudra, has been engaged for the protection (of the holy spot) from sinners like those who are inimical to Brāhmaṇas, those who raise futile arguments over devotion to Śiva, Brāhmaṇa-slayers, ungrateful ones, those who have no chance of redemption, those hated by the general public, those who are hated by the elders, the thorns unto the Tīrthas and shrines, those who are engaged in all kinds of sins and those of contemptible acts.

79-81. O goddess of Devas, the deity restrains sinners and

guards the holy spot. If men perpetrate sins in the holy spot and kill Brāhmaṇas, O beautiful lady, listen the fate they attain. O lotus-eyed one, they are born as sons of whores for ten thousand years according to the divine reckoning. At the end thereof, they become Brahmarākṣasas. Thereafter, when the sins are quelled they attain ignominous births.

82-85. Hence by all means one should avoid committing sins there. Sins committed elsewhere become quelled in this holy spot. But a sin committed in this Kṣetra brings about the state of Piśācas and fall into hells.

O beloved, the Lord is sympathetic to the devotees. He bestows the greatest position even on the lower types of creatures but not on those who hate Brāhmaṇas.

Those who meditate with concentration, those of souls practising Yogic rites after restraining the sense-organs, who perform the Japa of *Śatarudriya* residing in Prabhāsa, are undoubtedly blessed.

86. If anyone goes to the excellent Prabhāsa Kṣetra, he should continue to employ such means as will not necessitate going out of it.

87. O beautiful lady, this has to be guarded as a secret. It should not be given to anyone and everyone. O my beloved, this Śāstra has to be guarded well like one's own life.

88. He by whom this scriptural text that illuminates the Prabhāsa Kṣetra has been composed should be known as Śiva himself who has adopted human characteristics (form).

89. O Pārvatī, I stand occupying his physical form. He is honoured, adored and meditated upon like me. There is no doubt about it.

90. O goddess, in Kali Age the excellent Prabhāsa Kṣetra is very difficult to attain. It is the truth, nothing but the truth. Thrice I aver that it is the truth, O beautiful lady of Suras. Out of affection for you, now I shall expound something special.

91. Someśa is my favourite among those Liṅgas that are in Bhūrloka. The Guṇas (good qualities) present in this Liṅga are known to me.

92. Only I know. No one else at any rate knows it. I am worthy of being adored in other Liṅgas too by Suras and Asuras.

93. O goddess, we ourselves adore this Liṅga.

94. There is a time when there is neither Brahmā, nor the

earth nor the Sun; everything is the Lord of the worlds alone. At that time, O renowned one, we shall adore it.

95. After the dissolution of Brahmā, this great Liṅga will protect this holy spot by adopting the future role (existence).

96. Ten crores of Liṅgas come from the Gaṅgādvāra at midday. O lady of excellent countenance, and get merged in this Liṅga.

97. All the Tīrthas all over the earth and those in the sky always come (here) for the sake of the ablution of this Liṅga.

98. Blessed indeed are those men who have settled in Prabhāsa and who will visit Someśvara who releases people from the fear of worldly existence.

99. There is no doubt about this that all the sins perish in the case of those who remember Someśvara with mental purity.

100. O goddess, this Kṣetra is remembered always as the most favourite of mine. It is fascinating even unto the groups of sages, and Siddhas. O goddess, all those living beings that die in this holy spot, reach a spot beyond heaven. There is no doubt.

101. Even the Devas with Brahmā and Viṣṇu as their leaders do not know it either through Sāṁkhya or Yoga or the Pāśupata system.

102-103. *Kaivalya* (Salvation) which is devoid of dirt and attachment is obtained in this Liṅga. O renowned one, Devas and the others wander over mundance existence as long as they do not realize the Three-eyed Lord, Someśvara. The Kṣetra is mentioned as Prabhāsa. I am undoubtedly the Kṣetrajña.

104. This great prowess of Someśvara has been mentioned to awaken you. Those men who read this will attain that region of the Moon-crested Lord.

105. The men who have sought refuge in Someśvara with devotion, never again get involved in the fearful cycle of worldly existence of terrible features.

106. The twice-born ones who have resorted to Dakṣiṇāmūrti and perform the Japa of *Śatarudriya* are not reborn in this world. They have attained the other shore of this ocean of worldly existence.

107. Only a general outline of Śrīsomanātha has been narrated to you. It is partial. In the course of many years or many Yugas even, it cannot be told through one mouth.

CHAPTER EIGHT

The Glory of Someśvara

The Devī said:

1. Once more, do tell me the greatness of Śrīsomeśvaradeva, O Lord of Devas, O benefactor of the worlds. It is destructive of all sins.Tell me the trinity (Liṅga) that has Brahmā, Viṣṇu or Śiva as well as all the three as deities.

Īśvara said:

2-3. Listen with single-minded attention to my ancient lore that should be guarded as a secret. Listen to the great miracle that happened in that Liṅga.

Like an oblation (*Āhuti*) of clarified butter into sacred fire, sixty thousand crores of sages of sublimated sexuality entered that Liṅga.

4. These Śaktis also originated therefrom: *Siddhi* (Achievement), *Vṛddhi* (Enhancement), *Tuṣṭi* (Satisfaction), *Ṛddhi* (Prosperity), *Puṣṭi* (Nourishment), the fifth one, *Kīrti* (Reputation), *Śānti* (Quiescence) and *Lakṣmī* (Fortune). All these rose up from that Liṅga.

5-6. Seven crores of Mantras and Siddhis, Divine Yogas and *Rasas* (essences, elixir), divine medicines and potions, Bhūtatantra pertaining to Garuḍa, Khecarīs (sky-stalkers, evil spirits) and Vyantarīs (spirits)—all these originated together from that Liṅga.

7. The other eight Siddhis (e.g. *Aṇimā, Laghimā* etc.) also that have been glorified, rose up from that spot along with the Liṅga.

8. O goddess, I shall mention another thing. Those who attained Siddhi here and were born as parts of mine were merged in this Liṅga.

9-10. I shall mention their exploits in due order. The following seven are remembered as *Kutsikas:* Purākramas, Grahas, Muṇḍas, Guḍakas, Hetukas, Vimalas and Daṇḍikas. Through my Pāśupata yoga, these achieved Siddhi in this Liṅga formerly.

11. The following seven are glorified as Gārgeyas: Rudra,

Vipra, Dāna, Candra, Mantha, Avalokaka and Sūryāvaloka.

12-13. O lady of excellent complexion, they become Siddhas in Someśvara at Prabhāsa. The following are glorified as Pauruṣeyas: Mūkammanya, Śiva, Prakāśa, Kapila, Satkula and Karṇikāra. Formerly they became Siddhas in Someśvara at Prabhāsa that is destructive of sins.

14. In every Yuga formerly there appeared Siddhas in that favourite Liṅga of mine. These and other Brāhmaṇas will be born in Kali Yuga.

15. There they will attain Siddhi that is inaccessible even to Devas. Thus that Liṅga which bestows excellent Siddhis has been wholly explained to you.

16. It is difficult of access to all human beings. It is well-established in Prabhāsa. No one who is engaged in inauspicious activities understands it.

17-21. All the (following) malefic evil spirits and ailments perish when one visits Someśvara Liṅga, like fuel consigned to fire. The malefic spirits etc. are as follows: troubles caused by Bhūtadoṣas, Ḍākinīs, Pretas, Vetālas, Rākṣasas, Graha, Pūtanas, Piśācas, Yātudhānas,mothers called Jātahārikās (those who snatch away the new-born ones), Bālagrahas, and Buddha Grahas. The evil spirits of ailments are : Jvarabhūtagrahas, Atisāras (diarrhoea), Bhagandaras (fistula), Aśmarī (stones), Mūtrakṛcchra (strangury), and thousands of other ailments such as ulcers, leprosy, tuberculosis, rheumatism, gout, piles etc.

22. All other torments from serpents, scorpions, Ghoṇapas (insects drinking through snouts, i.e. hogs etc.)—all these perish by visiting Someśvara.

23-24. The last Bhairava is remembered by the name Someśvara. He is well-known by the synonyms of Kālāgni, Rudranātha etc. I stand thereon, O goddess of Devas, conferring blessings on devotees. Undoubtedly I devour all the evil deeds of men.

25. The Prāṇa (vital breath) present in the body, that moves about in the bodies of living beings, is one in the whole of the Cosmic Egg and also in diverse forms.

26-27. All the Vedas and the great sages praise this Lord. The form of the great Brahman is attained through that deity and that Lord is established in Prabhāsa. It is like a well concealed gem in the house which no one knows.

28. That Liṅga is stationed in Prabhāsa. It is like a gem. In the former Kalpa it pierced through the seven Pātālas.

29. It is mentioned as resembling the refulgence of a crore of suns and the fire at the time of annihilation. Therefore Someśvara is mentioned as Kālāgni Rudra.

30. Thus, O goddess Pārvatī, the greatness of Someśvara has been briefly described to you. It is destructive of all sins.

CHAPTER NINE

The Garland of Skulls and Tattvas

The Devī said:

1-3. I bow down to that divine refulgence originating from Śaṅkara. It was visible to me as stationed in the middle of Kālāgni Rudra in the ancient holy spot of Prabhāsa.

I seek refuge in Someśvara, the Lord of Devas, the cause of the destruction of sins. It is this deity who is being worshipped by sages of hoary antiquities with the collections of the Vedic texts and the Yogas mentioned in the Vedas.

O Lord of Devas, O Lord of the worlds, O Lord and cause of the blessings to the devotees! There is a certain doubt in my mind. It behoves you to clarify it.

Īśvara said:

4. O goddess of great renown, what is the doubt that has arisen in your mind. Tell me, O lady of great weal, I shall expound everything.

The Devī said:

5. If you are the great Lord, the creator without beginning and end, the cause of creation and annihilation, how is it that a garland of skulls has been worn (by you)?

6-7. Thereupon, Śaṅkara, the Lord of Devas, laughed and spoke these words: "This garland of mine that shines with many crores of skulls has been made out of skulls of thousands of Nārāyaṇas and ten thousand Brahmās. Therefore, it is devoid of beginning and end.

8. A new Viṣṇu is born in every Kalpa. So also a new Brahmā. In every Kalpa, Viṣṇu and Prajāpati are created by me.

9. In this form, O goddess, I am stationed at the root of Kālāgni Liṅga in Prabhāsa. I am adorned with the garland of skulls.

10. I am quiescent without beginning, middle and end. I hold a rosary. I am seated in the lotus-posture. I am the bestower of boons. I resemble (in complexion) snow, a jasmine flower and the moon.

11. Viṣṇu stands to my left and Pitāmaha to my right. The four Vedas are present in my belly and the eternal Brahman in (my) heart.

12. The fire, the moon and the sun are settled in the eyes.

13. In this manner, O great goddess, I am stationed at Prabhāsa that has been brought into being through Āpya tattva (element called water). Let there be no doubt in you anywhere."

14. On being told thus, the goddess became glad. With great devotion she eulogized the Lord of the Chiefs of Devas in words choked due to delight.

The Devī said:

15. Be victorious, O Lord, O great Lord, O Īśvara, O creator and sanctifier of all. Obeisance to you, O Lord of Suras, Obeisance to the great Īśa.

16. Obeisance to the creator, the beginningless one. Obeisance to one occupying everything, stationed in everything, Obeisance to you, the abode of refulgence, Obeisance to you.

17. Obeisance to you of sixfold nature, Obeisance to you, *Dvādaśānta* (One present at the extreme point of exhalation in Prāṇāyāma). Obeisance to you, O Haṁsa (seer of lofty principles?); Obeisance to you, O bestower of salvation.

18. While the Lord was being eulogized by the goddess thus, the crescent moon in his crest was moving (expressing satisfaction). Then the delighted Lord spoke these words:

Īśvara said:

19. Well! Well! O highly intelligent lady, I am pleased. May a boon be chosen.

The Devī said:

20. If you are pleased, O Lord of Devas, if I am eligible to receive a boon, once again do expound in detail the greatness of Prabhāsa Kṣetra.

21. O Lord of goblins, Lord Viṣṇu is the leader of the slayers of Daityas, Why then did he leave Dvārakā and resort to Prabhāsa Kṣetra?

22. There are sixty hundred crore sixty thousand Tīrthas which exist in the centre of Dvārakā. Why did Hari disrespect these?

23. Dvārakā is a holy city surrounded by Immortals and resorted to by meritorious persons. This being so, why has he left it and come to Prabhāsa?

24. Hari is the leader of Devas and human beings. He is the source of origin of heaven and earth. Why did he abandon Dvārakā and meet with his death in Prabhāsa?

25. He is the only one who creates motion (mental activities) in the discus in the form of minds of men. He is the excellent one among the wielders of discus. Why did he meet with death at Prabhāsa?

26. How (is it that) Lord Viṣṇu who gives universal protection all over the worlds resorted to Prabhāsakṣetra?

27-29. He is the Lord who at the time of the dissolution (Pralaya) of the universe, takes in water and makes all his body aqueous and makes the world a vast expanse of water through his vision, with his Ātman realized. How did he meet with death at Prabhāsa, O Consort of Pārvatī? In days of yore, this primordial soul assumed the form of a boar and lifted up (from the ocean the sinking) Earth along with mountains and forests. Why did he, the destroyer of sins, cast off his body at Prabhāsa?

30. How did the Lord of the chiefs of Devas, who adopted a leonine form and killed Hiraṇyakaśipu, resort to the holy spot of Prabhāsa?

31-33. In every Yuga, the Vedas call him thousand-footed, thousand-eyed, thousand-headed and highly lustrous. How did that Lord cast off his body in Prabhāsa?

The abode of Pitāmaha (god Brahmā) arose from the Araṇi in the form of Viṣṇu's navel. That lotus (Paṅkaja—mud-born) was not born (grown) from mud as the whole world formed an expanse of water. How is it that Hari who lifted up in a moment such a lotus, resorted to Prabhāsa?

34. He is the slayer of hostile warriors. He adopts the eternal Yoga and lies down in the northern part of the Milk Ocean, the ocean of nectar. Why did that great Lord abandon his body in Prabhāsa?

35. How did the Lord of chiefs of Devas, who made the Suras Havyādas (those who partake of Havyas or offerings in Yajñas) and the Pitṛs Kavyādas (those who partake of Kavya or oblations etc.) resort to Prabhāsa Kṣetra?

36. How did that Lord who adopts form befitting the Yuga for the purpose of the welfare of the worlds and redeems Dharma, happen to resort to this Kṣetra?

37. How did the Lord who created the three Varṇas, the three worlds, the three Vidyās, the three types of Pāṭhakas (teachers, readers, reciters), the three divisions of time, the three Karmas, the three Devas, and the three Guṇas, resort to the Kṣetra?

38-39. He is the goal of the righteous but is unattainable to sinners. He is the source of the origin of four Varṇas and is the protector of that system (of castes). He is the knower of four lores and abides by four stages of life. Why did such (great god) abandon Dvārakā and meet with death at Prabhāsa?

40-42. He is identical with the quarters, sky, earth, water, wind, fire, the pair of luminaries i.e. the moon and the sun. He is the Lord of the Yugas, his body is like the night in complexion. He is reported to be the greatest refulgence. He is mentioned in the Śruti as the greatest penance. He is spoken as greater than greatest. He is the greatest Ātmavān (possessor of soul). He is the divine Āditya etc., and is the Lord and slayer of Daityas. How did that son of Devakī attain siddhi in Prabhāsa?

43-46. He is the annihilator at the conclusion of the Yugas. He is the slayer of the destroyers of the worlds. He is the bridge for the existence of the worlds. He is the purest unto those of pure activities. He is the knower of the scholars of the Vedas. He is the Lord of those who exert influence unto the living beings. He is like Soma. He is like Agni (Fire-god) unto those who follow the path of Agni. He is the mind of Manuṣyas (human beings). He is the tapas of the *Tapasvins* (Sages). He is *Vinaya* (discipline) among those that become tacticians. He is the fiery refulgence of the brilliant ones. He is the *Vigraha* (idols, physical form) of all *Vigrahas*. He is activity of those who are active. How did he forsake Dvārakā and resort to Prabhāsa Kṣetra?

47. Vāyu is born of Ākāśa (Ether). Hutāśana (fire) has Vāyu as the vital essence. The vital essence of Devas is fire and Madhusūdana is the vital essence of fire. He is also the vital essence of the Lotus-born (Brahmā). Why did he resort to Prabhāsa Kṣetra?

Sūta said:

48. O excellent Brāhmaṇas, on being asked thus by the goddess, Śaṅkara, the benefactor of the worlds, laughingly spoke to Pārvatī:

Īśvara said:

49. Listen, O goddess, I shall explain the extent of Prabhāsa Kṣetra. It is a sin-destroying secret. It is difficult of access even to Devas.

50. O goddess, O beautiful lady, there are many Tīrthas over the earth. There are many Kṣetras. The Tīrthas are crores in number and their power is limited.

51. Prabhāsa is glorified as one of unlimited power. There are all the Tattvas therein such as the Brahma Tattva, Viṣṇu Tattva and Rudra Tattva.

52. There, the association is much more, O Pārvatī. It is rare in the other Tīrthas. O goddess of Devas, the three Tattvas are present in Prabhāsa.

53. Brahmā, the grandfather of the worlds, is himself stationed there in the form of a lad along with the twenty-four Tattvas.

54. The Lord of twenty-five Tattvas, the leader of Devatās, the slayer of Daityas is directly stationed there, O auspicious one.

55. O goddess, O highly esteemed one, I reside along with you and also the thirty-six Tattvas in Prabhāsa that is destructive of sins.

56. Understand that Prabhāsa alone is the Kṣetra full of all

the Tattvas and all the Tīrthas. It is auspicious. Do not entertain any doubt anywhere.

57. Men and even worms and insects who die there attain the greatest region. There should be no doubt in this respect.

58. Women, barbarians, Śūdras, beasts, birds and animals that die in Prabhāsa go to the world of Śiva.

59-61. Those who are bound by lust and anger, those who are under the influence of covetousness, those who are assailed by the darkness of ignorance, those who are deeply set into the Māyā Tattva, those who are bound by the noose of Kāla, those who are deluded by thirst (covetousness), those who are engaged in unrighteousness, those who remain as sinners, Brāhmaṇa-slayers, ungrateful ones, those who defile the beds of their preceptors—all these great sinners attain the greatest goal.

62. A man who kills his mother and a slayer of his father all of them attain salvation. Still more so in the case of those who are of auspicious rites.

63. It is because he realized this, O great goddess, that Hari, the slayer of Daityas, came to Prabhāsakṣetra and cast off his body.

CHAPTER TEN

Supreme Excellence of Prabhāsa

Īśvara said:

1-4. O beautiful lady, I shall tell you another secret. O lady of excellent countenance, I am telling you what has never been mentioned to anyone else.

Brahmā is stationed in the *Pṛthvībhāga* (part of the Earth). Janārdana stays in the aqueous part. Rudra abides in the *Tejobhāga* (fiery part). Īśvara is stationed in the Vāyu Bhāga (gaseous part). Sadāśiva is directly present in the Ākāśabhāga (etherial part). The Tīrthas in the respective parts belong to the respective deities. There is no doubt about it. He is remembered as the Īśvara thereof.

5-7. The following eight are located in the Pṛthvī Tattva:

Chāgalaṇḍa, Dugaṇḍa, Mākoṭa, Maṇḍaleśvara, Kāliñjaravana, Śaṅkukarṇa, Sthaleśvara and Śūleśvara which is well-known.

O lady of excellent countenance, these holy eight are stationed in the aqueous part: Hariścandra, Śrīśaila, Jalpeśa, Annāntikeśvara, Mahākāla, Madhyama, Kedāra and Bhairava.

8-10. The following group of eight are the Ādiguhyāṣṭaka which is well settled in the *Tejas* Tattva: Amareśa, Prabhāsa, Naimiṣa, Puṣkara, Āṣāḍhī, Daṇḍi, Bhārabhūti and Lāṅgala.

Gayā, Kurukṣetra, Tīrtha (?), Kanakhala, Vimala, Aṭṭahāsa, Māhendra and a Tīrtha called Bhīma—these are mentioned as Vāyvaṣṭaka. They are great secret, yet they have been enumerated to you.

11-12. Vastrāpatha, Rudrakoṭi, Jyeṣṭheśvara, Mahālaya, Gokarṇa, Rudrakarṇa, Varṇākhya, Sthāpasaṁjñaka—these constitute the sacred eight stationed in Ākāśa, O lady of excellent countenance. All these Tattva Tīrthas (Tīrthas based in five elements) have been enumerated.

13. The deity of a Tattva Tīrtha shall indicate the greatness thereof. The great Tattva of aqueous features is a great favourite of Viṣṇu, O my beloved.

14-15. It is mentioned in the Śruti that Nārāyaṇa is remembered as lying down in water. O goddess of the Devas, the Tīrthas pertaining to the *Āpyatattva* (water principle) have already been enumerated to you. Certainly they are dear to Nārāyaṇa. Prābhāsika is remembered among the *Audaka* (Āpya i.e. aqueous) Tattvas.

16. There, Lord Hari gets dissolved in every birth. Vāsudeva is subtle-souled and is stationed in what is greater than the greatest (i.e. Brahman).

17. Śiva is the Lord without beginning and end. He is the greatest *Vyoman* (sky). There is none greater than he, as mentioned in all the scriptural texts and Āgamas.

18-19. So also (is said) especially in (Śaiva) Siddhānta, Āgamas, Upaniṣads and the Darśanas (systems of philosophy). In all these, Hari is not different from me, O lady of good renown. Hari is stationed in that holy spot along with me in directly perceptible form. He is connected with four Liṅgas but is not known by anyone.

20. By visiting Bhallukā Tīrtha one obtains that merit which is attained by Naiṣṭhikas (persons of permanent and steady

religious practice) of all castes through Vratas performed for the sake of salvation.

21. That spot measures a Gocarma (i.e. 150 Hastas by 150 Hastas) all round. O beautiful lady, without the help of scriptural texts no one can know this.

22. O Pārvatī, there are five Liṅgas there. Some of them have five faces. Viṣuva exists there even today among men (The equinox is fixed for the purpose of performing rites).

23. Some of the (faces) are very big, as large as the eggs of hen. They are entwined by serpents and marked by tridents.

24. Merely by visiting them, one gets the merit of the worship of a crore of Liṅgas. Hence this great holy spot is always resorted to by Brahmā and others.

25. Leading Brāhmaṇas of great renown (well-versed in the Vedas) and sages endowed with great Siddhi resort to it on the eighth and fourteenth lunar days of every month.

26. O lady of excellent countenance, the Liṅgas in Prabhāsa are adorned then and more so at the times of lunar and solar eclipses and on the Kārttikī day.

27-28. Puṣkara, Naimiṣa, Prayāga, Sampṛthūdaka and other Tīrthas numbering sixty hundred crores and thousands meet together at the place of the confluence of Sarasvatī and the ocean as well as in Sannihatī at Kurukṣetra on every Māghī day (Full-Moon day in the month of Māgha).

29. O lady of excellent holy rites, people cast off their sins by remembering that Tīrtha or by repeating the names thereof at the time of death.

30-32. O dear one! The name of this Kṣetra is different in the different Kalpas such as Ānartasāra, Saumya, Bhuvana, Bhūṣaṇa, Divya, Pāñcanada, the meritorious Ādiguhya, Mahodaya, Siddharatnākara, Samudrāvaraṇa, Dharmākāra, Kalādhāra, Śivagarbhagṛha and Sarvadevaniveśa that is destructive of all sins.

33-38. O beautiful lady among Suras, know that the lengths (and other dimensions) are to be guarded as secret:

In the first Kalpa, O goddess, this Kṣetra was remembered as Pramodana. All round it there was Nandana park. Beyond that was Śiva. Beyond Śiva was Ugra. Further beyond it is Bhadrika. Beyond that is Samindhana and beyond that is Kāmada.

Then there are Siddhida, Dharmajña Vaiśvarūpa which is

Muktida (bestower of salvation). Then Śrīpadmanābha and the highly refulgent Śrīvatsa. Then Pāpasaṁhāra and Sarvakāmaprada. Then, O lady of beautiful features, Mokṣamārga and Sudarśana. This Prabhāsa is the centre of all piety (Dharma) and it is destructive of sins. Hereafter there shall be Utpalāvartikas. In the centre of the Kṣetra is stationed my Garbhagṛha (*Sanctum Sanctorum*). O goddess, its names have been mentioned to you in due order.

39. By listening to all the names and to the greatness of the Kṣetra people shall undoubtedly attain the desired Siddhi.

40. To one who glorifies this thrice a day it accords great rise in fortune. If it is glorified during dusk, the sin of the whole day (i.e. one day and one night) perishes.

41. Hypocrites, men of poor intellect who reside here, deluded Brāhmaṇas solely concerned about their sustenance—all these go to heaven when they die.

42. In the centre of this holy spot within the range of twelve Yojanas, O goddess of Devas, there are thousands of Upakṣetras (subsidiary shrines).

43. Some of them are in the form of lotuses. Some are shaped like barley. Some are hexagonal; some triangular. Some are in the shape of sticks.

44. These have Brahmā etc. as the presiding deities.They are stationed in the middle of the Īśakṣetra, some in the shape of crescent and some in the shape of squares.

45. Some of them extend to half a Yojana. Some are one-fourth of a Yojana in extent. Some have the dimensions of a Nivartana (i.e. twenty rods) and some the measure of a Daṇḍa (four Hastas).

46. Some have the measure of a Gocarma (i.e. 150 Hastas by 150 hastas). Some have the space of a Dhanus in the middle (4 Hastas). There are crores of holy sites of the size of a sacred thread.

47. O lotus-eyed one, there is not even a space of an eighth of an *Aṅguli* (finger) in the sky where the divine Tīrthas are not present.

48-53. Even after Pralaya (ultimate annihilation) all these following holy spots resort to Prabhāsakṣetra and survive: The Liṅga that is at Kedāra, O goddess and that which is at Mahālaya, that which is at Madhyameśvara, the Pāśupateśvara Liṅga,

Śaṅkukarṇeśvara, Bhadreśvara, Someśvara, Ekāgra, Kāleśvara, Ajeśvara, Bhairaveśvara, Īśāna, Kāyāvarohaṇa, the meritorious Cāpaṭeśvaraka, Badarikāśrama, Rudrakoṭi, Mahākoṭi, the auspicious Śrīparvata, Kapālin the Lord of Devas, then Karavīra, Oṁkāra the highly meritorious, Vasiṣṭhāśrama where, O goddess, there are a crore of Rudras who can assume any form they desire. All these and other holy spots and shrines of mine all over the earth stay in Prabhāsa keeping Prayāga at their head.

54. Raviputrī is in the north. The ocean is remembered in the south. This is the south-north extent of this holy spot.

55. To the east of Rukmiṇī and to the west of Taptatoyā—this is the east-west extent of Prabhāsa that is glorified.

56. Keeping within this limit, O beautiful Sura lady, those Tīrthas reside in beginning with Pātāla and ending with Kaṭāha.

57. O great goddess, after realizing this, Hari who comprises within him all the Devas came to Prabhāsakṣetra and cast off his body.

58. Those who listen to this divine Carita of Rudra always or on Parvan days (festival days) go over, by my grace, to heaven, the abode of meritorious persons.

59. Thus the wonderful Carita full of merit has been completely described to you, O goddess. If anything else is there dear (interesting) to you or conducive to the prosperity of the sages, tell me. I shall expound it.

CHAPTER ELEVEN

Origin of Rājabhaṭṭāraka

Sūta said:

1. O Brāhmaṇas, on being told thus, the goddess, having charming eyebrows was struck with wonder. Her eyes became blossomed and she felt horripilation covering her body. She asked again:

The Devī said:

2-5. I am blessed. I am highly meritorious. Great penance

has been performed by me since this greatness of the holy place was heard by me from Mahādeva.

O Lord Hara, O Lord of the chiefs of Devas, O redeemer from the ocean of worldly existence, everything that was asked by me earlier has been explained.

Further, O Lord of the chiefs of Devas, I have been delighted by the nectarine words of yours. O Maheśvara, O Lord of Devas, I am not adequately satisfied.

I am inclined to ask something regarding the details of the Prabhāsa Kṣetra. Hence, O Kāmeśa, O Lord of the worlds, take pity on me and do describe it.

Īśvara said:

6. What is remembered as Jambūdvīpa is exactly at the centre of the earth. It is divided into nine regions, O beautiful woman, known as the different Varṣas (regions).

7. Therein, the first Varṣa is Bhārata. It is also remembered as being divided into nine parts. From south to north it measures nine thousand Yojanas.

8. The distance from east to west is eighty thousand. Himavān is in the north. The Kṣīroda (ocean) is in the south.

9-10a. O goddess, Bhārata, the excellent Kṣetra, is in between. There are four Yugas, viz. Kṛta, Tretā, Dvāpara and Tiṣya (i.e. Kali). The division of Yugas exists only here. So also the classification of the people into four Varṇas.

10b-12. O goddess, the men here live upto four hundred, three hundred, two hundred and one hundred years, in the Yugas Kṛta, Tretā etc. respectively. I told you about the earth likened to a lotus with four petals. The Varṣas Bhārata etc. are the petals in the four quarters, viz. Bhārata, Ketumāla, Kuru and Bhadrāśva.[1]

13. The southern-most Varṣa that has been mentioned by me by the name Bhārata has oceans to its south, west and east. Himavān is to the north like string unto bow.

14. This Bhārata Varṣa is the seed of everything, O lady of excellent countenance. It is Karmabhūmi. The consequences of incurring merit and sins are not obtained elsewhere.

---

1. This is the earlier Purāṇic theory.It preceded the later theory of seven continents of the earth.

15. O goddess of Devas, even Devas wish. 'We would rather attain human birth in Bhārata or in the earth.'

16. Viṣṇu is stationed in Bhadrāśva Varṣa as Aśvaśiras (horse-headed). In Bhārata he is stationed as Kūrma (Tortoise); as Varāha (Boar) in Ketumāla. He is in the form of a fish in the northern (Kuru).

17. In all those four Varṣas, the Viṣayas (regions) are set up on the basis of constellations. O great goddess, the *Vigraha* (the physical form) is Navapādaka (nine-limbed).

18. O great goddess, I shall tell you the distribution of the constellations in regard to Bhārata which is constituted in the form of Kūrma (Tortoise).

19. The holy Lord in the form of a Kūrma is stationed facing the east. O my beloved, he thus occupies Bhārata Varṣa of nine sectors.

20. Learn from me the constellation basis of this (Varṣa) set up in nine sectors. Kṛttikā, Rohiṇī and Saumya (i.e. Mṛgaśīras) the third—these have their positions on the back of the Kūrma.

21-23. Ārdrā, Punarvasu and Puṣya—these three constellations are on the mouth (face). Āśleṣā, Maghā, and Pūrvā Phalgunī—these three constellations, O my beloved, have their bases on the south-east Pāda(sectors), Uttarā Phalgunī, Hasta and Citrā—these three constellations are remembered as having bases assigned to the right belly (side) of the Kūrma. Svātī, Viśākhā and Maitra (Anurādhā)—these three are in the south- west sector.

24-26. Aindra (i.e. Jyeṣṭhā), Mūla and Pūrvāṣāḍhā are remembered as based on the back part. O lady of renown, the three constellations Uttarāṣāḍhā, Śravaṇa and Dhaniṣṭhā are mentioned in the north-west sector. Śatabhiṣak, Pūrvāproṣṭhapadā and Uttarāproṣṭhapadā—these constellations are stationed in the left part of the belly of the Kūrma, O my beloved. Revatī, Aśvinī and Yāmyā (i.e. Bharaṇī) are assigned to the north-east sector. Listen to the auspicious and the inauspicious benefit.

27. If a planet, the Lord of the constellation of a region happens to occupy a low position, it indicates a danger to that region, O great goddess. If it is ascendant, it indicates the advent of good future.

28. As has been mentioned by me, this Kūrma is the Lord in Bhārata. It is Nārāyaṇa, the Supreme Soul, who cannot be adequately thought of. Everything is firmly established therein.

29. The zodiacs Meṣa and Vṛṣa (ie Aries and Taurus) are in the centre of the heart; Vṛṣa and Mithuna (Taurus and Gemini) in the face.The signs of Cancer and Leo are in the south-east Pāda (sector).

30. Three zodiacs are remembered as stationed in the belly, Leo, Virgo and Libra. Two zodiacs, Libra and Scorpio are in the south-west sector.

31. Scorpio and Sagittarius are stationed in the tail. The three beginning with Sagittarius (i.e. Sagittarius, Capricorn and Aquarius) are in the north-west left sector.

32. Aquarius and Pisces occupy its northern belly, O great goddess. Pisces and Aries are stationed in the north-east sector.

33. In these regions, O my beloved, the constellations occupy Kūrma parts. The zodiacs influence the constellations and the planets are influenced by the zodiacs.

34. One can point out the affliction of the regions based on the high and low positions of the planets and the constellations. At that time devotees take holy ablution, make religious offerings and perform Homa etc.

35. O goddess, it is the Vaiṣṇava Pāda where the *Graha* (planet) is in the centre. It is the Lord of the worlds named Nārāyaṇa, the supreme soul who cannot be adequately thought of.

36. The Lords of the zodiacs Meṣa (Aries) etc. are respectively Mars, Venus, Mercury, Moon, Sun, Mercury, Venus, Mars, Jupiter, Saturn, Saturn and Jupiter.

37. O great goddess, Janārdana in the form of Kūrma is of such a nature. The region well-known as Saurāṣṭra is in the south-west sector.

38-39. O beautiful lady, based on the difference in the city it is of nine types. Its ninth part is near the ocean and well-known as Prabhāsa. O goddess, it is dear to me always. Its overall extent is twelve Yojanas.

40. The Pīṭhikā is said to be five Yojanas in area. It is in the centre. My abode is in the middle of it. It is near the ocean.

41. O great goddess, I reside at its centre in the form of a Liṅga.

42. Three hundred *Dhanus* (i.e. 300 x 4 Hastas) to the west

of Kṛtasmara, I stay along with you (there). O goddess of Devas, of excellent countenance.

43. O great goddess, that spot of mine is dearer to me than even Kailāsa. There too even an area extending to a *Gocarma* (150 Hastas by 150 Hastas) is to be guarded as secret, O Lady of excellent countenance.

44. Ordinarily it should not be mentioned. But it has been revealed (to you) out of love for you. This Prābhāsika[1] Kṣetra is illumined by my refulgence.

45-47. Therefore, O lady of excellent countenance, it is called Prābhāsika in the first Kalpa. In the second (Kalpa) my Prabhā (Bhā, refulgence) was obtained (seen) by all the Devas including Vāsava, O goddess of Devas. Therefore it is remembered as Prābhāsika, It is the place where the great Suras are *Prabhāvavantaḥ* (influential, powerful). Therefore it is glorified as Prabhāsa in the worlds. O goddess, the first among all the refulgences i.e. the first Tīrtha among all the Tīrthas shines. Hence it is glorified as Prabhāsa.

48. Or since Bhānu (the Sun) *prakṛṣṭam bhāsitaḥ* i.e.is made to shine all the more by Viśvakarman and the fierceness of brilliance was lessened there, therefore it is Prābhāsika.

49-50. Or, O goddess, *Prabhā* (lustre) was regained there by the Moon who had been cursed by Dakṣa and therefore had become lustreless. Therefore, it is remembered as Prābhāsika.

Goddess Bhāratī lifted up the Vaḍavāgni (submarine fire). Therefore, O goddess of Devas, it is glorified as *Prabhāsa.*

Since the *'Prakṛṣṭa Bhāratī'* (i.e. the most excellent Vedic text) is always heard on the pathways, O great goddess, therefore it is glorified as Prabhāsa.

51. O my beloved, the ocean always shines there with brilliant waves. Therefore, the name Prabhāsa became well-known in all the three worlds.

52. O lady of great lustre, there the sun always stands perceptible. Therefore, it gained renown in the earth as Prabhāsa.

53. To those who meditate perfectly I grant all desires there. Therefore, the Tīrtha became well-known in all the three worlds by the name Prabhāsa.

---

1. Various popular etymologies (explanations) of the term '*Prābhāsika*' are given in the following verses.

54-55. O my beloved, O beautiful lady of the Suras, the names differ due to the difference in the Kalpas as well as due to the etymological explanations. There are many reasons thereof.

But whatever name has to be given is remembered as the name Prabhāsa.

O goddess, it is well-established in the aqueous principle, the first body of Viṣṇu. Thus, O goddess, the cause of origin of the name of the Kṣetra has been explained to you succinctly.

56. O lady of excellent countenance, I shall explain further whatever you ask. Hence, O woman of excellent countenance, tell me quickly whatever is in your mind.

The Devī said:

57. O Hara, tell me in detail how the Prābhāsika Kṣetra originated in this Kalpa and the cause of it's origin.

Īśvara said:

58. Listen, O goddess, I shall duly explain the origin of the holy spot which, if a man listens to with devotion, will rid him of all sins.

59. O beautiful lady, O fair one, I shall narrate the greatness of the primordial Kṣetra which is to be kept a secret and is destructive of sins. Out of love for you I shall narrate.

60-62. In this Kalpa in the first Manvantara of the Svāyaṁbhuva Manu, when Brahmā was engaged in creation earlier, the sun was born of his right eye, O my beloved. In due course he had two wives. One of them should be known as *Dyau* (Heaven) the Queen. The other is remembered as *Nikṣubhā,* Earth. On the seventh day in the month of Mārgaśīrṣa, Dyau gets herself united with Sun.

63. On the seventh day in the month of Māgha Ravi shall be in the company of Earth. Then Bhūḥ and Āditya have their union.

64. Fresh after her bath in the *Ṛtu* (menstrual cycle) Earth conceived from Sun. During the rains *Dyau* gives birth to water flowing over Earth.

65. Then for the sustenance of all the three worlds, Earth gives birth to vegetation and food-grains. Brāhmaṇas become

delighted by making use of the vegetation. They begin to offer libation to fire.

66-67a. They begin to worship Pitṛs and Devas by uttering the words Svāhā and Svadhā (at the time of offering libations).

67b-68a. I shall narrate to you completely how she became a queen, whose daughter she was, and who were her children. Since Bhūḥ renders human beings, Pitṛs and Devas free from hunger through the medicinal herbs from her womb, and nectar, it is remembered as Nikṣubhā.

I shall explain fully how Rājñī (Queen) became so, how the sons were born etc.

68b. Marīci is the son of Brahmā and Kaśyapa is remembered as Mārīca (son of Marīci).

69. From him was born Hiraṇyakaśipu. Prahlāda was his son. The son of Prahlāda is remembered by the name Virocana.

70. Virocana's sister is the mother of Saṁjñā. She is remembered as the granddaughter of Hiraṇyakaśipu, son of Diti.

71. That daughter of Prahlāda is mentioned as the wife of Viśvakarman by learned ones.

72. There was a splendid daughter of Marīci, Atirūpā by name. She was the wife of Aṅgiras and the mother of Bṛhaspati.

73. Bṛhaspati's sister Viśrūtā was an expounder of Brahman. She was the wife of Prabhāsa, the eighth one among Vasus.

74. She gave birth to Viśvakarman, the most excellent one among artists and craftsman. By the name of Tvaṣṭṛ, he became the Architect of Devas.

75. The daughter of the preceptor of Devas is well-known in all the three worlds as Sureṇu. She became the wife of Viśvakarman.

76. The daughter of Prahlāda who has been mentioned earlier is remembered as the wife of Tvaṣṭṛ. He begot of her the daughters (called) Lokamātaraḥ (Mother of the worlds).

77. She is known as Dyau, Saṁjñā, Rājñī, Tvaṣṭrī and Prabhā. Valayā is her shadow. She is noble-minded Nikṣubhā.

78. She was a chaste divine lady and wife of the noble-souled Mārtaṇḍa. She was endowed with beauty and youth.

79-80. He did not approach her in the form of a man. Āditya blazed with his fiery refulgence. That refulgence scorched her unrivalled limbs. On being looked at by Ravi, Saṁjñā used to close her eyes. Hence Sun got angry and spoke these words to Saṁjñā:

Ravi said:

81. Whenever I am seen, you close your eyes. Hence, O foolish woman, you will give birth to Yama, the restrainer of the subjects.

Īśvara said:

82. Thereupon, the terrified lady made her eyes tremulous. On seeing her with tremulous eyes, Ravi said to her again:

Ravi said:

83. Since, on seeing me you made your eyes tremulous, you will give birth to a daughter, an unsteady river.

Īśvara said:

84. Then, due to the husband's curse, Yama and the well-known great river Yamunā were born of her. She gave birth to a third son, the auspicious Manu Śrāddhadeva.

85. Unable to endure red-hot iron-ball like refulgence of Ravi, Saṁjñā began to think within her mind:

86. 'What shall I do? Where shall I go? Where will I get relief? How can it be that my husband Arka does not get angry?'

87. After thinking thus in various ways, the daughter of the Patriarch, the highly esteemed lady, approved of the plan of resorting to her father.

88-89. After deciding to go to her father's house, the lady of great renown looked at her own reflection (*Chāyā*), which appeared to be made similar to her in every limb. Seeing that divine being in front of her, her own Chāyā, she spoke these words:

Saṁjñā said:

90. Welfare unto you. I am going to the abode of my father. O splendid one, at my bidding you should stay here without any change (in behaviour).

91. These two sons of mine and this girl of excellent

complexion should be well looked after. This should not be mentioned by you to my Lord.

92. Even when asked, this departure of mine should not be divulged by you.If you are to be addressed by my name Saṁjña behave accordingly (as if you are Saṁjña) to carry out my part.

Chāyā said:

93. Unless and until I am caught hold of by my tresses, until I am cursed, I will not mention your secret.You may go wherever you desire.

Īśvara said:

94. On being told thus, the great lady went to her father's abode. There she saw Tvaṣṭṛ who had washed away all sins by means of penance.

95. For a thousand years she stayed in the abode of her father. Due respect was paid by Viśvakarman. The uncensured lady still continued her stay in the abode of her father.

96. Not long after that stay, the father said to the lady of beautiful limbs. He praised his daughter with affection and consideration.

Viśvakarman said:

97. My dear, on seeing you even many many days appear as though half a Muhūrta. But thereby there is violation of Dharma.

98. Continued stay with kinsmen is not conducive to the reputation of a woman. Her stay in her own husband's house is what is desired by all the relatives of a woman.

99. You are united in wedlock with your husband Sūrya, the Lord of the three worlds, O my dear daughter, it does not behove you to stay in the abode of your father for a long time.

100. Hence do go to your husband's place. You have seen me and have been duly honoured by me.You should come again, O lady of pure smiles, to see me.

Īśvara said:

101-105. On being told thus by her father, "Do go! Do go!

repeatedly, she duly took leave of her father with due veneration.

She assumed the form of a mare. There is a Varṣa (continent) to the north of Meru. It has the shape of a bow. O lady of renown, it is well-known in the world as Uttara Kuru.

The chaste lady in the form of a mare, abstained from food and performed penance there.

In the meantime, her Chāyā, the divine lady, wished to abide by her own promise to Saṁjñā and stayed near Vivasvān (Sun).

Lord Sūrya, the Lord of the heaven, became enamoured of her exalted beauty. He begot of this second wife two sons and a daughter.

106. Of the two sons, O beautiful lady of Suras, he who was born first from Sun became similar to Manu. Therefore, he became (known as) Sāvarṇi.

107. The second son who was born became the planet Śanaiścara (Saturn). The girl was Tapatī whom King Saṁvaraṇa wooed.

108. This river named Tāpī rose from the foot of Vindhya. Her waters are always auspicious for a bath. She flowed into the western ocean.

109-111. This daughter of great refulgence was extraordinarily blessed and prosperous.

The Pārthivī (Earthy) Chāyā did not show the same affection as Saṁjñā had shown towards her children by means of fondling and feeding well. The lady did not behave towards the others as she did towards her own children. O Pārvatī, the future Manu continued to forbear this behaviour of hers.

112. O lady of excellent countenance, he (Manu) continues to stay on Meru even today performing penance. He was patient with his mother forbearingly but this was not the case with Yama.

113-114. He used to beg for his requirements (of food or eatables) many times. Due to his childishness and anger as well as due to the inevitability of the destiny, the foot was raised by him to kick her but, due to forbearance, he did not place his foot on her person.

115. Yama, the son of Saṁjñā, threatened Chāyā with his foot.

116. The earthy Chāyā became excessively angry. With lips throbbing slightly and the sprout-like hands moving, she cursed:

Chāyā said:

117. O Amaryāda (one who transgresses the bounds of propriety), you threaten me, your father's wife, with your foot. Hence this foot of yours will drop down today itself.

Īśvara said:

118. Tormented much in his mind due to that curse, Yama, the righteous Soul, intimated everything to his father along with Manu.

Yama said:

119. Dear father, this is indeed highly surprising. It has never been seen by anyone that a mother gives up her maternal affection and heaps a curse on her son.

120. Mother does not behave impartially with us. Ignoring the seniors, she tends to become more affectionate towards the juniors.

121. Due to childishness, it may be, or due to delusion, I lifted up my foot against her, Of course. But it was restrained from touching her. You may be pleased to forgive me.

122. This is clear that I, a son, have been cursed by her in anger. Hence, O foremost one among the eloquent ones, she is obviously not mother.

123. A son may be unmannerly but the mother ought not to be bereft of consideration for him. How did she manage to utter, "Son, your foot shall drop down."

124. O Lord of rays, O holy Sir, with your favour, let not the foot fall down as a result of this curse of my mother. Think out means to this effect.

Ravi said:

125. Dear son, undoubtedly there must be a strong reason in this matter, since you, a noble-souled one conversant with Dharma, got enraged.

126. There is a remedy too in the case of all curses, but there is no redemption to those cursed by mother.

127. It is not proper to make your mother's words false and so ineffective. But out of my filial affection for you, I will try to bring about some blessings.

128. Worms will scrape up some flesh from your leg and go down to the earth. Thereby her words will be true and you will also be not affected.

Īśvara said:

129-131. Āditya said to Chāyā, "When all the children are equal, why should partiality be shown towards one?

Certainly you are not the mother of these children. That Saṁjñā has gone away somewhere. Even in the case of her defective children, a mother does not utter a curse.

A son may commit thousands of blunders and misdeeds. He may even threaten her life. But the mother should not react sinfully. Hence tell me the truth. Do not get cursed (by me)."

Īśvara said:

132-134. On seeing the Lord of the Day ready to curse the Reflection (Shadow) of Saṁjñā, she trembled with fear. She narrated what had happened.

The great chaste fair lady said: "I am the daughter of Tvaṣṭṛ, O Vibhāvasu (Sun), O Divākara (Sun), I have my husband in you."

Though Vivasvān (Sun) asked many times, she said only thus and not otherwise. He became angry and got ready to curse her.

135. On seeing Sun ready to curse, Chāyā told everything regarding Saṁjñā's well designed act to Vivasvān.

136. On hearing it Lord Sun went to the abode of Tvaṣṭṛ. He honoured (Sun) who is adored by all the three worlds.

137. O Pārvatī, when the Sun-god came to his house and intending to burn down him (Viśvakarmā) with his dazzling refulgence demanded, "Where is Saṁjñā" ? He (Viśvakarmā) pacified him and told:

138-140. "Let my words by heard by you. Indeed she came to my abode. Unable to endure this fiery, well-known refulgence of yours, Saṁjñā performs penance roaming about in the forest.

You will see your wife of auspicious activities today itself, performing a great penance for the sake of (your) excellent form.

This I became aware through the words of Brahmā, O Lord, if it is approved of by you, O Lord of heaven, I shall make your refulgence attractive."

Īśvara said:

141. Since Bhāsvān's earlier form was of the nature of an orb, Lord Hari (the Sun-god) said to Tvaṣṭṛ, "So be it".

142. On being permitted by Vivasvān, Viśvakarman placed him on a lathe and prepared to whet his refulgence in Śākadvīpa.

143. While Bhāsvān, the Lord of all living beings, began to whirl, the oceans along with all the materials within became agitated all round.

144. O highly esteemed goddess of Devas, everything including Moon, the planets and the stars was pulled (by Sun) who was whirling. They began to fall down and become upset.

145. The waters in all the rivers were thrown up. The mountains split with all their peaks and ridges broken up.

146. O lady of excellent complexion, all the heavenly abodes having the support of Dhruva went down in their thousands when the rays that bound them together snapped in the course of their whirling.

147. When the sky and the surface of the earth became shaky as Bhāsvān whirled the massive clouds became shattered producing terribly loud thunders.

148. Then, O lady of excellent complexion, the whole universe became extremely confounded and chaotic. O goddess, as the entire range of the three worlds whirled the great sages and Devas eulogized Bhāsvān along with Brahmā.

Devas said:

149 -150. You are the primordial Lord of Devas. This entire universe was born of you. You stand in three different forms at the times of creation, sustenance and annihilation.Hail unto you, O Lord of the universe, who are the source of heat, rain, shower and cold (i.e. three seasons, Summer, Rains and Winter).

Indra came and eulogized that Lord as he was being whetted: "Be victorious, O Lord, O Lord of the universe, be victorious, O master of the universe."

151. Then the seven sages with Vasiṣṭha, and Atri as leaders, eulogized with different kinds of prayers. They began to say loudly, "Hail! Hail!" Then the Vālakhilyas eulogized with the excellent words of the Vedas:

Vālakhilyas said:

152. Obeisance to you in the form of Ṛks. Obeisance to you of the form of Sāmans. Obeisance to you having the form comprising Yajus Mantras. O Dhāmaga (one who has occupied the abode) of Sāmans, obeisance to you.

153. Obeisance to one whose sole form and body is perfect knowledge. Obeisance to one who has quelled darkness (or ignorance). Obeisance to one whose form is the pure refulgence. Obeisance to one who is personified Trinity. Obeisance to the Ātman free from impurities.

154. Obeisance to the most excellent one, Obeisance to one who is to be considered the most excellent one. Obeisance to the Supreme Ātman identical with all. Obeisance to one whose form pervades the entire universe. Obeisance to one of endless forms.

155. Obeisance to one who has become the cause of all. Obeisance to one stationed as knowledge in the minds. Obeisance to one in the form of the Sun. Obeisance to one whose form is very difficult to look at due to the dazzling brilliance.

156. Obeisance to you, Bhāskara (Creator of brilliance). Obeisance to *Dinakṛt* (the cause of day). Obeisance to the entire cause of all. Obeisance to the creator of twilight and moonlight.

157. O Lord, you are all this universe. When you whirl everything in the universe, the entire Cosmic Egg including mobile and immobile beings moves. On being touched by your rays all this becomes purified.

158. Through the contact with your rays purification of waters etc. is brought about.

159. O father, as long as this universe does not come into contact with your rays, the holy rites of Homa, Dāna etc. do not come to help (i.e. prove efficacious).

160. All these Ṛks, all the Yajus Mantras, and all the Sāmans fall from your person.

161. O Lord of the universe, you are Ṛṅmaya (full of Ṛks,

identical with Ṛks). You alone are Yajurmaya (full of Yajus, identical with Yajus). You are Sāmamaya and therefore, O Lord, you are Trayīmaya (identical with the three Vedas).

162. You alone are the forms of Brahman viz. *Para* (the greatest) and *Apara* (the least); *Mūrta* (embodied), *Amūrta* (disembodied), *Sthūla* (gross) and *Sūkṣma* (subtle). You abide in all these forms.

163. You are identical with the units of time such as Nimeṣa, Kāṣṭhā etc. You are the forms of Kāla such as Kṛṣṇa etc. Be pleased and change your form. Subdue your refulgence willingly. O Lord, for the sake of the worlds, you endure unbearable pain.

164. O Lord, you are salvation unto those yearning for salvation. You are the most excellent *Dhyeya* (object of meditation) of those who regularly meditate. You are the goal of all living beings who desist from Karmakāṇḍa (rituals).

165. O Lord of Devas, let there by happiness and prosperity unto the subjects. O Lord of the worlds, let us have happiness and welfare.

166. You are the creator. You alone create the universe. You are the protector ardently engaged in its sustenance. All this universe will get dissolved in you at the end. O *Tapana* (Burning One), there is no one other than you who bestows everything.

167. You are Brahmā. You are termed Hari and Hara. You are Indra. You are the Lord of Wealth (Kubera). You are Pitṛpati, Aṁbupa (Varuṇa), Wind-god, Soma (Moon), fire, one having the forms of sky, great mountain etc. Are not you the bestower of all desires?

168. Brāhmaṇas assiduously engaged in their respective duties eulogize you with diverse kinds of *Padas* (words, songs, prayers) and perform *Yajñas* everyday. Men engaged in Yogic practice meditate on you with humility in their minds and attain the greatest goal (*Mokṣa*).

169. You scorch and cook the universe, protect it, reduce it to ashes and make it manifest. You delight the universe with your rays filled with water. You create as the Lotus-born (Brahmā). You protect with the name Acyuta. At the end of the Yuga, you annihilate everything in the sole form of Rudra.

Īśvara said:

170. Even as he scraped and whetted *Bhānu* (Sun) Viśvakarman, the patriarch, experienced horripilation. He eulogized Vivasvān thus:

[Viśvakrman's Prayer:]

171. Obeisance to Vivasvān who shows mercy on the people who bow down. Obeisance to the noble-souled one who has seven horses of equal speed. Obeisance to the brilliant one, the kinsman of the clusters of lotuses and bees. Obeisance to the destroyer of the curtain of darkness.

172. Obeisance to the Lord who surpasses all in sanctity, who has an eye on everyone (is all-seeing); who bestows many objects of desire, who has a number of shining rays devoid of impurities, and who does everything conducive to the welfare of all living beings.

173. Obeisance to the excellent Lord of rays who is unborn, who is the conceiver and creator of the three worlds, who is the soul of the living beings, who is the most excellent of all compassionate ones. Obeisance to Sūrya, the source of origin and dissolution of all objects.

174. Obeisance to Vivasvān who possesses perfect knowledge, who is the immanent soul, who is the support of the universe, who desires the welfare of the universe, who is self-born, who is the eye of the world and free from impurities, who is the most excellent of all Suras and whose refulgence is unlimited.

175. In a moment you shine on the top of *Udayācala* (Mountain where the Sun rises) even as the groups of Suras sing about you in excellent songs. You are like the Lotus-navelled Lord in the world covered with thousands of rays.

176. O Mihira (Sun), your physical form assumes red hue due to the inebriation resulting from the drinking of the liquor of darkness. By your refulgence you are intent on sanctifying the three worlds.

177. You ride on a chariot of symmetrical parts having divine shining horses, not at all defective. O Lord, you always move among the hordes of enemies because of your interest in the welfare of the universe.

178. You propitiate the Pitṛs of Devas too with the nectareous juice. O destroyer of enemies, therefore,I bow down to you and whet and scrape your body.

179. O Ravi fond of the people who bow down, O sanctifier of the three worlds, I bow down to you. I am dejected[1]. Make me one with splendid complexion and one rendered very holy through the dust from your feet. Oh, protect me.

180. Thus, I bow down to Ravi, the most excellent one among Devas. You are Lord of Devas. You are a light unto the whole of the world. You are the progenitor of the entire universe. You are the sole cause of the refulgence that creates the three worlds.

Īśvara said:

181. Those who were expert in the art of music such as Gandharvas, Hāhā and Hūhū as well as Nārada and Tuṁburu, began to sing in praise of Ravi.

182-188. While Vibhāvasu (Sun), the Lord of the worlds, was being scraped, the songsters sang elaborately[2]. They were experts in the three *Grāmas* such as *Ṣaḍja, Madhyama* and *Gāndhāra.* Their songs caused pleasure through *Mūrchanās* and *Tānas* well produced. The seven notes of the gamut evolved them and embellished them with the three *Yatis* (pauses). The seven *Dhātus,* six *Jātis* and the three Guṇas were at the basis. The four types of Gīta rose out of the four Varṇas. The four Varṇas (*Vargas*) were duly repulsed. The seven Alaṅkāras embellished the songs. There was the purity of the three *Sthānas.* The three *Kālas* were perfectly set up. In every mind and dance item the *Rasas* and the *Layas* were in harmony.

The most excellent Apsarās such as Viśvācī, Ghṛtācī, Urvaśī, Tilottamā, Menakā, Sahajanyā and Raṁbhā duly danced the four types of *Padas* with three kinds of *Tālas* and *Layas* as well as *Yatis.* There were *Ātodyas* (musical instruments) and the *Nāṭya* was of four types.

189. These Apsarās were experts in depicting many Bhāvas. There were sounded hundreds of *Devadundubhīs* (drums) and thousand of conchs.

---

1. The reading *vyathitam* preferred to *racitam* in the text.
2. These terms which follow have been explained in previous Khaṇḍa. For details see Śārṅgadhara's *Saṅgīta-ratnākara.*

190. They sounded without being played and their sounds resembled the rumblings of clouds while Gandharvas sang and groups of Apsarās danced.

191. *Veṇus* (flutes), *Vīṇās* (lutes), *Jharjharas* (drums and cymbals) and various kinds of drums like Paṇava, Puṣkara, Mṛdaṅga, Paṭaha and Ānaka were sounded.

192. There was a lot of confused sounds from the different musical instruments of *Tūrya* and *Vāditra*.

All the people joined their palms in veneration and bowed down humbly due to devotion.

193. All the Devas had assembled and there was clangorous hubbub. Viśvakarman kept Ravi on the lathe for a year.

194. Even as he was being eulogized by Devas, he continued the whetting and scraping. Sūtrakṛt (i.e. Tvaṣṭṛ) made the Lord get on to the wheel and whirled him.

195. This was like the work of a potter with a lump of clay. Viśvakarman continued to scrape with the sharp edge of his chisel even as he eulogized *Pataṅga* (Sun), the Lord of heaven.

196. A sixteenth part of the fieriness of the solar disc was scraped off even upto the feet, O lady of excellent countenance.

197. The part of the fieriness comprising Ṛks fell over Prabhāsa Kṣetra, O my beloved.O goddess of Devas, heaven was sanctified by the refulgence comprising Yajus Mantras of the great Lord.

198. Svarga was sanctified by the part comprising Sāman songs. Thus Bhūḥ, Bhuvaḥ and Svaḥ were set up. Then the refulgence was split into sixteen parts. Out of the first fifteen parts, the following were made.

199-201. The discus of Viṣṇu, the highly refulgent huge trident of Hara, the *Śibikā* (palanquin) of Kubera, the staff of Pretapati (Yama), Śakti of Devasenāpati (Kārttikeya) and the various weapons of the other Devas as well as Yakṣas and Vidyādharas—all these were made by Viśvakarman. Thus Lord Ravi now had only a sixteenth of his early brilliance. It is this brilliant light that is seen in the sky as of Ravi, O my beloved.

202. On being whetted thus by his father-in-law with the excess of refulgence scraped off, Mārtaṇḍa (Sun) had a very splendid body, as charming as that of the Flower-arrowed One (i.e. Kāmadeva).

203. Bhānu (Sun) with a lovely body went to Uttarakuru region. There he saw Saṁjñā in the form of a mare.

204. She was free of sins of all living beings due to her penance and restraint. On seeing him coming in the form of a horse, she had the suspicion of his being another male and so went forward facing him.

205. Their union thereupon was through the nose (of Saṁjñā) Two sons, Nāsatya and Dasra, with horse-faces were born.

206. At the culmination of the coitus Revanta[1] the son appeared with a sword, umbrella and coat of mail. As soon as he was born he seized the excellent horse of his father and fled.

207. Once he mounted the horse he never left it.Thereupon Daṇḍanāyaka and Piṅgala were commanded by Arka (Sun):

208-209. "Both of you, do bring back the horse to me not using force but through a loophole (i.e. by cunning device)." Though they stood at his side waiting for the loophole in regard to the horse, till today they did not find a loophole in regard to the noble-souled one. While Revanta went ahead Daṇḍa and Piṅgala closely followed.

210. They had speedily come out of Uttarakuru region and had come to the south of India where there was the holy spot Prabhāsa.

211. They as well as Revantaka were weary and distressed due to the rapidity. Gasping for breath with profuse perspiration all over the body, Revanta stationed himself there.

212. O goddess, from north to south a distance of a hundred thousand Yojanas was traversed in a Muhūrta by the noble-souled Revanta.

213. With profuse perspiration all over the body, O goddess, he stationed himself in Prabhāsa, riding the horse and accompanied by Daṇḍa and Piṅgala.

214. He is stationed to the south-west of Sāvitrī not very far.Since he was the son of Rājñī (Queen), O goddess, he was called Rājabhaṭṭāraka.

215. He has earned fame in the world as Rājabhaṭṭāraka. Revanta was employed in the post of Guhyabhaṭṭāraka (a venerable person as a confidant).

---

1. The name of their third son Revantaka is recorded in the Viṣṇu P. III.2.Mbh is silent about him.

216-218. Then Lord Sun, the scorcher of the worlds, approached him and said thus: "O dear one, you will also become a person worthy of the adoration to all the worlds.

Whether in a forest or in a great forest-fire or during danger arising from the enemies and robbers, if men remember you they will become liberated from the great disaster.

On being adored by men you will become greatly pleased and bestow on them prosperity, welfare, happiness, kingdom, health, fame and advancement."

219. Aśvins were made the physicians of Devas by their noble- souled father. Yama had pious and righteous outlook. He was impartial towards friends and enemies.

220. Then the destroyer of darkness employed him likewise. He made Yamunā, the river flowing through the Kālinda mountainous region (near the source of Yamunā).

221. Sāvarṇi, the highly esteemed son of Chāyā Saṁjñā, shall (in the future) become the eighth Manu, Sāvarṇika.

222-225. The Lord is performing a terrible penance on the top of Meru even today.His brother Śanaiścara became a planet, O my beloved.

After giving them boons thus and also to Revanta, Lord Bhāskara further explained his name. The son of Saṁjñā, a bestower of peace on her, goes like this. He was employed as the commander of horses by Bhānu. He who adores him on the path, traverses the way safely. O lady of excellent complexion, he can be easily propitiated always by men.

CHAPTER TWELVE

Creation of Yameśvara

Īśvara said:

1-2. She who was Saṁjñā was remembered as Rājñī and she who was Chāyā was Nikṣubhā.The root $\sqrt{\text{Rājṛ}}$ (Rāj) is remembered as meaning Dīpti (Shining). Rājā is one who shines always. He is superior to all living beings. Hence he is called Rājā. Since she was the wife of a Rājā she is glorified as Rājñī.

3. The root $\sqrt{\textit{Kṣubh}}$ is used in the sense of agitation. Since (the earth) is motionless it is called Nikṣubhā. Or (it may be thus) since members of her family shall be devoid of Kṣut (hunger).

4-7. Chāyā the divine enters it (the earth).Hence it is remembered as Nikṣubhā.

The (Lord) holding conch, discus and club is born in the family of (that king) who is the Manu in the world now, O highly intelligent one.

On being cursed by his mother, Yama became deficient of foot. He came to Prabhāsa Kṣetra on the earth and performed elaborate penance. O my beloved, he adored the Liṅga for more than ten thousand years.Becoming pleased, I granted him a hundred (i.e. a number of) boons. O goddess of Devas, Yameśvara is well-known there even today. One who visits it on the Yamadvitīyā day never sees Yama's world.

CHAPTER THIRTEEN

Origin of Arkasthala

The Devī said:

1-2. O great Lord, Savitṛ stationed on the lathe was whetted and scraped by his father-in-law lovingly. The particles of fieriness of the son-in-law fell in Prabhāsa profusely. O Lord, what was it transformed into at Prabhāsa? Do tell me.

Īśvara said:

3-4. O goddess of great renown, I shall narrate to you the ancient ancedote, the physical incarnation of Lord Arkasthala in Prabhāsa.

Listen, O goddess, I shall expound the excellent greatness of Sūrya. If a man listens to it with devotion, he is liberated from all sins.

5-6. O great goddess, Ravi was fixed on the lathe in Śākadvīpa for more than a hundred years.While Vibhāvasu (Sun-god) was being whetted and scraped, O my beloved, particles of his fiery splendour fell down in Prabhāsa, which took the shape of a *Sthala* (holy ground).

7. O goddess, earlier it was completely of gold on the earth, but due to the (evil) influence of the Kali Age it has become a mere rock now.

8. Actuated by a desire for welfare of all beings on the earth, Lord Divākara assumed the form of Arka and manifested himself.

9. Though actually named Hiraṇyagarbha he is glorified as Sūrya in Kṛta age. In Tretā his name was Savitṛ. He is remembered as Bhāskara (in Dvāpara).

10. In Kali Age he is glorified in all the three worlds by the name Arkasthala. The deity was self-installed soon after the incaranation.

11. O goddess, formerly the second Manu was Svārociṣa. Lord Divākara took the incarnation at that time.

12-14. O goddess, the deity is the bestower of worldly pleasures and salvation. He is the destroyer of ailments and misery. The particles of his fiery splendour spread over in an area of five Yojanas from south to north and five Yojanas from east to west. It extends to the north of the ocean upto Māheśvarī Nadī (river) and to the west of Nyaṅkumatī upto Kṛtasmara, O great goddess. This area was completely overspread by the auspicious particles of his fiery splendour.

15. O great goddess, twelve Yojanas were covered by it. Its subtlest refulgence issued forth from the primordial splendour.

16. To the north is the daughter of Bhāskara (i.e. the local river Yamunā). The ocean is to the south. To the east and west are the two Rukmiṇīs.

17. Within this area, O goddess, the solar splendour has spread. Thereby the holy spot extending to twelve Yojanas, was rendered sacred.

18. The middle of its centre is my abode, O beautiful woman. O great goddess, my holy spot exists in the centre of the refulgent solar zone.

19. O goddess, it is like the pupil in the middle of the eye. From the east to the west, O goddess, it extends from Gomukha to Āśvamedhika.

20. From the south to the north it extends from the ocean

to Kauraveśvarī. In the holy spot in the midst of all these I stay as Kṣetrajña (Soul), O lady of excellent countenance.

21. Since that abode of mine is illuminated by the refulgence of Arka (Sun), it has become well-known by the name Prabhāsa in this Kalpa, O my beloved.

22. An excellent man who sees Sūrya in the form of Arka there, shall be rid of all sins. He is honoured in the world of Sun.

23. It is as though he has had his ablution in all the Tīrthas and performed great Makhas (Yajñas). All the Dānas have been offered by him and the ancestors have been propitiated by him.

24. Since the Sun was born in the world there in the form of *Arka* (the plant *Calotropis Cigantea*), so in the course of taking food there, a leaf of Arka plant should always be avoided.

25. After a visit to Arkasthala, if a man takes food on Arka leaves, it is as though cow's meat has been eaten by him, O beautiful lady.

26. It is as though Bhāskara (the Sun-god) has been eaten by him. That man becomes a leper. Hence all efforts should be made to eschew the leaves of Arka (from food).

27-28a. If a pilgrim visits Arkabhāskara for the first time, O goddess, he should, after the visit, give a she-buffalo to a learned Brāhmaṇa. The buffalo may be copper-coloured. It should be offered along with a red cloth. Thereby Bhāskara becomes pleased.

28b-29. In the vicinity thereof, O highly esteemed one, not very far off in the south-eastern corner, there is the Liṅga remembered as Siddheśvara, O goddess, this Liṅga bestows all Siddhis. It is adored by all the three worlds.

30. Formerly in Kṛtayuga it was known by the name Jaigīṣavyeśvara. O my beloved, it becomes well-known as Siddheśvara in Kali Age.

31-33. On seeing the deity, O goddess, a man attains all the Siddhis.

O goddess of the chiefs of Devas, there is a crevice leading to Pātāla. It is not far from it. It is to the south and south-west of the deity Sun.

On being scorched by the brilliance of the Sun, the Rākṣasas named Mandehas and the Śālakaṭaṁkaṭas went to Pātāla. O my beloved, in Kali Age only the crevice exists but there is no passage leading to Pātāla.

34. Yoginīs and Mothers Brāhmī etc.guard that place. One should worship the groups of Mothers at night on the fourteenth lunar day in the dark half of the month of Māgha, by means of oblations and floral offerings. Thereby Siddhi is achieved.

35. Thus, by listening to the story of the whetting of the body of Bhānu, eulogized by Hara, Brahmā and Viṣṇu, one goes to the world of Divākara at the close of one's life.Indeed Bhānu is the cause of all holy rites and feelings.

CHAPTER FOURTEEN

Creation of Siddheśvara

The Devī said:

1-5. What has been narrated by you as the greatness of the deity Sun, may be further expounded in detail, O Lord of Devas, O Lord of the worlds.

How did Arkasthala, the ornament of Prabhāsa Kṣetra, take shape? The great Lord has to be worshipped by those desirous of the benefits of a perfect pilgrimage.

What are the Mantras? What is the procedure of worship? What are the *Parvas* (festive occasions) during which one should offer worship? How did the deity become Siddheśvara after having been Jaigīṣavyeśvara originally. O Lord of Devas, narrate this to me in full detail.

How was the crevice leading to the nether world created formerly? How did the Yoginīs and the groups of Mothers come there? O Lord Virūpākṣa, O Hara, O Lord of the worlds, have mercy on me and describe everything to me, if I am your beloved.

Īśvara said:

6. You have put a pertinent question, O goddess. I shall narrate briefly how Jaigīṣavyeśvara Hara became Siddheśvara.

7-8. Listen even as I expatiate upon the procedure of worship.

O goddess, in this Kṛta Yuga there was a son of Śatakalāka well-known by the name Jaigīṣavya. He was an expert in all the lores (branches of knowledge). He came to Prabhāsakṣetra and performed a very difficult penance.

9. He stood for a hundred years with air alone as the sole intake, a thousand years with water constituting his diet and ten thousand years with green vegetables for his food.

10. A thousand Cāndrāyaṇas were performed and Sāntapana thereafter. With meagre intake of food, he dried up his body and became *Digvāsas* (nude).

11. There is a Liṅga well-known as Mahodaya which was self-born in the previous Kalpa. He installed this Liṅga of the Lord of Devas and worshipped it.

12. He used to lie in holy ash. He smeared his body with the holy ash. He propitiated the deity with dances and songs. He performed Japa and made sounds like the bellow of a bull[1]. By means of penance he sanctified himself and remained pure.

13. Even as he was endowed with great devotion and propitiated the Lord thus, the Lord came to him and spoke these words:

14. "O Jaigīṣavya of great intellect, look at me with your divine vision. I am pleased with you. I shall grant you boons. Tell me whatever you cherish in your mind".

15. On being told thus by the Lord, he looked at the Three-eyed Lord, bowed down to his feet and spoke these words:

Jaigīṣavya said:

16. O Holy Lord, O Lord of the chiefs of Devas, if you are pleased with me, impart to me Jñānayoga that cuts off (the bonds of) worldly existence.

17. O Holy Lord, there is nothing more beneficial than Yoga and I do not wish for anything else. Let me have permanent devotion unto you, Skanda, Gaṇeśvara and the goddess.

18. Let there be no fear of ailments nor insult to (my) brilliance. Grant me absence of haughtiness, forbearance, restraint and quiescence.

19. O Lord, O great Lord, O Three-eyed One, I wish for these boons from you.

1. This is the Pāśupata procedure of worship.

Īśvara said:

20. You shall be immortal, free from old age and free from all griefs. You shall be a great Yogin of great power. You will become endowed with Yogic supernatural powers.

21. By the power of this well-protected holy spot of mine, you will attain the eight Yogic powers such as *Aṇimā, Laghimā* etc.

22. O most excellent sage, you will become a well-known Yogācārya (Master of Yoga).

23. He who regularly worships this Liṅga consecrated by you, shall be liberated from all sins. He will attain the divine Yoga.

24. He who comes to this cave of Jaigīṣavya and practices Yoga shall become a liberated soul in seven days. He shall cross the ocean of worldly existence.

25. Within a month he will begin to recollect the previous birth and everything that has happened before. Within a single night he will get a pure body. Within two days he will be able to redeem the Pitṛs and when three nights elapse, he will redeem seven succeeding generations.

26. Further, O Brāhmaṇa sage, you will become invincible to other yogins. You will have my vision whenever you wish.

27. After granting the boons thus, the Lord vanished there itself. This is what happened in Kṛta Yuga. It is thus explained to you, O goddess.

28-30. O great goddess, the same happened in Tretāyuga as well as Dvāpara. After the advent of Kaliyuga, the great sages, Vālakhilyas numbering eighty-eight thousand, came to this Prābhāsika Kṣetra. Near Sūryasthala they propitiated the Lord of Devas who resided in the middle of the cave. Practising strict celibacy these sages performed penance for ten thousand years and attained the Siddhi in the form of identity with the Supreme Soul.

31. Therefore, O lady of excellent countenance, it became well-known in Kali Age as Siddheśvara Liṅga. O goddess, rare indeed is the vision of that Lord on Śivacaturdaśī—the fourteenth lunar day in the dark half which has conjunction with the Moon.

32. By worshipping the Siddhaliṅga, O goddess, one gets that merit which accrues from donating the entire Cosmic Egg.

CHAPTER FIFTEEN

Origin of Pāpanāśana

Īśvara said:

1-3. To the south-east thereof, O goddess of Devas, there is the Liṅga installed by Aruṇa, the charioteer of Sūrya. It is very near the Siddhaliṅga, say three *Dhanus* (12 Hastas) away. It dispels the sins in Kali Age by mere vision. It's name is Pāpanāśana.

A person should worship it duly with great faith and devotion, O lady of excellent countenance, on the thirteenth lunar day in the bright half of the month of Caitra. He shall obtain the fruit of the Pauṇḍarīka Yajña.

CHAPTER SIXTEEN

Origin of Sunandā and Other Mother Goddesses

Īśvara said:

1-4. Now listen to the greatness of the *Pātālavivara* (Crevice leading to the nether worlds). O great goddess, this was already asked earlier by Brahmā, the creator of the Universe.

When there arose prevalence of darkness, Rākṣasas were born there too. They were innumerable, very powerful. All of them hated Sūrya.

They had Dhūmra as their leader. On seeing the noble-souled Divākara (Sun) rising, all of them immediately laughed at him: "Who is this perpetrator of evil deeds who may be our destroyer?" Standing before Sūrya, they spoke these and various other similar words.

5. On hearing this, the Lord got angry and his lips throbbed. Divākara appeared to swallow the words of the Rākṣasas.

6. Like a killer lion, the destroyer of darkness wanted to annihilate the cruel Rākṣasas. He looked at them with wrathful eyes.

7. Sūrya traversing the sky with great rays thought of killing

them, but the Lord of heaven did not know the weak point of the Rākṣasas till the end.

8. Then he saw these ones fallen from Dharma, having minds overwhelmed with sins. After considering this, Lord Prabhākara began to meditate.

9. The *Rajanīcaras* (demons) came to know that the three worlds were swallowed (pervaded) by the splendour. Then they were looked at by Bhānu with eyes (as if) burning with anger.

10-11. Slipping down from the sky they fell like the planets with dwindling merit. Dhūmra surrounded by the Rākṣasas falling down from the sky, shone like a half ripe *Tāla* fruit surrounded by monkeys. They fell automatically like stones released from a machine.

12. Thereafter, they fell further, dislodged and carried off by the wind. After reaching Prabhāsa Kṣetra, they pierced through the earth and went to the nether worlds, O lady of excellent complexion.

13. It is there that Lord Arkasthala, the bestower of all Siddhis, is present. O goddess, the great Pātāla cavity is in its vicinity.

14-15. There were crores of other cavities but, O beautiful lady, they had become lost. Beginning with Kṛtasmara and ending with Arkasthala with the Sun as the deity in between these two, O goddess, is the holy place of Sūrya. Attaining the boon from Devamātṛ (i.e. Aditi) the eight Siddhis had set up there.

16. It is remembered, O goddess, as the middle part of the splendour of Sūrya. It is fully golden. No one without merit sees the place, O goddess.

17. O great goddess, a hundred and one cavities and crores of *Sparśa* gems (philosopher's stones) are there, and Siddheśa guards them.

18. O great goddess, this holy spot is always dear to Sūrya. O my beloved, in the *Sūrya Parva* (festival day of Sun), it is more efficacious than Kurukṣetra.

19. Brāhmī, Hiraṇyā and the confluence of the great ocean, these three meeting places together, bestow the fruit of visiting Koṭitīrthas (a crore of Tīrthas).

20. The Devamātā and Maṅkīśā are there. So also it is cited that Nāgasthāna (holy spot of Nāgas) and Nagasthāna (holy spot of the mountains) are also there.

21. Thus the great origin of Arkasthala has been narrated. It is also explained how the cavity came into existence due to the fall of Rākṣasas.

22. O goddess of Devas, the other cavities there have become lost but this is clearly manifest even today, O beautiful woman.

23-24. That cavity named Śrīmukha is guarded by the Mothers, O my beloved. A devotee should worship the groups of Mothers beginning with Sunandā in accordance with the injunctions on every fourteenth lunar day for a period of one year, through the offerings of animals and flowers and excellent incense and lights. Brāhmaṇas should be fed. O goddess, he will achieve Siddhi.

25-27. Hence, if one desires achievement of Siddhis by oneself, one should assiduously worship all the Mothers. All these Mothers become famous by the name Sunandāgaṇa in this Prabhāsa Kṣetra, O lady of excellent complexion. It is to the north and middle of Pātāla. It has been briefly told. On hearing it an excellent man becomes rid of all dangers.

CHAPTER SEVENTEEN

Procedure of Worship

Īśvara said:

1-5. O lady of great renown, now I shall tell you the injunctions regarding the worship of the Lord of Arkasthala as to how he should be adored by excellent men.

Āditya (Sun) is called the primordial one among all the Devas. Since he is the Ādikartā (first creator) he is called Āditya.

Without Āditya there is neither day nor night, no libation, no holy rite, no unrighteousness and no living beings whether mobile or immobile exist.

Āditya protects everything always. Āditya creates. Āditya annihilates everything. Hence he is identical with Trayī (Triad).

O great goddess, I shall tell you the procedure of the worship of the noble-souled Bhāskara by means of the extensive Vedic Mantras. O beautiful lady, listen to it. It is destructive of all sins.

6. I shall tell you fully, O great goddess, how Dvādaśātman (i.e. Sun) is to be adored duly as (incorporated in) an icon.

7. At the outset one should cleanse the mouth, Then one takes the bath. After wearing washed clothes and with purified body one should touch Sūrya (i.e. the idol of the Sun-god).

8. First I shall explain the procedure for cleansing the mouth through *Dantakāṣṭha* (a twig used as toothbrush)[1]. If Madhūka tree is used (i.e. a twig thereof), there shall be the acquisition of a son. O my beloved, if Arka twig is used, it is good for the eyes.

9. By using Badarī twig, one shall attain eloquence, by using Bṛhatī twig one defeats wicked people. If a Bilva twig is used, there shall be good fortune. Undoubtedly so with Khadira twig also.

10. By using a Kadamba twig ailment is reduced; by using Atimuktaka twig there is acqusition of wealth. If Āṭarūsaka twig is used, one receives greater respect.

11. If a Jāti twig is used, one attains chiefship of one's community; Aśvattha yields fame; by resorting to Śirīṣa one gets all glory.

12. Conjugal felicity shall be attained by one using a Priyaṅgu twig. By resorting to a Plakṣa twig always, one attains what one desires.

13. One should never use a twig if it is split, damaged, crooked, or dried in the upper part or if the bark is peeled off.

14. One should chew the twig a *Vitasti* (i.e. a span or 12 Aṅgulas) long, neither more nor less. One should sit comfortably facing the north or the east. One should remain silent while chewing.

15. One may have some specific desire cherished in the heart, in which case one should recite the following Mantra. An intelligent (householder) shall chew the twig always in this manner.

16. "O *Dantakāṣṭha* (toothbrush twig), obeisance to you. O *Vanaspati* (tree or plant), you have granted me the boon. Hence you know my desire. Grant me the full *Siddhi* (accomplishment of desire) always."

---

1. See HD II. i. pp. 653-656.. With minor differences, Smṛtis present a consensus on this procedure. Vide *Smṛti Candrikā*, p. 105-6.

17. After repeating the above Mantra three times, one should begin to chew the twig. After cleansing the mouth, the twig is washed and kept in a clean place.

18. O goddess of Devas, the tongue should not be cleaned by means of this twig. If one desires good reputation, one should do these two acts separately..

19. Cleansing the teeth with finger, taking in salt by itself directly and eating mud—all these are on a par with eating cow's meat.

20. If the mouth remains stale (i.e unwashed) a Brāhmaṇa always becomes impure. Hence one must use a dry or damp tooth-brush twig.

21. On days when *Dantakāsṭha* is prohibited one must gargle sixteen times with sixteen mouthfuls of water. One should cleanse mouth with water rendered fragrant by means of lotus.

22. A Brāhmaṇa who touches (the idol of) Bhāskara without cleaning the mouth, becomes a leper for three thousand years.

23. After washing clothes etc. a person should take his bath. A lump of clay should be extracted from a clean pleasing spot with the *Astra Mantra* repeated.

24. The letter H(ह) along with the letter U(उ) and Anusvāra(ं) and *Phaṭ* is called *Astra Mantra* (i.e. *Huṁphaṭ*). One should gather a lump of clay by repeating this Mantra and then take bath.

25-26. The lump of clay should be without grass blades or gravel.Three parts thereof are made.One part is to be rubbed well repeating the *Astra Mantra;* another part with the *Bhāskara Mantra.* The third part is to be charged with the ancillary Mantras once each. After uttering the *Astra Mantra,* the clay is to be thrown in different directions. Now the water has become free from impediments.

27. A man should cover (ritualistically) the Sūryatīrtha with the second and third parts once each. Then he shall take his bath in the Ravitīrtha.

28. The sounds of musical instruments and conch should be thought of when the devotee meditates on Lord Divākara. After the bath, the Ācamana rite is performed again with royal ostentatiousness.

29-30. The bath is performed along with the utterance of

the *Mantrarāja*[1]. The *mantrarāja* is as follows: Letters H(ह) and R(र) along with *Bindu* (dot) and Lakṣmī.Then the vowel is lengthened.The letter S(स) with the *Visarga*. Ultimately *OM HRĪṀ HREṀ SAḤ* becomes the Mantrarāja.[2]

31. Then the devotee propitiates all the Mantras with the fingers.The Devas are to be meditated on the point where all the finger tips converge. The sages are to be meditated on the left side *(Savya)* and the Pitṛs should be propitiated anticlockwise *(Apasavya)*.

32. *Akṣara* (Imperishable) is that which is sung about by learned men as the most excellent of all letters. It has nineteen *Mātrās*.

33. After taking the holy bath thus in accordance with the injunctions, the person should offer the Sandhyā prayers duly.Then the learned devotee offers water with palms joined together (as a cup) to Bhāskara.

34. Then he should perform the Japa of the three-syllabled and six-faced *Mantra* casually (or as he pleases). O beloved, this has already been mentioned to you as *Mantrarāja*.

35. Afterwards the person concentrates the mantras and ritualistically touches the heart with the Tīrtha (holy water). Through the Mantras, he concentrates in the soul and offers the Arghya.

36. The devotee remains clean after the bath. He makes a circular diagram on the ground by means of sweet scents and red sandalpaste. He then sits there with mental concentration.

37. Karavīra flowers are placed in a copper vessel, scented water is poured into it and gingelly seeds, Kuśa grass and raw rice-grains are put into it.

38. The materials of worship are fumigated with incense and red sandal. The devotee places that pot on his head and kneels down on the ground.

39. He then offers the Arghya to Bhānu (the Sun-god) uttering the Mūla Mantra. He who makes this offering is rid of all sins.

40. By offering *Arghya* to the Sun, one obtains that benefit, O goddess, which one gets by offering *Arghya* in Jyeṣṭha Puṣkara

1. Comparison of the details of Bath in HD II. 1 pp. 656 -668 shows that the cryptic description of Snāna is different - special to this Tīrtha.
2. As the editor of the Text notes, this Mantra of three syllables is a Sūrya Mantra in *Meru Tantra*.

in the course of a thousand Yugādis, a hundred Vyatīpātas and a thousand Ayanas (transits of the Sun).

41. There is no doubt about it, O goddess, that even if one be without the initiation and utterance of the Mantra, the devotee obtains the benefit through the *Arghya,* if offered with devotion for a year.

42. In the case of a devotee who is learned and has due initiation, if he offers Arghya to the Sun, he is not reborn on the earth, even when Bhāskara gets dissolved.

43. Along with his wife, O goddess,he attains ere long happiness in this very birth, conjugal felicity, long life, riches and freedom from illness.

44. Thus for the sake of the welfare of good men, the procedure regarding holy bath for the propitiation of the Sun god has been succinctly told to you. It is destructive of all sins.

45. Or, an excellent Brāhmaṇa who is unable to perform the Snāna-rite with elaborate utterance of Mantras without the requisite Dīkṣā (initiation) can perform Snāna following the Vedic procedure.

Īśvara said:

46. Now, O lady of good renown, I shall tell you the procedure regarding the Pūjā (worship) in accordance with the holy Vedic way. It is conducive to the welfare of Brāhmaṇas.

47. After the devotee has gathered together all the requisite things and has arranged in proper order the flowers etc. he should install the deity Bhānu on the Karṇikā and invoke him.

48. For the *Upasthāna* (waiting on the deity for the prayers to begin) the Mantra, beginning with *udutyam jātavedasam* (RV I. 50.1) is to be used. This is the Mantra glorified, O lady of good holy rites.

49. The deity is to be invoked by the Mantra beginning with *agniṁ dūta* etc. O lady of beauty, and adored by the Mantras beginning with *ākṛṣṇena rajasā* etc. (RV I. 35.2)

50. The Pūjā should be performed with the Mantra beginning with *haṁsaḥ śuciṣaṭ* (RV IV 40.5.). Special Pūjā should be performed with the Mantra beginning with *apatye tāyavo vathā* (RV I. 50.2) etc., O goddess.

51. The excellent *Samārcana* of Sūrya should be performed,

O goddess, with the Mantra beginning with *adṛśramasya* (RV I. 50.3.) etc. There must be constant Japa with the Mantra beginning with *taraṇir viśva darśa* etc. (RV I. 50.4).

52. Bhadrā Devī should always be adored with the Mantras beginning with *citraṁ devānām udagāt* (RV I.115.1). Vibhūti (glory) should always be adored with the Mantra beginning with *yenā pāvaka cakṣasā* etc. (RV I. 50.6)

53. Vimalā should always be adored with the Mantra beginning with *vidyām eṣi rajaspṛthu* etc. (RV I. 50.7), O lady of excellent holy rites. Amoghā should always be worshipped with the same Mantra.

54. Siddhidā (The bestower of Siddhis) in all the holy rites should be worshipped with the Mantra beginning with *sapta tvā haritaḥ* (RV I. 50.8) etc. With the same *sapta tvā haritaḥ.* one should worship the Lord of *Vidyuts* (Lightning).

55. With the Mantra beginning with *ud vayam tamasas pari* (RV I. 50.10) etc. one should worship the ninth goddess Sarvatomukhī always, O goddess.

56. The first *Bījākṣara* should be repeated after uttering the Mantra beginning with *udyannadya mitramahaḥ* (RV I. 50.11). The second should be adored, O goddess, with the Mantra *śukeṣu me harimānam* (RV I. 50.12).

57. With the Mantra beginning with *udagādayam ādityaḥ* etc. (RV I. 50.13) one should worship the third Bījākṣara. It is glorified that the fourth Bījākṣara should be worshipped with the Mantra beginning with *Tat Savitur Vareṇyam* etc. (RV III. 62.10).

58. It is proclaimed that the fifth should be adored with the Mantra beginning with *mahāhivo mahāyā* etc. With the Mantra beginning with *hiraṇyagarbhaḥ samavartata* (RV X. 1.1) etc. the sixth one should be adored.

59. O lady of excellent complexion, the seventh Bīja should be adored with the Mantra beginning with *savitā paścāttāt savitā* (RV X. 36.14) etc. After performing the rite of Nyāsa thus, O splendid lady, Āditya should be installed.

60. After installing Āditya, the devotee should perform the Nyāsa of the Aṅgas.

61. The Nyāsa of the heart is in the south-east, that of Śiras in the north-east, that of *Śikhā* (tuft of hair)in the south-west and that of *Kavaca* (coat of mail) in the north-west.

62. After the Nyāsa of the *Astra* in the quarters the *Karṇikā* (pericarp) should be adored with its *Bīja*. One should perform the Pūjā of the *Hṛdaya* with the Mantra beginning with *amosi prāṇitena* (*Āśvalāyana Śrauta Sūtra*)

63. One should worship the head, O goddess, with the Mantra beginning with *āyuṣyam varcaseti vaī* etc. (RV, Khila X. 128.2). *Śikhā* set up in the south-west should be worshipped with the *Gāyatrī* Mantra.

64. One should worship *kavaca* separately with the Mantra beginning with *jīmūtasyeva bhavati* etc. (RV VI. 75. 1.) The Astra should always be adored with the Mantra beginning with *dhanvannāgā dhanvanā* etc. (RV VI. 75. 2.).

65. *Netra* (eye) should be worshipped, O goddess, with the Mantra beginning with *aśvinā tejasā* etc. (*Vājasaneyī Saṁhitā* 20.80). Externally the Nyāsa of Soma (Moon) is in the east, that of Budha in the south.

66. Guru (Jupiter) should be placed *(Nyāsa)* in the west, the *Nyāsa* of Bhārgava is in the north. The *Nyāsa* of Maṅgala is in the south-east and that of Śanaiścara is in the south-west.

67. The *Nyāsa* of Rāhu is in the north-west and that of Ketu is in the north-east. One should always worship Soma with the Mantra beginning with *āpyāyasva* etc. (RV I. 91.16.17). The Pratīka is common to both.

68. O great goddess, Budha should be always worshipped there with the Mantra beginning with *udbudhyadhvam* etc. (RV X. 101.1). Guru should always be adored with the Mantra beginning with *bṛhaspate* etc.

69. O goddess, Bhārgava should be worshipped with the Mantra beginning with *śukraḥ śuśukvān* etc. One should always adore Maṅgala (Mars) with the Mantra beginning with *agnirmūrdhā* etc. (RV VIII.44.16).

70. One should adore the son of Bhāskara (i.e. Saturn) with the Mantra *śam agni* (RV VIII.18.9) etc. O goddess, one should always worship Rāhu with the Mantra *kayā naścitrā* (RV IV. 31.1).

71. A sensible man should always worship Ketu with the Mantra beginning with *ketum kṛṇvanti* (RV I. 6.3). etc. Externally the following deities are installed: Śakra in the east, Yama in the south.

72. Īśvara should be known in the north-east, Agni in the

south-east, Virūpākṣa in the south-west and Pavana in the north-west.

73. One should adore Indra with the Mantra beginning with *tamuṣṭavāma* etc. and one should always worship Vaivasvata (i.e. Yama) with the Mantra beginning with *udīratām avara* etc.

74. O goddess, one should always worship Varuṇa with the Mantra beginning with *tattvāyāmi* (RV I. 24.11) etc. and worship Dhanada with the Mantra beginning with *indrāsomāvata.*

75. O goddess, one should worship Pāvaka (Fire) with the Mantra beginning with *agnim īḷe purohitam* (RV I. 1.1). etc. and worship Virūpākṣa with the Mantra beginning with *rakṣohaṇam vājinā* (RV X. 87.1). etc.

76. O goddess, one should always worship Vāyu with the Mantra beginning with *vāyavāyāhi* etc. A sensible man should always worship these Devas in this order.

77-79. Externally the adoration of Indra etc. from the east etc. should be performed thus all round:

Āditya's *Rūpa* (form) should be meditated upon on the ground where the mystic diagram *(Maṇḍala)* is drawn. It is red in colour and highly brilliant. It is stationed on a white lotus. It has all the characteristic features and is adorned with all ornaments. It has two arms and a single countenance. The hands hold *Saumya Pañcaka.* The radiant disc is circular and is stationed in the centre. The cloth is red in colour. This form of Āditya is adored in all the worlds.

The Devī said:

80. The procedure of the adoration of Bhāskara as stationed in the Maṇḍala (mystic diagram) has been mentioned by you. You have explained how he should be worshipped devoutly by men, O Suraśreṣṭha.

81. O Śaṅkara, tell me how one should duly worship Bhāskara, the omnipresent Lord stationed in (represented as) the idol and arising from the lotus[1].

Īśvara said:

82. Well! Well! O great goddess of good holy rites, I have

1. Two forms of Sun-worship:
(i) drawn in a Maṇḍala, (ii) as represented in an idol.

been well asked. O goddess, listen attentively. I shall tell you how to worship the Lord stationed in an idol.

83. The *Uttamāṅga* (head) should always be worshipped with the Mantra beginning with *ise tvā* etc. The right hand should be worshipped with the Mantra beginning with *agnim īḷe* etc. (RV I. 1.1).

84. The feet of the Lord should be worshipped with the Mantra beginning with *agnā ā yāhi* etc. One should adore the deity with flower garland with the Mantra beginning with *ājighra* etc.

85. Handfuls of loose flowers should be scattered with the Mantra beginning with *yoge yoge* (RV I. 30. 7) etc. The devotee bathes Ravi with the Mantra *samudrāgaccha* etc.

86. O beautiful lady, the deity can be bathed with the Mantra beginning with *imaṁ me gaṅge* etc. also. The bathing rite (with medicinal herbs) is to be duly performed with the mantra beginning with *samudrajyā* etc.

87. One should bathe with water from a conch with the Mantra beginning with *sinivālī* etc. Uttering *yajñam yajñena* etc. ointments and unguents are smeared over the idol.

88. O goddess, one should bathe the deity with milk uttering the Mantra beginning with *āpyāyasva*. One should duly bathe Ravi with curds uttering the mantra *dadhikrāvṇa* etc.

89. It can also be done, O beautiful lady, with the Mantra beginning with *imaṁ me gaṅge* etc. It is remembered that the bathing with herbal medicines is performed with the Mantra *samudrajyā* etc.

90. Then one should anoint the body of the (Sun) deity with perfumes etc. uttering *Dvipadas* (two-footed verses etc.) The simultaneous bath with several liquids shall be performed with the Mantra beginning with *manastoke* etc.

91. One should bathe with scented water with the Mantra *viṣṇo rarāṭa* etc. and offer Arghya and Pādya with the *Sauvarṇa* Mantra.

92. The Arghya is offered with the Mantra *idam viṣṇur vicakrame* etc. *Upavīta* (sacred thread) is offered with the Mantra *vedosi* etc.

93. One shall offer garments to Bhānu uttering the Mantra *bṛhaspate* etc. One shall adore with flower garland with the Mantra *yena śriyam prakurvāṇaḥ*.

94. *Dhūpa* (Incense) is offered with Guggala uttering the Mantra *dhūrasi* etc. One shall offer *Añjana* (collyrium) with the Mantra beginning with *śamiddhoñjana* etc. (*Vāj. Saṁhitā* 29.1).

95. One should rub Bhānu with *Rocana* (Yellow pigment) uttering the Mantra *yuñjāna* etc. For the sake of longevity *Ārārtika* (waving of lights) is offered.

96. The Sun is worshipped at the head uttering the Mantra *sahasraśīrṣā puruṣaḥ* (RV X.90.1) etc. The eyes of Ravi should be wiped (or touched) with the Mantra *śambhavāya*.

97. The whole body of Bhānu is rubbed with the Mantra *viśvataścakṣuḥ* etc. Ravi is worshipped in all the limbs with the Mantra *srīśca lakṣmīśca* etc.

Īśvara said:

98. Now, O great goddess of holy rites, I shall briefly tell you the Mantras relevant to the adoration of the eight-peaked Meru.

99. O great goddess, the Aṣṭaśṛṅga (eight-peaked mountain) is to be adored in this manner. One shall adore the first peak in the middle by the following Mantra, O lady of good holy rites.

100. Uttering the Mantra *mahāhivomahāya* etc. diverse kinds of flowers are offered. One should always adore the eastern peak with the Mantra *trātāram indra* etc. (*Vāj. Saṁhitā* 8.46).

101-102. O beautiful lady of the Suras, Pūjā should be performed unto him uttering the Mantra *tamūṣṭavāma* etc. One should adore the south-east peak with the Mantra *agnim iḷe purohitam* (RV I. 1.1). It can be adored either with Āgneyī Gāyatrī or this Mantra. One should adore the southern peak with the Mantra *yamāya tvā makhāya tvā* etc. (*Vāj. Saṁhitā* 37.11).

103. The Pūjā can also be done with the Mantra *udīratām avare* etc. or with this Mantra. One should adore the south-western peak with the Mantra beginning with *āyaṁ gauḥ*.

104. Asurāntika can also be worshipped with the Mantra *rakṣohaṇam vājinam vā* (RV X 87.1) etc. or with the Mantra *indrāsomā ca vo* etc.

105. One should worship the north-eastern peak with the Mantra beginning with *abhi tvā śūra nonuma.* etc. (RV VII. 32. 22) or the Mantra beginning with *yenedam bhūtam* etc. (*Vāj. Saṁ* 34.4.)

106. One shall always adore Merupīṭha uttering *namostu sarpebhyaḥ* etc. Again one should always adore in the centre with the Mantra *hiraṇyagarbhaḥ samavartatāgre* etc. (RV X. 121.1.).

107. One should offer flower garland uttering the Mantra *savitā paścāttāt* etc. (RV X 36. 14) The *Arcanā* should be performed thrice a day, O goddess, and the Arghya is offered with great respect.

108. In the forenoon, the Pūjā is performed uttering the Mantra *mātā rudrāṇām duhitā vasūnām* etc. (RV VIII. 101.15). O goddess, at midday, the Pūjā is done with the Mantra beginning with *tad viṣṇoḥ paramaṁ padam* etc. (RV I. 22. 20).

109. In the afternoon the Pūjā is offered with the Mantra beginning with *haṁsaḥ śuciṣat* (RV IV. 40.5.) etc. Thus, O lady of excellent complexion, one should adore Bhānu along with the planets.

The Devī said:

110. O Lord of Devas, do me this favour of telling me the names of the flowers always recommended in the adoration of Bhāskara. What are the flowers mentioned in this connection?

(Sub-Chapter: Puṣpādhyāya)

Īśvara said:

111. Listen, O goddess, I shall expound the excellent *Puṣpādhyāya* (Chapter on flowers). O goddess, on being worshipped duly, Arkasthala, the Lord, becomes pleased thereby.

112. The Pūjā performed with *Mālatī* flowers causes the *Sānnidhya* (proximity to the Lord). If the adoration is through *Mallikā* flowers, the man becomes an enjoyer of pleasures.

113. Worship with *Puṇḍarīka* flowers causes conjugal felicity and permanent wealth. Through *Kadaṁba* flowers, O goddess of Devas, one attains the greatest *Aiśvarya* (glory, power).

114. If worship of Ravi is performed through *Bakula* flowers, one acquires everlasting foodgrain. Adoration through *Mandāra* flowers destroys all types of leprosy.

115. Through the flowers and leaves of *Bilva,* one attains the greatest fortune and wealth.Through a garland made of *Arka* flowers, one acquires wealth that yields the fulfilment of all cherished desires.

116. On being worshipped with *Bakula* garland, Lord Bhāskara shall bestow a beautiful daughter. On being adored with *Kiṁśuka* flowers, he desists from troubling the devotees.

117. On being adored with *Agasti* flowers the Lord becomes favourable.O goddess of Devas, by adoring with *Karavīra* flowers, one becomes a follower (servant) of Sūrya.

118. O goddess, through a garland of *Śatapatra* one attains *Sūryasālokyatā* (sharing the same world as that of Sūrya). O great goddess, through *Baka* flowers poverty is ever averted.

119. By worshipping Divākara through the seasonal flowers and scents, one enjoys this earth with the four oceans as its boundary.

120. One who devoutly plasters the shrine of Sūrya with *Gairika* (red chalk) shall attain great fortune and is rid of ailments.

121. If the shrine is smeared with clay, all the eighteen types of leprosy and many other ailments of men get cured completely.

122. Of all unguents Kuṁkuma and red sandalpaste are the best. Of all flowers, O lady of excellent countenance, *Karavīras* are the most praiseworthy.

123. Nothing is more pleasing to Bhāsvān than *Kuṁkuma* (flowers), *Jāti*, *Śatapatra* and *Agaru*.

124. If one worships Ravi with all these, what is it that he will not get. The devotee should smear and plaster the shrine and draw the auspicious *Maṇḍalaka*.

125. If one such Maṇḍalaka is drawn, one shall attain wealth.With two such,one attains normalcy of health. With three, one acquires all lores,and with four,one shall enjoy all pleasures.

126. Through five, one attains plenty of food grains; through six, Longevity, strength and fame; and one who draws seven Maṇḍalas, shall become a Maṇḍalādhipati (a sovereign).

127. By offering a light with clarified butter, a man becomes one with good vision. A man offering light with mustard oil defeats his enemy.

128. By offering light with gingelly oil, one is honoured in the world of the Sun. One will attain great *Saubhāgya* (conjugal felicity) through the light with *Madhūka* oil.

129. *Jāti* is the most excellent one of all flowers. *Vijaya* (yellow myrobalan) is the greatest among the incenses. *Kuṁkuma*

(saffron) is the most excellent of all sweet scents. Red sandalpaste is the most excellent one of all unguents.

130. Among light offerings that of clarified butter is the most excellent. Among food offerings, sweetmeat is the best. The Lord of Devas becomes pleased with all these and grants *Sānnidhya* (proximity).

131-133. After duly adoring thus, the devotee circumambulates the Pitṛs and bows down to the deity. Facing Ravi, he sits comfortably and surveys Arkasthala (the region). He then should put a grain of white mustard in water taken on the palm. Wishing for whatever he has in the heart in the presence of Arkasthala, he should drink that water once, O goddess, without letting the teeth touch it.

134-135. By doing thus, O goddess, the man attains the benefit of a crore pilgrimages. O lady of excellent holy rites, Brahmā, Viṣṇu, Mahādeva, Jvalana (Fire-god) and Dhanada (Kubera) resort to Bhānu (the Sun-god) and all of them rejoice in heaven. Hence I do not see any deity on a par with Bhānu.

136. After the performance of all these, O great goddess of excellent countenance, the devotee circumambulates Bhānu seven times again uttering the Mantras.

137-140. The Mantras to be uttered during the circumambulation: For the first, the Ṛk beginning with *taṁuṣṭavāma* (RV VIII, 96.6) etc. the second with the Ṛk beginning with *etonvindram stavāma* (RV VIII. 95.7). The third is *indramśuddho na āgahi* (RV VIII. 95.8) and the fourth is *indraśuddho hi no rayim.* O splendid lady, the fifth one is *asya vāmasya* (RV I. 164) etc. The sixth one is *tribhiṣṭvam deva.* The devotee makes the seventh circumambulation chanting all the ten Sāmans sung about by the learned men following the *Sāman Śākhā* as the greatest.

141-144. O beautiful lady, I shall tell you those ten Sāmans, *Huṁkāra, Praṇava, Udgītha, Prastāva* are the first four. The fifth one is *Prahara* and the sixth one is *Āraṇyaka.* The seventh of the Sāmans is *Nidhana* remembered as *Saptasiddhi.* The eighth one is the *Pañcavidhya* uttered along with Hrīm and Praṇava. The ninth one is *Sādhya* and *Jyeṣṭha Vāmadevaka* is the tenth Sāman excellent and dear to Vedhas (Brahmā). The *Japa* of all these Sāmans should be performed in accordance with the injunctions.

145. Listen to my explanation of another Jyeṣṭha Sāman, the second. It should not be (loudly) chanted. The *Japa* should be performed by one who wishes for salvation.

146. That *Jāpya* is mentioned as the greatest by Lord Bhānu himself.The application and the definition of the Jāpya are being mentioned. Even as I expound it, listen and understand. *Stobha* (a division in the Sāman text) is its essence. *Aukāra* etc. get merged in the breath. It is remembered so by learned men.

147. *(Obscure)* Urbhānu, dharmam, Dharma, Satya, Ṛta, *dharmaṁ ye, dharmavaddharme, dharme vai dhanaṁ gatāḥ)*. (These are the allusions to the different passages.)

148. With these words one should worship. It is so practised by the Brāhmaṇas following Sāman Śākhā. This *Jāpya* has been mentioned as the greatest by Lord Bhānu himself.

149. One who performs the Japa of this is never reborn in the world. Rid of all ailments he is liberated from the sin of Brāhmaṇa-slaughter.

150. Another characteristic of the Jyeṣṭha Sāman is *ājyado hādyado ha* etc.

151. After worshipping the Lord of Devas thus, another prayer is recited by means of five Ṛks. Listen to them attentively.

152. The first proclaimed is that which begins with *ukṣāṇam pṛsnim* etc. (RV I. 164.43). The second one is the Mantra beginning with *catvāri vāk parimita* etc. (RV I. 164.45).

153. The third Ṛk proclaimed is *idam mitram* etc. The fourth one proclaimed is *kṛṣṇam nīyānam hi* etc. (RV I 164.47).

154. The fifth one proclaimed is *dvādaśa prathama* etc. Uttering the Ṛk beginning with *yo ratnavāhī* etc. the devotee puts the crown on Ravi.

155. With the Ṛk beginning with *gatehanām* etc. the devotee performs the *Nyāsa* (concluding rite of the adoration) of the unmutilated (idol of) Ravi. Thus, O goddess, one should duly worship Ravi in accordance with this procedure.

156. Thus the entire procedure for the worship of the idol has been described to you by me.

157. He who always worships in accordance with this procedure, attains most of his desires in this world as well as in the world hereafter.

158. One who seeks a son gets a son.One who seeks wealth

gets wealth. One who seeks a daughter gets a daughter. One who seeks learning becomes fully conversant with the Vedas.

159. By the greatness of this Kṣetra and by the power of Sun-god at Arkasthala, one who worships without any specific desire certainly gets liberation.

160. By feeding one Brāhmaṇa in Arkasthala, the benefit gained is the same as is obtained elsewhere by feeding a crore of Brāhmaṇas.

161. Snāna, Dāna, Japa, Homa—all these performed in *Sūrya Parva* have the benefit increased a crore times, by the power of Sūryakoṭi (Arkasthala).

162. A man who faithfully performs the rite of *Jāgara* (religious vigil) on the seventh lunar day on Sunday in the dark half of the month of Māgha, in the vicinity of Arkasthala, attains the greatest goal, O great goddess.

163. By visiting Arkasthala one attains that benefit which one obtains by making the gift of a hundred cows in Kurukṣetra.

164. Arkasthala should be worshipped through Arka flowers and Japā flowers by the permanent residents of that holy spot, especially the sick ones.

165. Divākara should not be worshipped with flowers like Patrorṇa, Unmatta and Āmrātaka.

166. A flower of Āmrātaka is looked upon as *Nirmālya* (used up for worship and kept aside). Since it is not fresh externally, it should be avoided.

167. If one desires prosperity, one should not offer a garland of flowers, if it is not from known (familiar) variety. If it is faded, defiled or stale, it should not be offered.

168-169. If a man makes the sweet-smelling flowers disappear from the idol of the Lord immediately due to greed for flowers, and in the case of the regular priest any flower, the priest enamoured and covetous incurs the sin of Brāhmaṇa-slaughter. He falls into Mahāraurava and is cooked there for many years.

170. Oh, I shall now explain to you, the procedure for offering incense. I shall tell you which incense yields which fruit on being offered to the Lord of Devas.

171. If Lord Ravi is offered incense always, he stays nearby and bestows all desires, whatever the man may wish for.

172. If *Aguru* incense is offered, the Lord bestows the desired

treasure. One who seeks health and wealth should always burn *Guggala*.

173. Bhānumān is always pleased with the offering of Piṇḍāta incense. He himself grants freedom from ailments. Thus there will be greatest happiness.

174. Through the incense of *Śrīvāsaka* one gets the monopoly of trade. One who burns *Sarjarasa* incense shall get wealth.

175. One who burns *Devadāru* gets everlasting foodgrains. Smearing with *Kuṁkuma* (saffron) as unguent yields all desires.

176. Remaining very happy in this world, he shall attain everlasting heavenly pleasures. By the unguent of sandalpaste one gets fortune and longevity.

177. The unguent with red sandal is very efficacious. Divākara grants everything. Even if one is affected by hundreds of ailments, one gets happiness and welfare and health.

178. By offering (powder or) unguent of musk, one gets unparalleled prosperity, good goal, scents and highest conjugal felicity.

179. Through scents together with camphor one becomes an emperor.If all the four types of scents are offered, one realizes all one's desires.

180. Thus, O goddess, the excellent greatness of Sūrya has been described to you in detail by me. What else do you wish to ask?

The Devī said:

181. O my Lord, if, in this way, Lord Sūrya is the most excellent of all luminaries, why is he swallowed by Rāhu, the son of Siṁhikā?

Īśvara said:

182. Listen, O goddess, I shall explain the cause of an eclipse. It destroys all sins and resolves all illusions and mistakes.

183. O beautiful lady, Rāhu is (positioned) beneath the disc of the Sun. He seeks nectar and so is stationed in an aerial chariot till the liquid nectar drops down.

184. He is therefore hidden by the disc. It is the solar

eclipse. No one can swallow him. Āditya certainly burns (all).

185. Those beginning with Brahmā worship him (the Sun-god). He is the primordial one among all heaven-dwellers. All other Devas and Dānavas are born of the body of Āditya.

186. He is called Āditya because he is the first and primordial agent. The Lord, the destroyer of all sins, is stationed in Prabhāsa.

187. The Lord is the bestower of worldly pleasures and salvation. He is the destroyer of ailments and evil deeds. There in the holy spot, O goddess, the guardians of the world and great sages became Siddhas.

188-192. Siddhas, Vidyādharas, Yakṣas, Gandharvas, sages, Dhanada (Kubera), Bhīṣma, Yayāti, Gālava and Sāṁba attained the great Siddhi from this place.

O goddess of Devas, this, the excellent greatness of Sūrya, is a great secret. It should not be divulged to people of wicked intellect and sinners in particular. This story should be told neither to an atheist nor to one who has no faith, nor to a ruthless man at any cost.

If one is not ardently devoted to Śiva, it is not to be passed on to him. This story should be told to a son, to a disciple, to a righteous one and to one who abides by justice.

The great Brahman should be mentioned to a devotee of Sūrya and to one of good holy rites. This greatness of the Lord of Arkasthala is excellent.

193. He who recites this to Brāhmaṇas at the time of Śrāddha, to persons of esteemed holy rites, shall attain infinite bliss as though through a Dāna.

194. Where this is being glorified, there will be affluence always. Yātudhānas become terrified. They do not violate that Śrāddha.

195. If a person has been earlier declared a Paṅktidoṣaka i.e. a defiler of a row at meals, he will become holy and esteemed. He will beget sons. He will become charming and possessor of all desired objects.

196. A man who has been away in alien lands will become reunited with kinsmen. He will regain the lost wealth and other things that caused him worry.

197. He is protected by Yoginīs. He is not separated from

dear ones. A Brāhmaṇa should listen to the story after sipping water ritualistically and becoming clean. He will get all desired things. No doubt should be entertained about this.

198. O lady of excellent countenance, by the glorification of the origin of Sūrya, a Vaiśya gets unlimited prosperity, a Kṣatriya becomes Lord of the earth. Merchants will flourish hundred times more in their trading activities.

199-200. O beautiful lady, Śūdras will attain all desired objects. All fear of premature death and terrible death due to accidents perishes. There is no doubt that what is done at the royal palace gets nullified (i.e. complaints against a devotee do not stand. He is acquitted). Richly endowed with all desired objectives, he is honoured in the world of the Sun.

201. Thus, O goddess, the greatness of the deity Sun has been narrated in the context of Arkasthala.What else do you wish to hear?

202. May the Solar Disc protect you all. It is the permanent abode of vigour. It is the goal unto waters, eternal light unto the quarters. It is the gateway to Siddhis. It destroys obstacles, dangers. It is the common eye for all the worlds. It is the golden lotus in the lake of the vast firmament. It is the brilliant earring unto heaven. It is the means of reckoning the time. It has no destruction nor has it any boundary.

CHAPTER EIGHTEEN

The Birth of Moon-God

Sūta said:

1. O leading Brāhmaṇas, on being told thus by Śaṅkara, the goddess of great renown further asked him about the details of the greatness of the Kṣetra.

The Devī said:

2. O my Lord, today my birth has become fruitful. My penance too has borne fruit. O Śaṅkara, with your favour, divinity has been attained.

3. Today I have become one who has done an auspicious act. Wisdom-eye has been granted by you. Today my ears have

become adorned with the ear-ornaments in the form of the greatness of the Kṣetra.

4. Today my brilliance has become a solid entity as knowledge has been fixed in the heart. Today my decorum and nobility, beauty and characteristics have become well-defined.

5. Today my delusion about the pilgrimage to holy places has become dispelled. O most excellent one among honoured ones, my mind has become steady in regard to Prabhāsa.

6-7. The Lord of Suras was propitiated by me earlier. Today the Lord has become pleased. I was surrounded by fire (in Pañcāgni penance). I have been standing on a single foot. That penance has become fruitful today. O Lord to whom devotees are favourites, the greatness of Prabhāsa Kṣetra has been revealed to me today.

8. I am asking you again, O Lord of Devas. O Lord, do tell me the exact facts.

9. Still, O Lord, I entertain doubts regarding the greatness of the Kṣetra and the Tīrtha. O Lord Maheśvara, do tell me if there is any other interesting thing.

10. Here this Candra (Moon) is on your head. Of whom is he born and how? At what time? Do tell me, O Lord!

Īśvara said:

11-12. This is the period (Kalpa) well-known as Vārāha. The second Parārdha of Brahmā is current now.At the beginning of the second month, this is the Pratipad (first lunar day). Lord Varāha (the divine Boar, Viṣṇu) redeemed and lifted up Dharā (the Earth) on this day, O my beloved. Therefore, this Kalpa came to be known by the name Vārāha Kalpa on the Earth.

13-14. In that Kalpa, O great goddess, O my beloved, the *Sandhyāṁśa* (twilight period i.e. interregnum of two Kalpas) has passed. The first Manu Svāyaṁbhuva was reigning, O goddess. The Ocean of Milk was being churned by Devas and Dānavas. Gems, fourteen in number, were born (recovered) therefrom.

15. Among them the highly refulgent Candra is one born of the *Tattva* (eternal entities, principles). O goddess, O my beloved, he was held and kept on the head by me where he still continues to be.

16. O great goddess, when the poison (Halāhala) was swallowed

by me while I was stationed in Prabhāsa, Candra was formerly made my ornament for the relief (from the effects of poison).

17. Since I have been adorned with the Moon (Śaśī), I came to be known as Śaśibhūṣaṇa (Moon-ornamented). Even today I am stationed in that holy spot in the form of Svayambhūliṅga.

18. I am the bestower of all Siddhis, O my beloved. I continue to stay through the duration of the Kalpa.Thus it has been narrated, O goddess; what else do you wish to ask?

CHAPTER NINETEEN

Incarnations of Śrī Viṣṇu

The Devī said:

1. If it is so, O Lord, why was the Full-Moon with all its digits not worn by you? Tell me the reason for (liking) the last part of the digits.

Īśvara said:

2-5. *Amā* (New Moon) is mentioned as the *Mahākalā* (greatest digit as distinguished) in sixteen types (of *Kalās*), O goddess. It is the greatest Māyā and the supporter of the bodies of the embodied ones.

Beginning with *Amā* and ending with *Paurṇamāsī*[1] (Full-Moon) there are sixteen Kalās pertaining to the Moon.They are called *Tithis* (Lunar days). The sixteen Kalās are thus glorified.

Amā is the greatest and subtlest *Śakti.* O goddess, it is acclaimed that you are that *Śakti.*

There are sixteen primordial *Svaras* (Notes). They are mentioned in the due order of time units, beginning with creation (of the world) and ending with its annihilation. O my beloved, they should be known by the experts on time as units of time.

6-8. They are *Truṭi, Lava, Nimeṣa, Kalā, Kāṣṭhā, Muhūrtaka, Rātri* (night), *Ahaḥ* (day), *Pakṣa* (fortnight), *Māsa* (month), *Ayana, Vatsara* (year), *Yuga, Manvantara, Kalpa* and *Mahākalpa* the sixteenth. *Kalā Visarjanī* (the creative one) is based on the

---

1. This shows that the author accepted Paurṇimānta Calendar.

Jīva (the individual soul). It creates the entire universe, the two Vīṣuvas (equinoxes) being included. *Kalā Saṁvaraṇī*[1] (that which conceals and covers), O my beloved, annihilates the universe.

9. A fourth of the winking time is called *Truṭi*. Understand, O Maheśvarī, that *Nimiṣa* is twice that (*Lava* is included in between).

10. Thirty *Nimiṣas* make a *Kāṣṭhā* and twenty *Kaṣṭhās* make one *Kalā*. A *Muhūrta* consists of twenty *Kalās* and fifteen *Muhūrtas* make a *Dina* (day).

11. Night is of the same duration as *Dina* (day) and these two together make one *Ahorātra* (night plus day=24 Hours). Fifteen *Ahorātras* make one *Pakṣa* (fortnight). Two *Pakṣas* together make what is called *Māsa* (month).

12-13. Six months make one Ayana and two *Ayanas* make one *Varṣa* (year).Four million three hundred twenty thousand years should be known as one *Caturyuga* according to the solar reckoning. Seventy-one *Caturyugas* can be cited as constituting one *Manvantara*.

14. This period along with the end of a month is acclaimed as the span of life of Indra.The period covered by the lives of fourteen Indras constitutes a *Kalpa* and it shall be one day of Brahmā.

15. The same period of a thousand *Caturyugas* constitutes his *Rātri* (Night) of Brahmā. O my beloved, he (Brahmā) lives for a hundred years calculated thus.

16. Along with half of a *Nimiṣa* pertaining to me, fourteen thousand Viṣṇus and unlimited number of Pitāmahas (Brahmās) die.

17. O goddess of Devas, this universe is created (and maintained) in this order. The reckoning may be lunar and solar; the universe is infinite and variegated.

18. O goddess, the Kalā is unborn, beginningless and immutable and Śaśin (Moon) is established therein with face down and accompanied by it.

19. Thus the waxing and waning of the Moon and the Sun should be known. It is the order of creation that has been narrated by me.Now listen to the annihilation.

20-23. *Mahākalpa* is struck (becomes extinct) by passing

---

1. Śaivism regards that the universe is not destroyed but withdrawn within himself by Śiva. Hence the word "*Saṁvaraṇī*".

away of *Kalpas* constituting it and a *Kalpa* is destroyed by *Manvantaras*. *Māsa* gets annihilated by *Pakṣas* and that (Pakṣa) is divided through *Ahorātras*. This *Ahorātra* is divided by *Muhūrta* and a *Muhūrta* is struck down by *Kalās*. Kalā is made extinct through *Kāṣṭhās* and *Kāṣṭhā* is divided through *Nimiṣas*. *Nimiṣa* is ended through *Lavas* and the *Lava* is divided by means of *Truṭi*. Thus that (which is beyond that) remains quiescent, *sans* characteristics and devoid of aberrations. The *Kalā* thereof, the great *Māyā* has been held over the head. O my beloved, it is the *Śakti* of the Lord of Devas. It has the form of the universe. O Pārvatī, it deludes the *Santāna* (series, progeny) and makes it undergo worldly existence.

24. Thus this universe, O goddess, has its characteristics of origin and sustenance. The entire universe gets dissolved wherein it is born.

25. Such is the *Śakti* in the form of Māyā. It's features are *Śuddha* (pure) and *Aśuddha* (impure). To you, O goddess, it reveals itself as staying in the form of *Candra* (Moon).

The Devī said:

26. I performed penance in which I got myself scorched by five fires for many crores of years. O Lord, O Lord of the universe, that penance has become fruitful today.

27. The Sṛṣṭiyoga (process of creation etc.) is understood by me, O Maheśvara, and that of the annihilation too (is understood). The origin of the Moon and the magnitude of Kalā also (is understood).

28. Now, O Lord of Devas, there is a doubt in my mind. O Lord Maheśvara, my curiosity is very great. Do tell me.

29. Śaśin (Moon) that delights everyone is born of nectar. O Lord of Devas, this Candramas is your dear favourite.

30. In regard to the word Candra, the root generally taken is $\sqrt{\text{cad}}$ 'to delight', but I think it means whiteness and aqueousness.

31. *Śaśin* is the Lord of all herbs. He pleases the *Pitṛs* much. He is your devotee. He is eager to serve you. He has resorted to you.

32-33. You are the Lord whose crest is embellished by groups of Cosmic Eggs coming into clash with one another. Yet he has a stigma despite being established on your head. This arouses my curiosity. If such a Candra too has to suffer, then why should a miserable one in the world be bewailed and pitied.

34-37. A parallel instance is not seen in all the three worlds, nor can it be so. This is a case where you can bring about an end to this. (Yet you do not do so.) In this regard, O Maheśvara, everyone has a grave doubt as it is in my case. What is the cause of the origin of the stigma in the Moon? O Lord Maheśvara, do tell me what caused it. How comes it that one who has issued forth from nectar has a stigma? He is your favourite, O Lord of Devas, yet the stigma continues to be there. My curiosity is great, O Lord. It behoves you to tell me the truth.

38. On being enquired thus by Pārvatī, Maheśvara, the Lord of Devas, became highly pleased. He spoke to the Daughter of the Mountain lovingly:

Īśvara said:

39. O goddess of excellent complexion, how is it that a great doubt such as this has occurred to you ? No aspersion should be cast on me. O my beloved, do not be agitated. It is due to the power of your father (i.e. Dakṣa) that *Śaśin* contracted this stigma.

40. O goddess, it is due to the inevitability of the destined *Karma.* The Moon was told: "You should be impartial in regard to all your wives." Since the Moon transgressed this command of Dakṣa (he had to incur this curse).

41. O my beloved, *Śaśin* did do something against his words (of advice).So he was cursed. And, O goddess, it is this that you have asked me, the cause of the stigma (on the Moon).

42. In every kalpa,O beautiful lady, there is difference due to various reasons. It is numberless and hence cannot be narrated. O my beloved, it cannot be mentioned by me.

43. Innumerable Moons come into existence again and again and they perish. In every Manvantara this happens, O goddess of Devas.

44. Innumerable are those (periods) called Kalpa. The Pitāmahas (Brahmās) are innumerable and Haris too are innumerable. But Maheśvara is one and only one.

45. Like formations of bubbles in water, O my beloved, crores and ten thousand crores of Brahmāṇḍas (Cosmic Eggs) issue forth from me in my sport.

46. In different places (Cosmic Eggs), four-faced Brahmās,

Haris and Bhavas are created by the *Pradhāna* (Māyā). Then the proximity to Śaṁbhu was obtained.

47. He (Maheśvara) brings about the mutual merger and dissolution of beings as well as the beginning and end. Lord Maheśvara is the agent of creation, annihilation and sustenance.

48. I get combined with Rajas at the time of creation. I am established in Sattva while maintaining it. I am united with Tamas during the annihilation (of the world). Thus I abide in three forms.

49. Hence Brahmā is the son of Maheśvara. Śiva is the Lord, master of Brahmā. Sadāśiva may become Viṣṇu and Brahmā, because he is *Sarvātmaka* (the immanent soul of all,identical with all).

50. He alone is Lord Rudra and Viṣṇu, the Lord of the entire universe.These worlds are in this Cosmic Egg, this world is within the universe.

51. O goddess, O highly intelligent one, it is impossible to count the Moons,Suns and Planets which are (now) in existence, and those that have come and gone and those which are as yet to come.

52. In the present Vārāha Kalpa, O intelligent lady, six Moons have already come and gone in the Cosmic Egg.

53. O great goddess, the present one issued forth from nectar and is seen now weak and wearied due to the curse of Dakṣa and is the seventh one.

54-56. In the second Parārdha of Brahmā, the thirtieth Kalpa was well-known as Pitṛkalpa, In the beginning of the Svāyaṁbhuva Manvantara therein, you were (known as) Satī. O great goddess, the Dakṣa who was then your father was born of Prāṇa, the patriarch. But in this Manvantara, O goddess, Dakṣa was born of Pracetas.

57. Now, O my beloved, Dakṣa will be born of the right Aṅguṣṭha (thumb). All the Brāhmaṇas beginning with Dakṣa are born in every Yuga.

58. They will again die. A sensible man does not become deluded thereby. O goddess, on being insulted by him (Dakṣa) formerly you abandoned your body.

59. Thus bereaved of you formerly, O my beloved, I was separated from you till the Cākṣuṣa Manvantara of the Vārāhakalpa.

60. This is the twenty-first Manu (i.e. beginning from

Svāyaṁbhuva of *Pitṛkalpa* and ending with Cākṣuṣa of Vārāha Kalpa) in the Kalpa called Vārāha. O great goddess, in every Kalpa you will have a different name.

61. In this Vārāha Kalpa, O goddess, you became Pārvatī obtained by Himavān through his penance, when the Cākṣuṣa Manvantara has passed off.

62. O beautiful lady, due to the anger of Dakṣa you had to be separated from me for the duration of a day of Brahmā. Your span of life is the period of his six months.

63. O goddess, the sages who were formerly cursed by me out of my anger in your case, are also born along with you in the Vaivasvata Manvantara.

64. They are the eight sons of Brahmā, viz. Bhṛgu, Aṅgiras, Marīci, Pulastya, Pulaha, Kratu, Atri and Vasiṣṭha.

65. Formerly, in the Svāyaṁbhuva Manvantara they had been cursed at the time of the Yajña of Dakṣa. O goddess, they are reborn in this Kalpa after the Cākṣuṣa Manvantara has elapsed.

66-67. Adopting the Vāruṇī body in the course of his Yajña, the great Lord Brahmā performed the Homa of his Śukra (semen) with a desire to get progeny.

Then the sages with the refulgence of the solar disc were born again. O my beloved, in order to woo you, they were sent by me to your father (Himavān). I hope you remember it, O lady of holy vows.

68-69. Why digress with profuse verbosity? I shall give reply to your excellent question. In the present second Parārdha of Brahmā beginning with Śveta Kalpa and ending with the Vārāha Kalpa, many Candras have come and gone. O lady of excellent countenance, listen to them.

70. O goddess of Devas, four hundred and twenty-six Moons have come and gone. O my beloved, the present one is the four hundred twenty-seventh.

71-73. The Moon who is present now is born in the tenth Tretāyuga of Vaivasvata Manvantara along with Dattātreya.In the context of the origin of the Moon, I shall describe the human incarnations of Viṣṇu. O my beloved, I shall describe (later) the earlier physical incarnations. The fifth incarnation was in the fifteenth Tretā Yuga.

74-77. He was Māndhātā, the emperor, along with Utathya (as preceptor).

In the nineteenth Tretā Yuga was born Jāmadagnya who was the slayer of all Kṣatriyas. It was the sixth incarnation with Viśvāmitra as the leader (teacher?).

In the twenty-fourth (Tretā) Yuga, Rāma was born with Vasiṣṭha as Priest. That was the seventh incarnation. He was the son of Daśaratha and the incarnation was for (the slaying of) Rāvaṇa.

Viṣṇu was born as Vedavyāsa, the eighth incarnation[1]. It was in the twenty-eighth Dvāpara and he was born of Parāśara with Jātūkarṇya as the leader (priest).

The ninth incarnation of Viṣṇu was also then born as the son of Aditi and Kaśyapa.

78-80. He was born of Devakī and Vasudeva with Brahmagarga as leader (priest, preceptor). It was in the twenty-first Dvāpara towards its close. When Dharma was spoiled Viṣṇu was born in the Vṛṣṇi dynasty. He was born in order to establish Dharma. He destroyed the Asuras.

He who was the powerful one named Pramati will be born as Kalki in the Gotra of Candramas, (with) the name of Viṣṇuyaśas. He will have the exploit of Pārāśarya (Vyāsa).

81. He will be the tenth incarnation. He is not yet born. With Yājñavalkya as the priest he will be dragging (taking with him) an army full of elephants, horses and chariots.

82. He will be accompanied by hundreds and thousands of fully armed Brāhmaṇas.He will exterminate all the Śūdra kings.

83. Thousands of heretics, barbarian tribes and robbers will be slain including the haters of Brāhmaṇas and the Vedas, those who are not very religious and pious.

84. The powerful hero will move about on the earth remaining invisible to all living beings. He will establish his soverignty.The mighty one was (will be) a destroyer of many brave enemies.

85. With a part of Mānava Deva (Lord and incarnation of Manu) he will undermine all those already so destined. Along with his followers he will disappear in the middle of Gaṅgā and Yamunā.

86. When Kalki passed away along with his ministers and army, when all the kings were also slain, the subjects became helpless (leaderless).

---

1. The author does not recognize the popular belief of Buddha being the ninth Avatāra. By making Vyāsa as the eighth and Kṛṣna as the ninth incarnation, Buddha is deleted from the list of Avatāras.

87. Succour and protection having been denied they (people) began attacking one another and continued killing one another in fights. They were highly miserable and lamented much.

88. When this Kaliyuga of thousand years according to the divine reckoning becomes diminished and when it becomes extinct along with the Sandhi (intervening period) Kṛta Yuga will begin.

89. When the Sun and the Moon as well as Jupiter come to the same zodiac with the Puṣya Star, Kṛta Yuga will set in.

90. When Janārdana was born the constellation was Abhijit, the night was Jayantī and the Muhūrta was Vijaya.

The Devī said:

91. The entire (story of incarnation) has not been narrated as it happened as a result of the curse of Bhṛgu. O Maheśvara, narrate to me the earlier incarnations not yet mentioned.

Īśvara said:

92-94. When the earth was occupied by highly powerful Dānavas, Viṣṇu took birth again and again with the curse of Bhṛgu as an ostensible cause.He took the incarnation in order to establish piety (Dharma).

Nārāyaṇa should be realized through Dharma (piety). He was then born in the Cākṣuṣa Manvantara. He propagated Yajña in the Vaivasvata Manvantara. At the time of his manifestation, Brahmā became his priest.

95. During the fourth quartet of Yugas, when Suras became distressed, he issued forth from the ocean for killing Hiraṇyakaśipu.

96-97. The second incarnation was Narasiṁha. Rudra was his priest.

In the seventh quartet of Yugas when all the worlds were under Bali, in the Tretāyuga when all the three worlds were overcome by Daityas. Viṣṇu became Vāmana reducing his limbs in size. Bṛhaspati was his priest.

98. In the tenth Tretā Yuga, Dattātreya was born when Dharma had disappeared in the fourth part. Mārkaṇḍeya was his priest. All these divine incarnations in the mortal world have been narrated earlier.

CHAPTER TWENTY

Creation of the Moon

Īśvara said:

1-5. Henceforth, the order of the lineage of Daityas is being described again. Hiraṇyakaśipu shone as the king for one hundred seven million two hundred eighty thousand years. He was the emperor of the three worlds.

During the Aśvamedha of Kaśyapa, the Atirātra sacrifice was performed.On the *Sautya* day (day when Soma juice is extracted) thereof, a golden throne was assigned to the Hotṛ. A deep pit occurred there. Hiraṇyakaśipu sat there.

He performed a very severe penance for a hundred thousand years. Formerly he had stayed in the womb of Diti for ten thousand years.

6-9. An old verse has been sung about Hiraṇyakaśipu by Daityas: "The Suras along with the sages used to pay respect to that direction which Hiraṇyakaśipu, the king, looked at."

After his term was over, Bali became the king for ten million three hundred sixty thousand years. While Bali continued to be the king, Prahlāda was held as hostage by the Suras. Indra and other famous (Suras) killed the Asuras with their valour.

10-12. The rule of the Daityas continued thus for ten Yugas without any enemy. Then for eighteen Yugas, the entire region of the three worlds was protected carefully by Mahendra. In the tenth Tretā Yuga, Kārtavīrya[1] was the extremely powerful king for eighty-five thousand years. He was an emperor in possession of seven gems.

13. During his reign that king used to go round in all the seven *Dvīpas* (continents) armed with a sword, shield and bow in his chariot, accompanied by his followers. By his Yogic power he used to detect thieves.

14-15. If he is remembered, men will never lose their wealth. After the lapse of a quartet of Yugas (Caturyuga) the eleventh Manu became the Lord. Half the period of his reign elapsed

1. It is surprising that Kārtavīrya, a disciple of Datta, is regarded as a Daitya. He is a seer of Mantras (Nārada Purāṇa). He belonged to Haihaya dynasty. His greatness is described in Mbh, *Śānti* 49.

and Dvāpara Yuga ensued. Mada was the son of Nariṣyanta, the son of Manu.

16. His ninth successor was remembered as Tṛṇabindu. He became the king at the beginning of the third Tretāyuga.

17. His daughter Ilavilā was unrivalled in beauty. The saintly king gave his daughter to Pulastya.

18-20. Sage Viśravas was born of her and he is known as Ailavila too. He had four wives and they were ornaments to the family of Pulastya: Bṛhaspati's splendid daughter named Vedavarṇinī, the two daughters of Mālyavān named Puṣpotkaṭā and Bīkā and Kekasī, the daughter of Mālin. O goddess, listen to her progeny. The lady of excellent complexion gave birth to the eldest son of Viśravas.

21-22. The boy had eight teeth and three feet like those of a dog. He had green moustache and pike-like ears. His hands were small. He was tawny in complexion but had pure ornaments. His body was huge and the head was large with a great chin. She saw the son so very ugly as this (and felt sad).

23-24. On seeing him,she said to herself: "This is Kubera". The word Ku is used to denote contempt. Bera means the body. He was named Kubera because of his ugly body. His wife was Vṛddhi and son Nalakūbera.

25-26. Kaikasī (Kekasī is an alternate form) gave birth to Rāvaṇa who later became Lord of Rākṣasas. His ears were like pike. He was tawny in colour with red hairs. He had ten heads, eight feet and twenty arms. He was very powerful with a huge body. He had complexion resembling black collyrium. He had curved fangs and his eyes were red.

27. He was endowed with the vigour of Rākṣasas.He was naturally terrible in features and strength. He was cruel. He was remembered as Rāvaṇa because his cry was shrill.

28. He was King Hiraṇyakaśipu in his previous birth. He was a king for fourteen Yugas as a Rākṣasa.

29-31. O my beloved, in terms of years, the time extended to five crore sixty-one lakh sixty thousand years. During this period, Rāvaṇa terrified Devas and the sages and made them sleepless. Rāvaṇa's penance (i.e. power of penance) dwindled and in the twenty-fourth Tretā Yuga, he met with his death along with his followers at the hands of Rāma, the son of Daśaratha.

32-36. O goddess, this same ten-headed Rāvaṇa, a suppressor of enemies, was reborn as son of the saintly king Damaghoṣa. His manliness was well-known. He was born of Śrutaśravā as Śiśupāla and became king of Cedi (modern Bundelkhand, Madhya Pradesh). Kaikasī gave birth to four children, viz. Rāvaṇa, Kuṁbhakarṇa, Vibhīṣaṇa and Śūrpaṇakhā.

Puṣpotkaṭā's children were Manohara, Prahasta, Mahāpārśva, Khara (four sons) and one daughter Kuṁbhīnasī. Triśiras, Dūṣaṇa, Rākṣasa Vidyujjihva and a daughter named Śyāmikā are remembered as the children of Bīkā. Thus in the family of Pulastya nine Rākṣasas were of ruthless activities. Vibhīṣaṇa, an extremely pure soul, is glorified as the tenth.

37. The children of Pulaha were all the deer, all tigers with curved fangs, Bhūtas, Piśācas, serpents, boars and elephants.

38. It is remembered that Kratu was issueless in this Vaivasvata Manvantara. Atri had ten wives. All of them were beautiful and chaste.

39. The ten celestial damsels ending with Ghṛtācī were born of Bhadrāśva.

40-41. O great goddess, Prabhākara is well-known as the husband of these ten: Bhadrā, Sūdrā, Madrā, Naladā, Jaladā, Uṛnā, Pūrṇā, Gopucchalā, Tāmarasā and Raktakoṭikā the tenth.

42-44. When Sūrya was struck down by Svarbhānu (i.e. Rāhu) and the Lord fell to the ground from heaven, the whole world was assailed (enveloped) with darkness. At that time the Brāhmaṇical sage said: "Hail unto you". Divākara (the Sun god) who was about to fall did not fall. Hence the sage was called Prabhākara because he caused light to function. The great sages called him so. Lord Prabhākara begot of Bhadrā the reputed son Soma.

45. The refulgent Lord Soma was a son unto Dharma.His rays are cool. He was born of Kṛttikās.He is cause of night (Niśākaraḥ).[1]

46. O goddess, Atri held the Lord of all the worlds in his eyes and stationed himself thus. In this way the holy sage Atri became the father of Soma.

47. Mentally, verbally and physically, whatever he performed was only auspicious.

---

1. The reading is Niśācaraḥ - one who moves at night.

In the course of his penance the highly lustrous sage remained motionless like a wooden piece or a wall or a rock. He kept his arms raised up.

48. The penance performed by him formerly was very severe and great. O beautiful goddess, he performed that penance for three thousand years according to the reckoning of Devas.

49. O auspicious lady, the highly intelligent one remained winkless thus. He had sublimated his sexual energy. His body attained the state of Soma (Moon).

50. As his body attained the status of Soma, the Moon rose up and the Soma juice flowed out of his eyes illuminating the ten directions.

51. The ten delighted directions duly conceived it in their wombs. They received it collectively but they could not hold it.

52. That eternal foetus, the cool-rayed Moon, the delighter of all, suddenly fell down from the directions and illuminated the worlds.

53. When those ladies were unable to hold the foetus, Śītāṁśu (the cool-rayed Moon) fell on to the ground from the directions.

54. Brahmā, the grandfather of the worlds, saw the fallen Soma. With a desire for the welfare of all the worlds, he placed him into a chariot.

55. O goddess, O beautiful lady of Suras, the chariot was fitted with a thousand white horses by me for the purpose of establishing piety. He was truthful in speech.

56. O goddess, when the great soul, the son of Atri, fell down, the well-known mental sons of Brahmā eulogized him.

57. These as well as all the Aṅgirasas and sons of Bhṛgu eulogized him with the Mantras of Ṛg Veda, Sāmaveda and Atharva Veda.

58. As he was being eulogized, the splendour of the refulgent Soma became well-nourished and enhanced. He illuminated all the three worlds.

59. The excessively renowned one circumambulated the ocean-girt earth twenty-one times (riding) in that excellent chariot.

60. From the part of (his) Tejas that reached the earth, arose (were born) medicinal herbs which shone with great lustre.

61. With them, he (i.e. Moon) enlivens this world and the

four types of subjects (creations). These *Oṣadhīs* (medicinal herbs) are of seventeen varieties (in the form of cereals and lentils). They mature and bear fruits.

62-64. They are: *Vrīhi, Yava* (barley), *Godhūma* (wheat), *Aṇu, gingelly seeds, Priyaṅgu* (the sixth), *Kovidāra, Koradūṣa, Tinaka, Māṣa, Mudga, Masūra, Niṣpāva, Kulattha, Āḍhakī,* and *Caṇaka* and *Kaṇa.* These are remembered as the rural varieties of Oṣadhīs.

65-68. Oṣadhīs pertaining to Yajñas are both *Gràmya* (rural) and *Āraṇya* (grown in forests).They are fourteen: *Vrīhi,Yava, Godhūma, Aṇu, Tila* (gingelly seeds), *Priyaṅgu* forming the sixth variety, *Kulattha* the seventh variety, *Śyāmāka, Nīvāra, Jartila, Gavedhūka, Uruvinda, Markaṭaka,* and *Veṇuyava.* These are the fourteen varieties grown in village fields and forests.There are crores and crores of varieties of grass and creepers etc. Candra is the Lord of all these. He sustains the entire universe.

69. Lord Soma sustains the entire earth by means of *Jyotsnā* (Moonlight) with a desire for the welfare of the universe. Therefore, Brahmā the foremost among the knowers of Brahman, gave a kingdom unto him.

70. O lady of excellent countenance, the highly resplendent *Niśākara* (Moon) was crowned in the kingdom of seeds and medicinal herbs, Brāhmaṇas and *Mantras.*

71-74. The foremost among the refulgent luminaries sustained the three worlds with his lustre. Nine *Devīs* (goddesses) viz. *Sinī, Kuhū, Dyuti, Puṣṭi, Prabhā, Vasu, Kīrti, Dhṛti* and *Lakṣmī* served him.Dakṣa, the son of Pracetas, gave him his twenty-seven daughters of great holy rites, whom they (people) knew as constellations.

After attaining the great kingdom, Soma, the most excellent one among those endowed with Soma juice, performed a Rājasūya Yajña. The monetary gifts consisted of hundred thousand (gold coins). Hiraṇyagarbha was the *Udgātṛ* and Brahmā accepted the *Brahmatva* (the post of the presiding priest).

75. Lord Hari, Nārāyaṇa was his *Sadasya* (member of the sacrificial assembly). He was surrounded by the primordial sages, the chief of whom was Sanatkumāra.

76. O splendid lady of excellent countenance, Soma gave the three worlds as the *Dakṣiṇā* to those *Sadasyas* of whom the Brāhmaṇical sages were the chief ones.

77. After the *Avabhṛtha* bath, unperturted and honoured by all the Devas and the sages, the leader of Rājās (kings) excelled all the kings illuminating the ten directions.

78. Therefore, he attained that *Aiśvarya* (power and affluence) which persons lacking self-control find it impossible to obtain. Thus is Candra well-known as the son of Atri.

CHAPTER TWENTYONE

Advice to Propitiate Śiva

The Devī said:

1-5. The origin of Candra has been listened to entirely. Now do narrate how he acquired the stigma.

Īśvara said:

O goddess, formerly Brahmā had a son named Dakṣa. Earlier Dakṣa was instructed by the Self-born Lord (Brahmā): "Create the subjects".

Dakṣa, the patriarch, begot of Vairiṇī sixty daughters. He gave ten of them to Dharma, thirteen to Kaśyapa, twenty-seven to Soma, four to Ariṣṭanemi, two to the son of Bhṛgu, two to the intelligent Kṛśāśva and two to Aṅgiras. O goddess, listen to their names. Listen to the expansion of progeny of the mothers from the beginning.

6-8. O beautiful lady, the following are mentioned as the wives of Dharma: Marutvatī, Vasu, Jāmī, Lambā, Bhānu, Arundhatī, Saṁkalpā, Muhūrtā, Sādhyā and Viśvā. Dakṣa, the son of Pracetas, gave them to him.

The wives of Kaśyapa are: Aditi, Diti, Danu, Ariṣṭā, Surasā, Surabhi, Vinatā, Krodhavaśā, Ilā, Kadrū, Tviṣā and Vasu. I shall enumerate their sons.

9. Viśvedevas are the sons of Viśvā. Sādhyā gave birth to Sādhyas. Marutvantas were born of Marutvatī, Vasus were the sons of Vasu.

10. Bhānus are the sons of Bhānu; Muhūrtakas are the sons of Muhūrtā; those named Ghoṣas were born of Laṁbā; Nāgavīthi was born of Jāmī.

11-12. Saṁkalpa was the son of Saṁkalpā.

These ten are remembered as the ten sons of Dharma. The eight Vasus are: Āpa, Dhruva, Soma, Dhara, Anala, Anila, Pratyūṣa and Prabhāsa.

Vaidaṇḍya, Śrama, Śānta and Dhvani are the sons of Āpa.

13. Lord Kāla, the reckoner of time, is the son of Dhruva. Soma's sons are Bhagavān, Śarva, Dhruva and Gṛhabodhana.

14. Hutahavyavāha is also the son of Soma. Draviṇa is remembered as the son of Dhara. Manojava and Avijñātagati were born of Anila.

15. Devala, Bhagavān and Yogī were the sons of Pratyūṣa. Bhuvanā, the sister of Bṛhaspati, was an expounder of Brahman.

16. She became the wife of Prabhāsa, the eighth of the Vasus. Viśvakarmā was his son. He is the patriarch and the architect of Devas.

17-18. I shall mention the names of the Sādhyas called the Tuṣitas (the delighted ones). They are Mana, Anumantā, Prāṇa, Nara, the powerful Apāna, Bhakti, Bhaya, Anagha, Haṁsa, Nārāyaṇa, Vibhu and Prabhu. The twelve Sādhyas have been mentioned.

19-20. O lady of excellent complexion, I shall enumerate the progeny of Kaśyapa.The following are remembered as the twelve Ādityas (sons of Aditi): Aṁśa, Dhātṛ, Bhaga, Tvaṣṭṛ, Mitra, Varuṇa, Aryaman, Vivasvān, Savitṛ, Pūṣan, Aṁśumān and Viṣṇu. They are thousand-rayed ones.

21-22. The following are called Rudras, the eleven leaders of Gaṇas: Ajaikapāt, Ahirbudhnya, Virūpākṣa, Raivata, Hara, Bahurūpa, Tryaṁbaka, Sureśvara, Sāvitra, Jayanta, Pinākī, Aparājita (unconquered).

23. From Kaśyapa, Diti obtained two sons very arrogant of their power viz. Hiraṇyakaśipu, the elder and Hiraṇyākṣa, the younger one.

24-25. A verse has been sung about Hiraṇyakaśipu by the ancient Daityas: "The Suras together with the great sages paid respect to that direction which was looked at by Hiraṇyakaśipu." Hiraṇyakaśipu had four very powerful sons.

26. Prahrāda was the eldest among them.The next one was Anuhrāda. Then Hrāda and Hrada. Thus the sons have been enumerated.

27. Sunda and Upasunda were the two sons of Hrada. Hrāda had only one son well-known as Mūka.

28. Mārīca, the son of Sunda, was born of Tāḍakā. He was killed in the Daṇḍaka forest by the powerful scion of the family of Raghu.

29-31. Mūka was killed by Savyasācin (i.e. Arjuna) in the course of his encounter with the divine Kirāta (hunter) (i.e. Lord Śiva). There were three crores of Nivātakavacas of the family of Daitya Saṁhrāda. They were killed by Savyasācin (Arjuna). The following are remembered as the sons of Prahrāda: Gaveṣṭhī, Kālanemi, Jambha, Valkala, Jṛmbha and a younger brother (the sixth) of them. Śumbha and Niśumbha are remembered as the two sons of Gaveṣṭhin.

32. Dhanuka and Asiloman are glorified as the two sons of Śumbha. Virocana had only one powerful son named Bali.

33-34. (The following) five sons of Hiraṇyākṣa were very powerful and valorous: Andhaka, Śakuni, Kālanābha, Mahānābha the valorous and Bhūtasantāpana. Hundreds of hundred thousands of these Daityas were killed in the course of the hostilities pertaining to Tāraka[1].

35. Thus the lineage of Kaśyapa has been succinctly narrated. The entire universe consisting of Devas, Asuras and human beings is pervaded by these children.

36. O great goddess, among the twenty-seven daughters given to Indu (Moon-god) Rohiṇī was his greatest favourite.

37. Among them, the fair lady Rohiṇī was the dearest darling of the Lord of Constellations, greater than his own vital airs.

38. He forsook all the others and sported about secretly with her in forests and gardens. He was so passionately infatuated that he took her to beautiful lands, caves and crevices and sported about.

39. Thereupon, O renowned lady, the remaining miserable wives sought refuge in Dakṣa and spoke these words:

40-43. "Soma has eschewed all of us and is rejoicing with Rohiṇī alone. Ever since our marriage, for these thousand years he has been sporting about with her as he pleases. Ever since our marriage, all the twenty-six of us are devoid of glory

---

1. This war was caused by the abduction of Bṛhaspati's wife Tārā by Candra (Moon-god).

and we have been rendered devoid of lustre and dirty, though we are faultless. He seems to consider this entire period of a thousand years a mere night. O dear father, though we are blameless, we have been abandoned. He diverts himself with that Rohiṇī alone. Hence our unhappiness. So, in view of this that we have already been burnt by misery, death itself would have been more welcome."

44. On hearing these words of these distressed ones, the patriarch endowed with Brāhmaṇical splendour, urged by his affection for his daughters, went to the place where the Lord of Constellations was present and spoke these words:

45. "O *Niśākara* (Moon), be have impartially in respect to all my daughters.If not,youwill undoubtedly be incurring the fault."

46. On hearing these words, the Lord of Constellations stood with his head bowing down due to shame and spoke thus to Dakṣa:

47. "Of course, O Brāhmaṇical sage, from this day onwards I shall behave impartially with your daughters. It is the truth. I solemnly take this pledge."

48. O Aṁbika, when the Lord of Night took this oath, all the daughters endowed with beauty were duly informed.

49. Dakṣa went back to his abode, experiencing great relief and happiness. But, O goddess, Candra remained indulgent towards Rohiṇī as before.

50. With his mind deluded by infatuation he discarded all of them. So, once again, all of them complained to Dakṣa:

51. Even before it, on seeing them all emaciated and distressed, dusty and gloomy, Dakṣa fell into a swoon.

52-53. On regaining consciousness he spoke to all those daughters of his with the hair bristling due to anger: "Why are you in dirty garments? Why are you so pale in your faces? O my sinless dear ones, do tell me. O my daughters, whether they be the Asuras with their followers, or the other excellent Suras, I shall strike them all down by means of my curses."

54. On being told thus by Dakṣa all of them uttered thus:

55-56. " O Lord, the Lord of Night does not approach us even after menstruation. Hence we have come to you. He has ignored your advice. Again he is addicted to Rohiṇī secretly. Causing us increased grief he diverts himself with her in his lasciviousness."

57. On hearing their words, Dakṣa became furious. He went to Candra, O great goddess, and cursed him even as he stood face to face:

58. "Since you ignored my advice and are going on in your exclusive indulgence with Rohiṇī by excluding the other faultless daughters of mine, the consumptive disease will assail you. There is no doubt about it."

59. In the meantime, O Daughter of the Mountain, the consumptive disease, at the behest of Dakṣa, penetrated the body of Candra.

60. With his body assailed by consumptive disease Candra waned day by day.

61. O goddess, on being cursed thus by Dakṣa Soma became lustreless and motionless. He fell down on the ground along with Rohiṇī.

62. Regaining consciousness after a short while, he spoke to Rohiṇī:

63. "O fair lady, what is to be done now? I have been cursed by your father. O my beloved, afflicted by consumption and leprosy what can I do now?"

64. On being told thus, Rohiṇī's eyes became dimmed with tears. Glancing at Soma struck down by the curse of Dakṣa, she spoke these words:

65-66. "Seek refuge in him alone, by whom you have been cursed. Indeed, now that you have been afflicted by his curse, he will bring about your welfare by all means. With his favour, you will regain your lost splendour, the splendour with which you were formerly so pleasurable."

67. On hearing the words of Rohiṇī, Candra went near Dakṣa and stood there humbly with tears rendering his eyes turbid.

68-70. "O great sage, Dakṣa, do bless me with a delighted heart. Cast off your anger and take pity on me. You had been extremely furious with or without reason. It behoves you to take pity on me and redeem me from the curse. O highly esteemed one, I am fully aware of the reason why I have been cursed. But I am distressed and I implore you, do bless me."

71. When the noble-souled Soma lamented thus, Dakṣa felt inclined to bless him and spoke these words:

Dakṣa said:

72. O Soma, no one who has been struck down by my curse can be saved by Devas. O Soma, whatever I say remains as it is (i.e. unchangeable). There is no doubt about it.

73. Span of life, Karma, wealth, learning and death—all these have been pre-destined and they remain so.

74. Asuras, Suras, Yakṣas and Rākṣasas—none of these can save you, except Maheśvara.

75. Śaṅkara will bless even those whom I curse. No one except Bhava, Paśupati, is competent to grant succour. Hence, go quickly and propitiate Śaṅkara.

76. Excepting Mahādeva, the blue-throated consort of Umā, O Candra, none can free you from impurities.

77. On hearing the words of Dakṣa, Soma stood there with palms joined in reverence. With an over-delighted mind he replied thus:

78-79. "O holy sage of excellent pious rites, if you are pleased with me, your devotee, and if you have decided to bless me, then tell me where is Śiva. O Dakṣa, where can I find Maheśvara? I shall go to those places. Tell me what those places are."

Dakṣa said:

80-81. O Soma, listen carefully. After hearing, understand it well. In the west, in the vicinity of the ocean and the marshy land nearby beyond Kṛtasmara, within a distance of three hundred *Dhanus*, there is a Liṅga of great power. It has come up by itself and has stationed itself there.

82. It's lustre is like that of the solar disc. It is adorned by a girdle of serpents. Its magnitude is that of a hen's egg. It is stationed within the ground.

83. Understand that it is a *Sparśa Liṅga* (a Liṅga to be known by touch). You will know it through devotion. Śaṅkara, Parameśvara is present therein.

84. Do go and propitiate the Lord of Suras by means of severe penance.

85. Make yourself free from impurities after eulogizing the Lord of the chiefs of Devas. He will grant you a boon and thus, you will regain your excellent form.

CHAPTER TWENTYTWO

Soma Gets a Boon

Īśvara said:

1-2. On being thus instructed by Dakṣa, Soma who bewailed his misdemeanour and was utterly grief-stricken, came to Prabhāsa. He went to the southern shore of the sea and saw nearby the mountain well-known as Kṛtasmara.

3-6. The whole region was occupied by Yakṣas, Vidyādharas and Kinnaras. It was beautified by trees such as sandal, agallocham, camphor, Aśoka, splendid Tilaka, Kalhāra and Śatapatra in full bloom. It appeared beautiful with trees laden with fruits such as Āmra, Jaṁbū, Kapittha, Dāḍima, Panasa, Niṁba, Jaṁbīra, Nāga, banana, Kramuka, Nāgavallī etc., Śāla, Tamālaka, Bījapūra, date palm, grape-vines sweet and pinkish in colour. There were Bilva, Campaka, Tindu, Kadamba and Kakubha trees.

7. The mountain shone with different kinds of trees—Dhava, Aśoka, Śirīṣa etc. The trees were splendid with pleasant fruits and flowers.

8. The place was resonant with the chirping sounds of various kinds of birds such as Haṁsa, Kāraṇḍava, Cakravāka, cuckoos, and parrots.

9-10. Some birds having power to remember previous births spoke with human voice. The excellent mountain shone with couples of Gandharvas, Kinnaras, Siddhas, Vidyādharas, Serpents etc. who were playing different kinds of divine sports. Devas and Gandharvas were engaged in dances. The notes of flutes and lutes echoed all round.

11. It was resounded with the chanting of Vedas. It was enveloped with smoke which rose up from the fires of sacrifices and *Homas* emitting pleasant smell of clarified butter (oblated in them).

12-19. The mountain was graced by the divine sages and excellent Brāhmaṇas, experts in the four lores (or four Vedas). They were: Atri, Vasiṣṭha, Pulastya, Pulaha, Kratu, Bhṛgu, Marīci, Bharadvāja, Kaśyapa, Manu, Yama, Aṅgiras, Viṣṇu, Śātātapa, Parāśara, Āpastamba, Saṁvarta, Kātya (Kāvya? i.e. Śukra), Sage Kātyāyana, Gautama, Śaṅkha, Likhita, Sage Vācaspati, Jāmadagnya, Yājñavalkya, Ṛṣyaśṛṅga, Vibhāṇḍaka, Gārgya, Śaunaka, Dālbhya,

Vyāsa, Uddālaka, Śuka, Nārada, Parvata, the fierce ascetic Durvāsas, Śākalya, Gālava, Jābāli, Mudgala, Viśvāmitra, Kauśika, Jahnu, Viśvāvasu, Dhaumya, Śatānanda, Vaiśampāyana, Jiṣṇu, Śākaṭāyana, Vārdhikya, Agnika, Bādarāyaṇa and the noble-souled Vālakhilyas. In fact all the sages existing on the earth, reside there on Mountain Kṛtasmara. O my beloved, all the righteous sages and the refulgent sons of Brahmā (stayed there).

20. By their penance, all the ascetics were (refulgent like) blazing fire devoid of smoke. Some observed fasts for a month and some for a fortnight.

21. Others took food once in three days. Yet others performed Sāntapana expiatory rite. Some abstained from food. Some had fruits and flowers for food. Some ate only dried and scattered leaves.

22. Some subsisted on cowdung (Pañca-gavya?) and some on mere water. All were excellent scholars performing Agnihotra rites. They pondered over matters pertaining to salvation.

23. There were other sages with Mārkaṇḍeya as the leader. These and many others were experts in Śruti, Smṛti, Itihāsa, Purāṇa etc.

24. All these sages, O goddess, came and stayed on the Kṛtasmara mountain in the holy spot of Prabhāsa. Thus Kṛtasmara is resorted to by all the Devas. Later in this Manvantara, it will be burnt completely by Vaḍavā fire, O fair lady.

25. On seeing the beautiful mountain and the great ocean, *Niśākara* (Moon) circumambulated it seven times. After circumambulating the mountain he went to the place where Maheśvara was present.

26. The deity was near the ocean, in the form of a *Sparśa Liṅga* (felt by touch?). He then propitiated the Lord with a delighted mind.

27-28. He resolved within himself: 'I seek refuge in Maheśvara for the annihilation of the curse or I shall meet with death or it is better that I meet with death from Śaṅkara'. After resolving thus Soma began to propitiate Śiva by means of penance for a period of a thousand years. He took in only fruits and roots as food.

29. O lady of excellent complexion, when the fourth round of a thousand years concluded Lord Rudra became pleased and spoke these words:

30. "O Candra of good holy rites, I am pleased with you. Do choose your boon.Do tell me what wish of yours shall I fulfill even if it be very difficult to acquire."

31. On seeing that Bull-emblemed Lord has come within the ken of his vision, *Niśākara* (Candra) devoutly bowed down and eulogized.

Candra said:

32. Om, obeisance to Śiva, the Lord of Devas, the supreme soul, the Lord whose form and features cannot be comprehended. Obeisance to the Lord whose form is both manifest and unmanifest.

33. Supreme God! You are the Lord of Yogins. Everything is well-established in you. You are Yajña. You are Vaṣaṭkāra. You are Oṁkāra and Prajāpati (patriarch).

34. There are two hundred twenty-four Bhuvanas (worlds). Above them the supreme refulgence of yours solely shines and keeps vigil.

35. Obeisance to thy refulgent Liṅga that became the pillar of support to the Cosmic Egg when, at the conclusion of the Kalpa, the primordial Varāha deserted it.

36. Obeisance to you having the name *Anāmaya.* Obeisance to Kṛttivāsas. Obeisance to Bhairavanātha. Obeisance to you, Someśvara.

37. You Amṛteśvara are eulogized by excellent Suras of the past, present and future, through these names worthy of being eulogized.

38. When there was the first Brahmā, the grandfather of the worlds called by the name Virañci, O Consort of Pārvatī, your name was Mṛtyuñjaya.

39. When the second Brahmā became well-known as Padmabhū, your name had been glorified as Kālāgnirudra.

40. When the third Brahmā became well-known as Svayaṁbhū, your name was glorified as Amṛteśa, a name causing enhancement of glory.

41. When the fourth Brahmā became well-known as Parameṣṭhin, O Lord of Devas, your name had been remembered as Anāmaya.

42. When the fifth Brahmā became known as Surajyeṣṭha, O destroyer of Tripura, your name was Kṛttivāsas.

43. When the sixth Brahmā was remembered as Hemagarbha, your name was glorified as Bhairavanātha.

44-45. Now the Brahmā who is present is known as Śatānanda. The Ādisoma (primordial Soma) who originated from your left eye brought that Brahmā when he was eight years old, in order to install your Liṅga. He was in the form of a boy. Hence your name is glorified as Somanātha.

46. Since then two Lakh two thousand one hundred six Somas have come and gone.

47. O Mahādeva, I am the seventh and am well-known as Ātreya. Being cursed by Dakṣa, the son of Pracetas, I seek refuge in you. O Lord of the chiefs of Devas, protect me suffering from the fell disease Phthysis.

48. As Candra eulogized thus, the compassionate Lord Rudra became pleased and spoke these words:

49. "O Candra of good holy rites, I am pleased with you. Choose you boon. What wish of yours shall I fulfill ? Tell me, even if it be very difficult to acquire.

50. These secret names of mine are dear to me. I will grant everything mentally cherished by those men who recite these.

51. In the case of Candras of the past and future, this Liṅga shall be worthy of being adored till another Brahmā of eight years arrives.

52. Henceforth, the four-faced Brahmā will be born; the name of the God will be Prāṇanātha then.

53. Winds are called by the name *Prāṇa*. The name for the sake of propitiation is called Prāṇanātha.That will be my name now.

54-56. Thereafter, these names will be used: Agnīśa, Kālarudra, Tāraka, Mṛtyuñjaya, Tryaṁbakeśa, Īśa, Bhuvaneśa, Bhūtanātha, Ghora, Brahmeśa, Pṛthvīśa and Ādinātha.

57. Then the Lord will have the names Kalpeśvara and Candranātha. The future names of the Lord have now been revealed.

58. These and other names have been self-reckoned as sixteen. Those that have gone by will be revived, since infiniteness is the nature of Time.

59. Each of the names continues to exist till the dissolution of Brahmā. Then another name crops up befittingly.

60. Of what avail is much talk? The secret has been revealed to you. O dear one, tell me entirely the purpose for which all this penance has been undertaken by you. I am pleased with you. I shall grant you the boon."

Candra said:

61. I have been cursed by Dakṣa for some reason. I have been reduced in size through Phthysis. It behoves you to save me therefrom.

Śaṁbhu said:

62. Now, do look upon all the daughters of Dakṣa impartially. Reduction in your size is inevitable per fortnight. There will be waxing in the next fortnight.

63-64. O Soma, with my favour, you will regain the lustre as it was previously. It is impossible to alter the utterance of Dakṣa, the son of Pracetas, the Brāhmaṇa whose sins have been destroyed by penance. No one else, not even Suras can alter his utterance. If infuriated Brāhmaṇas may kill, may reduce one to ashes by the power of their own refulgence.

65. They can reduce Devas to the position of non-Devas. They can destroy this universe. Brāhmaṇas and Devas constitute one mass of refulgence split into two.

66. Brāhmaṇas are Devas, the perceptible (ones) in the world. Devas are invisible and are present in heaven. Without Devas Brāhmaṇas are non-entities; without Brāhmaṇas Devas are non-entities.

67. Mantras are present on one side.Refulgence is present on the other. Brāhmaṇas are deities in the world. Brāhmaṇas are Devatās inheaven. Brāhmaṇas are the most excellent onesin all the threeworlds.Brāhmaṇas alone are the cause (of wefare).

68. Excellent Brāhmaṇas employed in the holy rites of Pitṛs, become Pitṛs and if they are engaged in the rites of Devas, they become Devas. With the water sprinkled with their palms, the excellent Brāhmaṇas become Devas.

69. The great fear and danger arising from *Pretas* (ghosts) do not assail Brāhmaṇas interested in the Vedic themes and engaged in the Ṣaṭkarmas (six duties of a Brāhmaṇa) due to their devotion to them.

70. Devas translate into real actions what highly praise worthy, Brāhmaṇas speak. When the perceptible (visible) Devas (Brāhmaṇas) are pleased the invisible Devas too always become pleased.

71. The excellent Brāhmaṇas in the world are on a par with Rudras, Devas, Maruts, Vasus, Aśvins, Brahmā, Soma and Sūrya.

72. All the subjects (people) are dependent on Devas; all the Devas are dependent on Yajñas. Those Yajñas are dependent on Brāhmaṇas. Hence the excellent Brāhmaṇas are Devas.

73. One should always adore Brāhmaṇas. One should propitiate Brāhmaṇas always. Brāhmaṇas are the redeemers in the world. One enjoys heavenly pleasures through Brāhmaṇas.

74. Brāhmaṇas guard and protect the ancient religious tradition that cannot be broken or cut off, that is beginningless and endless. A highly sensible man adores Brāhmaṇas and becomes invincible like the king of Devas in heaven.

75. An armour can be pierced through by a *Nārāca* (an iron dart or an arrow). But the Brāhmaṇical benediction cannot be split even by a thousand Vajras (thunderbolts).

76. A sin is quelled by *Homa*. Food subdues *Homa*. Food is subdued by the gift of gold and gold is subdued by the blessings of Brāhmaṇas.

77. If one wishes to go to hell along with his sons, cattle and kinsmen, one should assert undue authority over Devas, Brāhmaṇas and cows.

78. If due to delusion, a wicked-hearted person cherishes hatred for Brāhmaṇas, Devas, cows and Yajñas, he shall never attain the other worlds or even this world.

79. Brāhmaṇas, cows, gold, water, women and the earth do not deserve to be censured. He who reviles these, is a sinner.

80. Kings are the top of righteousness (Dharma) and Brāhmaṇas are the roots thereof. Hence one shall not injure the root. The top stands on the root.

81. Kings are the fruit of Dharma and Brāhmaṇas are the flowers thereof. Hence one should not harm the flower. It is from flower that fruit grows.

82. King is a tree of which Brāhmaṇas are the roots. Citizens are the leaves. Ministers are its branches. Hence Brāhmaṇas should be protected by king. If root is protected tree is not destroyed.

83. Indeed fire burns when it is in close contact, but Brāhmaṇas burn from afar (by curse). What is burned by fire may grow again but what is burnt by Brāhmaṇas never grows.

84. Hutāśana (Fire-god) became Sarvabhakṣa (omnivorous) due to the curse of Brāhmaṇas, so also the ocean became *Apeya* (water of which was not worthy of being drunk) and Purandara became *Viphala* (impotent).

85. O Candra, you became afflicted with Phthysis. Unfertile arid lands abound on the earth. There occurred fall of sun and moon again and there is redemption (for them).

86-87 The exudation of juice (sap) from vegetation, defeat of Dānavas, subjugation of elephants, the extermination of Kṣattriyas,origin anddeath ofDevasand upheavel of the world: These and other things constitute the refulgence of the noble-souled Brāhmaṇas. Hence a king should always bow down to Brāhmaṇas.

88. (A king) may be in the greatest of adversities. Yet he should not infuriate Brāhmaṇas. If infuriated they may kill him along with his army and vehicles.

89. Fire may or may not be consecrated with prayers. Yet it is a great deity. So also whether learned or not, a Brāhmaṇa is a great deity.

90. Refulgent fire is not defiled even in cremation ground. Fire in which Homa is performed blazes all the more in the course of Yajñas.

91. In the same manner, a Brāhmaṇa may be engaged in all undesirable activities. Yet he is worthy of being adored by all. He is a great deity.

92. A Kṣatriya greatly flourishes through the power of Brāhmaṇas. The Brāhmaṇical power is extremely adorable. Indeed the Kṣatriya's valour arises from that of Brāhmaṇa (power).

93. Fire originates from water; Kṣetra from Brahmā; steel from rock. The refulgence of these, which spreads everywhere gets dissolved in their respective sources.

94. What person desirous of remaining alive can dare to assail (Brāhmaṇas) on whose support Devas and the worlds stand up and whose words are the Vedas?

95. A king shall not levy and exact tax from a Brāhmaṇa even when he is faced by death. A Brāhmaṇa residing in his realm should not (be allowed to) languish due to hunger.

96. If in the realm of any king, a Brāhmaṇa languishes due to hunger, ere long his entire kingdom splits into a hundred parts and faces annihilation.

97. Brāhmaṇas well-versed in the Vedas staying in the realm of a king, suppress the sin a king commits due to inadvertence or delusion.

98. If holy rites (of *Agnihotra* etc.) are duly performed by Brāhmaṇas in the beginning of a day or at the close thereof, that king flourishes along with the entire kingdom, as a result of the Brāhmaṇical splendour.

99. Everyday a king should get up early in the morning and adore Brāhmaṇas. It is by the favour of Brāhmaṇas that Devas shine in heaven.

100. Of what avail is much talk? Brāhmaṇas constitute my person. The form of the Lord of Devas, Śiva the supreme soul, is glorified on the earth girdled by the ocean, as Brāhmaṇas.

101. The foolish ones who hate these Brāhmaṇas of praiseworthy holy rites indeed hate me. Through worshipping them, they adore me.

102. Hence no sensible man should dare to hate Brāhmaṇas. Men struck down by the curse of Brāhmaṇas perish instantly by hating them.

103. Thus, O Candra, the ocean-like expanse of the good qualities of Brāhmaṇas has been expounded to you. Carry out the subsequent work I am going to tell you.

104. O *Niśākara* (creator of night), I give you protection from the curse. The utterance of those Brāhmaṇas cannot be altered.

105. All Devas including Vāsava may be able to curse or bless but they cannot alter the words of Brāhmaṇas. Hence, O Candra, you are sensible enough not to grieve over this.

106. Your waning is inevitable during a fortnight but during the other fortnight you will wax. Listen, O Candra, to another task to be carried out by you.

107. This excellent Liṅga that is present near the ocean is in the centre of the earth. It is not in the range of the vision of Devas.

108. It has the size of a hen's egg. It is adorned by serpentine girdle. It has the refulgence similar to that of hen's egg. It is my primordial refulgence. No one else knows it.

109. But away from this side, in the centre of the ocean,

within a distance of three hundred *Dhanus,* there stands (another) Liṅga endowed with all characteristics and well-guarded.

110. In the first Kalpa, due to the curse of the great sages, my Liṅga (Penis) fell into the ocean. Do bring it quickly.

111-112. O Lord, summon Brahmā along with the leading sages. Make him perform great Makhas after placing it on my Liṅga called Sparśa (Touch) with effort in the company of Viśvakarman and cause the installation.

113. After saying thus, the Lord vanished there itself. Then, O lady of excellent countenance, the Lord of night regained his refulgence.

114. Thereafter that holy spot became well- known as Prabhāsa. Refulgence was given to one (who was) without lustre. Hence it is called Prabhāsa.

115. Nor was the curse of Dakṣa in vain. There is the stigma. Soma illuminates the worlds after receiving the boon from Maheśvara. That Lord of Devas became manifest only to Soma, the noble-souled one.

CHAPTER TWENTYTHREE

Installation of Someśvara

Īśvara said:

1-3. Although surprised, Candramas retained his mental calmness. With devotion to Śaṁbhu filling his soul, he reached and stayed at Prabhāsa Kṣetra.

Vidhu (Moon-god) duly carried out what he had been told earlier by the Lord. He went to the interior of the ocean and picked up the excellent Liṅga. Summoning Viśvakarman along with his attendants, Soma ordered Tvaṣṭṛ, the divine architect.

Candra said:

4. O Viśvakarman, this Liṅga has been given to me by Śaṁbhu. Take this, O mighty one, and install it at a proper spot.

5. Guard this, O Lord, I am going to my abode. I shall bring in the meanwhile all the requisites for the Yajña.

Īśvara said:

6-9. After saying this, Candra went to Candraloka. It is highly refulgent and extends to a crore of Yojanas. It is splendid and full of nectar always. O great goddess, he summoned the porter Sumedhas and the minister Hemagarbhāṅga who was on a par with Bṛhaspati in intellect, and ordered him: "Gather together everything necessary for a Yajña and hasten to Prabhāsa Kṣetra at my bidding. You should be accompanied by Brāhmaṇas with the sacred fires when you go to the excellent holy spot.

10-12. Gather everything together quickly so that the Yajña can be initiated duly. Send separate aerial chariots to everyone of the Brāhmaṇas residing in Candraloka. Ample wealth should be distributed among them. One million cows should be given along with their calves. Their lustre should be that of Kāmadhenu. They shall be bedecked with a *Bhāra* (weight) of gold. They must yield plenty of milk. Send one and one fourth million horses with black ears.

13. There should be ten thousand elephants fully resplendent with ornaments and bells. There should be four thousand chariots having the speed of wind.

14. There should be a hundred thousand camels laden with jewels and rubies. Ten million armies each consisting of four divisions should be sent.

15. For the Brāhmaṇas, there should be garments as pure as the sacred fire. For the Ṛtviks, there should be splendid divine ornaments.

16. Different kinds of articles of food and edibles and various kinds of beverages should be kept ready. There should be a hundred thousand servants and the same number of maid servants.

17. Whatever money is set apart for wooden pieces etc. as per my order and other things the Brāhmaṇas may ask for, should be brought there.

18-19. Let there be a general proclamation inviting Devas, Dānavas, Yakṣas, Gandharvas, Rākṣasas staying in the seven Pātāla worlds, Kings of the seven continents, thousands of kings elsewhere. Let there be repeated announcements requesting the people to come to Prabhāsa."

20. After saying thus to the minister, Candramas hurriedly went to Brahmaloka to the presence of Brahmā, for the purpose of Yajña.

21. Hemagarbha, the highly refulgent minister of Candramas, took the command of Soma earnestly with his head bowed down and gathered the requisites for the Yajña.

22. He duly arrived at Prabhāsa and engaged himself in making provisions and arrangement for the Yajña. He invited all the residents of *Bhūḥ, Bhuvaḥ* and *Svaḥ (Lokas).*

23-24. On hearing the invitation, all of them hastened to that place. Surveying the entire holy spot extending to twelve Yojanas, the minister of Soma addressed the Brāhmaṇas: "O Brāhmaṇas, all the ancillaries of the Yajñas have been brought here at the behest of Soma. What should be done next may be carried out by you venerable ones."

25. On being told thus, all the Brāhmaṇas who had rid themselves of the sins through penance met Tvaṣṭṛ, the divine architect, there itself.

26. On seeing him and the Liṅga too nearby, those Brāhmaṇas said: "How is this, O Viśvakarman, tell us. Why are you present here with a crores of other artisans?"

Viśvakarman said:

27. I have been commanded by Soma and so am engaged in guarding this Liṅga. Due effort is being done by me to carry out his command, O Brāhmaṇas.

Īśvara said:

28. On hearing this, the Brāhmaṇas understood the real purpose. Then they were glad and began the necessary preliminary rites of the Yajña.

29. The splendid place of sacrifice unto the Devas (Devayajana) extended to a Yojana. After making the *Devayajana* they made the *Patnīśālā* (chamber of the honoured wives of Yajamānas) ready.

30. They made ready all the parts of the sacrificial chamber such as *Havirdhāna, Sadas, Uttarā Vedī,* the abode of Brahmā and Agnidhrī.

31. Viśvakarman erected *Yūpas* (sacrificial posts) in various places over a distance of a Yojana. *Maṇḍapas* (pavilions) and various kinds of *Kuṇḍas* were made.

32-35. There were thousands of Kuṇḍas to the end of the

Maṇḍapas. All the Brāhmaṇas were experts in the rites of installation and Yajñas.

They were adorned with various kinds of ornaments. They referred to the scriptural texts frequently and performed the rites duly.

Trees, divine medicinal herbs, sacrificial twigs, flowers, Darbha grass, ingredients for Homa, plenty of ghee and fresh milk and all other requisite things for the purpose of Yajña were kept ready. *Vardhanīkalaśa* and other utensils were of gold and were auspicious.

36. Groups of Brāhmaṇas performed the holy Yajña of the installation duly. They were duly fed and honoured. They were delighted by the various kinds of foodstuffs.

37. The sounds of the chanting of the Vedic Mantras touched heaven and earth. The Maṇḍapa decorated with banners shone well.

38. There were divine thrones in the Maṇḍapa. Pearl strings, divine sandal garlands and festoons of the sprouts of Kalpa trees added to its beauty.

39. Scents of celestial fragrance transformed it into a heavenly place. Fourteen kinds of *Bhūtagrāma* (living beings) had arrived there.

40-42. *Sthāvara* (stationary beings), reptiles like those of serpent class, classes of birds, the fourth group of *Mṛgas* (deer etc.) the fifth one called *Paśus* (beasts), human beings constituting the sixth group, Paiśāca (ghosts) making up the seventh, the eighth one mentioned as Rākṣasas, the ninth group that of Yakṣas and the other groups in the fourteen referred to before, being Gandharvas, Gaṇas called Śākras, Saumyas, Prājāpatyas and the Brahma group (had arrived).

43. There were Viśvedevas, Sādhyas, Maruts, Vasus, the eight Guardians of the Quarters and the Constellations along with the Planets.

44. When the Yajña rite started at the Prabhāsaka Kṣetra all the Devas present in the whole Cosmic Egg had arrived there.

45. Rivers of ghee and milk flowed there. Curds and milk puddings constituted veritable quagmires there. Heaps of cooked food and fruits resembled mountains.

46. Various such heaps were seen in the place where the great festivity of the Yajña took place. The Gandharvas sang and the groups of celestial damsels danced.

47. The Devas, the sages and the fourteen types of *Bhūtas* (Beings) were fully satisfied with the different kinds of edibles and foodstuffs and beverages etc. as desired by them.

48. After having got together all the requisites for the Yajña, the minister (of Soma), appointing guards (for protecting) there itself, went to Brahmaloka to call Soma.

Īśvara said:

49-52. He saw the highly refulgent Soma standing by the side of Brahmā. He prostrated on the ground like a log of wood before Soma and Brahmā. With palms joined in reverence and bending down his neck (head) he spoke:

Hemagarbha said:

O holy Sir, at your behest the entire requisites for the Yajña have been collected together at the Prābhāsika Kṣetra by me. All the Brāhmaṇa-sages and the saintly kings are awaiting your arrival with great eagerness. It behoves you to carry out what should be done henceforth.

Īśvara said:

53. On being requested thus by the son of Samudra (i.e. Hemagarbha) Candra smiled and spoke to Brahmā, the witness unto all the worlds:

54. "O Lord, O Lord of all the Devas, be pleased to accept my hospitality with a desire to bless me. I am desirous of performing the Yajña of installation (of the Liṅga).

55. Today my birth has become fruitful, O Lord, and my penance has borne fruit. O Brahmā, with your favour, I will attain Devahood today.

56. With a very severe penance I have obtained this Liṅga of the Consort of Umā. It behoves you to perform the installation thereof."

Brahmā said:

57. Certainly I will perform the installation ceremony of Śaṅkara in the Someśa Liṅga which you have to propitiate with special emphasis.

58. It is the primordial deity of all belonging to the family of Soma, of all Niśākaras (Moon-gods) whether they be bygones or are yet to be born.

59. This Lord Someśvara bore the name Bhairava at the beginning, in the other Manvantara that has elapsed. I (shall) install it again and again (in every Manvantara).

60-61. When I went to the Prābhāsika Kṣetra, I was eight years old. I had been invited by Indra earlier for the purpose of the installation of Bhairava. My name is being mentioned as "Bālarūpin" since then. In all other Tīrthas I remain in the form of an elderly person.

62-63. But, O Candra, I stay in Prabhāsa ever since my childhood. I am the first among all the Brāhmaṇas in the Tīrthas all over the Brahmāṇḍa. I am well established at Prabhāsa. In every Kalpa I get a new name.

64. The name in the first Kalpa was Svayaṁbhū. In the second I am remembered as Padmabhū. In the third I am remembered as Viśvakartṛ and in the fourth as Bālarūpī.

65. There has been a repetition of these names again and again for two Parārdhas I settled in Prabhāsa.

66. It was there that the primordial Soma, arising from the eye of Śaṁbhu, performed penance in Prabhāsa and saw Īśvara directly.

67-69. Thereupon the delighted Trident-bearing Lord granted boon to the Full Moon: "O Soma, since I have been propitiated for a long time by you devoutly, so this Liṅga will be named Someśa. All the Moons who are yet to be born until Brahmā named Śatānanda is dissolved (dies) will repeatedly adore and propitiate me here."

70. After saying this Lord Śaṁbhu vanished there itself. O Soma, the first Liṅga was installed by me then.

71. Ever since then two lakh two thousand one hundred six Somas have gone by.

72. You are the seventh (202107th), O mighty one, O Soma now. As many Liṅgas too have been installed by me.

73. (I am enjoying) the benefit arising from his propitiation. Welfare unto you, O Soma.This is my duty. I shall install (the Liṅga).

Īśvara said:

74-78. After saying this, Lord Brahmā identical with all the Devas, equipped with all lores and accompanied by the Devas and Tīrthas summoned Bṛhaspati, the Purodhas. He was accompanied by the leading Yogins and sages, the chief of whom is Sanatkumāra, and also a crore of Brahmarṣis. He rode on his vehicle of *Haṁsa* (Swan). Thus Brahmā, the Lord of the Universe, came to the Prābhāsika Tīrtha along with Somarāja. In this Prābhāsika Tīrtha the region where there is Dāruvana grove as well as the river Ṛṣitoyā, the destroyer of great sins, is called Brahmabhāga. O my beloved, it has already been mentioned by me that this Kṣetra has three deities.

79. The Four-faced One came to *Brahmabhāga*, the purest portion, and invited the sages residing in higher regions.

80. On seeing *Vedhas* (Brahmā) coming in the company of celestial sages and the preceptor, all of them honoured and adored him through prayers on a par with the Vedic passages.

81-84. Then Brahmā, the grandfather of all the worlds, spoke to all those Brāhmaṇas: "Someśa, the destroyer of sins, was propitiated by Soma for a long time. When he was pleased the excellent Liṅga was obtained by Soma. O excellent Brāhmaṇas we have come here for the sake of the installation of the Lord. Just as the installation ceremony of Śaṅkara should be performed always by me, the ancillary service should be performed by you all who have resorted to my *Bhāga* (portion of the Kṣetra). Since the Liṅga (Penis) fell on to the ground due to your anger, the installation also should be performed by you. There is no doubt about this."

Īśvara said:

85-86. Somarāja brought Brahmā, the Lord of the universe, to the great Prābhāsika Tīrtha along with Sāvitrī and all the sages.Lord Brahmā then erected a hundred *Maṇḍapas* and caused a hundred *Kuṇḍas* to be dug.

87. Directed by Guru (Bṛhaspati), the priest of Devas, Brahmā assigned seventeen *Ṛtviks* to each of the *Maṇḍapas*.

88. Standing by the side, Brahmā initiated Lord Soma accompanied by Rohiṇī, in accordance with the injunctions laid down in the Vedic passages.

89. Rohiṇī who had all the (auspicious) characteristic features was given the due place of Patnī (sacrificer's wife). The fair lady wore deerskin and covered her face with a silken cloth.

90. She was brought to the *Patnīśālā* (chamber of the sacrificer's

wife) by the *Ṛtviks* who were the masters of the Vedas. Candramas who had been duly initiated, was eulogized by the sages and Gandharvas.

91. He was clad in deerskin and he held an *Udumbara* staff. In the middle of the Assembly he shone with excessive refulgence.

92. Then, O great goddess, Brahmā, the grandfather of all the worlds, performed the rite of *Ṛtvigvaraṇa* (formally selecting the *Ṛtviks* for starting their work) in the manner it has been enjoined in the Vedas.

93. Guru (Bṛhaspati) was selected as the *Hotṛ* there, Vasiṣṭha as *Adhvaryu,* Marīci as *Udgātṛ* and Nārada was placed in the position of *Brahmā.*

94-95. Sanatkumāra and others connected with him were made the *Sadasyas.* They were bedecked in good garments and ornaments such as crowns, rings etc. The *Ṛtviks* were adorned with many ornaments in the course of that Yajña. In each of the four entrances there were four *Ṛtviks.* Thus there were sixteen *Ṛtviks.*

96. Kaśyapa was the *Prastotṛ* there and Gālava the *Pratihartṛ.* Garga was *Subrahmaṇya* and Pulaha was made *Sadasya.*

97. Śukra was named *Hotṛ.* Kratha was cited as *Neṣṭṛ.* Durvāsas, Maitrāvaruṇa, and Kauśika were *Brāhmaṇācchaṁsī.*

98. Śākalya was *Acchāvāka,* Kratu was *Grāvastha,* Śālaṅkāyana was *Pratiprasthātṛ.*

99-100. Manu was *Agnīdhra;* Aṅgiras was made the *Unnetṛ.* The Lord thus made these the *Ṛtviks* in the *Maṇḍapas.* In the other Maṇḍapas too there were Ṛtviks similarly. After arranging thus in all the hundred *Maṇḍapas,* he caused the *Kuṇḍas* (to be prepared).

101. Each one of the *Maṇḍapas* was twenty *Hastas* in dimension. The ground was sprinkled with *Pañcagavya* after duly cleansing it with *Astra Mantra.*

102. O Pārvatī, the ground was covered with the sacred *Carman* (leather), the rites of *Ālekhana* and *Ullekhana* (scratching and engraving) were performed with *Astra Mantra.* Then water was sprinkled and the digging was performed duly.

103. O my beloved, for each *Maṇḍapa* eight Kuṇḍas were assigned. The *Maṇḍapa* was duly plastered and *Vajrākaraṇa* (making the ground firm like thunderbolt) was performed.

104. The shapes of the Kuṇḍas beginning with that in the east, were square, bow-like, circular and lotus-like.

105-107. The square-shaped *Kuṇḍa* was in the east. That in the shape of *Bhaga* (vagina) was in the south-east, that in the shape of a bow was in the south, the triangular one in the south-west, the circular one was in the west, the hexagonal one in the north-west, the lotus-like one was in the north, the octagonal one was in the north-east. In the centre one was made in accordance with the injunction. Everyone of the *Maṇḍapas* was splendid with sixteen pillars.

108-110. Banners and festoons were put up by Brahmā in accordance with the injunctions. The pillar of *Nyagrodha* tree was placed in the east, that of *Uduṁbara* in the south, *Aśvattha* in the west and *Palāśa* in the north. He fixed the banners in accordance with the length of the staff. A yellow-coloured banner was fixed in the east. (In the other quarters banners were of other colours.) Then Brahmā began the Agnisthāpana (installing or placing-sacred fires) rite in the Kuṇḍa.

111-115. (Brāhmaṇas belonging to different Vedas were made to recite certain *Sūktas* of their respective Vedas as follows.) He made the Brāhmaṇas sit in their respective places and employed them in the utterance of *Jāpya*. In the east the Ṛgvedins recited *Śrīsūkta, Pāvamāna, Vājina, Vṛṣākapi* and *Aindra Sūktas*. In the south the Yajuṣas (Yajurvedins) performed the *Japa* of *Rudra Mantra, Puruṣasūkta, Krokādhyāya, Vaikriya, Brāhmaṇa, Paitrya* and *Aindra*. The Chandogas (Sāmavedins) performed the *Japa* of the following in the west: *Devavrata, Vāmadevya, Jyeṣṭha Sāman, Rathantara* and *Bheruṇḍa Sāmans*. In the north the Atharvā (Brāhmaṇa of Atharva Śākhā) performed the *Japa* of *Atharvaśiras, Skaṁbhastaṁbha, Nīlarudra* etc. Then the Lord performed *Garbhādhāna* and other rites of Agni (Fire-god).

116-117. After the offering of the *Pūrṇāhuti* the rites for the holy ablution were begun. The waters from the *Tīrthas* were brought along with *Pañcapallavas* (sprouts of five specific trees), lumps of clay, *Kaṣāyas, Pañcagavyas* and the five *Amṛtaphalas*. With the utterance of the Mantras, the ablution started.

118-121. Eyes were fixed to the deity and the sacred *Tilaka* mark was put. He caused all the *Tīrthas* on the earth, Pātāla and Svargaloka to be brought. In the meantime, even as the Devas were watching Brahmā pierced the ground and entered the bowels (of the earth). There he saw the Liṅga called *Sparśa* (i.e. Tactile? Liṅga) which he covered with roots of Darbha grass and poured honey over. Above it he placed the *Brahmaśilā*. Over that he installed highly refulgent Liṅga and made it firmly stable. The self-possessed Lord made it fixed.

122. Stationing (i.e. concentrating himself in the Supreme principle) he performed the *Nyāsa* rite with the Mantras. After installing the Liṅga thus, Brahmā, the preceptor of the universe, performed the adoration rite by means of elaborate Vedic Mantras.

123. When the *Nyāsa* rite with Mantras was performed by Brahmā, the creator of the worlds, the groups of Brāhmaṇas became delighted. They hailed with words "Be Victorious" and other auspicious sounds, The fire became smokeless and it had the refulgence of crore of Suns.

124. In the great festivity of the sacrifice divine Dundubhi drums were beaten. The quarters and their Guardians became pleased. There was a shower of flowers.

125. After the installation ceremony of Śrīsomeśa the grandfather (Brahmā) caused plenty of Yajña Dakṣiṇā to be distributed among the Brāhmaṇas.

126. Surrounded by the ancient Brahmarṣis, the chief of whom was Sanatkumāra, Soma gave the three worlds to Brahmā as Dakṣiṇā.

127. Crores of gold pieces, jewels and plenty of cash presents were given to the *Sadasyas* (members of the sacrificial assembly) and principal Brahmarṣis.

128. After being crowned by all the Brahmarṣis, the most excellent one among the luminaries, illuminated the three worlds with his refulgence. He was endowed with excessive brilliance.

129. Nine goddesses viz *Sinī, Kuhū, Dyuti, Puṣṭi, Prabhā, Vasu, Kīrti, Dhṛti* and *Lakṣmī* served him.

130. The unperturbed Lord of the Night had his valedictory bath after the celebration of the Māheśvara *Makha*. He attained fullness and perfection and had his objects achieved.

131. Thereafter, O lady of excellent countenance, Brahmā, the grandfather, gave him the flourishing kingdom of seeds (of plants), medicinal herbs, Brāhmaṇas and cooked food.

132. To those kings who were present in that *Yajña*, he gave wealth, enjoyment of pleasures and everlasting Svarga.

133. The Lord of medicinal herbs himself fed the Brāhmaṇas and gave everything unto those who resided in Prabhāsa Kṣetra.

134. He made the great sixteen *Dānas* beginning with gold. Even an ordinary person, an uncultured rustic, got whatever he requested for according to his fate (past actions).

135. After the accomplishment of the Yajña, Devas along with Indra installed their own *Liṅgas* and went the way they came.

136-137. O goddess, Lord Candramas in the company of Brahmā, once again propitiated the Liṅga in Prabhāsa which quells all sins. Thrice a day he adored it with incense, garlands and unguents. O goddess of Devas, the Lord of the night bowed down to and eulogized the Lord.

CHAPTER TWENTYFOUR

Importance of Somavāra Vrata

The Devī said:

1. O Lord of the universe, at what time was the Liṅga installed? How did the contented Consort of Rohiṇī continue the propitiation?

Īśvara said:

2-5. In the course of the Manvantara of Vaivasvata Manu in the tenth Tretā Yuga, O my beloved, the Lord of Rohiṇī was born along with Durvāsas.

During the period he performed penance and when a thousand years elapsed (in penance) he made Lord Śaṅkara manifest himself to him.

He caused the Liṅga to be installed by Brahmā, the creator of the worlds. Then he adored Śaṅkara for a thousand years.

After adoring the Lord in accordance with the injunctions for the purpose of realizing his own objectives, the Lord of the night who could perceive Śaṅkara directly eulogized (thus):

Candra said:

6. Thereis no god on a par with Śaṅkara. There is no goal

or destination like Śaṅkara. There is no Lord on a par with Śaṅkara. There is no goal like Śaṅkara[1].

7. Obeisance to that *Jñeyātman* (the soul worthy of being realized) whom the Sāṁkhyas cite always and Yogins ponder over always as the supreme *Pradhāna* and *Puruṣa*.

8. Obeisance to that *Jñānātman* (the soul in the form of spiritual knowledge) whom learned men know as the cause of the origin and destruction of Devas, Asuras and human beings.

9. Obeisance to that Yogātman whom the learned men know as the unchangeable, permanent and steady, eternal, supreme Brahman without beginning and end, and free from impurities.

10. Obeisance to that Tīrthātman (the soul of all holy places) who is the purest of all pure things; to the primordial Lord Maheśvara who sanctifies by his mere vision.

11. Obeisance to that *Sarvātman* (the soul of all) from whom everything issues forth, who maintains the entire universe and into whom everything gets dissolved.

12. Obeisance to that *Yajñātman* (the soul of sacrifices) whom the twice-born adore by means of *Agniṣṭoma* and other *Yajñas* with the full complement of monetary gifts.

Īśvara said:

13. Thus *Niśākara* (Moon-god) continued to eulogize day and night when Lord Śaṅkara became pleased and said smilingly:

Śaṅkara said:

14. O Sītāṁśu (Cool-rayed One), O dear one, I am well-pleased with you due to this prayer. Welfare unto you! Choose your boon whatever may be in your mind.

Candra said:

15. O Lord, if a boon is to be granted to me, if you are pleased with me, O Lord of Devas, be present in this Liṅga for ever.

---

1. The first line is repeated for the sake of emphasis on devotion just as we say "Śiva, Śiva".

16. O Lord of Suras, let those have the greatest Siddhi, who are endowed with the most ardent devotion and view you stationed here in the Liṅga. Let those have the Siddhi with your favour.

Śambhu said:

17. O great Lord, even earlier I had been present in this Liṅga. It is all the more so, O Candra, now due to your incessant devotion.

18. From this day onwards, I have to stay in this holy spot along with Umā. The name of this holy spot shall forever be Prabhāsa because with my favour illumination was acquired by you in this *Kṣetra*.

19. Since, O Soma, the splendid Liṅga of mine has been installed by you, my name shall be well-known as Somanātha.

20-21. This name Somanātha of mine has already been well-known earlier and will be so till the end of Brahmā. Again will this become popular. O dear one, O *Niśākara,* listen to the benefit of those persons who view me installed here with great devotion. By my power, they will have no ailment, no poverty, no wretchedness, nor any separation from their beloved ones.

22. If they perform pilgrimage with a desire to view me stationed here with great devotion in their minds, their benefit is cited (as great) as that of a horse-sacrifice at every step.

23. O *Niśākara,* of what avail are the many Yajñas performed and fasts undertaken? Even those who view me only once, will attain the benefit thereof.

24-25. If one, imbued with devotion performs monthly fast (fast continuous for a period of one month during a year) for one thousand years and another (simply) views me, the benefit derived by both of them is the same. No hesitation need be entertained in this respect.

26. One may observe celibacy throughout his life, O Niśākara, and another may view me here, but once. Their benefit is remembered to be the same.

27. One makes all kinds of *Dāna*-offerings to the twice-born and another sees me here; their benefit is remembered as the same.

28. O *Mṛgalāñchana* (The Moon, marked with the figure of a deer), one may perform all the Vratas while another sees me

here; the benefits accrued to them is remembered as the same.

29. One person undertakes pilgrimage to all the *Tīrthas* and performs plenty of *Japas;* another views me here (in this *Kṣetra*); their benefit is remembered as the same.

30. One may certainly be keen to get salvation through *Jñānayoga* etc. Another sees me here. Their benefit is remembered as equal.

31. O *Niśākara,* one meets with death through the rite of *Bhṛgupāta* (falling from a precipice). Another views me here. The benefit of both is remembered as the same.

32. One excellent man takes holy bath always during the month of Māgha at Prayāga. Another views me here. The benefit of both is remembered as the same.

33. One may offer rice-balls (to the manes) in the Pitṛtīrtha (like Gayā). Another views me here. The benefit of both is remembered as the same.

34. One makes the gift of a thousand cows to a Brāhmaṇa who has mastered the Vedas; (while) another sees me here. The benefit of both is remembered as equal.

35. One may practise the penance amidst five fires during severe summer. Another views me here. The benefit of both is remembered as the same.

36. O Candra, if a person takes his holy bath devoutly at the time of lunar eclipse on a Monday and views me, he acquires the benefit of all these.

37. Five things beginning with the letter स (S) are very rarely achieved viẓ Sarasvatī (the river), Samudra (the ocean), Soma (Moon, Soma juice), Soma-graha (lunar eclipse) and the opportunity to view Somanātha.

38. If one offers worship duly and continuously for six months and another only on the Viṣuva (Equinox) day, both acquire the same meritorious benefit.

39. The same should be understood in the case of eclipse, northern transit and the (group of) Saṁkrāntis (Solar transits) of Dhanus, Mithuna, Kanyā and Mīna called "Ṣaḍaśītimukhas".

40. The benefit one gets by duly worshipping Śaṅkara for four months (of *Cāturmāsa*) is derived by Kārttikī (i.e. by viewing me present in the Someśvara Liṅga on the full-Moon day of Kārttika) alone and on the Caitrī it is remembered as twice.

The benefit and merit on Phālgunī and Āṣāḍhī is also the same.

41. If one adores my Liṅga, his merit is more than that of one who makes the gift of a hundred thousand milch-cows to one who has mastered the Vedas.

42. O goddess of Suras, one may take food only once in a month and continue thus throughout one's life. Another may adore my Liṅga but once. These two are equal (in merit). There is no doubt.

43. Through the offering of a flower, one gets the same benefit as is obtained by offering ten million pieces of gold to a deserving person who has mastered the Vedas and who is endowed with good qualities and is a regular practitioner of penance.

44. Even if a single *Arkapuṣpa* is offered to Śiva, one gets the same benefit as one gets by offering ten *pieces* of gold.

45. *Karavīra* (flower) excels thousands of *Arkapuṣpas. Droṇapuṣpa* excels thousands of *Karavīra.*

46. *Apāmārga* excels thousands of *Droṇapuṣpas. Kuśapuṣpa* excels thousands of *Apāmarga. Śamīpuṣpa* excels thousands of *Kuśapuṣpas.*

47. A *Śamīpuṣpa* and a flower of *Bṛhatī* are mentioned as equal. The flower of *Jāti, Vijaya* and *Pāṭalā* should be known as equal to *Karavīra.*

48. A flower of white *Mandāra* and those of *Nāga, Campaka, Punnāga* and *Dhattūra* are remembered on a par with white lotus.

49. One should avoid the following flowers: *Ketakī, Atimukta, Kanda, Yūthī, Madantikā, Śirīṣa, Sarja,* and *Jambūka* flowers.

50. One should avoid *Ākulī* flower, leaf of *Karañjendra, Vibhītaka* flowers etc.

51. *Kanaka* and *Kadambaka* flowers are to be offered to Śaṅkara at night, all the remaining flowers of deities during the day and *Mallikā* during the night.

52-54. *Malli* stays (fresh) for a *Prahara* (three hours). *Karavīra* for a day and night.

The following flowers should be abandoned: Those eaten and defiled by insects and hairs; those that have been kept overnight and so are stale; flowers that have automatically dropped down and those that are broken (mutilated). *Tulasī, Śatapatra,*

Gāndhārī, Damana and *Marubaka* are remembered as the most excellent ones among all leaves. Someśvara should always be adored by means of these flowers.

55. The person attains the benefit of pilgrimage (or religious procession). He is honoured in the heavenly world.

After saying this much, he (Śaṁbhu) vanished there itself.

56. Candramas was rid of Phthysis and he settled himself in his own place. He summoned Viśvakarman and made him build a palace of crystal-like splendour and sparklingly white like cow's milk.

57. The palace was named after Meru. It has gold-ramparts and ornamental gates. All round it fourteen other palaces were also built. Their names I shall mention separately. Do listen.

[Names of palaces of the Moon]

58-60. (*The names exceed fourteen - See Verse* 64) *Kesarī, Sarvatobhadra, Nadana, Nandīśālaka, Nandīśa, Mandara, Śrīvṛkṣa, Amṛtodbhava, Himavān, Hemakūṭa, Kailāsa, Pṛthivijaya, Indranīla, Mahānīla, Bhūdhara, Ratnakūṭaka, Vaiḍūrya, Padmarāga, Vajraka, Mukuṭojvala, Airāvata, Rājahaṁsa, Garuḍa* and *Vṛṣabha.*

61. Meru is the king of the palaces. Indeed it is the abode of the Devas. At the outset the palace by the name *Kesarī* should be known as having five *Aṇḍakas* (domes).

62. The height of the palaces goes on increasing to one fourth of the height of Meru.

63-64. After building these fourteen palaces separately, O lady of excellent countenance, he caused ten more palaces to be built for the Devas beginning with Brahmā, who were the residents of the neighbourhood. These ten are palaces beginning with *Bhūdhara* and ending with *Vṛṣabha.* They were constructed with Kapardin in view as the first.

65. Meru is the king of the palaces. It was constructed at Someśvara, in the tenth Tretāyuga in the Vaivasvata Manvantara.

66. After causing the *Maṇḍapas* to be made and having installed them duly, he caused a hundred *Nadas* (rivers, probably wide canals) and a thousand tanks and wells to be dug.

67. After causing thousands of houses, hospitals and orphanages duly, he offered them to the Brāhmaṇas severally.

68. Soma thus set up a city in the vicinity of Śrīsomeśvara

and requested the Brāhmaṇas for an elaborate performance of their rites:

69. "With the favour of Parameṣṭhin, I am Soma your king. Yet I humbly and devoutly submit to you.

70-71. I have placed at your disposal all these things: Wealth, cash, gold, jewels etc., foodgrains, cereals, barley etc., cows, buffaloes and other animals, different kinds of garments, plantains, coconuts, betal leaves, areca palms and parks, all round with charming border strips.

72. All the rulers of the Jaṁbūdvīpa will carry out your orders with heads bowed down. You who stay here can issue excellent orders which they will honour.

73. Your abodes are filled with camphor, agallocham, sandal and various other kinds of articles coming from other continents.

74. The merchants who are engaged in trading activities in hundreds of commodities will set apart *Brahmottaras* (a percentage of their profit) for the sake of you, Brāhmaṇas, because they desire for more gain.

75. Seeking their own welfare, they will be your well-wishers and behave like your servants.Thus they and the other citizens will never face failure and fatigue.

76. Thus equipped with full complements of the requisite materials, you should strive for my prosperity. Hence may the rites of Yajñas be performed duly with adequate monetary gifts.

77. May all the rites pertaining to Brahman (Vedas) such as studies and recitation of the Vedas be performed day and night. May the distress of the blind, disabled and wretched ones be alleviated.

78. Hospitality should be extended to the guests properly. Noble-souled ones who have assembled in the course of their pilgrimage should be honoured with due formalities.

79-84. May shelter be always given to Brāhmaṇas, sages in the hermitages. O learned Brāhmaṇas of steadfastness in the holy vows, may excellent Brāhmaṇas always worship with holy rites, the Liṅga installed by me here.

Eight persons of authority should look after the affairs of the citizens. They must be experts in the conventions laid down in the Smṛtis. You excellent Brāhmaṇas, the noble-souled ones, extend your support to the arrangement made by me here even as the Elephants of the Quarters do to the earth. Thus, O Brāhmaṇas, take up the leadership here, in this holy spot of Śiva and carry out the rites and activities mentioned in the Śrutis and the Smṛtis."

On hearing these polite words of Soma, the Brāhmaṇas, Kauśika, the first among the families there said: "Dvijarāja (Soma) has given us excellent advices in every respect.

85-86. We shall carry out all this. But listen to (consider) one matter. Even while we adore in accordance with the direction, if we make use of *Śivanirmālya* (remnants of the adoration of Śiva) it will result in our downfall as it is censured in the Śrutis and Smṛtis. And the Śrutis and Smṛtis constitute the two great commands of Rudra.

87. Which fool will transgress them even if the vital airs are at the throat (even if death is imminent)?

88. But we shall perform *Makhas* (sacrifices) in the sacred fire, one of the cosmic bodies of Aṣṭamūrti (Śiva) and the mouth of Devas. We shall perform Yajñas according to the Vedic path and propitiate the entire universe.

89. This universe is the manifest form of Lord *Puradviṣ* (Śiva). They are different from each other but all are non-different from Īśvara.

90. The *Āhuti* (oblation) consigned to the holy fire perfectly, goes over to Āditya (Sun-god). From Āditya shower of rain results and from shower foodgrains and the subjects are nourished thereby.

91-93. We are interested in the regular study and practice of Śruti, Smṛti, Purāṇa etc. Our activities are entirely conducive to acquisition of merit in regard to different pursuits of aims. We may not get enough time to worship the Liṅga. We do worship Īśvara by means of great Yajñas and *Rudrajāpyas*. We attend every moment in due course to our main symbol Veda. O Soma, you wish that we adore Someśvara. O highly intelligent one, that we assure you we will carry out specially.

94-95. Listen to the means whereby your desire can be fulfilled. On hearing the dialogue between Gaurī and Śaṅkara straight from the mouth of the Lord, Nārada told us earlier. We shall mention that to you.

Formerly hundreds of Daityas and Dānavas inimical to Brāhmaṇas and Devas resorted to Śaṅkara by means of different kinds of severe penances.

96. Īśvara, the veritable ocean of nectar-like compassion, granted favour to them as they performed very severe penance with the minds not attached to anything else.

97. Maheśvara, the Lord of Devas, the master of the three worlds, expects only continuous, firm devotion for the purpose of granting boons.

98. Although they were the enemies of Devas and Brāhmaṇas, the Lord became pleased with their devotions alone and granted them the desired boons pertaining to the Lordship of the worlds.

99. The limits of the power of the Lord cannot be comprehended either by Brahmā or by Viṣṇu. The Lord's prowess is thus incomprehensible. Who can then divine the intention of the Lord?

100. The pure-hearted Pārvatī asked Parameśvara who, due to their penance, granted boons unto Daityas although they were of wicked activities.

Pārvatī said:

101. O Lord, on receiving your favour (boons) the Daityas dare to assail the three worlds. They harass Indra and other Devas. They make them agitated.

102. Why do you grant boons to them, to the evil-souled ones like them? None of their activities brings even the slightest peace and welfare of the universe.

103. You have granted boons to these and they enjoy divine pleasures. How then does Viṣṇu disregard your lordship and kill them?

104. O Lord, tell me what will their ultimate goal be on being killed?

Īśvara said:

105. People of the world are of three types: *Sāttvika, Rājasa* and *Tāmasa.* Among them these are dominated by Tamas. Hence they are difficult to encounter (are invincible).

106. They compete with Suras. They are intent on exterminating the universe. Hence, out of delusion, they resort to me by means of penance of the *Tamas* quality.

107. That I grant them boons is because of their devotion. I can be easily won over by means of devotion. There is no doubt about it.

108. Those Daityas of sinful deeds acquire boons befitting their penance. Let me explain why then they are killed by Viṣṇu.

109. Hari and I are apparently different. The reason thereof is the difference of the Guṇa. In fact we are non-different. This is the greatest secret.

110-113. The difference due to being the adored and the adorer is common to both of us. For, I bear on my head devoutly this Gaṅgā that has issued forth from the tip of Viṣṇu's foot despite the fact that I have been viewed with suspicion by you.

Further, for the sake of protecting the three worlds, Viṣṇu adored me for a long time systematically and obtained the discus that kills the evil ones. You are the Mahāmāyā of Hari of incomprehensible nature. Out of devotion to him, I propitiate that Mahāmāyā, the cause of the origin of the three worlds. Similarly Hari also has another Śakti of mine placed on his head.

114-116. Though he is unborn, he resorts to births and carries out the protection of the world. In order to kill Hiraṇyakaśipu he adopted the form of the Man-lion. When he (Viṣṇu as Man-Lion) was about to destroy the universe, I adopted the form of the (fabulous lion-killer) Śarabha and subdued him. In my attempt to save Bāṇa I raised my trident aloft. But even in his human incarnation, he could sportively stun me then. Further, increasing my prowess and greatness he adores me daily, although the Lord is my immanent soul.

117. Moreover, I always meditate on him, the Supreme Soul, devoid of beginning and end, by means of *Dhyānayoga*.

118. Therefore, there is no real difference between us. Difference and comparison are resorted to by deluded persons alone.

119. Assuming the form of Viṣṇu, I kill those persons of evil deeds. Now, O great goddess, listen to their ultimate goal.

120. After the devotion to me has ended, they are assailed by (overwhelmed with) anger and arrogance on seeing Hari. So they do not attain salvation.

121. By our power, their sins become wiped off and they attain nativity in the families of Brāhmaṇa-sages, which in turn brings about their salvation.

122. Adopting the holy vow of celibacy, they resort to *Pāśupata* Yoga. In view of the latent impressions of previous actions, they begin to adore me once again.

123. Others adopt *Pāśupata* and other *Vratas* devoutly by means of *Bhaktiyoga* and reside in cremation ground. Some are nude and some wear a single cloth.

124. Eating what they get by way of alms and smearing the body with ash, they worship my Liṅgas. They keep their intellect concentrated on me alone. They adhere firmly to the vow of meditating on me alone.

125. I grant salvation at the time of death to those who bow down to you, the goddess of the worlds and mine.

126. To those who have directed their minds to me, I grant the salvation of *Sārupya* (similarity in form) and *Sālokya* (staying in the God's region) types. That is because this *Pāśupatayoga* is not conducive to the salvation of the *Sāyujya* type. So it has been censured by good sages, Smṛtis and good people.

The Brāhmaṇas said:

127. We shall receive with equal honour those Brāhmaṇas who come here during their pilgrimage and whose minds have become humble with devotion.

128. They will be duly received and offered pure alms, loin cloth, waterpot etc. After coming here those ascetics need not do any other work.

129. They will be carefree on account of the presents provided by you. They will be solely devoted to *Śivadharma* based on the twenty-four Tattvas.

130. By worshipping Śrīsomeśvara, they will enhance your *Śreyas* (ultimate welfare). In the end they will attain salvation which is very rarely achieved (by others).

131. Other ascetics will come after them. Many others after these.Many others thereafter. O Lord of the night, they will surely be tested by us.

The Brāhmaṇas said:

132-133. On being asked by the goddess, the Three-eyed

Lord said thus. Nārada heard this dialogue and when we asked him during our discourse, he narrated it to us. Now everything has been mentioned to you by us.

134. On being told thus by them Soma became pleased and went home. At his behest, they also began to carry out whatever he had ordered.

The Devī said:

135. The Lord of Devas, Someśa, has such a prowess, He is the destroyer of sins. By what means can he be pleased? By what *Vrata* or restraint?

Īśvara said:

136. I shall clearly mention the holy rite for the sake of the welfare of human beings. O beautiful Deva lady, listen to that by means of which the Lord becomes pleased.

137. There are various kinds of *Vratas* and *Upavāsas* (fasts). Fasts observed every day, at day time or only during nights? In a Tīrtha many gifts are made over to deserving persons.

138-139. But if the divine *Somavāra Vrata* is observed in one's own abode, it is as good as performance of all kinds of penance etc. It is like a holy bath in Puṣkara. It is as good as going to Kedāra and drinking the water thereof. It is as good as viewing the Jyotirliṅga of excessive refulgence, O beautiful lady.

140. Of what avail are many *Dānas,* though given to deserving persons, O beautiful lady?

141. If any one worships with devotion for eight Somavāras (Mondays) it is as good as performing everything and observing great *Vratas.*

142. O my beloved, O Mahādevī, in the context of *Somavāra Vrata* I shall narrate to you this *Itihāsa* (a true story) just as it has occurred.

Īśvara said:

143. O great goddess, to the north of Kailāsa on the mountain Niṣadha, there is a large city named Svayaṁprabha.

144. It has all the features of a city. It is splendid with various kinds of jewels. It is full of Gandharvas of different tribes.It is on a par with Indra's capital city Amarāvatī.

145. A Gandharva named Ghanavāhana stays there and enjoys great pleasures not available even to Devas.

146. His wife was in the prime of her youth. She was charming with stout and protruding breasts. Mature in her speech, she had splendid conduct.

147. The leader of Gandharvas enjoyed all pleasures along with her. After eight sons, a daughter was born to him in due course.

148. O Parameśvarī, she was well-known by the name Gandharvasenā. She had all her limbs in perfect proportion. She knew all lores.

149-150. She was the most excellent one among thousands of girls there. She was endowed with beauty. With enthusiastic fancy, she was told by the father: "O sweet girl, go and play. This park is very fascinating. It is full of different kinds of trees and creepers. Many trees grow there. They are in full bloom and richly laden with fruits."

151. Accordingly she used to play there always surrounded by other girls. Once looking at her daughter playing thus, the mother said to her husband:

152. "I feel my life, your life and the lives of other kinsmen is fruitless in view of the fact that such a daughter stays at home without a husband, O my Lord."

153. On being told thus, the Gandharva spoke these words to his wife: "I shall be on the lookout for a handsome husband for our daughter."

154-155. After saying so, Ghanavāhana sent for his daughter to come to him. On being called by her parents the beautiful girl hastened to them and fell at the feet of everyone in due order (and said): "Command me, dear father, what can I do for you now?"

156. The delighted Ghanavāhana said: "O my daughter, is there any bridegroom who appeals to you now? I shall look for a jewel among Gandharvas befitting you."

157. On being told thus, her eyes grew red in anger and she asked her father: "Is there anyone in all the three worlds having one-ten-millionth of my beauty ?" On hearing her highly

surprising statement, the father and the mother virtually fell into a swoon.

158. All the kinsmen and other people were sad. "What this girl uttered now is not good at all." Saying thus all the kinsmen and mother went away.

159. That beautiful girl continued to sport about in the park rocking herself in the swing during that vernal month.

160. In the meantime Śikhaṇḍī,the group leader (of Śiva Gaṇas) was going through the sky in his divine aerial chariot. He saw the girl with exalted beauty and charm.

161-163. She was having fun with songs, instrumental music and dance. The group leader got down from the aerial chariot for offering midday prayer. He wanted midday sporting-about with the celestial damsels. He got down from the aerial chariot and stood there in the park. He then heard the statement of the Gandharva girl: "No one on a par with me in beauty is seen.No Deva or Dānava possesses one-ten-millionth of my beauty."

164. On hearing this statement the group leader became angry. The Lord of Gaṇas cursed that girl of beautiful limbs but of arrogant nature.

The Gaṇa said:

165. Despite seeing me, O large-eyed girl, you disparage Gandharvas and Devas as well as others. You are so haughty on account of your excessive beauty and charm?

166. Hence,Ohaughtygirl, leprosy shall affect all your limbs.

On hearing this curse the poor girl became terrified.

167. She fell at his feet stretching to the full length and requested for blessing. "O kind Sir, bless me and withdraw the curse. I am a wretched girl. I shall not behave like this in future."

168. On being appealed thus, Śikhaṇḍī, the group leader, blessed the Gandharva girl out of compassion.

Śikhaṇḍī said:

169. A living being may be endowed with birth in high caste, beauty, learning and riches, but if he becomes haughty and proud thereby he perishes.

170. Hence one should not be puffed up and vainglorious. The result of haughtiness is this. O my girl, listen to my blessing (by way of redemption). After listening, ponder over it.

171. Gośṛṅga, a leading sage, is in the Himālayan forests. He will render help to you.

After saying this, O my beloved, he went away.

172. By that time it was evening in all the worlds.

173. Thereupon, the Gandharva girl lost all her enthusiasm. She left the beautiful park with head drooping down and came to her parents.

174. She told them everything that resulted in leprosy. On hearing it, the parents were grief-stricken with no lustre (pale in their faces).

175. They hastened to Mountain Himālaya along with their daughter. They found out the hermitage of Sage Gośṛṅga.

176-177. They saw the leading sage Gośṛṅga seated in the middle. They bowed to him and prostrated on the ground like a log of wood and eulogized him with many hymns. Sitting before him and saluting him again and again, he spoke words about what happened earlier.

178. When the story was heard, he asked the reason. When that was asked, the Gandharva said:

The Gandharva said:

179-180. The body of my daughter is afflicted with the fell disease of leprosy. It behoves you to do something that finishes it. O Brāhmaṇa-sage, be pleased. I am highly distressed now. The reason of our coming here is to see that the leprosy of my daughter is eradicated.

Gośṛṅga said:

181-183. In Bhāratavarṣa, there is the highly resplendent Lord Someśvara by name near the ocean. He is bowed down to by all the Devas. Resolve to worship him taking only a single meal for the sake of destroying all ailments and for the fulfilment of all objectives. Propitiate Śaṅkara by means of the *Somavāra Vrata.* If this is done the sickness of your daughter will be eradicated.

Īśvara said:

184. On hearing these words of the great sage of purified soul, he resolved to go there for the purpose of propitiating Someśvara.

CHAPTER TWENTYFIVE

Description of Somavāra Vrata

Īśvara said:

1. Desirous of propitiating Bhava, O goddess, that Gandharva asked the excellent sage about the *Somavāra Vrata* (vow to be performed on Monday).

The Gandharva said:

2. How is this *Somavara Vrata* to be observed? What are the injunctions regarding its procedure? At what time is it to be performed? Narrate everything in detail.

Gośṛṅga said:

3. Very well! Very well! O highly intelligent one! This is what has not been mentioned to anyone else. It is conducive to help all living beings.

4. What is called *Somavāra Vrata* is divine. It is destructive of all ailments and it confers all Siddhis. It bestows all the desired benefits.

5. It can be observed at all times. It causes auspiciousness to all the *Varṇas*. Seeing good result thereof, this has to be performed always by men and women.

6. This great *Vrata* has been performed by Brahmā, Viṣṇu and other Devas. Further, this has been performed by Somarāja when he was overwhelmed by Dakṣa's curse.

7. Fully devoted to the meditation on Śaṁbhu, Śaṁbhu was propitiated by him. The great Lord was pleased with the devotion of Somarāja.

8-9. He (Soma)said: "If you are pleased, be present in the

installed Liṅga permanently. May my Liṅga installed along with Umā, continue to stay as long as the Sun and Moon shine and mountains stand."

10. After praying to Maheśvara, the Liṅga was installed by him and known after his own name. Then he was rid of the ailments.

11. Thus he has got his body heated and purified and he now shines in the sky.

12. Ever since then, those men too who perform the Vrata on the earth, attain purity of body like Moon and go to his region.

13. Of what avail is much talk? I shall describe the mode of procedure thereof. It can be adopted and performed in any month on any Monday in the bright half of the month.

14. Earlier in the Brāhma Muhūrta, the devotee finishes cleansing the teeth with the toothbrush twig (of any tree) and performs the rite of ablution and all holy rites laid down in his own code of pious activities.

15. In a pleasant site on a clean level ground, one should place a polished pot. The pot is covered with mango shoots and beautified with sandalpaste.

16. The vessel is then embellished with all the ornaments and covered all round with a white cloth. Śiva (Liṅga) with its pedestal base is put therein.

17. There Lord Somanātha along with his Śakti and accompanied by Umā is worshipped with white flowers. In the (eight) quarters the *Aṣṭamūrtis* are also worshipped.

18. There shall be different kinds of foodstuffs and snacks. The fruit offered shall be Bījapūraka (pomegranate?). The rites are entirely performed with the following Mantra:

19-20. The adoration and the *Homa* are performed with this Mantra: "Om, obeisance to the Five-faced One with ten arms and three eyes. O Lord with half the body united with the body of Umā, O Lord riding on the bull, O Lord adorned with white ornaments, obeisance to you, the omniformed one."

21. Having performed thus during the day, the man should go to sleep at night after viewing the Moon[1]. He should be on a mattress of Darbha grass and meditate on Hara, Someśvara.

1. Read *candram* for *caivam.*

22. If the rite is thus performed the eighteen varieties of leprosy will be dispelled.

On the second Monday *(Somavāra)* the devotee shall use a twig of *Karañja* as toothbrush.

23. He should worship the subtle form of the Lord accompanied by *Jyeṣṭhaśakti* (the eldest Śakti) by means of lotuses and imbibe honey duly.

24. An orange fruit *(Nāraṅga)* is offered and all other rites are performed as before. If the rite is thus performed one shall attain the benefit of (gifting as *Dāna*) a hundred thousand cows.

25. On the third *Somavāra,* the tooth-brush twig is from an Apāmārga tree. After cleansing the teeth the devotee should worship *Trinetra* (Śiva—the three-eyed).

26. A *Dāḍima* fruit (pomegranate) should be offered and the deity is adored with Jāti flowers. At night the devotee eats grapes and worships God Śiva attended by Siddhis.

27. On the fourth Monday *(Somavāra)* the tooth-brush twig is that of *Udumbara* (Indian fig tree). The devotee should worship Gaurīśa accompanied by *Sūkṣmā* (the goddess in the subtle form).

28. A fruit of *Nārikela* (coconut) is to be offered and the adoration is performed with *Damana* (Artenisia indica—MW). At night the devotee eats *Śarkarā* (sugar granules) and keeps vigil at night.

29. On the fifth Monday the devotee worships the Lord of Gaṇas accompanied by *Vibhūti* (goddess of prosperity). The adoration is done with *Kunda* flowers.

30. The toothbrush twig is from an *Aśvattha* (Peepal) tree. The *Arghya* is offered through grapes. At night the devotee eats *Mocā (Phala)* (banana). One will get the benefit of a horse-sacrifice.

31. On the sixth Monday the devotee should worship the Lord named Surūpa. With great devotion he should eat camphor.

32. On the seventh Monday the toothbrush is a twig of *Mallikā.* The devotee should worship *Sarvajña* accompanied by Dīptā.

33. A Jambīra fruit is offered and the adoration is done with Jāti flowers. The devotee should eat Lavaṅga (cloves). It has infinite benefit.

34. On the eighth Monday Lord Amoghāyuta is to be worshipped with *Marubhaka* flowers. A *Kadalīphala* (banana fruit) is offered as *Arghya.* At night the devotee takes milk. He shall obtain the benefit of *Agniṣṭoma* (sacrifice).

35-36. When this Vrata is performed, the benefit is a crore times more than the benefit remembered as being derived from a crore times of perfect ablution in Gaṅgā or the benefit of gifting ten thousand gold coins to a Brāhmaṇa well-versed in the Vedas at the time of a solar eclipse in Kurukṣetra.

37. If the *Somavāra* (Monday) Vrata is performed the benefit is a crore times more than the benefit of the gift of a hundred elephants and a hundred thousand chariots and horses.

38. If the *Somavāra* is performed, one gets the benefit of fumigating *Guggulu* crores of times.

39. He shall be endowed with all the riches. He will have the same valour as that of Śiva. He shall reside in Rudraloka till the dissolution (death) of Brahmā.

40. When the ninth *Somavāra* falls the devotee performs the splendid *Udyāpana* (conclusion) rite. O Gandharva, I shall explain to you now how it is done.

41. A circular pavilion is erected and decorated with flags and banners splendidly. A Kuṇḍa is also made. Four ornamental gates are erected.

42. The altar is to be made in the centre. It should be square in shape and very splendid. There, in the middle, the mystic figure of *Padma* inside a circle is to be drawn.

43. In the eight quarters, eight pots are placed with gold therein. They are placed separately. *Vāmā* and other *Śaktis* are in due order installed in the pots in east etc.

44. In the pericarp of the lotus, the highly resplendent golden image of Śrīsomeśa along with Śakti is installed.

45. The Lord occupies a golden bed and is accompanied by *Manonmanī* (a form of Durgā). Vessels of gold etc. are filled with honey.

46. It is covered with a golden bedstead and the deity therein is duly adored.It is duly and serially adored uttering the names beginning with *Ananta* and ending with *Śikhaṇḍin.*

47-48. There shall be sweet scents, garlands, incense, lamps and different kinds of food offerings. With Someśvara in view the following are offered to the preceptor well-versed in the *Purāṇas:* garments, ornaments, betel-leaves, umbrella, chowries, mirrors, lamps, bells, canopies and bedstead with cotton cushion.

49. After adorning the preceptor, the devotee should perform the rite of *Homa.* At the conclusion of the rite of offering oblations, the devotee keeps vigil at night there itself.

50. Then he drinks *Pañcagavya* (the five substances got from a cow) and meditates on Lord Someśvara in his heart. At dawn he takes his holy bath and performs the meditation in accordance with the injunctions.

51. Thereafter, O Gandharva, he should feed Brāhmaṇas devoutly with various kinds of foodstuffs made of milk, sugar-candy etc.

52. He then should offer a pair of garments and a cow and see them off.

53. In this way the devotee performs the *Vrata* duly and acquires everlasting merit. He becomes richly endowed with wealth and foodgrain along with his sons and wife.

54. No one born in that family becomes poor and miserable. One without a son becomes blessed with sons. Even a barren woman bears sons.

55. This *Vrata* should be particularly performed by all these: a woman who is *Kākavandhyā* (one who has given birth to only one child), a woman whose child is dead, one disliked or maltreated by husband and one who gives birth to only girls.

56. After these Vratas have been duly performed, when he (or she) dies, the devotee shall go to heaven. He enjoys elaborate and unlimited pleasures for thousands and hundreds of crores of Kalpas, until the annihilation of all living beings.

57. Thus the entire procedure of *Somavāra Vrata* has been narrated to you in due order. O highly esteemed one, hasten to the place where Someśvara is present.

Īśvara said:

58. O lady of excellent countenance, on being told thus, the Gandharva arrived at Prabhāsa Kṣetra along with all requisite offerings and accompanied by his daughter.

59-60. There he visited Someśvara and his eyes became filled with tears of joy. In the course of his pilgrimage, he duly worshipped the Lord and performed *Somavrata* in the company of his daughter. Maheśvara became pleased with that highly esteemed devotee. He granted him the kingdom of Gandharvas and perfect devotion unto himself. All the ailments were dispelled and all the desires richly fulfilled.

CHAPTER TWENTYSIX

Greatness of Gandharveśvara

Īśvara said:

1-3. On the acquisition of the boon, the Gandharva named Ghanavāhana became contented. With great devotion he installed a Liṅga there.

It was to the north of Someśvara in the vicinity of Daṇḍapāṇi. The Liṅga was called Gandharveśvara. It bestows skill in *Gāndharva* (art of music). It is stationed to the west of Varadā at a distance of five Dhanus. A man who adores it on the fifth lunar day, never becomes miserable.

CHAPTER TWENTYSEVEN

Greatness of Gandharvaseneśvara

Īśvara said:

1-4. Further, O goddess of Devas, there is a Liṅga installed there itself by Gandharvasenā, the daughter of Ghanavāhana. It is in the vicinity of Gaurī, within a distance of three *Dhanus* in the east.

It is called Vimaleśvara and is destructive of all ailments.

A woman who adores it on the third lunar day is rid of all wretchedness. She obtains all that she desires. She will become well-established with sons and grandsons.

O goddess, this *Vrata* which is destructive of sins, was narrated to the Gandharva in the twilight (interim) period of Tretā Yuga. If this *Vrata* is heard, it destroys sins.

CHAPTER TWENTYEIGHT

Procedure of the Pilgrimage

The Devī said:

1-2. Thus, O Lord, this wonderful narrative has been heard by me from you entirely. Now it behoves you to narrate duly and in detail the greatness of Maheśvara, the Lord of Soma. How should men proceed to visit him? How is the religious pilgrimage to be performed? At what time, O great Lord? And what are the regulations?

Īśvara said:

3-4. Whether in *Hemanta* (early winter) or in *Śiśira* (late winter) or in spring, O beautiful lady, if a person feels inclined and has also the requisite money on hand and the festival season falls, the Yātrā (pilgrimage) should be performed. It is the keenness of the devotion that is the criterion. O lady of excellent complexion, the devotee himself should observe some sort of (religious) rules and regulations in his own house.

5. He bows to Rudra mentally and performs the *Śrāddha* in accordance with the injunctions. He circumambulates the holy spot, observing the vow of silence with great concentration.

6. He should be self-restrained. He should observe full control on the diet. The devotee should be rid of lust, anger, covetousness and delusion.

7. He must be free from rivalry, malice and indulgence. Thus the men should start on their religious procession. Undertaking pilgrimage is highly meritorious. It excels even (performance of) *Yajñas*.

8. By performing Agniṣṭoma and other Yajñas with plenty of monetary gifts, one gets that benefit which one acquires by means of pilgrimage to holy places.

9. In the extremely terrible Kali Yuga with its full complement of sinfulness, one cannot obtain piety and heavenly pleasures through any other means. O great goddess, there is no doubt in this that there is no other means except pilgrimage.

10. In the Kali age, men who undertake pilgrimage with

purity and faith, shall be ones who have achieved their objectives. Others are useless.

11. Just as there is no reservoir of water on a par with the great ocean, so also there is no Tīrtha equal to Prābhāsika Kṣetra.

12. One not observing the holy fast for three days, not undertaking pilgrimage to holy spots and not gifting gold or cows definitely becomes indigent.

13. If a devotee is desirous of the benefit of all the Tīrthas, but these are inaccessible and impossible places of pilgrimage, he should visit them mentally.

14. If one's hands and feet and the mind are fully under control, if one has learning, penance and fame, one attains the benefit of (pilgrimage to) holy spots.

15. A man of self-control, one with full diet control, one keenly interested in holy ablution and *Japa,* and one regular in observing holy vows and fasts, attains the benefit of pilgrimage to holy spots.

16. O goddess of Devas, one who is never angry, one who is habitually truthful and steadfast in vows and one who views all living beings on a par with his own self, attains the benefit of pilgrimage to holy spots.

17. A Brāhmaṇa should undertake pilgrimage to places like Kurukṣetra which can be traversed by means of chariots. There is no fault in making use of vehicles therein.

18. Those good men who have ample wealth and who constantly think of visiting Tīrthas, will have more benefit through making gifts in holy spots as well as by Yoga.

19. Those poor people who have no money but who are interested in pilgrimage, will have the acquisition of the benefit of Yajñas even without possessing ready cash.

20. It should be known that a Tīrtha bestows benefits to persons of all *Varṇas* and stages of life. No hesitation need be there in this matter.

21. If a person goes to a holy spot for some other task (of his own) but incidentally takes his holy ablution, he does not acquire the benefit of the pilgrimage but gets only that of the holy bath.

22. Undertaking pilgrimage on foot is considered the greatest penance. If the same is undertaken by means of vehicles, one gets only the benefit of the holy ablution.

23. O goddess, if anyone pays another the expenditure (for the *Yātrā*) and also places his vehicle at his disposal for the pilgrimage, he gets four times the benefit.

24. Having undertaken pilgrimage, O great goddess, if people control their sense-organs and subsist on alms, they acquire ten times the benefit.

25. A Brāhmaṇa (who undertakes a pilgrimage) without using umbrella and shoes, who subsist himself on alms and keeps his sense-organs under control, he is rid of all terrible results arising from committing Mahāpātakas.

26. Taking alms is not on a par with taking other people's cooked food. Accepting alms is not acceptance of gifts. Taking alms is on a par with imbibing Soma juice. Hence one should beg for alms.

27. In this world there are two types of holy spots: one type is created by self-willed ones; the other type is self-born (natural) like Prabhāsa etc. or created by deities.

28. In a great Tīrtha that is self-born i.e. natural and is by nature more exalted, a *Pratigraha* (gift) taken is as good as accepting all *Pratigrahas*.

29. In the case of one refraining from *Pratigraha* the benefit of the pilgrimage is ten times that of the pilgrimage. All gifts are made by him. The Devas are propitiated by means of *Yajñas*.

30-31. It is as though after reaching the holy spot great restraint is indulged in by him. If anyone is inclined to take *Pratigraha* because of his liking for the object, he is a wicked soul. He has neither this world nor the other world. But if a Brāhmaṇa weak for want of an avocation, accepts *Pratigraha* he shall make a gift of a tenth of what he got thus. Thereby he never become a loser.

32. If a Śūdra assumes the guise of a Brāhmaṇa and takes the *Pratigraha* of anything like grass or wood, he meets with a downfall.

33. He falls into crores of great hells such as Kūṁbhīpāka etc. He remains there, O lady of excellent countenance, till fourteen thousand Indras reign.

34. Hence no *Pratigraha* should be accepted in both the types of *Tīrthas, Kṛta* (created) or *Akṛta* (natural) even by other Brāhmaṇas.

35. One who is fully endowed with *Bhāva* (emotional purity) attains the full benefit. But one who goes (on pilgrimage) with another man's food, attains only a sixteenth (part of the benefit).

36. In the case of a blind man, a man of failing health and weakness, a lame man and a *Yāyāvara* (one who moves about from one village to another every night), a vehicle has been permitted for cogent reasons. Why should there be (such a concession) in the case of an *Acchidra* (having no holes, i.e. weakness, healthy, with no weakness) Brāhmaṇa?

37. One who visits Tīrthas, gives away the benefit of ablution, eating and drinking to those who bear him. But the benefit of the Tīrtha, he acquires entirely.

38. If he does not give away the entire sixteenth fraction of what he has acquired with effort, he shall give unto Brāhmaṇas a fifth (of this sixteenth).

39. If honouring the good wishes of preceptors, parents and deities, one gives away one's merit the person gets the same multiplied eight times as the benefit.

40. Whether in the case of holy ablution, *Dāna, Japa, Homa,* self-study of the Vedas and adoration of deities, it is the *Puṇya* (merit) that has to be given, demerit is never given.

41. If a pilgrim dips in a Tīrtha with his father, mother, brother, friend, or preceptor in view, that person gets a twelfth of the merit.

42. O great goddess, if a pilgrim makes an image of anyone and gets it immersed in the waters of a Tīrtha, that person gets one-eighth of the merit.

43. Those Brāhmaṇas deficient in learning who accept great gifts *(Mahādāna)* are reborn as trees or as Brahmarākṣasas.

44. One should not take interest in *Pratigraha* on the strength of Vedic knowledge. Whether due to ignorance or due to mistake, Karma burns, not the other things. (?)

45. On touching a log of wood in a funeral pyre or a Yajña *Yūpa* (sacrificial post) or one who sells Veda, bath is prescribed (by way of atonement).

46. One who reads command and the one who gives it—both of them are sinful ones, residents of the nether worlds (i.e. hells). (?)

47. He who reads command with a desire to collect *Pratigraha,* particularly in a holy place, is *Brahmaghna* (slayer of Brāhmaṇas),

none else. One may be staying at the entrance to the palace of a king but one should not make a sale of the Vedas.

48. A base Brāhmaṇa may very well kill a cow and eat its flesh, or one may live like fish, but one shall not sell the Vedas. There has never been and there will never be a sin like Brāhmaṇa-slaughter.

49. O goddess, one may commit that sin but one shall not make a sale of Vedas particularly in a holy spot, so also in a Mahākṣetra.

50. A person undertaking pilgrimage renders the *Tīrtha* holy and sacred if he abandons (refrains from accepting) a gift offered. He sanctifies his ancestors.

51. A sin committed elsewhere becomes reduced in Tīrtha. But what is committed in the Tīrtha is never destroyed anywhere.

52. A pilgrim shall guard himself like a pot filled with oil by not letting it spill. That Brāhmaṇa of self-control attains the benefit of the Tīrtha.

53. If a pilgrim eats cooked food from anyone whether in a large quantity or only very little, he gives a moiety of that benefit of bath to him.

54. If a Brāhmaṇa pilgrim does not beg for alms despite being in difficulties, if he is truthful and resolute in meditation, he renders service to the Tīrtha itself.

55. Puṣkara in Kṛta Yuga, Naimiṣa in Tretā Yuga, Kurukṣetra in Dvāpara and Prābhāsika in Kali Yuga (are most important and sacred).

56. A man may stand on a single leg for a thousand Yugas. Another performs the pilgrimage to the Prābhāsika Kṣetra. The latter may or may not be equal to the former.

57. O lady of excellent countenance, after reaching the centre of this holy spot a man must leave off his vehicle and walk on foot.

58. He should roll on where even the deities had rolled. Then as a true pilgrim, he should go to Lord Someśvara after visiting Kapardin. He should proceed ahead dancing, laughing and singing.

59. On seeing such a man standing before Someśvara, the Pitṛs always become pleased and the grandfathers shout for joy.

60. "One belonging to our family has set off towards Lord Someśvara, in order to redeem us." O goddess, after going to Someśvara, a devotee should get himself (i.e. his head) shaved.

61. In the Tīrtha the requisite *Upavāsa* (fasting) should be observed. Understand the procedure from me. There is no Tīrtha on a par with Gaṅgā. There is no resort on a par with a *Kratu* (Yajña).

62. There is no *Jāpya* (Mantra) like Gāyatrī; no *Homa* like that with the *Vyāhṛtis* (*Om bhūḥ* etc.). Within water there is nothing that quells sins more than the *Aghamarṣaṇa* (Mantra).

63. There is no meritorious act like non-violence. There is nothing greater than *Dāna.* There is no greater austerity (penance) than observing fast or resorting to Tīrthas.

64. O goddess of Devas, there is nothing superior to fast observed in a holy spot as a means of quelling sins and causing pleasure to the good.

65. Fast has been particularly prescribed in holy spots of deities. In the case of a Brāhmaṇa abstinence from food is called the greatest austerity.

66. Taking food once in three days is mentioned as the greatest austerity in the case of a Śūdra. In the case of persons born as a result of mixture of castes, one day is glorified (as an interval between two meals).

67. If at all anywhere a Śūdra performs a penance greater than (taking food) once in three days, it should be known that there is loss unto the nation and a great danger befalls the king.

68. A Śūdra should perform austerity within his capacity by regularly taking food once in three days. A Śūdra shall never pull out or uproot Darbha grass. He should never drink the milk of a *Kapilā* (tawny-coloured) cow.

69. O beautiful woman, he should never take food in the middle leaf of *Brahmavṛkṣa* (Mulberry or Palāśa tree). He should not utter the *Praṇava Mantra* (*Om*), nor shall he eat *Puroḍāśa* (sacrificial oblation).

70. He should not have a tuft of hair on the head nor should he wear the sacred thread. He should not even utter Saṁskṛta language. He should not read a Vedic passage nor should he resort to *Trairātra* (fast for three nights).

71. Certainly the fulfilment of the holy rites in the case of

a Śūdra is with a mere bow of salutation. If he does anything prohibited he sinks down (in hell)along with his Pitṛs.

72. One by whom the organs (of sense and action) numbering eleven have been controlled obtains the merit of (pilgrimage to) Tīrthas. The other one shall meet only with pain and distress.

73. One should take the holy bath in the same Tīrtha where Pitṛ Śrāddha is performed. He shall be one doing what is beneficial to all living beings. He shall attain the benefit of the Tīrtha.

74. A person who is a religious impostor, who is always covetous and is enamoured of other men 's wives shall be a sinner even if he undertakes pilgrimage.

75. O great goddess, one should know all these and then undertake pilgrimage in accordance with the injunctions. At the outset, he should observe fast at the pilgrim centre. He should be faithful and steadfast in his holy vows.

76. If he wishes for his welfare he should not take food at all on that day. No Brāhmaṇa should ever take another man's food.

77. One may accept elephant, horse, chariot, other vehicles, plot of land, cow, gold etc. but shall not take food.

78. Through uncooked food, one gets hundred times the merit of one who offers or takes food. Hence, O lady of excellent countenance, one should observe *Tīrthopavāsa* (fast at a holy spot).

79. O goddess, in the case of one who has undertaken holy vows, a pilgrim and a widow in particular, if food is taken from another persons the merit goes to that person whose food is partaken of.

80-82. I shall mention the procedure of pilgrimage to be followed by a widowed woman. She has to eschew *Kuṁkuma,* sandal, betel-leaves, garlands, all red garments, bedsheets, conversation with the uncultured, taking meal two times a day, seeing men, engaging in jokes in darkness. She has to avoid creaky sandals, dance and music.

83. She should not tie up tresses of hair nor should she apply collyrium to the eyes. No unguent is to be used. She will dissociate with unchaste women. She should not revel in too much of scholarship (scholarly discussions).

84. An ascetic, a religious student and a widow in particular, should take bath everyday and wear white clothes.

85. They (learned men) consider betel-leaves, honey and meat on a par with imbibing liquor. By avoiding these, O goddess, the merit of the pilgrimage will be complete.

The Devī said:

86. What are the austerities recommended in the holy place Prābhāsika? What types of gifts are made? How? In what holy spot?

Īśvara said:

87. Austerities are of a very great importance in Kṛtayuga. It is knowledge that is sought after in Tretā Yuga. In Dvāpara, performing Yajña is praised. Only *Dāna* (is regarded so) in Kaliyuga.

88. Sages and other people go to Prābhāsika Kṣetra and perform austerities called *Kṛcchra Cāndrāyaṇa* etc. in Kṛtayuga.

89. In Kali Age, gifts are made over to Brāhmaṇas duly. After reaching Prabhāsa Kṣetra the merit of the austerities is obtained.

90-94. At Prabhāsa, a king should make sixteen *Mahādānas* namely: *Tulāpuruṣa, Brahmāṇḍa, Pṛthvī, Kalpa tree, Kāmadhenu, Gaja* (elephant), *Vāji* (horse), *Ratha* (chariot), *Ratna* (jewel), *Dhenu*(cow), *Hiraṇya* (gold), *Aśva* (horse), *Sapta Sāgara* (seven seas), *Mahābhūta* (great elements), *Ghaṭa* (pot), *Viśva* (universe), *Cakra* (wheel), and *Kalpalatā* (wish-yielding creeper).

The following ten are remembered as *Parvatas* (mountains): *Dhānya* (grain), *Ratna* (jewel), *Guḍa* (jaggery), *Svarṇa* (gold), *Tila* (gingelly seeds), *Kārpāsa* (cotton), *Śarkarā* (sugar), *Sarpis* (ghee), *Lavaṇa* (salt) and *Rūpya* (silver).

The following ten are remembered as *Dhenus* (cows): *Guḍa* (jaggery), *Ājya* (ghee), *Dadhi* (curds), *Madhu* (honey), *Aṁbu* (water) (?), *Salila* (water) (?), *Kṣīra* (milk), *Śarkarā* (sugar) and those called *Ratna* in their own form.

One of these gifts is to be given at each Tīrtha separately. Or all should be given once in a place at the confluence of Sarasvatī and the sea.

95. To a great learned man should be given everything or a house with all the necessary paraphernalia; something whether it is much or little should be given to Brāhmaṇas in a social gathering.

96. Rites in the sacred fire are to be performed in that Tīrtha where Liṅga is obtained and where the waters are devoid of impurities. Thereafter the *Dāna* is to be made.

97. There is a definite injunction laid down that in every Tīrtha, propitiation of the Devas, offering oblations of water to the Pitṛs, Śrāddha and *Dāna* together with the monetary gifts and the gift of cows should be performed.

98. In regard to the Liṅgas well-known as extraordinary, *Vṛsadāna* (gift of a bull) is prescribed. Ablution, smearing of unguents and the adoration of the deities should be performed.

99. The *Jagatī* (Precincts of a temple) should be devoutly plastered and then the worship performed. The palace (temple) should be made white with lime and if it is ruined, it should be renovated.

100. A person who undertakes *Vratas* should keep the flower garden and the well for bathing pure and clean. Plenty of gifts to Brāhmaṇas as well as the priest worshipping the deity (be given).

101. In all pilgrimages everywhere, this injunction holds good. A Tīrtha in ruins should be renovated and swept clean. The merit of such good work is to be mentioned (to all).

102. In a well-known Tīrtha, one should give *Mahādāna;* in a medium type moderate type of gift. Gift of cows is made in all the Tīrthas. Gold is the means of expiation. The gift of gold is the best of all gifts.

103. By doing thus with devotion, a man's birth becomes fruitful. I shall now explain the gifts in various Tīrthas—what should be given, where and on what lunar days.

104. In Prabhāsa Kṣetra pure gold should be given on the first lunar day; garment on the second lunar day; a plot of land on the third day (should be given).

105. On the fourth day, foodgrains are to be gifted and a *Kapilā* (tawny-coloured cow) on the fifth day. A horse should be given on the sixth day and a buffalo on the seventh day.

106. A bull is to be gifted on the eighth day. It shall be blue-coloured and endowed with all characteristic features. On

the ninth day, the devotee should give a house, a discus, a conch and a club.

107. All types of sweet scents are to be gifted on the tenth day and pearl on the eleventh day. On the twelfth day cooked food etc. and corals are to be duly offered to a person of excellent *Vratas.*

108. Women (slave girls) are to be given on the thirteenth day and wisdom (knowledge, learning) is gifted on the *Bhūta* (fourteenth) day. On the *Amāvāsyā* day all *Dānas* are to be made.

109. By making these gifts one will get ten times more merit (benefit).

The Devī said:

110. Tell me the result experienced by those who have come to Prabhāsa Kṣetra without devotion and without making gifts and also those without holy baths and utterance of Mantras.

Īśvara said:

111. Irrespective of their being wealthy or without the utterance of the Mantras all those who meet with death at Prabhāsa proceed to Śiva's abode.

112. O my beloved, I allot a great chariot to those persons who die without utterance of Mantras and performance of sacred rites.

113. Men obtain the highest status in a manner befitting the holy bath and *Dāna.* Some men get it as a result of *Snāna* and some men by means of *Dāna.*

114. Some get it by means of bowing down to the Liṅga and some by means of the adoration of the Liṅga; some as a result of the power of meditation and some due to the power of Yoga.

115. O splendid lady, some (obtain these) due to the *Jāpya* (muttering) of the *Mantra* and some through penance; some as a result of renunciation in the Tīrtha and some in accordance with their devotion.

116. All these and many others, whether exalted, middling or the lowest, go to the city of Śiva by means of chariots resembling the Sun.

117. Their hands are marked by tridents. All of them have bulls for vehicle. By my power they sport about in the midst of divine groups of Apsarās.

118. Thus, in accordance with their devotion I grant perpetual benefit. This holy place Prabhāsa is stainless. It is not adversely affected by *Dharmas* or *Adharmas*.

119. Whether they perform holy rites or unholy acts they undoubtedly go to Śiva.

120. O goddess, a man may be blind ever since his birth. Meeting with death in my Kṣetra, he too, is honoured in the world of Rudra.

121. O goddess, a man may be devoid of both of his ears ever since his birth but meeting with death in Prabhāsa he shall be in my company (an attendant).

122. Now I shall mention the rules regarding *Sparśana* (touching or ritualistic imbibing)of the Tīrtha waters. Charged with a Mantra a Tīrtha comes near.

123. At the outset the devotee touches the Tīrtha, the pure water uttering the *Praṇava*. Thereafter, he should take the plunge and take his bath uttering this *Adhyātma Mantra* (the Mantra of spiritual efficacy):

124-125 "Om, obeisance to the Lord of Devas, to Śitikaṇṭha (Blue-throated Śiva) holding a staff and having the discus in the left hand. Obeisance to *Vedhas* (creator).

O Sarasvatī, O Sāvitrī, O mother of the Vedas, O Vibhāvarī (night), be present here in this Tīrtha, O destroyer of sins".

In the case of all the Tīrthas, this same Mantra is cited.

126. Uttering this Mantra, a pilgrim makes the salutation and takes the holy bath in accordance with the injunctions. O lady of holy vows, he should observe fast on that day.

127. For a whole year, the devotee should observe fast on that lunar day.

The Devī said:

128. O great god, tell me in detail. After coming to Prabhāsa Kṣetra, in which Tīrtha should the devotees take their holy bath?

Īśvara said:

129. So, I shall tell you about the first Tīrtha of great lustre, where men should take their bath at the outset.

CHAPTER TWENTYNINE

Reason why Sea Water Is not Fit for Drinking

Īśvara said:

1-3. Thereafter, a pilgrim should go to Agnitīrtha on the auspicious shore of the sea where the Bāḍava (submarine fire) was released by Sarasvatī, O lady of excellent countenance.

It is to the south of Somanātha and is destructive of all sins. It is the Tīrtha well-known in all the three worlds by the name *Padmaka.*

It is said that the Kuṇḍa is within the water at a distance of a hundred *Dhanus* from Someśa. It extends to a hundred *Hastas* and is destructive of sins. There the pilgrim takes his plunge into the sea and takes his bath.

4. First of all he should shave off the hairs (of his head) near Someśvara. Meditating mentally on Śaṅkara, he should cast off the hairs there. After casting off the hairs, he should take bath once again.

5. O Daughter of the Mountain, whatever sin a man commits when in straitened circumstances due to want of sustenance, all that sin remains on his hairs.

6. Hence one should assiduously cast off the hairs there. If the same is carried out in front of Somanātha, the benefit is twofold.

7. The place in the vicinity of Agnitīrtha, in the centre of *Kapardi Dvāra* should be known as the place where the benefit is twofold. At other spots, the benefit is only single.

8. O lady of excellent countenance, shaving off the hairs is not commendable in the case of women with husband alive. Listen to the rite in regard to them from me.

9. Hold together the entire tresses of hairs and cut off two

finger-breadths (of hairs in the end). Then oblations are offered to gods and libations to the Pitṛs duly.

10. In regard to shaving off and observing of fast, this alone is the procedure in all the Tīrthas.

11. Shaving off (the head) is laid down on seven occasions. It should be done when visiting Gaṅgā, in the holy spot of Bhāskara, at death of mother, that of father, that of preceptor, on impregnation and at the time of imbibing Soma juice.

12. Even if one performs a thousand horse-sacrifices, one does not get that benefit which is obtained by shaving off (the head).

13. O goddess, if one takes the holy ablution there without uttering Mantra on certain occasions, he may get benefit except the single occasion of the day of festival *(Parvan)*.

14. With the exception of Parvan occasions, O goddess of Devas, the great ocean should not be touched by men even with the tip of the Darbha grass without Mantra and without the rite of shaving off.

15-16. After the holy ablution in accordance with the injunctions and the offer of *Arghyas* to the great ocean, the pilgrim adores through sweet scents, flowers, garments and holy unguents and places a gold bangle there within his capacity.

17. After following this procedure, O goddess of Devas, the devotee ritualistically touches the salty ocean uttering this Mantra. Then (the deity) will grace the place with its presence.

18. "Ọm, obeisance to Viṣṇugupta (one protected by Viṣṇu). to you in the form of Viṣṇu. O Lord of Devas, be present in the salty brine in the vicinity."

19. He should utter the following truthful statement and take the plunge in the Lord of rivers: "Agni is the *Retas*(semen). The body is through Mṛḍā (the protecting deity). Viṣṇu, the navel of Amṛta, is the *Retodhā* (who deposits the *Retas*)"

20. "Om, obeisance to *Ratnagarbha*". With this *Mantra,* O beautiful woman, the pilgrim casts off the bracelet there and then takes his bath as he pleases.

21. Then he should offer libations to Devas, human beings and grandfathers with water mixed with gingelly seeds duly and with great faith.

22. By taking the holy bath once in the salty water of the sea, a man dispels the sins committed in the course of a hundred thousand births.

23. When the rite of shaving off is begun, a bull is to be gifted there. So also, the gifts of a yellow garment and one's own image (replica) should be made.

24-25. By this procedure the pilgrim should perform the rite of holy ablution. He should also touch the submarine fire. Otherwise he will incur a fault since Brāhmaṇas had formerly granted a boon and also imprecated him with a curse.

The Devī said:

26-28. O great god, I have a great curiosity as to why some evil effect is incurred by the bath in ocean water. Where (at what places) does a man get purity by watery bath? Why is defect (evil) incurred in the ocean? I have great curiosity: Why was the boon granted and curse hurled by Brāhmaṇas formerly in the case of the ocean where all the rivers beginning with Gaṅgā come to rest, where Viṣṇu himself lies down and where Lakṣmī personally resides? Tell me everything in detail. I have a great doubt in this regard.

Īśvara said:

29. Formerly, O goddess, the excellent Suras came to Prabhāsa Tīrtha and began a sacrifice of a long duration *(Dīrgha Sattra)*, with perfect faith.

30. At the close of the *Sattra,* they made gifts of many kinds and *Sarvasva* (the entire possession) to the leading Brāhmaṇas residing in the Prabhāsa Kṣetra.

31. By that time, other native Brāhmaṇas, residents of that place came there in hundreds and thousands for the sake of Dakṣiṇā.

32. Afraid of disappointing them in their expectations, those Devas including Vāsava vanished. On seeing the Suras disappear, the Brāhmaṇas pursued them.

33. Formerly, O goddess, Brāhmaṇas had the great power of moving through the sky. So they rapidly followed them to the place where the Suras had their abode.

34. Becoming aware of their ability to go everywhere, the Heaven-dwellers became frightened. They entered the ocean and said:

35. "O great Ocean, we are seeking refuge in you. We are afraid of the Brāhmaṇas. We do not have the wealth to make the gift. So protect us.

36. On one side are all the Kratus with all excellent monetary gifts, gathered together, and on the other side is the protection of the life of frightened living beings. Especially the protection of the Devas is highly meritorious."

Samudra (Ocean) said:

37. O excellent Suras, you should not be afraid of the Brāhmaṇas at all. I shall save you all. Enter my belly.

38. Thereupon, all the Devas became delighted at his words. They entered his bowels and remained fearless.

39. The Ocean increased his size very much and held the aquatic creatures near the shore.

40. Thereafter, he took steps to cause downfall of the Brāhmaṇas. He cooked the meat of fish and got it concealed with *Mahānna* (meal for honoured guests).

41-42. Then he bowed down to all the Brāhmaṇas. With palms joined in verneration he said: "O Brāhmaṇas, may it please you to accept my hospitality for a short while. I am in distress and am bowing down to you. I have this perfect meal ready for you all. Have your meals and then go in pursuit of the Heaven-dwellers."

43. Those Brāhmaṇas considered the Ocean to be very devout. "So be it" they said and partook of the food in gold vessels.

44. As they were distressed with hunger they were not aware that the tasty meal was meat concealed.

45. Once getting their hunger satisfied, the Brāhmaṇas became contented. All these Brāhmaṇas of praiseworthy holy rites offered their benediction.

46. The anger of a Brāhmaṇa comes to an end with a hearty meal. That of Kṣatriyas ends with death of the enemy. The fury of serpents is known to last only till the death of the person bitten. They let the Devas go saying, "You may go".

47-49. Then the Devas along with Gandharvas hastened through the sky while going.The Brāhmaṇas were duly saluted. But all of a sudden the Brāhmaṇas fell down. They had eaten prohibited food—they had taken in meat.

On seeing the Suras going, they jumped up to follow them for the sake of *Dakṣiṇā*.

50. They realized that it was roguery on the part of the Ocean. Highly infuriated, O great goddess, they became and hurled the curse:

51. "It is laid down in the Smṛti-texts that meat is a prohibited food unto Brāhmaṇas. But that has been served to us well-concealed in regular foodstuffs.

52. On one side are all the types of meat. On another side is the meat of fish. On one side are all the sins. On the other side is the (sin of) ravishing another man's wife.

53. We know fully well the evil result of (eating) meat. Yet all of us have been deceived. We did something without any test or probe whatsoever.

54. Since, O ruthless fellow, we have been deceived by you by feeding us with meat, you shall become impotable.

55-57. You shall become unworthy of being touched by leading Brāhmaṇas as well as other men on the earth. Men of crooked intellect who take bath in your waters will undoubtedly go to a terrible hell.

By touching your waters, men on earth will fall into the worlds set apart for ungrateful persons, into those worlds intended for men of sinful activities."

Īśvara said:

58. Thus the Ocean was cursed by those Brāhmaṇas, O Lady of excellent complexion. Then for a thousand years he remained untouchable.

59-63. Then becoming extremely frightened, he said to all of them: "O Brāhmaṇas, this is a work of the Devas. It has been carried out by me who am lacking in intellect.

I considered that giving shelter to those who seek refuge was the greatest piety. If, out of love, anger, convetousness or even adherence to truth anyone forsakes a person who seeks refuge, he should be known as one committing a great sin.

The Heaven-dwellers sought refuge in me because they were afraid of you. They were saved by me perfectly in accordance with my capacity but through a tricky means.

Since I have been cursed by you angrily I shall dry myself up. Having been denied contact by you all, I am not interested enough to remain alive."

After saying this, O goddess, Ocean, the Lord of rivers, dried himself up. He had been so miserable.

64. On seeing the great Ocean gradually turning into dry land, all the groups of the Devas became extremely terrified.

65-69. They went to Pitāmaha, the Lord of Devas, the Lord of the worlds and said: "The Ocean has been cursed by the Brāhmaṇas on account of us. He is overwhelmed with great sorrow and is drying himself up. You know that it is from the Ocean that clouds take water and then shower again. Thereby the vegetation (food-grains) springs up. Thanks to the vegetation, the work of Yajñas becomes possible. Through the Yajñas the Heaven-dwellers become (nourished and) satisfied. If the Ocean were to meet with destruction in this manner, it will result in our own destruction. So you do go and save him lest he should get dried up. See to this also, that those Brāhmaṇas are also satisfied by a means you will be employing."

70. At the instance of the Devas, Brahmā went near the Ocean and pleaded to the Brāhmaṇas, residents of the holy spot, on behalf of the Ocean:

Brahmā said:

71-73. O excellent Brāhmaṇas, be pleased with the Ocean. At my instance do that, whereby it becomes pure once again. He will give you various kinds of jewels. You will come to be known as *Bhūmidevas* (Devas on the earth) at my instance. Certainly the truth has been said by me.

The Brāhmaṇas said:

74. O Lord of the worlds, we do not wish to defy what you say. Nor shall our statements be false. You are the sole judge in this matter.

75. Hence, O excellent one among Suras, whether benefit or evil results from our utterance, do something, O Lord of the worlds, whereby there shall be welfare unto all the worlds and the Heaven-dwellers also and shall cause benefit to us too.

76. Then Brahmā, the grandfather of the worlds, spoke to the Lord of rivers. "Do not dry yourself up. Listen to my beneficial words.

77. By no other means can the words of the Brāhmaṇas be made inoperative. Certainly if made furious the Brāhmaṇas

may reduce everything to ash by means of their refulgence.

78-79. They may turn Devas into non-Devas. Hence one shall not infuriate them. For the same reason your touch shall be pure on three occasions viz. on Parva days, at the confluence of rivers as well as where there is a *Setu* (at Rāmeśvara?) and where you are in contact with other Tīrthas.

80. In all these cases and not during any other rite, one will get by your contact, the same benefit which results from all the Tīrthas and all the Yajñas.

81. By touching your water the merit of offering Śrāddha at Gayā or meeting death at *Gograha* (death while protecting cows) will be obtained.

82. Your impotability is only due to the (salty) taste. If a mouthful of water is drunk it is destructive of all inauspiciousness.

83. Your water shall increase the happiness of the men in the world. Listen to the meritorious benefit of a person who offers libation to the *Pitṛs* with your water in accordance with the procedure laid down before.

84. The ancestors who are propitiated by means of your nectarine waters will remain satisfied as long as you as well as the moon, the sun and the stars continue to exist.

85. If a devotee takes bath in your water every day in the month of Māgha with great purity and fervour, he shall attain the merit of *Pauṇḍarīka Yajña.*

86. In the course of pilgrimage or on *Parva* days, or on a day of lunar eclipse, if a man takes his bath here in the salty ocean, he will obtain the benefit of a thousand horse-sacrifices.

87. Men who die in the place between the ocean and Śrī Someśa will go to heaven with all their sins washed off.

88. O powerful one, I assure you that everything will always happen like this in your case. Give unto the leading Brāhmaṇas different kinds of jewels.

89. Pleased thereby they will grant you your desire."

Īśvara said:

90. On hearing the words of the Grandfather (Brahmā, the creator) the ocean said: "So be it" and with great faith gave excellent jewels to the Brāhmaṇas.

91. The entire suggestion of Brahmā was carried out by the Brāhmaṇas. All of them got the hairs shaved and performed the rite of ablution.

92. Thus the salt ocean attained sacredness and the status of a Tīrtha. O great goddess, there are five crores of Liṅgas within it.

93. O goddess, the Liṅgas in the ocean are not visible in this Manvantara. There itself there is the *Agnikuṇḍa* and another *Padmaka* lake.

94. O my beloved, everything in the centre is concealed in this Manvantara. In between the Cakra and Maināka is the southern quarter.

95. There is a golden pot ten thousand Dhanus in extent. There in the centre of that pot is what is called *Vaḍavānala* (submarine fire).

96. It has pointed countenance (mouth). It has a huge body and it always drinks the water. Thus they call it *Agni Tīrtha.*

97. It is within it that the Vāḍava fire of great power is present. Its face is like that of a mare. It is to the south of Śrīsomeśa within a distance of a hundred *Dhanus* to the east of northern *Mānasa* as far as Kṛtasmara.

98. O beautiful woman, this should be kept as a great secret. It should not be given to anyone and everyone. On hearing this, even a Brāhmaṇa-slayer is rid of his sins. There is no doubt about it.

99. Thus everything has been said as to how the curse was heaped by the angry Brāhmaṇas before but afterwards a boon was granted when they were pleased.

CHAPTER THIRTY

Efficacy of the Worship of Someśvara

The Devī said:

1. Which is the deity to be worshipped first after taking bath in the Agni Tīrthas? O Lord of Suras, it behoves you to

explain the procedure of the pilgrimage whereby it shall be free from obstacles.

Īśvara said:

2-3. After duly taking the holy bath, offering the *Arghya* in the great ocean and worshipping it with scented flowers, garments and floral unguents, the pilgrim should cast into it a golden bracelet in accordance with his capacity. Then he should offer libations to the Pitṛs and go to Lord Kapardin.

4. After devoutly worshipping with flowers, incense, scents and garments, the pilgrim should offer *Arghya* uttering the *Mantra: "gaṇānām tvā"* (RV.II.23.11) etc.

5. For Śūdras, O goddess of Devas, the Mantra prescribed by the Smṛti is the eight-syllabled one. There he should go to the greatest sin-destroying deity Someśvara.

6. After bathing (the deity) duly, he should perform the Japa of *Śatarudriya*, the Rudra Mantras with five Aṅgas and the other *Rudra Saṁhitās.*

7. The bathing should be done with milk and curds mixed with ghee. Then the deity is smeared with honey, sugarcane juice and *Kuṁkuma* (saffron).

8. Thereafter, the adorable one is adored with sweet scents and sandalpaste, along with musk mixed with camphor and *Uśīra* (fragrant root of a plant).

9. The Lord is fumigated with different kinds of incense and duly wrapped with garments. Then the excellent *Naivedya* (food offerings) should be offered.

10. Then *Ārārtika* (waving of light—Āratī) is performed. There should be a dancing programme as the devotee wishes. The deity is bowed down to in the *Aṣṭāṅga* manner (so that the eight limbs of the body touch the ground) and vocal and instrumental music follows.

11-13. A show should be arranged in front of the Lord, along with discourses on Dharma, and charitable gifts are then distributed in keeping with the financial capacity of the devotee, among the Brāhmaṇas, ascetics, the disabled, wretched ones, blind people, miserable ones and pilgrims. If a ruthless act (e.g. bloody sacrifice) is intended to be begun (*?pravṛtte krūrakarmaṇi*), a bull is to be offered. Then, O beautiful woman, the devotee undertakes fast for that day. For one full year, men of devout nature should observe fast on that lunar day, on which they first visited Someśvara.

14. By so doing with devotion, the man derives the fruit of his birth. In addition he acquires the entire benefit of pilgrimage to all the Tīrthas.

15-17. O beautiful woman, he redeems all the ancestors in the father's and mother's line. By visiting Someśvara, a man washes off all the sins committed during childhood, youth and old age. After viewing Lord Someśvara, no wretched, miserable or impoverished child is born in his family in seven generations. The devotee is reborn in a well-reputed family richly endowed with wealth and foodgrains.

18. He will again have devotion towards Lord Somanātha further increased. The bathing is carried at the outset with milk and then by means of a continuous current (of water).

19-20. During the first Yāma, this takes place and the *Mahāsnāna* (great ablution at midday) thereafter. Men who view this *Mahāsnāna* of the Lord of Devas at midday and the *Ārārtika* at dusk are not reborn. O lady of excellent countenance, considering the terrible nature of Kaliyuga with sins in plenty, it must be asserted that no man (will) avert wretchedness and misery by any other rite.

CHAPTER THIRTYONE

The Origin of the Submarine Fire: Devas Deposit Weapons at the Hermitage of Sage Dadhīci

The Devī said:

1-2. O Śaṅkara, my great doubt is in regard to the (Set of) five beginning with स(S). How did they happen to occur here? How and from where did Sarasvatī originate? How was that Vāḍava created? At what time and how did it happen? It behoves you to explain all this in detail.

Īśvara said:

3. Listen, O goddess, how Sarasvatī originated in that holy

spot and from where the destroyer of all sins (i.e. Sarasvatī) came out.

4-5. She was formerly called by the five sages Hiraṇyā, Vajriṇī, Nyaṅku, Kapilā and Sarasvatī. Listen how she came into contact with Vāḍava fire.

6. Formerly the fight that had broken out on account of Moon's conduct ceased and at the instance of Pitāmaha Candra surrendered Tārā.

7-8. Then the Suras went back to heaven looking at the earth with their faces turned down. Thereupon, the Devas saw on the earth something that was like another Svarga.

It was the hermitage of the eminent sage Dadhīci. It was well-known all over the world. It had flowers blossoming throughout the whole year. It shone with various kinds of trees. The fragrance from Ketakī, Kuṭaja and Bakula rendered it very pleasant.

9. After reaching that large penance grove all the Devas wanted to explore the whole of that charming region out of curiosity.

10. They left their vehicles (outside) and entered that holy hermitage like lay persons. They became humble and self- controlled and went in search of that sage.

11. All the Suras saw him who appeared like another Brahmā. All of them were received and adored with *Pādya* (water for washing the feet), *Arghya* etc.

12. All the Devas including Vāsava sat on the seats pointed out to them. Śakra then stood up from the middle and spoke to the sage:

13. Pākaśāsana (Indra) deposited all the weapons in front of the sage and requested, "Your Holiness may be pleased to take these". To him (Pākaśāsana) Dadhīci said:

14-17a. "Deposit the weapons with me and do go to heaven."

Śakra said to him: "When necessity arises, these weapons should be returned to us by you so that we can conquer our enemies in battle."

Śakra spoke this again and again to the excellent sage: "O sage, these should be given to us alone and not to anyone else." When he said so, the excellent sage replied: " So it shall be. I will give you everything especially at the time of war."

17b. Śacī's Consort (Indra) thought: The words of this sage will never be false. Thinking so, he left all the weapons with him and went to heaven.

18. A king who remains personally pure and with purified soul and listens attentively to this narrative of depositing the weapons, attains victory in battle and begets sons shining splendidly with the attainment of virtue, wealth and renown.

CHAPTER THIRTYTWO

Vaḍavānala Outwitted

Īśvara said:

1-3. When all the Devas had gone away, the sage remained there for a hundred years. Then the Brāhmaṇa set off for performing penance from the northern hermitage towards the divine northern quarter.

He had a servant-woman, the highly esteemed Subhadrā. That beautiful lady who could not carry the weapons said to the sage: "I am not able to lift and carry the weapons with my hand."

4. Thereupon, the sage drank the intrinsic power of the weapons along with water. After thus making all the divine miraculous weapons well-established within himself, the sage, the storehouse of austerities, went to the northern quarter.

5. He saw Mount Himācala, bestower of happiness on all people like Śiva. He held Gaṅgā, he was white (in complexion of) his body and his form (region) was full of serpents.

6. He also espied a hermitage surrounded by Aśvattha trees by the side of Candrabhāgā. It abounded in sacrificial twigs, flowers and Kuśa grass.

7. The tiger among the sages stayed there along with other sages and was accompanied by Subhadrā like the Moon with Moonlight.

8. Once, the servant-maid Subhadrā who had her monthly course, set off from his abode to have her bath on the fourth day.

9. As she was going ahead, she saw a loin cloth. Thinking

that it had been dropped down by chance, she took it up (as fate would have it).

10. The loin cloth was drenched with semen but she wore it secretly and went off to the river to have a bath as she pleased.

11. The good woman found herself moving lazily due to heavy weight. As she looked down she found that a foetus had developed within her belly.

12. She began to lament herself. "When I came here I did not have any foetus within. I am a luckless wretched woman. By whom have I been defiled?"

13. Completely overwhelmed with shame she entered the grove of *Aśvattha* trees. There she delivered herself of the foetus even without knowing where it had come from.

14. Not aware of any misconduct on her part, she took bath once again. She then began to heap an unbearable curse on the (unknown one) who had caused the conception.

15-16. "If I am a chaste woman loyal to my husband, may that person by whom this defilement was brought about knowingly or unknowingly die today itself.

If I do not love a person other than my husband even mentally, may that paramour face destruction, thanks to this truth of my statement."

17. Thus the good woman cursed the person who caused the impregnation without knowing him. She began to return to the abode of Dadhīci.

18. After casting off the foetus resembling the Sun there she returned to the beautiful hermitage where the eminent sage was present.

19. In the meantime all the highly powerful Devas, the Guardians of the Quarters came to the hermitage of the sage for the sake of the missiles.

20. Śakra said to the sage: "O sage of good holy rites, return to us quickly those miraculous weapons kept as deposit with you by us."

21-23. The sage said: "O Vāsava, those weapons still remain in that hermitage where they had been deposited. They were not brought here.

O Vāsava, O destroyer of enemies, I have taken in along with water all their power in battle, their prowess.

That being the case, O sinless one, if the miraculous weapons are to be given to you by me, I shall, O Lord of good holy rites, give my bones in the shape thereof."

24-29. On being told thus, the Thousand- eyed One (Indra) said to the excellent sage: "In nothing else is that terrific power which is vested in them. For the sake of the protection of the worlds Rudraśiva deposited a thousandth part of his refulgence and gave them to us. We therefore set up ourselves taking up all those weapons for the purpose of protecting the world. Hence our designation *Lokapāla* (Guardians of the Worlds). Among all these weapons *Vajra* (thunderbolt) is the most excellent one. It is because we hold it that the kingship of the Devas is vested in us. Still more excellent than the Vajra is that discus which is in the custody of Viṣṇu. The conquest of the groups of Daityas and Dānavas depends thereon. Hence, O excellent sage, O foremost one among those who know their duty, think about the matter on hand and manage it so that we regain those (weapons)."

30-32. When this was said, the sage spoke to Śakra standing before him: "I shall suggest another means for getting them.

Here are all my bones. Do fashion out all your weapons in their own shapes and sizes entirely out of these (bones). These (bones) have been strengthened thereby. They have more strength than they (had formerly). I wish that they will be more effective in your battle."

33-34. Then Śakra spoke to that storehouse of austerities, Dadhīci: "I cannot cause your death which you (seem to) wish. We have no power to take your bones and yet prevent your death. Hence think about everything and say what is to be done."

35-39. On being told thus the sage said: "I shall myself cast off this body of mine for the sake of realizing the cause of the Devas.

Since this (body) is the seat of all miseries, censured by everyone and by no means eternal or steady, it is but proper to abandon it just now.

By casting it off, I will not have the misery of worldly existence, because everyone who is born in the next birth, dies again.

Wife, sister and daughter all these are reborn as a result of one's own actions. Therefore, having keen attachment for them in the world is censured.

Anyhow this body is going to be cast off certainly. So its voluntary casting off (on my part) should be welcomed by you."

40. After proclaiming thus in front of Purandara, the great sage Dadhīci hurriedly brought about his own death.

41. Seeing him dead in this manner, the Devas thought how the body could be made free from flesh and blood.

42. Then the Lord of Suras said thus for the sake of the purification of the bones: "The tongues of Gaurīs (? from the context 'Cows') are hard and rough. Let them lick this clean."

43. Thereupon, Nandā stationed in the world (i.e. Goloka) was meditated upon by the Devas. She came there accompanied by her companions.

44. Nandā, Subhadrā, Surabhi, Suśīlā and Sumanā, the five cow-mothers, came there from Goloka.

45. They said to all those Suras: "We shall carry out any job which is assigned to us as our duty. Think well and say."

The Devas said:

46. Since his body has been abandoned by the sage himself, may the skeleton be got rid of flesh etc.

47. At the bidding of the Devas, they carried out the despicable and terrible duty. Then they went to meet the Grandfather (Brahmā). The excellent Suras too followed.

48. They said to Pitāmaha the whole story of the terrible duty duly carried out by them.

49. On hearing it, Pitāmaha summoned all the Suras. With a desire to purify them, he touched the cows all over their limbs.

50. On being touched by the Devas, they become very pure. Only their mouth was not touched. Hence it is remembered as impure.

51. Their mouth alone is unholy and censured. The remaining part of the body of all of them was made excellent by the Suras.

52. They were told by Sarasvatī: "You are slayers of Brāhmaṇas.

Otherwise, why was the mouth not touched by the immortal ones?"

53-54. Thereupon, Goddess Sarasvatī was told by them: "This utterance of yours describing the mouth as such is not proper. It is our heart that has been burned by you through this utterance. Hence, ere long you will be subjected to combustion."

55. After cursing Sarasvatī, those Surabhis (cows) honoured by the Suras went to Goloka.

56. Summoning Viśvakarman, the architect, the excellent Suras told him: "For the purpose of fighting, prepare weapons for us."

57. On hearing this statement, he caused the weapons to be fashioned out of the sets of bones of Dadhīci.

58. He made them of the requisite shapes and sizes as demanded by the Devas. He also ensured that they should be invincible in the course of hostilities. While making them, he had that in view.

59. He got ready all these perfect weapons: the *Vajra* for India, the Śakti for Vahni (Fire-god), the Daṇḍa (staff) for Yama, the sword for Nirṛti and the noose for Pracetas (Varuṇa).

60. Viśvakarman made the *Dhvaja* (flagstaff) for Vāyu, the *Gadā* (mace) for Kubera and the *Śūla* (trident) for Īśāna (Śiva).

61. The Devas took up these miraculous weapons and on the strength of those missiles, they proceeded to conquer Daityas and Dānavas.

62. In the meantime Subhadrā performed the funeral rites of Dadhīci and accompanied by those sages she went in search of that son.

63. She saw that charming child in the grove of *Aśvattha*. On seeing him alive, she quickly shed tears and cried.

64-67. The child addressed her as "Mother" and said: "O lady of good renown, do not weep. What you and I reap is the fruit of what was done formerly.

O illustrious lady, give up grief. An act, the manner in which it was done, the place where perpetrated by a person in a former birth must necessarily result in the enjoyment or suffering of the agent.

Do not be ashamed because you were compelled to cast me off, O beautiful lady. What was perpetrated by me earlier should be borne by me alone.

O mother, O lady of good renown, show your maternal affection to me as your son. By abandoning her son, a mother becomes guilty."

68-69. On being told thus by the child she meditated on Lord Janārdana and said with palms joined in reverence: "Let it be firmly disclosed to me. I do not know the truth as to the person from whose semen this child has been born. Hence, O Lord of Devas, tell me your definite opinion."

70. On being requested thus, Kṛṣṇa Janārdana said to Mother Subhadrā: "This is Dadhīci's son born of the Kṣetra (field, i.e. wife) of your husband."

71. On coming to know of his origin, Subhadrā was delighted in her mind. She placed the child on her lap and lamented with words of distress.

72-79a. The child born said: "Speak out the cause of sorrow." Then he was told: "How were you able to sustain your life without breast milk?

Four types of beings have been created by Brahmā—oviparous, viviparous, sweat-born and those that pierce through the ground and germinate.

Among the viviparous ones, there are the different types such as men, women and eunuch. The four-legged animals are of two types, wild and domesticated.

All the birds, fishes, tortoises and reptiles are oviparous. The sweat-born ones are the following: bugs, lice, flies and mosquitoes.

Those that pierce the ground and grow are the immobile ones such as grass, hedges, creepers etc. Thousands of other beings of similar nature can be included among these befittingly.

The young ones of the egg-born creatures survive by flapping the wings. All the sweat-born ones live by heat and the ground-piercing ones by water.

The *Udbhija* (ground-piercing ones) live by the collection of the five elements on the earth. The oviparous ones are incapable of living without breast-milk. Then, son, how could you sustain your life without it?"

79b. Thereupon, he spoke to his mother whose eyes were dimmed with tears:

80-82. "The vital airs were retained by me through the juice of Aśvattha fruits imbibed." Then she had the idea in her mind that his name should be Pippalāda for that reason.[1] This name of the noble-souled one became well-known. All the consecratory rites of Pippalāda as laid down in the Vedas were performed in due order by all the sages who had mastered all the Vedas and were present there. The Vedas along with the six Aṅgas as well as the *Upāṅgas* were perfectly studied by him from the sages residing in the hermitage.

83. In the course of his stay there he saw the children of the sages playing on the laps of their fathers. So he said to his mother of pure smiles:

84. "O Subhadrā, welfare unto you. Where is my father? Tell me clearly so that I can play on his lap like the other children."

85. When his mother was thus asked, she fell into a pitiable nervous agitation. Without saying anything by way of reply, she began to weep.

86. On seeing her crying, the son of the sage became furious and said: "Is he someone notoriously despicable and so you do not disclose him to me?"

87. When this was uttered by the son, she said to him: "Your father has been killed by the Devas. Welfare unto you. Do not be angry. It is about Dadhīci that I speak."

88. Blazing with anger he then said to his mother: "What offence did my father commit in regard to the Suras? Tell me about it."

Subhadrā said:

89. O (my son) of good holy rites, though the prominent sage offered them other weapons of the same shapes and sizes, he was killed by those deluded ones for the sake of the miraculous weapons.

90-92. On hearing this statement, the sage of fierce austerities (said): "Since my father was killed by the Devas I will

1. Similar birth of Pippalāda from Yājñavalkya's semen from his sister is told elsewhere.

create a very powerful *Kṛtyā* (a female deity of destructive power) and make her fall over their head taking away their lives.

If he does not deserve death I will spare Pitāmaha (Brahmā). I will thrash all the others collectively by means of this *Kṛtyā* weapon. If the Devas out of fear from me seek refuge in me, I will yet kill them collectively."

93. Finding the sage furious thus, all the excellent Suras sought refuge in Brahmā out of great fright.

94. On coming to know that the Devas had sought refuge in Brahmā, the compassionate Lord Janārdana himself hastened to that place and said to the Devas:

95. "The means of saving you all has been thought out by me now. Thereby I will get the *Kṛtyā* that has come, enchanted and deluded."

96. In the meantime, Pippalāda who continued to remember the reason for avenging his father and so determined to find a means of killing the Suras, entered the Himālaya mountain.

97. It was the unpleasant statement issued from the mouth of his mother, and heard by him which forced him to leave the place and go to Himālaya.

98. He reached the snow-capped mountain which is like a staircase unto Svarga for people. It appeared like the sky that has become a veritable ground, and which resembled the extensive (white) physical form of Śeṣa.

99. There he stood motionless like Sthāṇu (a fixed pillar) and vowed "I will kill those Cāraṇas (heavenly choristers, spies) who caused the death of my father."

100-103a. Standing angrily in that courtyard of the temple of Śiva (he vowed), I will kill all those who are proud of their immortality through the miraculous weapon of the *Kṛtyā*.

Standing here and thinking of her within my heart I will win over the *Kṛtyā*. Either I will bring the *Kṛtyā* under control or I will go to the abode of Yama. I will desist from food intake day and night, I will remain fearless and free of *Dvandvas* (mutually opposing pairs such as pleasure-pain). With my left hand I will massage and churn the left thigh and create the great *Kṛtyā*."

103b-106. Thus he remained motionless. When a year passed off, a *Vaḍavā* (a mare) issued forth from his body through the thigh. She was distressed due to heavy weight. She was followed by *Vāḍava* (submarine fire). After issuing forth from the (left) thigh, she *(Vaḍavā)* gave birth to a very powerful foetus from her womb. After discharging the blazing foetus emitting flames all round in front of the sage, the Vaḍavā went away. Even the sage did not know her (where she wents). Thus it was that the *Vaḍavānala* (submarine fire) in the form of a man (lit. Fire from mare) issued forth from her womb.

107-110. It looked like the end of the Kalpa unto the living beings. By means of its refulgence it resembled the *Kālāgni* (Fire at the end of a Kalpa). On seeing it in front resembling a mass of lightning streaks, he became surprised very much. "What is this?" he thought. Thereupon, sage Pippalāda was addressed by the Vāḍava fire present in front: "I have been evolved by you through your power (of penance). Now your task, whatever has been thought of, should be carried out by me. Even if it were impossible to achieve, I shall achieve it. Dear father, I have been evolved by you in the course of a year through the churning of your thigh. Hence, I am devoid of thighs. Yet I will carry out your wish."

111. On hearing his words, the infuriated sage said: "All the Devas have been offered to you by me. Eat them yourself."

112. The Suras were convinced that he had become very terrible because of his furious obsession due to the killing of his father. All of them gathered together immediately along with their womenfolk and resorted to the Purāṇa Puruṣa (the Ancient Being, Viṣṇu).

113. Viṣṇu consoled those Suras. Delighted within himself he approached (the *Kṛtyā*), the fire of fury. On seeing it resembling a mass of suns, Viṣṇu spoke these excellent words:

114-120. "O Lord of Suras, I have been sent to your very presence by the Devas who are afraid. Listen from me to the words wholesome unto the *Cāraṇas* (Devas) as well as unto you.

Your inconceivable and inordinate strength destructive of even self-possessed wise ones has become known certainly. This being the case, do as the Suras say. Everyday eat one of them.

There are thirty crores of leading powerful Suras. How will you eat them at the same time?

Hence, do eat them one-by-one. Then it is not impossible to eat them even if you are alone. (Read *aśakyā* for *śakyā*)

Further Hutabhuk (Fire-god) contracted the disease of jaundice. Overeating is not proper. So accept my suggestion.

Moreover if they are all eaten simultaneously, everyday hunger will prompt you to worry for the means of the next meal.

Thus, your vow can be successfully carried out. The statement of the sage will not be false even if you do like this. Further, your desire too will be fulfilled."

121. So said Janārdana. The *Vāḍava* said: "I will do so." The Vāḍava agreed to the suggestion that he should eat the Devas one by one.

122-123. Then the Suras bowed down to Viṣṇu, the Lord of Suras, of unmeasured prowess. "What is befitting and splendid has been accomplished by you. Further, you alone are competent to avert this danger. No one else can be the saviour of the Heaven-dwellers."

124. Thereupon, Mādhava who wears yellow garments and holds the conch, the discus and the club told the Suras: "I will remove the cause of your fear."

125. On hearing this, all the Devas became happy and their eyes beamed with delight.

126. Looking at the Devas Vāḍava said: "What should be done by me to you? May that be mentioned."

127. In the meantime the dignified and illustrious Lord of great prowess having the cosmic body enchanted that *Jvalana* (fire) by means of his (greater) intellect and said, "Eat up the *AP* (waters) created at the outset."

128. He who listens with concentration to this act of Viṣṇu shall be rid of the excessive fear of spies and attain salvation and perfect knowledge.

CHAPTER THIRTYTHREE

The Story of Sarasvatī

The Devī said:

1-2. Everything has been listened to by me with concentration. I have heard everything that was performed earlier by the great sage, whose anger was justifiably aroused by the killing of his father. What the son of Dadhīci, who wanted to take the revenge on Suras, did I have heard. It is now my curiosity to know similarly everything in due order that befell the Suras, which is of equal importance.

Īśvara said:

3-5. When he was thus addressed by that noble-souled one, "Swallow first of all Water because it was created in the world at first and so it is the eldest of all Suras and Asuras", he said, "O Suras, show me where it is stationed. After drinking it entirely, I shall carry out the task of eating the Suras. If you are able to take me to the place where the water has collected together (do so). I will not be one uttering falsehood. Even if the vital airs depart, I will carry out the behest of the sage".

6. When this was said, Puṇḍarīkākṣa (Viṣṇu) said to the Vāḍava Aurva, "O Vāḍava, by what vehicle can I take you to the place where the water is present?"

The Vāḍava said:

7. I am not eager to go there by means of horses and other vehicles. Excepting the contact with the hand of a virgin (no other means of transport is desirable). This is what I think.

Viṣṇu said:

8. This means of transport is easily available to you. I shall bring that girl who is certainly able to take you to the reservoir of water.

Īśvara said:

9. Sarasvatī who was distressed due to the curse of the (celestial) Surabhis and who suffered the result of the (false) step taken earlier, was turned into his (Vāḍava's) vehicle by Viṣṇu.

10. Then the Lord spoke to Gaṅgā who was present by his side, "O highly esteemed lady, take this fire quickly to the great ocean. O sanctifier of the worlds, except you, no one is competent to take it."

Gaṅgā said:

11. O Lord, O master of the worlds, I do not have the strength to carry Aurva. He is huge and terrific in form. This *Anala* (Fire) burns excessively.

12. Thereupon the liberal-minded Lord spoke to Yamunā first, to Sindhu thereafter, and to various rivers severally.

13-15. They were asked by the excellent one among Suras and they proved unable to take (Aurva). Then Janārdana, the Lord of Devas, spoke to Sarasvatī: "O auspicious one, you yourself go over to the west of the briny sea. If this is carried out, all the Suras will be rid of their fear. Otherwise they will be burned by the Vāḍava through its refulgence. So, save *Vibudhas* (Suras) from this terrible fear. O lady of excellent waist, like a mother you alone can bestow freedom from fear on the Suras."

16-18. On being told thus by Viṣṇu, the powerful one, she said: "I am not free. My father, the ancient one, is waiting. Being a daughter and having *Vratas* to be performed, I can only do what he orders. A daughter is never independent in the past, present and future. So learned men say. O Hari, without the specific command of my father, I will not move even a step, . So, may some other means be thought of."

19-20. Having known her attitude, Vāsudeva approached Pitāmaha (Brahmā) and said: "This is the task of Devas. Carry it out. Excepting this virgin daughter of yours, without any apparent defect, no one else can carry the Vāḍava fire of great prowess."

21. On hearing the words uttered by Viṣṇu, the Great-grandfather sniffed the head of his virgin daughter and said lovingly:

22. "O fair lady, do go. Save all the Devas caught in the midst of fearful danger. Take this Vāḍava with you and cast it into the salt sea."

On hearing her father's words she said:

Sarasvatī said:

23. At your instance, O dear father, I am now setting out undoubtedly. This Vāḍava fire is very horrendous. He will consume my body.

24. It is the advent of the terrible Kali Age now on the earth. O Lord, folks of evil conduct will be coming into contact with me.

25. What can be more painful than contact with sinners!

Brahmā said:

26. If you do not like the earth's surface fully infested with sinful folks, do take the *Vahni* (Fire) to the great ocean confining yourself to the Pātālatala (nether worlds).

27. If you find yourself exceedingly over-burdened and weary and get scorched by the *Vahni* pierce through the ground, O dear daughter, and reveal yourself.

28. O lady of wide eyes and excellent waistline, turn your face eastwards. Thereupon, the (other) Tīrthas will approach you in that weary state of yours, O lady of charming smiles.

29. O lady of excellent countenance, they will come to you for help. At my bidding thirty-three crores of them will render you help.

30. Do proceed ahead, dear daughter. Do not be worried at any cost. Let your path be free from misfortune and loss. May there be no antagonists.

Īśvara said:

31. On being told thus by Brahmā, Sarasvatī got rid of her nervousness and trepidation. Delighted in her mind, she got ready to go ahead.

32. At the time of her departure, the whole world was filled with the sounds of conch-shells and Dundubhi drums as well as similar auspicious sounds.

33-36. The divine lady had white garments. She had smeared herself with white sandalpaste. She resembled the autumnal cloud; she was adorned with pearl necklaces. Her face was like the full moon. Her eyes were large like the petals of a lotus. Like the renown of Mahendra, she filled all the ten quarters. Shining with her own refulgence, she illuminated the entire universe. O lady of excellent complexion (Gaurī), Gaṅgā, following her was addressed by her: "Dear friend, where shall I see you staying again?" On being asked thus by her, Gaṅgā spoke in affectionate words:

37-43. "As soon as you come to the east and espy me, O lady of excellent holy rites, I shall appear before you surrounded by all the Suras there. O lady of splendid smiles, cast off your grief." She then took leave of Gaṅgā saying, "May there be a meeting later on, O fair lady, go to your abode. O sinless one, I should be remembered by you."

Similarly Yamunā, the highly charming Gāyatrī and all friends including Sāvitrī were sent back by her.

After sending them away, the goddess became the river Sarasvatī and reached the mountain Himavān. There she came out of the Plakṣa tree and descended on the surface of the earth. There she (the river) abounded in fish, turtles, crocodiles, Ḍiṇḍīras (cuttlefish), whales and groups of alligators. The great goddess (river) appeared to smile as she flowed with foams all round.

The splendid divine river with sacred waters, was eulogized by twice-born ones. Holding the Vāḍava fire, she flowed on gallopping like a horse trotting swiftly.

44. With the rapidity of her current, she pierced the ground and came to the surface of the Earth. Whenever she (the river) became weary and got scorched by the Vāḍava fire, the river became visible in the mortal world[1].

45-46. Thereupon, Prācī (Eastern quarter) became scorched by the Vāḍava. Thereat all the Tīrthas glorified by the ancient seers, O beautiful woman, the Tīrthas of heaven, intermediate space and the earth asserted their presence there. On being consoled by them, the river Sarasvatī went over to the nether worlds and passed over to the ocean, the abode of sharks and crocodiles.

47. O beautiful woman among the Suras, she (river) reached *Khadirāmoda* and there saw the ocean. Afterwards she took up the *Vahni* and began to proceed onwards.

48. She thought of the fact that it was at the behest of the Lord that she had herself taken up the burden and was therefore delighted. With a clear conscience, she went ahead facing the South.

---

1. This is to explain why Sarasvatī had no continuous flow but appeared intermitently (at the time of this Purāṇa). Obviously the author has confused the Vedic Sarasvatī with Prācī Sarasvatī which joins Arabian Sea at Prabhāsa.

49. In the meantime, O great goddess, four sages who had mastered the Vedas reached the holy spot Prabhāsa Kṣetra.

50. They were Hariṇa, Vajra, Nyaṅku and Kapila. After stationing themselves there, they began to perform penance, with their minds engrossed in the self-study (of the Vedas).

51. Sarasvatī was severally summoned by them for the sake of holy bath. Suddenly the Ocean appeared before her face-to-face.

52. Thereupon, she began to reflect, 'How can I attain some merit!' Further the chaste lady (river) was afraid of the curse (of the sages). She then turned herself into one of five channels.

53. O lady of excellent complexion (Gaurī), she propitiated each of the sages. Then, she had five different names on the earth.

54-56. They are: Hariṇī, Vajriṇī, Nyaṅku, Kapilā, and Sarasvatī. The river Sarasvatī flowing in five channels shall dispel all the five sins of men if they plunge into it or drink the waters. The sins are those of Brāhmaṇa-slaughter, imbibing liquor, committing theft and ravishing the wife of the preceptor. The fifth sin accrues from contact with these sinners. Sarasvatī (flowing in five channels) accompanied by her friends dispels these sins.

57. Sarasvatī flowing backwards dispels the terrible sin of Brāhmaṇa-slaughter entirely, through drinking her water and bathing in it.

58. The river Kapilā flows dispelling the sin of imbibing liquor committed by the twice-born, if they had drunk it inadvertently.

59. If the twice-born perform *Japa* and *Homa,* if they observe fast and if they take their holy bath in and drink her water, the river dispels the sin in seven days. Whatever they perform, shall be performed with fervour and devotion in the mind.

60. By resorting to the river Nyaṅku, the devotees get rid of the great sin committed by them if they perform everything as mentioned.

61. By observing fast, taking the holy bath and drinking the holy waters Vajriṇī redeems a sinner who has violated the sanctity of the preceptor's bed. She annihilates the entire sin of men despite its massiveness and terrible nature.

62. The river Hariṇī dispels the sin resulting from having contact with other sinners. The river has sacred and meritorious waters. By taking the holy plunge in her for seven days, the sin is removed. Hence the river is remembered as Hariṇī (the remover).

63. Thus, O beautiful goddess, the river Sarasvatī with five channels dispels all the sins. It is the truth.

64. Then, further ahead, the fair lady (river) saw a beautiful mountain standing in her path near the ocean, as if to obstruct her way.

65. 'So, here is this excellent mountain. It is the measuring rod for the whole Cosmic Egg. It has now come as an obstacle before me even as I was going ahead on the errand of Suras.' (Thought Sarasvatī.)

66. The river Sarasvatī looked at the great lofty mountain. The chaste lady (river) became surprised, when the mountain held up the speed of her current.

67. Even as she was contemplating on this miracle in her mind, Kṛtasmara, the mountain, woke up (became aware of it) through the auspicious sound.

68-69a. She (the river) saw a being walking over a pair of peaks of the mountain. The mountain said to her (the river), the divine lady: "O lady of excellent holy rites, there is no way here. O fair lady, go somewhere else where you please".

69b. When this was said the divine lady (river) spoke to the being stationed on the top of the mountain:

70. "O Mountain, I have come here at the behest of the Lord. I should not be hindered by you." When this was spoken, the Mountain said to that charming divine lady (river):

71-72. "O fair one, haven't you come to know that I am the Mountain Kṛtasmara. O sinless one, there is no fault in touching you because you are a virgin. So, O lady of excellent holy rites, I woo you. Become my wife."

Sarasvatī said:

73. Since my father is alive and active I cannot be a *Svayaṁvarā* (a girl choosing her own groom) and become your wife. Leave the path free unto me now.

74. On being told thus the Mountain said: "O fair one, I

will forcibly marry you, though you do not wish it. Who can come to help you now?"

75-76. With her divine eyes, she came to consider him overwhelmed by *Manobhava* (Passion, Lord of love) and said: "There is no one to save me. I seek refuge in you. O highly powerful one, if I am to be certainly married thus, O Lord, do not marry me before I take my bath. Permit me to take my bath."

77. Then, the Mountain in the fullness of his pride of his rich assets said: "O fortunate one, O beautiful lady (river), you can find all pleasing amenities in me.

78. Yonder where pairs of Kinnaras sing in an enchanting manner, another highly pleasing note of the musical instrument, the lute, is heard.

79. There the charming trees laden with fruits and flowers are seen—*Tālas, Tamālas, Pippalas* and *Panasas.*

80. All round, the Mountain shines well with *Kuṭajas, Kovidāras, Kadambas* and *Kurabas.* All of them are reverberating with the humming sounds of the swarms of inebriated bees.

81. In some places, with the buds of *Kuṭaja* it appears as though the unguent of Hara (i.e. the holy ash) has been smeared. In some places it appears to have the lustre resembling that of the robes of Viṣṇu, on account of the Karṇikāras.

82. Covered with the *Tamāla* leaves in some places it has the lustre of Vaivasvata (Yama). In some places, its parts are smeared with minerals. So the mountain appears to have the body like that of *Gaṇādhyakṣa* (Vighneśvara).

83. In some places, with *Haritāla* (Yellow, Orpiment) over its body, it appears like the Four-faced Lord. In some places, with the *Saptacchadas,* the mountain appears to have the body of Viṣṇu.

84. In some places abounding in *Priyaṅgu,* it resembles the refulgence of Kātyāyanī. In some places, with the trees having flower filaments it resembles *Anala* (Fire).

85. In some places is shine with *Bilvaka* fruits that look like the breasts of women, circular (globular), glossy and horripilant. They are inaccessible to those who are deficient in merit.

86-87. In some places, it shines with lions, tigers, deer, elephants, boars and monkeys coming into contact with one another and rendering the sky pierced and covered with roasted meat sticking to pikes."

When this was said, Śāradā (i.e. Sarasvatī) replied to the excellent Mountain:

88. "I am alone and isolated. I lament. Still if you are inclined to marry me, hold this Vāḍava in your hands while I take my holy bath."

89. When this was said, Kṛtasmara, the excellent Mountain, seized the Vāḍava handed over by Sarasvatī. Due to its contact, Kṛtasmara was reduced to (a heap of) ash instantly.

90. Ever since then all the rocks therein became soft. They are being taken by the artisans for use in (building) houses and temples.[1]

91. After burning Kṛtasmara and holding the Vāḍava once again, the divine lady (river) came near the sea and stood there with hairs standing on end due to delight.

92. Stationed there, the great goddess (river) spoke to the Vāḍava fire: "O Vāḍava, see the roaring sea standing before you."

93. He saw the roaring sea lashing with its waves. He spoke to her, "What is this, O fair lady? The briny sea is afraid of me."

94. The girl (river) laughed and said: "O Fire, who is not afraid of you? O highly powerful one, it has been assigned to you by the Devas as your food."

95. On hearing her words the Fire was highly delighted. He said: "O fair one, I shall grant you a boon. Make a request as you please."

96. On being told thus by that Vāḍava fire, the divine lady (river) remembered the lotus-eyed Viṣṇu, the soul that is the cause (of all).

97. Immediately on being remembered by her, by Sarasvatī, Lord Janārdana, the great Lord of the three worlds, was seen by her as stationed in her own heart.

98. Looking at Acyuta stationed within, by means of her mind's eye, she said, "The Vāḍava wishes to give a boon. What shall I ask him?"

99. Sarasvatī, the goddess, was addressed by the Lord sta-

1. Mythological explanation for the softness of local rocks thereof.

tioned in the heart, "O fair one, *Sūcīvaktratva* (state of having a mouth like a needle) should be respectfully requested for."

100. Then (the Fire) was addressed by the goddess, "O highly powerful one, if you wish to grant a boon, then become *Sūcīmukha* (one with the mouth like a needle) and drink the waters."

101-103. On being told thus, the mouth was rendered like a needle by him. It was like the minute hole in the Ghaṭikā[1]. That mouth drank the water. Thus the Vāḍava fire that attempted to devour Suras was deceived by Viṣṇu. He then proceeded (to the holy spot) assiduously taking care of his intellect. He who listens to this holy *Sarga* (chapter) as it is being read attains Viṣṇuloka and rejoices with him.

CHAPTER THIRTYFOUR

The Descent of Sarasvatī

Īśvara said:

1. The noble- minded Sarasvatī received the excellent boon from Vaḍavānala and thereafter she proceeded ahead to hurl him into the ocean.

2. Desirous of handing over the Vāḍava at the behest of the Lord, she stationed herself before the holy place of Prabhāsa and invoked the ocean:

3. "O Arṇava (Ocean), you are the primordial one among Devas. You are the vital air of all living beings always. Do come and accept the Vāḍava at the behest of the Lord."

4. When the Lord of waters was thus thought of by the divine lady (river), the ocean of great lustre, rose up from the water and came there.

5-7. On seeing the highly fascinating Ocean like another blue-complexioned, lotus-eyed, divine Viṣṇu the divine lady was surprised. He had ornaments and garlands of various kinds.

---

1. Ghaṭikā: As the editor explains: For calculating the period of one Ghaṭikā (24 minutes) a copper pot with a small hole is kept in water. Water coming in from that small aperture fills the pot which indicates the period of one Ghaṭikā.

He had garments of diverse colours and (was smeared with) unguents of various sorts. He was surrounded by the *Āpagās* (Rivers) in physical forms like ladies.

On seeing the Ocean of this description, the divine lady, the daughter of Brahmā, spoke to the Ocean with pure smiles:

8. "You are the eldest of all beings born in the world. You are the vital life of all the men born. Hence carry out the task desired by Suras. Receive the (Vāḍava) Vahni brought here."

9. In the meantime he too considered mentally everything to be carried out. 'By accepting the *Anala* (fire) the task of the Suras will be carried out by me'.

10. Contemplating thus *Samudra* (Sea-god) liked the acceptance of the Vaḍavāgni to stop the affliction caused to the Suras.

11. Then the Devī was addressed by him as he stood in front, "O Sarasvatī, hand over this Vāḍava, the enemy of Suras."

12-13. Then Sarasvatī of variegated limbs (beautiful) immediately bowed down to Cāraṇas standing in the firmament with Pitāmaha as the leader. Then she spoke to the Vāḍava held in her hands: "You have been asked to devour the *ĀP* (Waters) by Suras. These are they (the waters)."

14. After saying this the divine lady Sarasvatī handed over the highly powerful Vaḍavāgni to the Ocean at the behest of Suras.

15. After handing over the Fire to him, the divine lady Sarasvatī transformed herself into a river and entered the *Sāgara* (Sea) along the path of Nāradeśvara (the deity of that name installed there).

16. In the vicinity of Daityasūdana (Viṣṇu) she offered Arghya to the Salt Sea and installed Arghyeśvara to the west of Daityasūdana.

17. Then the great river of five channels entered the ocean. Already meritorious and holy in her own original form, she became now still more sacred.

18. She became holier due to the contact of the Prabhāsa Kṣetra and the confluence with the Ocean. After receiving the Vāḍava from Sarasvatī, *Sāgara* (Ocean) thought in the manner of a poor man who suddenly got much wealth: 'Where shall I place this?'

19. With that fire held in the hand and blazing brightly

the Sāgara appeared like another Meru with the fire held on the head.

20. On seeing him in that position, all the aquatic beings, the sea monsters etc. howled loudly as they were afraid of being scalded.

21-22. On hearing that terrific sound, Daityasūdana (Viṣṇu) came there and told all the aquatic beings, "O highly powerful ones, do not be afraid, since, at the outset, only the waters are to be taken in by this (Vāḍava Fire) and not those beings living therein. At my bidding, do not get afraid."

23. On being told thus by Kṛṣṇa, the aquatic beings kept quiet.

24. When all the aquatic beings became silent, Acyuta said to the Lord of Waters, "Do hurl the Vāḍava in the midst of the waters."

25. The Vāḍava Anala was hurled into the deep waters. The highly powerful one remained drinking the water along with Varuṇa.

26. That water shaken by the exhalation of the breath began to move about outside the ocean like a young woman who has set at nought all bounds and curbs of behaviour.

27-28. As time passed on, O Goddess (Gaurī), the water began to dry up and evaporate slowly. The Storehouse of waters (the Sea) became aware of the fact that the (store of) waters are getting dwindled. He spoke to the Lotus-eyed Lord: "Do make the waters perennial. Otherwise, O Janārdana, if all the waters disappear, this Vāḍava fire will at the very outset swallow me."

29-30. On hearing these awful, panicky words of the Ocean, the water was rendered perennial (by Acyuta). The Suras knew that the water thus rendered everlasting dispels their grief. They knew these activities (of Keśava) which bound the Kṛtyā Fire to a tempting promise. They worshipped Keśava who moved about there tempting their enemy (i.e. the Vāḍava Fire). In this they kept the waters as their leaders.

31. Thus, O great goddess (Gaurī), from the world of Brahmā, Sarasvatī, the destroyer of all sins, reached the excellent Prabhāsa Kṣetra.

32. The great goddess holding the Vāḍava fire stationed herself to the south-east of Someśa near the ocean.

33-34. At the outset, a pilgrim should take his bath in the

Agnitīrtha and then worship her in accordance with the injunctions. He should feed a couple and give them garments along with bodice. Then he should worship the great Lord Kapardin. O goddess (Gaurī) this incident happened formerly in the Cākṣuṣa Manvantara.

35-37. This incident refers to the Vāḍava born in the family of Dadhīci. O great goddess, when this Vaivasvata Manvantara began, Aurva, the great Brāhmaṇa, was born in the family of Bhārgava. The Aurva of great refulgence was controlled (within limits) by Sarasvatī, the mother of Devas. Till the end of this Manvantara he will stay within the womb of the waters[1].

Thus, O goddess, the origin of Sarasvatī has been narrated to you. If it is listened to, it dispels the sins of men. It gives reputation and increases merits.

CHAPTER THIRTYFIVE

Greatness of Agni Tīrtha

The Devī said:

1-4. O holy Lord, an Aurva of the Bhārgava family was mentioned by you. O Lord, do narrate his nativity in this Vaivasvata Manvantara.

Īśvara said:

Brāhmaṇas had been killed by Kṣatriyas for the sake of wealth. They were entirely exterminated along with sons and children in the womb.

Among the many who were killed, there was a woman who concealed the foetus within the region of the thighs and protected it.

O beautiful lady (Gaurī), the foetuses of all other women were aborted by the base Kṣatriyas for the sake of monetary gain.

5. At a later time, the highly refulgent foetus pierced through the region of thighs (Read *urudeśam* for *kurudeśam* in the Text)

1. According to Mbh, *Ādi.* 179.21 it was Aurva who threw his fiery wrath in the form of Vaḍavānala in the Sea. Aurva was not drowned in the Sea.

and came out with the head propped up. He was extremely terrible and his face (mouth) blazed.

6. With the feelings of enmity cherished in his heart, he performed penance and created a terrible Aurva fire that could devour water. With this he scorched the surface of the earth.

7. O lady of excellent complexion (Gaurī), Indra flooded him with incessant heavy downpour. When he was not successful in driving him away, Indra became quiet (ceased to shower).

8. Then all the Devas and Gandharvas became excessively frightened. All of them sought refuge in Brahmā and stood with palms joined in reverence.

The Devas said:

9. O holy Sir, a highly refulgent one is born of the family of Bhārgava. In the form of fire, he has burnt the surface of the earth.

10. O most excellent one, formerly attempt was made by us to destroy him. But his (destructive) power enhances with (shower) of water. Hence we are afraid.

11. O Lord, if the terrestrial region is destroyed, *Agniṣṭoma* and other holy rites will be stopped altogether. Thereby our destruction is certain.

12. Hence, O Lord, do something urgently for the benefit of the three worlds.

13-14. Thereafter, Brahmā arrived there along with the Suras and the sages, Bhārgava and others, and said: "O Aurva, O most excellent one among Brāhmaṇas, why do you burn the earth. May this be stopped immediately for my sake."

Aurva said:

15-16. O most excellent one, O Lord, at your instance I have desisted (from burning). Let some means be found out so that the fire discharged by me reaches the vicinity of the ocean at your behest.

17. The Lotus-born Lord summoned his daughter, the goddess, and said: "O my highly refulgent daughter, take this fire and go to the great ocean. My instruction should not be disobeyed. Go quickly."

Sarasvatī said:

18a. Here, O Lord, I am setting out undoubtedly at your instance.

18b. When this was said the words "Excellent! Excellent!" were uttered by Brahmā.

19. Brahmā, the grandfather, himself deposited the fire inspired by Mantras in a gold pot and handed it over to Sarasvatī. After offering diverse kinds of benediction, he said thus again and again:

20. "Do go, dear daughter. You need not strain yourself on any account. May you traverse the path without obstacles. Let there be no antagonists."

Īśvara said:

21-23. On being told thus by Brahmā, Sarasvatī reached Himavān. From the hermitage of Pippalāda she proceeded ahead. The goddess (river) came out from beneath the *(Plakṣa)* tree.

There were Brāhmaṇas at the place near the hollow of the tree, in their numerous huts. Their chanting of the Vedas was heard and their minds were engrossed in chanting in good taste. Lord Viṣṇu, the excellent preceptor of Devas, was present there.

24[1]. From that spot, the goddess (river) proceeded westwards. After vanishing (for a while) she reached Kedāra in the midst of snow.

25-26. After flooding the peak of the mountain Kedāra, she stood before it. Being burnt by that fire held in the hand, Sarasvatī pierced the ground and entered beneath. Along that hidden path, she proceeded with face towards the west with the gait of an elephant.

27. After crossing the sinful region, she pierced the ground and came out. It became a well (Kūpa) by name *Gandharva* there.

1. The Vedic Sarasvatī has no continuous water flow. It disappears at some places. This intermittent course of the river as known to the Purāṇa author is given here, as that of Prācī Sarasvatī. The confusion between two Sarasvatīs is obvious.

28-29. The great river became visible beyond that well. Six *Upāsikās* (servants, tributaries) of Sarasvatī started therefrom, viz. *Mati, Smṛti, Prajñā, Medhā, Buddhi* and *Girādharā*. Further, that river proceeded ahead from the pierced sector towards the West.

30. She (River) came to Bhūtīśvara where there was a great sage, a Siddha. There is a charming region near Bhūtīśvara.

31. It is stationed in the southern quarter. It contains a crore of Rudras. Then she reached the famous Śrīkaṇṭha Deśa (Kurujāṅgala) abounding in all herbs.

32. From that highly meritorious region Śrīkaṇṭha, the noble-minded Sarasvatī came to Kurukṣetra along with the fire.

33. Then the charming river proceeded from Kurukṣetra and vanished when nearing the city of Virāṭa[1] She further came up at the place where the mountain Gopāyana is situated.

34. It was at this place that the sons of Pāṇḍu were concealed by Keśava, while they carried on their activities. They were not noticed (found out) by anyone.

35. There the goddess (river), the destroyer of great sins, stayed in a *Kuṇḍa*. Again from Gopāyana the goddess (river) reached a highly splendid holy spot.

36-37. She (river) reached *Kharjūrīvana* where she became well-known by the name Nandā. Sarasvatī left *Kharjūrīvana* and came to Merupāda (foot of the mountain Meru) and reached Mārkaṇḍāśrama. At this place there is the Mārkaṇḍaka Tīrtha situated at Merupāda.

38. From the splendid hermitage of Mārkaṇḍeya Sarasvatī proceeded to *Arbudāraṇya* (Mt. Abu) and went to the charming *Vaṭavana*.

39. It was here that Vasiṣṭha performed a penance. From that meritorious *Vaṭavana* that had been resorted to by Vasiṣṭha, she came to *Udumbara Vana*. It was there that Taṇḍi performed a penance on *Merupāda*.

40. From that *Udumbara Vana*, the great holy river Sarasvatī went ahead concealed and reached another peak.

41. This *Merupāda* too is very great and it is resorted to by

1. 40 Miles north of Jaipur, Rajasthan.

Suras and Siddhas. It resembles split collyrium and it is remembered by the name Golāṅgūlam (cow's tail).

42. It is a very fascinating spot. The lady of excellent middle line (i.e. river) rose up from the *Vaṁśastaṁba* (Bamboo cluster), spread widely and proceeded to the South.

43. The *Vaṭa* (holy fig tree) from which it came up is well-known as *Udgamavaṭa*. Thenceforth, that goddess (the river) continues to be manifest with excellent lustre.

44. She has now abandoned the state of concealment, due to her compassion for all living beings. On her beautiful banks, there are crores of Tīrthas.

45. In all those Tīrthas, the spiritual character is derived from Sarasvatī. On this path, Rudrāvatāra is remembered as the first and the foremost.

46. The *Kāka Tīrtha* of great refulgence designated as Tara Taraṅga is a great Tīrtha. There is a Tīrtha remembered as Dhāreśvara.

47. Another Tīrtha beyond *Dhāreśvara* is remembered as *Gaṅgodbheda*. It is the place where the waters of Sarasvatī and Gaṅgā mingle together. There is another greater Tīrtha beyond it called Puṇḍarīka.

48-50. The highly meritorious Mātṛtīrtha is fully destructive of all worries and fears. The Tīrtha by the name *Anaraka* is situated not very far from *Mātṛtīrtha*. It dispels the distress and fear caused by hell. Beyond that *Anaraka* Tīrtha, the other Tīrtha named *Saṅgameśvara* is situated. It is very well-known all over the earth. Beyond it is again another Tīrtha named *Koṭīśvara*.

51. Beyond it, O great goddess, *Śaṁbhukuṇḍeśvara* is remembered among the Tīrthas on the banks of Sarasvatī. So also is *Siddheśvara*.

52. From Siddheśvara, the river (Sarasvatī) flows westwards in order to reach the Western ocean. There she remembered her companion and wept for her.

53. The goddess (river) stood facing the east and lamented, "Alas! Gaṅgā, I am lonely without you! Unlucky and bereft of kinsmen, how shall I go?"

54. Becoming aware that she was rendered lean due to grief and was lamenting, Gaṅgā hastened from heaven along with a crore of Tīrthas.

55. Thereupon, Prācī (Eastern) Sarasvatī gave up grieving.

She stationed herself there accompanied by all the groups of Devas.

56. There, in front of *Vaṭeśvara* is the Tīrtha of Pitāmaha named *Siddhavaṭa.* It destroys all sins.

57. Thrice every day, Rudra arrives there and stays. It is the holy spot of that great Soul and is called *Mahālaya.*

58. There is an excellent ancient Tīrtha named *Piṇḍatāraka* situated on the mountain Kuṁbhakukṣigiri. It accords great Siddhi in rites connected with the Manes.

59. It is well-settled in front of Lord *Prācīneśvara.* What other thing need be sought after in a place where Prācī Sarasvatī is present!

60. When the Mahābhārata war was concluded Kirīṭin (Arjuna) performed expiatory rites in that Tīrtha on being directed by Viṣṇu earlier.

61. By that rite he became rid of that sin incurre earlier. Therefore, it is well-known as *Naratīrtha.* It dispels all fears of sins.

62. O my beloved, there is another Tīrtha remembered as *Puṇḍarīka* different from *Naratīrtha.* Hari came there along with Arjuna and took his holy bath.

63. Beyond *Prācīneśa* there is a great Tīrtha (named) Vālakhilyeśvara. Beyond that great Tīrtha there is another Tīrtha of great efficacy.

64-65. There is another Tīrtha of great efficacy named *Gaṅgāsaṁgama.* On seeing the goddess (river) with a gloomy face and dejected in mind, Brahmā created for her a companion of wide eyes named Kapilā. Hari hastily created Hariṇī and the Lord of Devas (Indra) Vajriṇī. Hara gave Nyaṅku to Sarasvatī in order to humour her.

66. Thereupon, the goddess (river) Prācīna Sarasvatī became happy. At the behest of the Lord, she, the destroyer of sins, proceeded to go.

Īśvara said:

67. At the outset, the river flowed towards south and then turned westwards. Sarasvatī, the great goddess continued to hold the Vaḍavānala. On her northern bank is the Tīrtha remembered as Ekadvāra.

68. It is so called because the army went to Svarga through *Ekadvāra* (single door) from that forest. There is another Tīrtha beyond, where the deity is *Guheśvara*.

69. Formerly it was installed by Guha, at the place where Lord Maheśvara is present. Not far from *Guheśvara* is the Tīrtha named *Vaṭeśvara*.

70-71. It is a divine Tīrtha on the banks of Sarasvatī. Formerly it was propitiated by Vyāsa. The great Tīrtha where the river Āmardakī unites with Sarasvatī, accords benefit to all embodied beings. No one without merit can know the confluence of Āmardakī. A Liṅga named *Saṅgameśvara* has been installed there.

72-73. It became famous over the earth by the name *Muṇḍīśvara*. In the vicinity of *Muṇḍīśvara* there is an east-facing Tīrtha on Sarasvatī. It is situated on the banks of Sarasvatī. It is named *Mahodaya*. The Lord installed there is known by the name *Māṇḍavyeśvara*.

74. There is another Tīrtha named *Pīlukarṇika* on the banks of Sarasvatī. It is a great Tīrtha resorted to by sages.

75. There is another Tīrtha on the banks of the river. It is remembered as Dvāravatī. O goddess (Gaurī), it is the foremost of all Tīrthas and Hari is present there.

76. Further, situated nearby is the Tīrtha called *Govatsa*. It was here that the Consort of Aṁbikā (i.e. Śiva) descended in the form of a calf.

77. The storehouse of refulgence stayed there in the form of *Bhūliṅga*. On the south-west of *Govatsa* is seen a *Lohayaṣṭikā* (Iron Post).

78-80. Rudra himself is stationed there in the form of Bhūliṅga.

By performing a single Śrāddha there men obtain the benefit that is usually derived by devoutly offering rice-balls twenty-one times in Gaṅgā.

Then from that great Tīrtha, the river proceeds ahead along with her friends like a child with its toys. Sometimes she flows southwards, sometimes northwards. Thus she flows backwards and forwards.

81-82. After reaching Rulla, the goddess (river) becomes charming once again. It was here that the city Rulla was created by Lord Śaṁbhu. He played for a period of a thousand years with Pārvatī and the Devas jetting out water from the *Dhārāyantra* (a pump like instrument from which water is jetted out against other players).

83. Rulla is a whirlpool of great efficacy in Sarasvatī. Mahādeva is directly present there by the name of Ānandeśvara.

84. To the west of the temple of Śaṁbhu, on the southern foot-hill of Meru, there is a nail-like mark. It is highly glorified.

85. Men who view this perfectly, become rid of sins. They certainly attain the benefit of a thousand horse-sacrifices.

86. Beyond it is the great hermitage of Sage Kūṣmāṇḍa. The Tīrtha called Kūṣmāṇḍeśvara is famous all over the three worlds.

87. It is there that the goddess Kollā is stationed. She dispels all sins and fears. The great river reached the vicinity of Kollā, by proceeding under ground (in a concealed manner).

88. Again she became hidden (went underground) and reached a very charming tableland called Madana. It is a holy spot resorted to by Siddhas.

89. Going under cover once again, she (the river) reached a snow-clad mountain named Khādirāmoda. This place remarkably shines with the flowers of all the seasons.

90. Mounting it she espied the highly fascinating *Kṣāroda* (Sea) lofty like a clustre of clouds in the western quarter.

91. On seeing this in this manner, the highly refulgent (river) became five-faced (five currents, mouths of the river) in her delightShe then got ready to accomplish the task of Devas.

92. The five channels are Hariṇī, Vajriṇī, Nyaṅku, Kapilā and Sarasvatī. On being told by the sage, Sarasvatī stood there with the five channels.

93. The places where she stood dispelling the fatigue of sages, are each called after the name of the sage concerned (the Tīrtha of that sage). O lady of excellent countenance (Gaurī), these Tīrthas dispels all the sins of the men desirous of (undertaking pilgrimage) to them.

94. Reaching Khādirāmoda and tarrying there she looked at the ocean. Then, O beautiful goddess, she took the fire and began to proceed ahead.

95. After burning Kṛtasmara, the goddess (river) took up the Vāḍava once again and stood in the vicinity of the ocean. In her delight, her hairs stood on ends.

96. Then goddess entered deep into the salt sea. She took the Vāḍava fire and cast (Vāḍava) off into the middle of the waters.

97. Then *Hutāśana* (Fire-god) himself became pleased with her. On seeing that difficult task accomplished, he spoke these words:

98. "O fair lady, I am pleased with you. O lady of excellent holy rites, choose your boon. That I shall gladly grant you even if it be very difficult to get."

Īśvara said:

99. She took off a bangle from her forearm and spoke these words: "O *Vahni,* this bangle of mine should always be worn round your mouth.

100. Draw only that much water which can be drawn through this. *Samudra,* the Lord of rivers, should not be dried away by you."

101. After saying "So it shall be", he entered the storehouse of waters. It is thus, O great goddess, that Sarasvatī came to Prabhāsa taking the Vāḍava for the sake of the pleasure of noble-minded ones.

102. O beautiful lady, that great river halted and rested at Kurukṣetra, Bhadrāvarta and Śrīsthala.

103. In this Manvantara, O goddess, formerly in the first Tretāyuga she merged within the salty ocean in the form of Devamātā (Mother of the Devas).

104. This is what took place in the case of Sarasvatī and Vāḍava fire. When this Manvantara passes off another Vāḍava will be born.

105. It will be born of the fury of Rudra under the name *Jvālāmukha.* Then the name of Sarasvatī will become well-known as Brāhmī.

106. Now in the world, the name current is Sarasvatī. Her name in the past was Kamaṇḍalubhavā ('born of the water-pot'). It is true that another earlier name of *Samudra* (ocean) was *Ratnākara* ('storehouse of jewels').

107. O goddess, in this Manvantara it is glorified as *Sāgara.* It has been proclaimed, O goddess, that the future name is *Kṣāroda.*

108. Whoever knows it thus attains the benefit of the Tīrtha.

In the holy spot Prabhāsa Sarasvatī has become a ladder unto *Svarga* (heaven).

109. The great river cannot be attained (reached) by persons without merit. O goddess, Prācī Sarasvatī is everywhere very difficult of access, and especially so in Kurukṣetra, Prabhāsa and Puṣkara.

110. That goddess (river) holding the Vaḍavānala has such efficacy. The goddess Sarasvatī stood very near *Agni Tīrtha.*

111. One who worships her at the outset attains the benefit of the Tīrtha. That Sāgara Tīrtha is destructive of sins and it augments merit.

112-113. By its mere sight, one attains the benefit of a great *Kratu.* An *Agnicit* (performer of Agnihotra), a *Kapilā* (the tawny-coloured cow), a *Sattrī* (one who performs a *Sattra* sacrifice), a king, a holy mendicant and the great ocean—these sanctify on being merely viewed. Hence one should view them with purity.

After taking the holy bath in Agnitīrtha a man should cast into the holy fire a Bhāra weight (twenty Tolas) of *Guggula.* He is honoured in Agniloka.

114. Thus has been briefly described the prosperity arising from Agnitīrtha and the greatness of Sarasvatī that is destructive of all sins.

115. After taking the holy bath duly in Agnitīrtha, O great goddess, one should cast into it a gold bangle as permitted by one's funds.

116-119. Then after worshipping Sarasvatī, the devotee should adore Kapardin.

Then the deity named Kedāra and Bhīmeśvara thereafter, then the deity named Bhairaveśvara and then Caṇḍīśvara, thereafter the man should duly adore Lord Someśvara. After worshipping Navagraheśvaras and the eleven Rudras, one should adore Lord Brahmā in the form of a boy. Thus the Yātrā (Pilgrimage) called *Rādrī* (Raudrī ?) is accomplished. It is destructive of sins.

120-122. An excellent man who resides within the Kṣetra and fully knows the greatness, obtains the benefit of the Tīrtha. After doing thus, the devotee goes to the great goddess Sarasvatī. Where else can the merit on a par with that of residence in Sarasvatī be obtained? Where else is pleasure on a par with that of residence in Sarasvatī? Men who went up to heaven after reaching Sarasvatī, will again remember the river.

CHAPTER THIRTYSIX

Greatness of Prācī Sarasvatī

The Devī said:

1-2. It has been said by you that Prācī Sarasvatī is difficult of access everywhere, especially in Kurukṣetra, Prabhāsa and Puṣkara. How did this river destructive of all sins reach Prabhāsa and halt there eventually? O Lord Maheśāna, describe fully the greatness that is destructive of sins, of that Prācī, if I am your beloved.

Īśvara said:

3. O fair lady, you have said pertinently. Prācī is difficult of access everywhere, in Kurukṣetra, and Puṣkara and more so in the holy spot of Prabhāsa.

4. O great goddess, O goddess of Devas, no one devoid of merit obtains in Prabhāsa, Prācī the destroyer of sins and capable of rooting out (adverse) Karmas.

5. It is the truth, (I repeat) it is true that men who drink the water of Prācī Sarasvatī should never be thought of as mere men, O lady of excellent countenance.

6. Blessed indeed are those sages and meritorious ascetics who drink the waters of the Sarasvatī everyday.

7. They are gods. They are not human beings, but gods who drink the waters of the three rivers, namely Gaṅgā, Candrabhāgā (Chinab) and the divine Sarasvatī.

8. This can be after taking food or while abstaining from food. It may be by day or at night. In Prācī Sarasvatī there is no time restriction (for drinking water).

9. Even those animals that drink Prācī Sarasvatī always will go to Svarga as in the case of excellent Brāhmaṇas (who do so) through Yajñas.

10. In the case of laymen, that excellent holy place serves

the purpose of fulfilling all desires. There, Prācī Sarasvatī is on a par with *Cintāmaṇi* (the fabulous philosopher's stone yielding everything wished for).

11. Just as the Kāmadhuk (wish-yielding) cows accord the benefit of achieving all desires, so also the divine Prācī Sarasvatī through heavenly pleasures and absolute salvation.

12. What else can be regarded as superior to this (holy spot) where eighty-eight thousand sages of sublimated sexuality have stayed on, renouncing the idea of leaving for other holy spots?

13. It is the place where Maṅkaṇaka attained Siddhi. He observed restrictions and self-control in Prācīna (a holy spot on the Prācī river). O lady of excellent countenance, I performed the expiatory rite for (the sin of) Brāhmaṇa-slaughter in that place.

14. When the Mahābhārata war concluded, Kirīṭin (Arjuna) performed expiatory rite on being directed by Viṣṇu (Kṛṣṇa). He performed the rite in that Tīrtha, the highly meritorious Tīrtha situated on the banks of Prācī.

15. Among all the Tīrthas of the three worlds, that Tīrtha is remembered as the most excellent. It destroys the sins of living beings. It generates (confers) merits and it accords meritorious renown.

Sūta said:

16. On this being told thus, the goddess spoke to Śaṅkara, the benefactor of the worlds: "O Lord, how did Pārtha (Arjuna), the conqueror of the cities of the enemies, undergo the expiation? How did the sin caused by the killing of the kinsmen get dissolved?"

17. On being asked thus, Nīlalohita, the Lord of the universe, spoke of the manner in which he realized the expiation as obtaining there.

Īśvara said:

18. O fair lady, listen with attention to the story that destroys sins. By listening to this devoutly, a man becomes one of purified soul.

19. O goddess, he who is called Kirīṭin and Śvetavāhana

(i.e. Arjuna) conquered all the Kauravas and slaughtered horses and elephants.

20. Thereafter, with the help of Bhīma he got Suyodhana (killed). This Nara along with Nārāyaṇa set off homewards from the battlefield and reached the abode.

21-23a. With a desire to meet the son of Dharma, the delighted Arjuna bowed down to him and stood ready with palms joined in reverence. On coming to know that both of them, Nara and Nārāyaṇa were coming, King Yudhiṣṭhira spoke to the sentries at the entrance gate: "You who are at the gate should prevent these two from entering. Nara and Nārāyaṇa are cruel. They are smeared with the mire of sins".

23b. They said, "It will be so". When the two came near the gate, they were told thus:

24. "The king does not wish to see both of you because you are guilty of misconduct." Nara himself who was standing there asked the sentry:

25. "What is the reason? Why does our king not wish to see both of us (who are) completely under his control?" Then the King who was bowed to, said to the sentry standing before:

26. He also spoke to Nara who was dauntless of even hell and who was accompanied by Nārāyaṇa: "Since all the kinsmen including Duryodhana and all the kings on a par with the parents were killed by you, you have incurred sins."

27. When this was spoken, he (Nara) looked at the face of Hari. Hari said, "What has been uttered by the king is the truth."

28-29. When this was uttered, Nara spoke to Janārdana once again: "O Kṛṣṇa, say, how are we going to get free from the sin? O Kṛṣṇa, tell me clearly how I will get purified through the holy bath in a Tīrtha viz. Gaṅgā etc. which is destructive of sins."

Kṛṣṇa said:

30. O Kaunteya, do not go to Gayā. Do not go to Puṣkara. O most excellent one among the scions of the family of Kuru, go to that place where Prācī Sarasvatī flows.

31. Brāhmaṇa-slayers, those who imbibe liquor as well as other sinners, become rid of the sins by taking the holy bath at the place where Prācī Sarasvatī flows.

32. On being told thus by Nārāyaṇa, Nara, immediately in compliance of his words, reached the excellent Prācīna Tīrtha accompanied by him.

33. He observed fast for three nights and took his holy ablution thrice a day with full self-control. Thereby he got rid of the sins accumulated earlier.

34. On realizing that he had become pure, King Dharmaputra, accompanied by his brothers came there to see the leading Nara.

35. Then Dharmaputra saw him in front bowing down. With a delighted soul, he embraced him and enquired after his health.

36. Nara endowed with many good qualities, was surrounded by the group of elders. He was embraced by his delighted brothers Bhīma and others.

37. Such is that great Tīrtha called Prācīna. It is the purifier of men and others through regular holy ablution.

38. Even one who is a slayer of a Brāhmaṇa, but takes his bath in this Tīrtha and observes fast for three nights, becomes rid of that sin. He rejoices in heaven like Rudra.

39. O goddess, O beautiful woman, I reside along with you in this great ancient holy spot Prabhāsa.

40. He who casts off his body, O beautiful lady, in the holy spot Prācīna on the northern bank of Sarasvatī, does not come here again.

41. If he takes his plunge he will get the full benefit of a horse-sacrifice. He should get his body dried up by means of restraints and fasts.

42-43. There are ascetics of various kinds: some take in only water; some take in only air; others have leaves for diet. They observe many restraints such as always lying down on the dry bare ground. If the people who reside in the hermitage of Maṅki, meet with death, they are no longer men. They are Devas. I speak the truth.

44. In this Tīrtha, if anyone offers a bit of gold with great faith to a leading Brāhmaṇa, he will obtain the benefit thereof on a par with Meru.

45. Men who perform Śrāddha in this Tīrtha will certainly go to heaven in the company of twenty-one generations.

46. Those propitiated with a single rice-ball in this Tīrtha

that is a favourite of the Pitṛs, will go to Brahmaloka like those who perform Gayāśrāddha.

47. Holy bath on the fourteenth day in the dark half is always laid down. If a devotee offers balls of *Piṇyāka* or *Iṅgudaka,* the Pitṛs are eternally satisfied. The devotee goes to Pitṛloka.

48. If they offer much rice (food), they go along the path to salvation.

49. He who offers excellent curds there to a Brāhmaṇa, reaches Agniloka and enjoys splendid pleasures.

50. He who devoutly offers a woollenblanketto an excellent Brāhmaṇa attains great Siddhi very difficult for othersto acquire.

51. If men enter the waters here for getting rid of dirt, one can easily predict the benefit acquired on a par with the gift of cows.

52. A man who takes the holy bath with ardent fervour, shall be rid of all sins and will be honoured in Brahmaloka.

53. The Pitṛs detained in Narakas can be redeemed by an excellent son by means of libations and offerings of rice-balls. They go to Svarga.

54. If anyone who has gone to Prācī Sarasvatī turns to Himālaya, he forsakes what he has in his hand and begins to lick with the elbow *(obscure).*

55. He who casts away his life thinking of anything whatever before death, obtains it entirely, thanks to the greatness of the Tīrtha.

56-58. Another thing, O goddess. This has been said by Gāṅgeya (Bhīṣma) to Yudhiṣṭhira: "It is true that we are born of Gaṅgā, O Yudhiṣṭhira, but out of all the rivers in the world, Sarasvatī is the greatest and the most meritorious of all of them. Sarasvatī is the most meritorious of all the rivers. Sarasvatī always accords happiness to all the people. After reaching Sarasvatī, even a most miserable man never grieves here or hereafter.

CHAPTER THIRTYSEVEN

Importance of Offering a Bracelet

The Devī said:

1-2. O Lord, what for is a gold bracelet thrown into the

Salt Sea? The merit acquired thereby has not been mentioned before. It behoves you to tell it exactly. What are the *Mantras*? What is the injunction? At what time is it highly efficacious? What is the episode associated with the gold bracelet, O holy Lord?

Īśvara said:

3. Formerly there was a king well-known as Bṛhadratha. He had a beloved wife, a chaste lady named Indumatī.

4. O great goddess, neither among the Deva women nor in Gandharvīs nor in Asurīs nor in Kinnarīs is (was) there a slender-waisted lady like her (in beauty.).

5. She was endowed with good manners, beauty, and other qualities. She was always chaste. Like the chaste lady Arundhatī, she possessed all the womanly good qualities.

6. She was the most important one among a thousand inmates. Naturally she was proud of her conjugal felicity. Without her, the king did not divert himself even for a moment.

7. Once, she was occupying half the throne of the saintly king, when a sage named Kaṇva came near the saintly king. He was an ascetic of great refulgence and was a master of the Vedas.

8-9. Seeing him coming, the king promptly got up. He duly adored him and offered excellent *Arghya*. Assured that the leading sage was comfortably seated and relaxed, the king enquired after his health and well-being and the sage congratulated him.

10. Then the sage held discourse on piety in the audience with the king.

11. At the end of the discourse, the wife of the king stood there with palms joined in reverence and spoke these nectarine words:

Indumatī said:

12. O holy Sir, O Lord, you know everything past and future. Urged by curiosity I am asking you. So it behoves you to excuse me.

13. Do narrate to me all my Karmas done in the earlier bodies. Mine is such a great conjugal felicity. My husband is comparable to a son of Devas.

14. Due to my good fortune, I am having a husband as a Lord unto me whose good conduct is well-known all over the three worlds. Is this the result of any Vrata or that of a religious fast?

15. O leading sage, is this the efficacy of a Dāna that I possess excellent conjugal felicity? The mighty king is under my control. He always acts according to what I say.

16. Do explain this to me entirely. My curiousity is excessive.

Sūta said:

17. On hearing her words, the sage meditated for a long time. Ultimately Kaṇva, the most excellent one among knowers of the Vedas, laughingly spoke these words:

Kaṇva said:

18. Listen, O queen. I shall tell the details of your previous birth. O lady of slender waist-line, you must not be angry. Nor is there any need to feel ashamed.

19. In the previous birth you were a cowherdess with five husbands in the land of Saurāṣṭra. When you became *Hīnā* (a widow devoid of husbands) you went to the deity Someśvara.

20. Then, for your holy bath, you entered the salty sea. On being struck by a series of waves, you became agitated.

21. From your forearm the gold bracelet slipped down and got lost in the waters of the ocean. You began to regret it.

22. After a long time, you met with your death. Then, O beautiful woman, you were born in the abode of the king of Daśārṇa.

23-24a. Thanks to the power of the gold bracelet (lost in the sea), you were married to Bṛhadratha. O splendid lady, no *Vrata*, penance or *Dāna* was undertaken by you before. Here everything has been mentioned to you, all which you had asked me.

24b. On hearing those words the large-eyed lady stood with face down due to bashfulness. On hearing those words, the fair lady remained silent.

25. After intimating this to the wife of the king, O lady of excellent countenance (i.e. Gaurī), the sage took leave of the king and went to his abode.

26. Having understood that the benefit was a result of (offer of) gold bracelet by the power of the sage, she went to Lord Someśvara and took her holy bath in the salty ocean.

27. O lady of great refulgence, every year she used to throw down a gold bracelet. Then she attained the state of Deva, thanks to its power, O lady of great beauty.

Īśvara said:

28. This great power of (offering to sea) a gold bracelet has been described. O goddess, it accords all desires. It is destructive of all sins.

CHAPTER THIRTYEIGHT

Kapardi-Vināyaka

The Devī said:

1-2. In regard to your earlier statement that one should visit Kapardin at the outset, I have a doubt. It behoves you to clarify it. O Lord of Devas, O Śaṁbhu, is he not your attendant though highly lustrous? According to a convention the honouring of a servant should take place only after that of the master.

Īśvara said:

3. Listen, O goddess, I shall explain how Kapardin is the most adorable. He is the foremost of all the Devas. He is Lord Vighneśvara.

4. O great goddess, Someśvara, Sadāśiva who is stationed in Prabhāsa Kṣetra in the form of a Liṅga is beyond the ken of sense-organs.

5. On his left is stationed Viṣṇu who is remembered as Varāha (the Boar). Brahmā, the Prajāpati (Lord of the subjects), is stationed on his right. Since he is angry with Sāvitrī he has adopted the form of Kapardin.

6. In Kṛta Yuga, his name was *Heraṁba*; in Tretā he was *Vighnamardana*. In Dvāpara he was *Laṁbodara* and he is remembered as *Kapardin* in Kali Age.

7. Thus his incarnation is distinct in every Yuga. He is born again and again in accordance with the task on hand.

8. At the advent of the twenty-eighth *Caturyuga* Kapardin was born there as *Kāraṇātman* (in the form of the original cause). Listen how he was born so.

9. Formerly at the junction of Dvāpara when Kaliyuga began, women, barbarians, Śūdras and those who were sinners used to go to Svarga quickly after viewing Lord Someśvara.

10. There were no Yajñas, no austerity, no Dāna, no study of the Vedas and no *Vrata*. Men who never performed any of these things, O goddess, used to go to the abode of Śiva.

11. As a result of this power of Someśvara, O goddess of Suras, all holy rites beginning with *Agniṣṭoma* (sacrifice) became extinct.

12. Thereupon boys, old men, sages who had mastered the Vedas, Śūdras and even women used to attain the highest state.

13. At a time when the festivities of Yajña were extinct, the whole of the earth became vacant and heaven became filled with persons of raised arms (Since there was no living space left in the crowded heaven, all could stand only with raised arms).

14. Thereupon, the Devas beginning with Mahendra, became miserable on being attacked and defeated by human beings as it were. They sought refuge in Śaṅkara.

15-18. With palms joined in reverence all the excellent Suras beginning with Indra said: "O Śaṅkara, due to your favour this Svarga has become over-crowded with human beings.

They are boasting to one another, "I am the most excellent one, I am the most superior one" and move about everywhere as they please. O Lord, suggest some place for us to stay.

Dharmarāja, the highly virtuous one, is reviewing their auspicious and inauspicious Karmas recorded by himself. He keeps quiet with extreme surprise.

The extremely terrible Kuṁbhīpāka, Raurava and Śālmali hells had been kept ready by him for these sinners. But on seeing those very persons well-settled in heaven he felt embarrassed. So he has abandoned his work.

Śrī Bhagavān said:

19. When I was pleased with the devotion of Soma I had

promised him everything. My presence (proximity to Soma) in this holy spot was promised.

20. What has been promised by me cannot be altered. Those who visit me there will thus go to Svarga.

21. Agitated by fear, the Devas looked at Pārvatī present everywhere and spoke to her with palms joined in reverence, "Do be our refuge".

22. After saying so, they knelt on the ground. With joined palms kept over the head all those Devas eulogized her by means of this prayer.

The Devas prayed:

23. Obeisance to you, O goddess of the chiefs of Devas. Obeisance to you, O mother of the Universe. Obeisance to you with eyes like lotus-petals. Obeisance to you, O goddess with golden lustre.

24. Obeisance to you, O great annihilatrix and creatrix. Obeisance to you, O beloved of Śaṅkara. Obeisance to you, O Kālarātri (Durga identified as the goddess of the night of annihilation) Obeisance to you, O daughter of the Mountain.

25. O fair lady, O noble lady, O Viśālākṣī (large-eyed one)! Obeisance to you, to the most beautiful lady of the world. You are *Rati* (pleasure). You are *Dhṛti* (fortitude). You are *Śrī* (fortune). You are Svāhā. You are Svadhā and Satī.

26. You are Durgā, you are *Mati* (intellect) you are *Medhā* (retentive power of memory). You are everything. You are the earth, the repository of rich wealth. This entire range of the three worlds consisting of mobile and immobile beings has been pervaded by you.

27-28. We have been looking for you in rivers, tops of mountains, oceans, caves, forests, altars and sanctuaries, battlefields, hermitages—all those places in the three worlds where, O goddess, you were not present. In view of all this, O Viśālākṣī, save us from the great danger.

Īśvara said:

29. That goddess was prayed to thus by the Devas with Indra as their leader. Out of mercy you caused your own body to be massaged and pressed by those Devas.

30. A great deal of dirt issued forth as you were being pressed and massaged. It was there that the four- armed charming *Gajendrāsya* (one with the face of a leading tusker) appeared.

31-33. You mercifully spoke to all the Suras: "This is the being created by me with a desire for your benefit. He will cause all obstacles to the living beings. Men overwhelmed with great delusion, with intellect overpowered by lust, will never see Somanātha. Hence they will fall into hell."

34. All the Devas were delighted in their minds on hearing these words of yours. They went back to their respective abodes shedding off all fear arising from human beings.

35. Then, O goddess, the Elephant-faced One spoke to you humbly: "O large-eyed one, what shall I do? May some command be given to me."

Śrī Bhagavatī said:

36-38. Go to the holy place of Prabhāsa where Hara is present and protect it. See that the Liṅga of the Lord of Devas which is installed by the Moon himself does not fall within the range of vision of human beings.

On being commanded by you thus, he causes obstacles to men always. Kapardin begins to cause great obstacles to everyone on seeing him proceeding to Somanātha, the Lord. Hence Kapardin is highly adored by people.

39. He creates unto him the great infatuation of sons, wives, houses, fields, wealth and foodgrain. As a result the man does no see Hara.

40. Or he may generate some illness like goitre, swelling in the neck etc. and the man afflicted with those illnesses becomes deluded and never sees Hara.

41. Hence with a desire to (attain) Someśvara one should assiduously worship him (Kapardin) always and remember him day and night.

42. Gaṇādhyakṣa, the protector of Prabhāsa Kṣetra, should be propitiated, O goddess of Devas, by means of this prayer that destroys all obstacles.

43. O great goddess, I shall proclaim to you that prayer which suppresses obstacles, the prayer to Kapardin. Listen with attention.

Prayer (44-51): *(Prayer to Kapardin)*

44. Oṁ, obeisance to the Lord of obstacles. O Kapardin, obeisance to you. Obeisance to the Lord of great and fierce fang-like teeth, to the resident of the holy spot of Prabhāsa.

45. After bowing down to Kapardin for the sake of freedom from obstacles in the course of the pilgrimage, I shall eulogize Vighnarāja, the splendid lover of *Siddhi* and *Buddhi*.

46. (I adore) Mahāgaṇapati, heroic one, unconquered one, one who enhances victory, single-toothed one, double-toothed one, four-toothed one, four-armed one.

47. (I adore) the three-eyed one, the trident-armed one, the red-eyed one, the bestower of boons, the invincible one, the pike-eared one, the fierce one, the leader of the army, one with iron staff held up, *Hutavaktra* (one in whose mouth the sacrificial articles are consigned), and *Hutapriya* (one fond of the performance of Homa).

48. I bow down to that Gaṇādhyakṣa, the terrifying and fierce son of Umā, who, if not worshipped, causes obstacles in all the activities of men.

49. I bow down to that Vināyaka who is full of inebriation, who has uneven (three) eyes, whose lustre is befitting the elephant-faced deity, who is firm and motionless, and who is quiescent.

50. With a previous physical form you adopted the guise of an elephant for the fulfilment of the tasks of Devas. You then terrified all the Dānavas.

51. You have revealed your leadership of the sages and the Devas.

52-55. O son of Bhava, you are adored at the outset by the Suras after being eulogized thus.

A devotee shall propitiate you, O Gaṇādhyakṣa, having the lustre befitting the elephant-faced Lord. The devotee should eulogize the steady, motionless, quiescent Lord surrounded by the glory of victory. For the realization of any task the devotee should wear red garments and worship with red flowers and the waters (rendered fragrant) with red sandalpaste. He should restrain himself and restrict his food intake. He can worship once a day or twice a day. The Lord of all obstacles shall control everyone, be it a king, king's son, king's minister or the kingdom.

56. By remembering Lord Vināyaka, one obtains that benefit which results from visiting all the Tīrthas and performing all the Yajñas.

57. He will never meet with difficulty. He will face no defeat or discomfiture, nor will he have any obstacle. The man shall become competent to remember the previous birth.

58. He who recites this hymn shall be granted boons within six months. He will obtain *Siddhi* within a year. There is no doubt about this.

59. Lord Someśvara favours him and comes within the view of that devotee. Since his belly has the shape of a *Kaparda* (a courrie used as a coin, a shell) the noble-souled one has come to be named *Kapardin*.

CHAPTER THIRTYNINE

Kedāreśvara Liṅga

Īśvara said:

1-4. After duly adoring Kapardin, the Lord of Devas, O great goddess, a pilgrim should go to the Liṅga situated in Kedāra and set up in its south-east sector. It is near Bhīmeśvara. It is self-born *Kalpaliṅga,* O great goddess, and is my favourite. This Vṛddhiliṅga of great lustre was worshipped by me, O goddess. If any devotee abstains from food and keeps vigil on the night of the fourteenth lunar day, his worlds shall be eternal. But the name of this Lord in the earlier Yuga was Rudreśvara.

5. When at the advent of this *Tiṣya* (Kali Yuga) the Lord became afraid and agitated about contact with barbarians, he, Lord Kedāra, got merged into this Liṅga in the vicinity of the sea.

6-8. Hence, the name of the Lord became well-known as Kedāra.

In the month of Māgha, the pilgrim should restrict his diet and take his holy bath in the great *Padmaka Kuṇḍa* within the salty sea. It is situated at a distance of ten Dhanus to the south of Rudreśa.

O goddess, after taking the holy bath in accordance with the injunctions he should adore Rudreśa. Thereby he shall derive the benefits of the perfect performance of the pilgrimage to Kedāra.

9-10. By adoring the Lord, the sins of Brāhmaṇa-slaughter etc. shall be dispelled.

Now, O beloved of Suras, the ancient legend of the same Lord is being told. It yields the fulfilment of all the cherished desires unto men.

Formerly, O goddess, there was a king well-known as Śaśabindu.

11. He was born during the junction of Kali and Dvāpara. He was an emperor and Lord of all kings. He was competent to slay all antagonists and their hosts.

12-14. He had a chaste wife dear to him more than his own life. O beautiful lady (Gaurī), neither a Deva lady nor a Gandharvī, neither an Asurī lady nor a Pannagī was as beautiful as this lady of splendid eyes, the queen of the king. He had a hundred-petalled charming lotus moving through the sky. It was a fast vehicle of that noble-souled king. O goddess, he wandered over all the worlds as he pleased by means of that (lotus-vehicle).

15. Once, O lady of excellent countenance, on the fourteenth lunar day in the bright half of the month of Phālguna, he arrived at the excellent Prabhāsa Kṣetra.

16. He saw all the sages gathered before Śrīsomeśa. They were engaged in *Japa* and *Homa* at night for the purpose of keeping awake.

17. After viewing Somanātha and making the bow of veneration in accordance with the injunctions, he adored all of them in a fitting manner with devotion.

18-19. Then, O my beloved, he proceeded to Kedāra and bathed (the deity) duly. He worshipped Īśvara with flower garlands of various kinds, Various kinds of food-offerings were made. Charming robes and ornaments were dedicated to the deity. Thereafter, with great concentration he made arrangements for *Jāgara* (keeping awake at night).

20-21. Sages Cyavana, Yājñavalkya, Śāṇḍilya, Śākaṭāyana, Raibhya, Jaimini, Krauñca, Nārada, Parvata and Śīla were filled with eager curiosity. Keeping Mārkaṇḍa at their head, they approved him.

22. They conducted diverse kinds of discourses mostly in mythology and old legends. After remaining thus for some time, they asked the excellent king:

The sages said:

23. O king, why did you ignore Lord Someśvara and perform the rite of keeping awake before Lord Kedāra? Do tell us this. Certainly you know the efficacy of this Liṅga, in conferring prosperity.

The King said:

24. May all the Brāhmaṇas listen to the details of mine in the other body (i.e. earlier birth). Formerly I was a man of Śūdra caste, venerating Brāhmaṇas.

25. It was in the splendid land of Saurāṣṭra in a family possessing much wealth and foodgrains. Then, O Brāhmaṇas, on another occassion a state of drought overran it.

26. Then I came to the Prabhāsa Kṣetra. I was afflicted with hunger. Then I espied a splendid lake situated near the Hariṇī river.

27. The name of that lake was Rāmasaras. It was adorned with clusters of lotuses. It resembled the Ocean of Milk. As I was tired, on seeing it, I took my bath there.

28-29. After offering libations to the Pitṛs and Devas, I drank the clear water. Then my wife told me thus: "Take these lotuses. Here, nearby an excellent charming holy spot is seen. We can sell these after going there so that, O dear Lord, we shall get our food."

30. Thereupon, I got down into the water, O Brāhmaṇas, and plucked plenty of lotus flowers. Then I started towards the city.

31-32. O excellent sages, in order to sell the lotuses in full bloom, I went along the roads and places where three roads and four roads met. No one came forward to take (the flower). By that time, the sun also set. Accompanied by my wife, I went to a big building and slept there.

33-34. While sleeping I heard the sound of music. My wife and I were very hungry. It occurred to me that certainly the ritual of keeping awake was on, in a certain temple and that I shall go there to the temple with the lotus flowers. If anyone buys them, we can have our means of sustenance (food).

35. O leading sages, I got up and came to this place and saw this Liṅga adored with splendid flowers.

36-38a. This Vṛddha Liṅga is a self-born one and is named Rudreśvara.

A harlot named Anaṅgavatī was celebrating Śivarātri. With songs, dances and other festivities she kept awake before the deity.

I saw someone (and asked him): "Is this the ritual of keeping awake? Who is this lady seen here very ardently engaged in songs, dances and festivities?"

38b-42. He replied: "This is the ritual of Śivarātri mentioned in the scripture as *Śivadharma*. It yields great merit.

This is the harlot named Anaṅgavatī. She is very pious. She keeps awake at night after performing the splendid *Śivarātri Vrata*.

A man who perfectly celebrates this *Śivarātri Vrata* never meets with misery or poverty. Nor does he get into bondage.

He does not suffer due to malefic position of Planets, illness or anything fearsome. The man becomes richly endowed with good luck and happiness and is born in a good family.

He becomes refulgent, famous and recipient of everything by way of welfare. With the favour (of this deity) all this happens, so say learned men.

The King said:

43. Then I became finally inclined to perform that *Vrata*, O excellent Brāhmaṇas. I thought thus in my mind.

44. As there was no food I was compelled to observe fast. Then I took my holy bath in the *Padmaka Tīrtha* in the salty ocean.

45. I thought, I shall worship Lord Maheśvara by means of these lotuses. Then Rudreśa was duly adored by me along with my wife.

46. The Lord was worshipped devoutly by means of the lotuses. Further, my wife had accompanied me in the adora-

tion. Throughout that night, I had kept awake along with my wife.

47-48. After the day had dawned and the disc of the sun had risen, that harlot told me: "Take the three palas of silver as the price of the lotuses." But I did not accept it, O excellent Brāhmaṇas. A Sāttvika feeling arose in me and in my wife.

49. Then I began to beg for alms and thus I sustained my life. Then after a great deal of time, O leading sages, I met with my death.

50. This chaste wife of mine who is dearer to me more than my own life, entered fire along with my dead body.

51. Thanks to its power, I was born as an emperor. Along with my wife I could remember the earlier birth. O excellent Brāhmaṇas, this is the truth.

52. It is for this reason that my devotion is concentrated on this Liṅga permanently along with my wife too. I am speaking the truth to you.

53. O excellent ones, this *Vrata* was performed by me who (as a Śūdra) had been excluded from all holy rites and devotional fervour. This is the great benefit yielded by it.

54. Now I am fully endowed with devotion and I have all essential requisites. What benefit is in store for me in the future, I do not know, O leading sages. Therefore, I have ignored Someśvara and became devouted to this deity (Kedāreśvara).

Īśvara said:

55. On hearing this, those Brāhmaṇas wondered much. With their eyes beaming, they said: "Excellent!Excellent!" They praised the king.

56. They always worshipped that self-born Liṅga. Thanks to the favour of this Liṅga, the most excellent king attained great Siddhi inaccessible even to Devas.

57. Thanks to the favour of the holy Śivarātri and the greatness of that Liṅga, the harlot became the celestial lady Raṁbhā.

58. Hence a sensible man should adore that Liṅga with all means and efforts, if he desires Puruṣārthas viz. virtue, love, wealth and salvation. The deity bestows everything.

CHAPTER FORTY

Bhīmeśvara

Īśvara said:

1-2. Then, O great goddess, a pilgrim should go to the Liṅga of great power installed by Śvetaketu. It was propitiated earlier by Bhīma.

It is in the vicinity of Kedāreśvara and is installed not very far therefrom.

One should worship it in accordance with the injunctions in due order, by means of bathing with milk etc. The pilgrim desirous of getting the benefit of the pilgrimage (here) and the benefit of heavenly pleasures after death, should do so.

The Devī said:

3. O Lord, you have mentioned about the Liṅga of Śvetaketu. How did it come to be named Bhīmeśvara also?

4. How was it evolved before? What is the benefit of viewing it?

Īśvara said:

5. Formerly, in the course of the Svāyaṁbhuva Manvantara, in Tretā Yuga there was a king well-known as Śvetaketu. The saintly king had performed a very severe penance.

6. He came to Prabhāsa, installed Maheśvara and performed a very severe penance on the splendid shore of the ocean.

7. This continued for fourteen years. During the summer he practised the *Pañcāgni* (i.e. four fires were kindled on all sides and the sun blazed above when he performed the penance). During rainy season he remained under the open sky. During winter, he remained in water.

8. In the fourteenth year, I became highly pleased with his penance and observance of restraints. O goddess, I told him, "O sage of good holy rites, choose your boon."

9. Then Śvetaketu said: "O Lord, grant me a steady devotion. If the Lord is pleased, do stay behind in this holy spot."

10-11. After saying "So be it", I vanished there. Later on Śvetaketu of great refulgence propitiated this Liṅga and attained highly prosperous state. Thereupon, It became well-known by the name Śvetaketvīśvara.

12-14. It was in the highly meritorious Agnitīrtha that is destructive of all sins. Thereafter, when Kali Yuga[1] (?) arrived, in the course of his pilgrimage the mighty Bhīmasena, the son of Vāyu, born of a part of mine came to Prabhāsa. Realizing that the Tīrtha is highly meritorious, he installed his own deity Jāgeśvara near the sea, but adored that Liṅga.

15-16. Ever since then the splendid name of the Liṅga was Bhīmeśa. O beautiful lady, if that Liṅga is viewed even once, all the sins committed in earlier births perish. So also those (committed) hereafter.

CHAPTER FORTYONE

Bhairaveśvara

Īśvara said:

1-3. To the east thereof and to the south-east of Someśa, there is a Liṅga of great power, installed by Sarasvatī.

The Vāḍava fire kept in a pot in the form of Bhairaveśvara, was brought by the goddess near the sea.

She left it for a moment to take rest and then the Liṅga was installed. After worshipping it in accordance with the injunctions, she took the Vāḍava fire and cast it into the Sea with a desire for the welfare of the Devas.

4. Thereupon, the Devas became extremely pleased. They adored the goddess with showers of flowers and filled the sky with the sounds of Śaṅkha and Dundubhi drums.

5-6. The Suras named her *Devamātā* (Mother of the Devas) and said to her: "You have accomplished a terrific task that could not be accomplished by Devas and Dānavas and installed

1. It must be Dvāpara Yuga when Pāṇḍavas lived and ruled.

here the Liṅga of great power. You are the most excellent of all rivers and the destroyer of all sins. Hence this Liṅga will become famous by the name Bhairava."

7-9. On being told thus, the goddess stationed herself in the form of an image to the south-east of Bhairaveśvara on the charming shore of the ocean.

A pilgrim should worship her as well as Bhairaveśvara in accordance with the injunction on the Mahānavamī day with great effort. After duly bathing and worshipping Sarasvatī, one becomes rid of all defects of speech.

If the Liṅga is adored after bathing it with milk, uttering the *Aghora Mantra* duly, one will get the benefit of the pilgrimage.

CHAPTER FORTYTWO

Caṇḍīśa

Īśvara said:

1. Then a pilgrim should go over to the excellent Lord Caṇḍīśa, O great goddess. It is situated within a distance of seven *Dhanus* to the north-east of Someśa.

2. It was installed by Caṇḍī formerly not far from the abode of Daṇḍapāṇi. It was then adored by Caṇḍa.

3. After performing a very difficult penance, O goddess of Devas, Caṇḍa, a Gaṇa of mine, propitiated it. Therefore, the Liṅga became well-known all over the earth as Caṇḍeśvara.

4. The pilgrim should at the outset bathe the Liṅga with *Payas* (milk, water), then with curds mixed with ghee, then with honey and sugarcane juice. He should smear it with *Kuṁkuma* (saffron).

5. Then he should apply the liquefied musk mixed with camphor and *Uśīra (Khus)*. Sweet-scented sandalpaste is then applied. The pilgrim should then adore it with flowers.

6. O goddess, incense and agallocham should be fumigated before the Lord. Thereafter, garments are offered during the worship in accordance with one's wealth.

7. The "best cooked rice"[1] (sweet rice pudding) is offered as *Naivedya* along with a lamp. Thereafter, the pilgrim should give monetary gifts to Brāhmaṇas within his capacity.

8. O beautiful lady, the pilgrim should face the southern quarter. Whatever is offered then to Caṇḍīśa, shall become everlasting in its benefit.

9. If the pilgrim performs *Śrāddha* on the right side of Caṇḍīśa, O beautiful lady, the Pitṛs become satisfied for the period of a *Kalpa*.

10. In the course of the *Uttarāyaṇa* (northern transit of the Sun) the pilgrim should perform the rite of *Ghṛtakaṁbala* (wool-like thick application of ghee over the idol or Liṅga). He will never again take up the terrible worldly birth.

11. Thus, the pilgrim performs the Yātrā (pilgrimage) of the Trident-bearing Lord. Thereby the creature becomes rid of various sins such as those caused by overstepping the remnants of the adoration of Śiva, eating unwittingly the prohibited food etc. All the entanglaments due to earlier Karmas perish (get dissolved).

CHAPTER FORTYTHREE

Ādityeśvara

Īśvara said:

1. Then, O beautiful lady, a pilgrim should go to the shrine named Ādityeśvara, destructive of all sins. The Liṅga was installed by Sūrya (the Sun god) himself. It is situated within a distance of seven Dhanus to the west of Someśa.

2. O beautiful woman, O my beloved, O great goddess, the Liṅga was worshipped by the noble-souled Ocean in Tretāyuga for a period of ten thousand years.

3. Therefore, now it is well-known over the earth by the name *Ratneśvara*. The deity should be bathed with *Pañcāmṛta* and worshipped with five jewels.

---

1. *Paramānna* - Rice boiled in milk and mixed with sugar.

4. Then the man should duly worship it with all royal offerings of services. If it is done so, O great goddess, one shall obtain the benefit of *Merudāna* (gifting the great mountain Meru).

5. There is no doubt in this that he will get the merit of performing all *Yajñas* and *Dānas.*

6. He shall get the fruit of (pilgrimage to) all Tīrthas and he will derive every merit on the earth. The man will redeem all the generations on his father's side as well as on the mother's side.

7. By viewing *Ratneśvara,* a man shall wash off all the sins committed during childhood, youth and old age.

8. Great sages praise *Dhenu Dāna* (gift of cows) at that holy spot. The donor of cows redeems ten preceding and ten succeeding generations certainly.

9. He who worships the Liṅga duly and performs the *Japa* of the *Śatarudriya* on the right side of the deity is never born again.

10. Thus, the great prosperity arising from *Ādityeśa* has been succinctly spoken. It should be listened to attentively and retained carefully. The pilgrim is rid of the bondage due to his Karmas.

CHAPTER FORTYFOUR

Someśvara

Īśvara said:

1. After adoring *Ādityeśa,* a pilgrim should once again go to Someśvara and worship the deity duly with all five ancillary features.

2. After viewing Someśvara, the pilgrim prostrates (before the deity) and then circumambulates (it). Again he should view the Lord repeatedly. A pilgrim who, with purity circumambulates the Liṅga of (installed by) the Sun and the Moon gets the same benefit as when *Agniṣṭoma* rite has been performed by him.

3-4. Then the pilgrim proceeds to goddess Umā in the vicinity of Someśvara. He should also proceed to a second image of the goddess in the vicinity of *Daityasūdana* (Viṣṇu).

CHAPTER FORTYFIVE

Aṅgāreśvara

Īśvara said:

1-4. Then, O great goddess, a pilgrim should go to the excellent Aṅgāreśvara established by the Son of the Earth (or Maṅgala) on the north-east of Someśa.

Formerly, O lady of excellent countenance, I was desirous of burning down the Tripuras. Due to anger, tears came out of all the three eyes. They fell down and therefrom arose *Bhūmiputra* (Mars).

He went to Prabhāsa and ever since his childhood, he propitiated Śaṅkara for many years, by means of his penance.

O my beloved, Mahādeva was pleased with him. With his soul extremely delighted he granted him a boon.

5. He said: "O Lord, O Bull-emblemed One, if you are pleased, grant me the state of being a planet. O Lord of all, I am not eager to have any other boon."

6-9. He (the Lord) promised: "So it shall be" and again spoke to him these words: "A man who comes here and devoutly adores me will never get afflicted by you at all. The devotee should perform *Homa* with many red flowers soaked in honey and ghee with great devotion before the deity. With the mode of offering the five types of services, he should strenuously worship you. For the whole of that life, he will never get troubled by you. Further, through the gift of a piece of coral, he will get the desired benefit."

10. After saying thus the Lord vanished here itself. Bhauma (Mars) shines amongst the Planets by means of the aerial chariot.

11. Thus, the excellent greatness of Bhauma has been succinctly spoken. On being listened to it dispels sins and yields freedom from illness.

CHAPTER FORTYSIX

Budheśvara

Īśvara said:

1-3. Then, O great goddess, a pilgrim should proceed towards the Liṅga of great efficacy well-known as Budheśvara.

It is situated to the north of it (Aṅgāreśvara) not very far, say within a couple of *Dhanus* in distance, O beautiful lady.

This Liṅga dispels all sins by its mere vision. O goddess of Devas, Budha (Mercury) performed a great penance there and this pure Liṅga was installed. He then propitiated Sadāśiva.

4. Worshipping the Lord for forty thousand years in accordance with the injunctions, he kept his mind quiescent without straying into anything else. He had the direct vision of Bhava (Śiva).

5. Pleased with him, the Lord granted him the status of being a Planet. The devotee who worships the deity installed by the son of Soma (i.e. Budha) especially on a Wednesday coinciding with the eighth lunar day derives the fruit of (performing) Rājasūya sacrifice.

6. Due to the favour of the deity, no one in the family of the devotee becomes wretched or separated from near and dear ones. He will never have any cause to fear from enemies.

7. Thus, the greatness of the deity installed by Budha has been succinctly spoken. One who listens to it, delights in it and remains pure attains the greatest region.

CHAPTER FORTYSEVEN

Bṛhaspatīśvara

Īśvara said:

1-3. Then, O great goddess, a devotee should go over to the Lord resorted to by *Guru* (Jupiter). It is situated to the east of Umā and south-east of Siddheśa.

This great Liṅga was installed by the Preceptor of Devas.

With great devotion, he propitiated the Liṅga for a thousand years and pleased Śarva, the consort of Umā, the Lord of the Devas. He attained all the cherished desires inaccessible to those who have no self-control.

4. Now he has the knowledge pertaining to Īśvara and the state of being adorable by Devas. He has attained the status of a planet. He rejoices in heaven only.

5-7. A man who views that Lord, never meets with a distressed condition. The affliction brought about by an adverse Bṛhaspati will never torment those excellent men who view the Liṅga installed by Bṛhaspati.

O my beloved, one who duly worships the Liṅga with royal attendance and service, or with devotional fervour, on the fourteenth lunar day in the bright half coinciding with a Thursday attains the greatest region.

8. The man who ritualistically bathes the deity with a thousand *Palas* of Pañcāmṛta devoutly, is rid of the three types of indebtedness.

9. O goddess, he becomes purified of all sins inherited from or pertaining to his mother, father or preceptor. He is rid of all *Dvandvas* (mutually opposed pairs such as pleasure-pain) and he attains salvation.

10. Thus, the greatness of the deity pertaining to (i.e. resorted to by) *Guru* has been succinctly described. He who listens to this with devotional fervour, *Guru* will become pleased with him.

CHAPTER FORTYEIGHT

Śukreśvara

Īśvara said:

1-3. Then, O Great Goddess, a pilgrim should go towards the Liṅga installed by Śukra, to the west of Vibhūtīśvara.

It dispels all sins. It is not far off and it has been created by Śukra himself. At this holy spot, thanks to the power of Rudra, he obtained the Vidyā (secret formula) called Sañjīvanī.

The wise one performed a very severe penance for a thousand

years and propitiated the Odd (three)-eyed Lord. He then attained the status of a Planet.

4. He was swallowed by Śaṁbhu for the sake of accomplishing some task of the Devas. Even as Śukra was held inside the belly, he performed a very severe penance.

5. When more than ten thousand years elapsed Maheśvara was pleased. Thereafter, he was discharged quickly by Śaṁbhu through the seminal path (tube).

6-7. Thereupon, the noble-souled Bhārgava got the name Śukra. The devotee shall keep his mind steady and propitiate the Liṅga. He shall repeat the *Mṛtyuñjaya Mantra* (death-defying formula) one hundred thousand times. He shall (thereby) obtain what is desired.

8. By viewing him and touching him, O beautiful woman, a man becomes rid of all sins committed from birth till death.

9-11. A person whose devotion is highly steady shall undoubtedly obtain the power of *Mṛtasañjīvana* (resuscitating the dead) and *Aṇimā* (becoming as small as an atom) and other supernatural powers *(Siddhis)*.

A devotee who bathes the deity installed by Śukra with Pañcāmṛta and worships with sweet-smelling flowers, will never have seminal affliction.

Thus the greatness of the deity installed by Śukra has been fully described to you, O lady of excellent buttocks. On being heard, it dispels the fear resulting from sins.

CHAPTER FORTYNINE

Śanaiścareśvara

Īśvara said:

1-3. From that Śukreśvara shrine, O Goddess, a pilgrim should go to the highly lustrous Liṅga named Śanaiścareśvara. It is destructive of all great sins.

It is to the west of Budheśvara and to the south-east of Ajādevī from which it is not very far. It is situated only five *Dhanus* away.

It is a *Kalpa Liṅga* (i.e. existing ever since the beginning of the *Kalpa*), O Great Goddess, worshipped by Devas and Dānavas. A very severe and most difficult penance was performed by the Son of Chāyā (i.e. Saturn or Śani).

4. The Lord without beginning or death was brought down to the Liṅga by him. Due to his devotion to Śaṁbhu, he gained his favour and the status of a Planet.

5-7. The great community of Devas and Asuras is afraid of his (adverse) look. In the whole of the Cosmos consisting of mobile and immobile beings, there is no living being, Deva or Dānava who is not afflicted by *Sauri* (i.e. Saturn).

The devotee should worship Saurīśvara Śiva devoutly on Saturdays with Śamī leaves and rice cooked with gingelly seeds, black gram and jaggery. After offering libations in accordance with the injunctions, he should offer a black bull to a Brāhmaṇa.

8. The deity may be eulogized with hymns of diverse kinds taken from the Purāṇas and Śrutis. Or it is possible to propitiate the Lord of Devas with a single hymn.

9. Lord Saurīśvara should be eulogized with a single *Stotra* composed by the powerful King Daśaratha. The Lord should be eulogized for the sake of subduing all afflictions.

The Devī said:

10. How did King Daśaratha compose the hymn of Śanaiścara? How did Lord Śanaiścara become pleased with him?

Īśvara said:

11. There was a very powerful king named Daśaratha in the dynasty of Raghu. He was a very well-known emperor, a former overlord of the seven continents.

12-13. When Śani was at the extremity of Kṛttikā the king was informed by astrologers: "Now Śani will pierce through Rohiṇī and go beyond. This is what is called *Śakaṭabheda*[1] which causes fright even to Suras and Asuras. There will be an extremely disastrous famine lasting for twelve years."

14-15. On hearing the words of the astrologer-sage he in the company of his ministers saw the entire world including

1. The shape of the constellation Rohiṇī is like a cart (Śakaṭa).

the citizens and rural folk got agitated. People said: "This always occurs regularly. The lands, cities, and villages become terrified all round". The king asked the sages beginning with Vasiṣṭha:

Daśaratha said:

16. O most excellent one among Brāhmaṇas, what is the solution of this problem?

Vasiṣṭha said:

17. When the constellation pertaining to Prajāpati (i.e. Rohiṇī) is pierced, how can the subjects (survive)? This combination (of planets etc.) has no remedy to be devised by Brahmā, Indra and others too among the Suras.

18-19. The king pondered over it and decided to take a great risk. He took up his divine bow fitted with divine missiles. He got into his divine golden chariot and hurried towards the stellar zone.

20. His chariot was adorned with jewels. It was decorated with banners, Cāmaras, umbrellas and tinkling bells. There was a lofty flagstaff there. It was fitted with swan-coloured horses.

21. Dazzling with great jewels and refulgent with coronets, he shone in the sky like another Sun.

22-23. He bent the bow as far as his ears after fitting it with a *Saṁhārāstra* (destructive missile). He saw that Śani had already come to the extremity of Kṛttikā and was about to enter Rohiṇī. Daśaratha stood before him with knitted eyebrows. Śani looked at the *Saṁhārāstra* that could suppress Suras and Asuras.

24-26. After laughing (to himself), Saturn spoke these words (as though) out of fear for it: "O great king, your manliness is terrifying to your foes. I looked at the Devas, Asuras, human beings, Siddhas, Vidyādharas, Uragas etc. and found all of them terrified. I am now pleased with your bravery and the power of penance, O great king. Tell me what boon you will like to have. I shall grant you whatever you desire."

Daśaratha said:

27-28. O Śani, as long as the rivers and oceans are in

existence, as long as the moon, sun and earth are present, you must not pierce through Rohiṇī and go beyond.

O Sauri, no other boon is desired from you by me.

On being told thus, Śani granted him a boon of permanent benefit.

29. After receiving this boon, the king became gratified. Sauri once again told him, "O king of excellent holy rites, choose your boon."

30-31. (The king) delighted in his mind requested for this boon from Śani: "O son of Bhāskara, the *Śakaṭa* (Cart-shaped constellation, Rohiṇī) should not be pierced through by you. Never should the famine lasting for twelve years be caused. This fame of mine shall spread all over the three worlds."

Īśvara said:

32-33. The king experienced horripilation on receiving the two boons. He put the bow in the chariot and stood with palms joined in reverence. Meditating on Goddess Sarasvatī and Vināyaka, the leader of Gaṇas, King Daśaratha composed this prayer of Sauri (Śani).

The king said:

(King Daśaratha's prayer to Saturn)

34. Obeisance to the blue-rayed one, to the one resembling a blue lotus. Obeisance to one with the body bereft of flesh, to one with long beard and matted hairs.

35. O dry (lean)-bellied one, O terrible one, obeisance to the one with large eyes. Obeisance to the rough-limbed one. Obeisance to the thick-haired one.

36. Obeisance to one, always distressed with hunger. Obeisance to one who is satisfied always. Obeisance to one in the form of *Kālāgni* (Black fire i.e. Fire at the end of the world).

37. Obeisance to the long one, to the dry one. O black-eyed one, (I offer) obeisance to you. Obeisance to the hollow-eyed one. Obeisance to one very difficult to look at.

38. Obeisance to the frightening one, to the terrible one, to the awe-inspiring one, to the appalling one. Obeisance to

you the all-consuming one. Obeisance to you, O wrinkle-faced one.

39. Obeisance to you, O son of the Sun-god. O Bhāskari, the frightening one. O one with downcast eyes, obeisance to you, O one black in body, obeisance to you.

40. Obeisance to you, O slow-gaited one. Obeisance! Obeisance to the pitiless one. Obeisance to you, the fierce-formed one. Obeisance to you fierce in refulgence.

41. Obeisance to the one always burnt with penance. Obeisance to one always sitting in Yogic posture. Obeisance to you with vision of knowledge, the offspring of the son of Kaśyapa (Sun-god).

42-45. When pleased, you grant a kingdom; when angry you deprive one of it in and instant.

Devas, Asuras, and human beings, beasts, birds and reptiles looked at (adversely) by you, O Sauri, immediately become wretched.

Brahmā, Śakra, Yama, the seven redeeming sages—all these become ousted from their kingdoms on being glared at by your eyes.

The lands, cities, villages, continents, and mountains—when looked at with horrible eyes perish in an instant.

46. Be favourable to me, O Sauri, I have resorted to you for the sake of boons. O Sauri, forgive my fault for the sake of the welfare of all living beings.

Īśvara said:

47. On being eulogized thus by King Daśaratha, Śani, the son of Sun, the king of Planets, spoke these words with hairs standing on ends:

Śani said:

48. O great king of good holy rites, O scion of the family of Raghu, I am pleased with this prayer of thine. Tell me what boon you will like to have; I shall grant that voluntarily.

Daśaratha said:

49. O tawny-eyed one, from now onwards no one should

be afflicted, none among the Devas, Asuras and human beings, among beasts, birds and reptiles.

Śani said:

50. I should be known as an evil Planet among all the Planets. I cause affliction as a Planet. O king, something that should not be given has been requested for. I am ready to grant something which is appropriate.

51-53. To men or women who recite the hymn composed by you on me after being afflicted with fear of mine, to Devas, Asuras and human beings, to Siddhas, Vidyādharas and Uragas I shall grant permanent welfare. I may be staying in the House of Death or I may be in the House of Nativity (in their horoscopes), they should recite the hymn once or twice a day, the devotee should worship me and repeat the Stotra in all reverence with palms joined together.

54. I will not cause affliction to him at any time whether I am present in the House of Nativity or in the House of Death (in his horoscope).

55. I shall always grant him protection from other Planets too and their affliction in the Constellation of Nativity or Lagna or in the *Daśās* (aspects of Planets) or *sub-Daśās*.

56. In this manner he shall be rid of afflictions. Thus the boon asked for by you has been granted by me, O scion of Raghu's family.

Īśvara said:

57. After acquiring the pair of boons formerly, King Daśaratha considered himself blessed. He bowed to Śanaiścara with reverence.

58. After eulogizing Śani and on being permitted by him, the powerful king got into his chariot and went back to his abode. He was duly honoured by the Heaven-dwellers.

59. If any man gets up early in the morning on a Saturday and recites this *Stotra* he will never suffer from affliction caused by any Planet.

60. One should always remember Lord Śaṇaiścara with great devotion. One should recite the Stotra after adoration. The Son of Bhāskara (Śani) becomes pleased with him.

61. Thus, O goddess, the greatness pertaining to the deity

Śani (or deity installed by Śani) has been told to you. It suppresses all sins. It yields all the desired benefits.

CHAPTER FIFTY

Greatness of Rāhvīśvara

Īśvara said:

1-3. Thereafter, O great goddess, the pilgrim should proceed to the Liṅga well installed by Rāhu to the north-west of Śanaiścara.

It is situated within a distance of seven *Dhanus* to the north of Ajādevī. It is also in the vicinity of Maṅgalā, not very far off.

The Liṅga installed by Saiṁhikeya (Rāhu) is of great efficacy. Vaipracitti (Rāhu) performed a penance there for a thousand years.

4-5. That mighty and great Asura, Svarbhānu, adept in crooked fighting propitiated the great Lord by means of his wonderful penance and caused Maheśvara, the light of the Universe, to come down in the Liṅga.

He who worships it with devotion and views it clearly shall get his sin reduced to nothing, even if it be the result of Brāhmaṇa-slaughter.

6. If he is viewed, the devotee, the man, never becomes blind, deaf, dumb, sick or poor.

7. He becomes handsome and richly endowed with happiness and conjugal felicity. With all his desires richly realized, he rejoices like a Deva in heaven.

8. Thus, O goddess, the greatness of the deity installed by Rāhu has been spoken to you. One listening to this, comes out of delusion and becomes free from sins.

CHAPTER FIFTYONE

Greatness of Ketvīśvra

Īśvara said:

1-3. Then, O great goddess, a pilgrim should go to Ketuliṅga of great lustre. It is on the north of Rāhvīśāna and the south of Maṅgalā.

It is situated not very far off, say, within a few Dhanus. This Liṅga is of great efficacy and is destructive of all sins.

The Planet named Ketu is extremely ferocious but sanctified by means of *Śivasadbhāva* (good feelings towards Lord Śiva). He is extremely terrible with round large eyes.

4. He resembles in colour smoke emitted by burning straws, dispels the afflictions caused by evil Planets, and O my beloved, he performed a severe penance there for a hundred years according to divine reckoning.

5. Mahādeva was pleased with him and granted him the status of a Planet and also the overlordship of eleven hundred *Grahas* (Planets).

6-7. At the time of the terrible rise of Ketu, especially when he is seen, and also during the horrible afflictions caused by evil Planets, one should worship the deity in accordance with the injunctions.

The devotee should adore the deity with flowers, sweet scents, incense and splendid *Naivedyas* of various kinds.

8. He should duly propitiate Lord Ketu, the destroyer of sins.

9. Thus Ketuliṅga granting great prosperity has been succinctly mentioned. It suppresses the afflictions caused by the Planets and destroys all sins.

10. Thus the nine Liṅgas of the Planets have been spoken to you. If a man views them all everyday, whence can he have the fear of afflictions?

11. O goddess, wretchedness never occurs in his family. No sick or miserable one is born in his family. The great Planets protect him like a son.

12. Thus, O my beloved, the fourteen shrines beginning with Vighneśvara and ending with the shrine installed by Ketu, have been described to you.

13. The greatness of the deities of the nine Planets is destructive of sins. So also is that of the five Liṅgas. By listening to it, one is rid of all sins.

14. A man devoid of merits never knows the five *Mudrā Liṅgas* beginning with *Kapardin* and ending with *Caṇḍanātha.*

15. No one else knows the Liṅgas of the nine Planets beginning with Sūryeśvara and ending with Ketuliṅga.

16. Thus the fourteen types of shrine setting have been described. He who attentively knows this, attains the benefit of (visiting) the holy spots.

CHAPTER FIFTYTWO

Greatness of Siddheśvara

Īśvara said:

1-2. O glorious lady, I shall describe to you the five *Siddha Liṅgas,* which on being seen make the pilgrimage of men fruitful or perfectly accomplished.

Lord Siddheśvara is stationed to the east of the deity remembered as Varārohā situated to the north-east of Someśa. A man who visits with devotion this great Siddheśvara shall acquire supernatural powers like *Aṇimā* etc.

3. By devoutly viewing the Liṅga installed by Siddhas, a man is rid of all sins. He goes to the Siddhaloka.

4-6. All obstacles of the residents of those holy spots are destroyed. The obstacles are lust, anger, fear, covetousness, passion, rivalry, jealousy, hypocrisy, lethargy, drowsiness, delusion and egotism. These are obstacles to the achievement of (spiritual) perfection.

By worshipping the Siddheśvaras there all these obstacles disappear. One should undertake the pilgrimage strenuously after knowing this very well.

7. Thus, O goddess, the great rise and prosperity of Siddheśvara has been spoken. It yields all cherished desires unto men. If listened to (attentively), it is destructive of sins.

CHAPTER FIFTYTHREE

Greatness of Kapileśvara

Īśvara said:

1-4. Then, O great goddess, a pilgrim should go to the

excellent shrine of Kapileśvara. It is stationed not far from it (i.e. Siddheśvara) in the eastern quarter.

This Liṅga is of very great power. It destroys sins by its very sight. A saintly king named Kapila performed a great penance there after installing Maheśvara. He attained great Siddhi (spiritual achievement). Hari always worships Īśāna in the presence of the Devas in that Liṅga.

Especially on the fourteenth lunar day in the bright half of a month, he worships, Mahādeva seven times, for the sake of the welfare of all the worlds.

One who remains pure and clean and visits Someśa named Kapileśvara shall attain the merit of gifting cows.

5. O my beloved, one who is mentally pure and offers *Tiladhenu* (cow made of gingelly seeds) in that holy spot, remains in heaven for as many Yugas as there are gingelly seeds.

CHAPTER FIFTYFOUR

Greatness of Gandharveśvara

Īśvara said:

1-3. Then, O great goddess, one should go to the excellent Gandharveśvara. It is situated very near, to the north of the abode of Daṇḍapāṇi.

It was here that the king of Gandharvas well-known as *Ghanavāha* (ruled). His daughter well-known as Gandharvasenā was highly lustrous.

She was arrogant due to her beauty and so was cursed by a Gaṇa named Śikhaṇḍin. Thereupon, blessings were given to her by Sage Gośṛṅga.

4-5. He directed her to propitiate Someśa by means of the *Somavāra Vrata*. Thereafter, the king of Gandharvas himself came to the holy spot and performed very difficult penance and installed a Liṅga. Another Liṅga was installed by his own daughter.

6-7. O goddess of Devas, one who scrupulously worships the Liṅga named Ghanavāheśvara there itself in the vicinity of Daṇḍapāṇi and/or visits the deity, himself being clean and pure, attains Gandharva world. Thus, O goddess, the excellent Gandharva Liṅga has been spoken to you.

8-9. It is the third Liṅga (in this context). It is destructive of all sins and it increases merit. A man who bathes in the Agnitīrtha and worships the Liṅga adored by Gandharvas at the time of the northern transit of the Sun, attains salvation. By listening to and approving the greatness of it, one is rid of great danger.

CHAPTER FIFTYFIVE

Greatness of Vimaleśvara

Īśvara said:

1-3. Then, O great goddess, one should go to Vimaleśvara (stationed) to the east thereof. It is very near, not far from Gaurī's shrine.

It is situated on the south-west of Guru (Jupiter). It is destructive of sins. Even after committing a great sin, a devotee, be it a woman or a man, becomes pure.

Even one who is afflicted with pulmonary consumption, attains the destruction of all miseries by adoring the deity with devotion. He shall attain the region devoid of impurities.

4. It was there that Gandharvasenā who was afflicted with phthysis got rid of impurities. That Liṅga has become famous all the world over by the name Vimaleśvara.

5. Thus the greatness of Vimaleśvara has been entirely spoken to you, O beautiful lady of Bhava. It is the fourth (Liṅga) destructive of all sins.

CHAPTER FIFTYSIX

Greatness of Dhanadeśvara

Īśvara said:

1-3. Henceforth I shall describe the fifth *Siddha Liṅga* of great lustre. It is situated on the south-western side of Brahmā at a distance of about sixteen bows.

The Liṅga installed by *Dhanada* (i.e. Kubera, the bestower of wealth) is near Rāhuliṅga. Here he performed great penance and attained the status of Dhanada (Giver of wealth).

He installed the Liṅga and duly worshipped it for a thousand years. With the favour of Śaṁbhu, he became the Lord of Alakā.

4-7. He remembered his previous birth and knowing the merit of supplying a wick for lamp and the power of Śivarātri, came to Prabhāsa.

Knowing the great power of it he installed Śaṅkara. By means of penance, he made Śaṅkara manifest. O great goddess, by means of his great devotion he caused Śaṅkara to come down in that Liṅga. A man of devotion should visit it and perform worship duly observing the five *Upacāras* (varieties of service) and offering scents, incense and unguents with great devotion. Never will a destitute person be born in his family.

8-9. Those men who with devotion worship the Liṅga become invincible to enemies whose arrogance they will destroy.

Thus the greatness of Dhandeśa has been fully spoken to you. By listening to this and approving of it, one shall avert poverty.

CHAPTER FIFTYSEVEN

Greatness of Varārohā

Īśvara said:

1-4. Thus, O my beloved, five Siddhaliṅgas have been spoken to you. He who understands this convention is called *Kṣetravāsin* (a resident of holy spot).

Henceforth, I shall describe in detail the three Śaktis of Rudra to you. They are: *Icchā* (Volition), *Jñāna* (Knowledge) and *Kriyā* (Action) of the Liṅgas mentioned to you previously. Listen to the sequence of their worship. A devotee duly worships fourteen, five, four, three or one in accordance with his capacity and thereafter adores the three *Śaktis*.

5. The deity stationed on the north-east of Someśa and remembered as Varārohā is the digit *Amā* of Soma (Moon). It is later glorified as Umā.

6. The deity is to be known as *Icchā Śakti*. She is stationed in Prabhāsa Kṣetra, O goddess, for the welfare of all the living beings on the earth.

7-9. Now I shall fully narrate the greatness of that deity to you. O lady of excellent countenance, a penance was performed by the twenty-six wives ignored and abandoned by Soma. For many years according to the divine reckoning, Gaurī was propitiated in the splendid holy spot of Prabhāsa. Pārvatī, the great goddess, became manifest to them and said: "I am the bestower of boons. Do tell me what has been thought of in your minds."

10-11. Then they said: "O goddess Pārvatī, if you are pleased, grant unto us the utmost conjugal felicity and excellent loveliness. O splendid goddess, though guiltless, all of us have been deserted by our Lord and master. We have been scorched by the fault of unluckiness and afflicted by adverse fate."

Gaurī said:

12. From now onwards the Lord of the Night (Soma) will treat all of you alike, with my favour. O ladies of exquisitely beautiful limbs, this will never be false.

13-16. On account of this granting of the boon, my name will be Varadā. If any woman comes here and adores me, the splendid one, the women in her family will never meet with bad luck.

A woman of excellent hips who observes fast on the third lunar day in the month of Māgha and views me, will be on a par with me.

A woman who scrupulously offers garments to sixteen couples and feeds them with fruits and various foodstuffs as well as sixteen types of sweetmeats will definitely become Umā.

17. A woman of ill-luck and one who has not yet given birth to any child, should perform this holy rite named *Gaurīvrata* on the third lunar day.

18. A man who performs this Vrata frequently shall obtain the desired things.

After saying this, that goddess of beautiful eyes stood by.

19-21. The Lord of the Night began to treat all of them as he treated Rohiṇī. Another woman scorched by misery and blighted by misfortune worshipped Goddess Umā and she became happy and lucky thereafter.

Thus the greatness of *Śakti* has been succinctly described. The name Varārohā of thine, has been mentioned in the holy spot of Someśvara. It causes the destruction of all sins and of poverty of all sorts.

CHAPTER FIFTYEIGHT

Greatness of Ajāpāleśvarī

Īśvara said:

1-4. Henceforth, O goddess, I shall describe unto you the *Śakti* of the nature of *Kriyā (Action)*. It is stationed in Prabhāsa as the great goddess bestowing pleasure on Devas.

The deity is situated within a distance of sixty *Dhanus* in the north-west direction of Someśvara. O great goddess, the pedestal there is honoured by groups of Yoginīs.

At that spot, O goddess, there is a great *Pātāla Vivara* (the great crevice leading to the nether worlds). In that highly lustrous spot, she is stationed for protection and security.

One engaged in adoring that deity shall obtain excellent medicines and valuable treasures of Pātāla, present in the centre of the holy spot.

5. The earlier name of that goddess was Bhairavī.

There was a king named Ajāpāla in the beginning of the Tretā Yuga of the twenty-eighth set of four Yugas *(Caturyuga)* in this Manvantara.

6. O beautiful woman, he was afflicted by diseases. So he came to this holy spot. Goddess Bhairavī was adored by him in this Kṣetra for five hundred years.

7. The goddess who was pleased said to that excellent king: "Do not strain yourself, O saintly king, I am pleased with your devotion."

8. On being told thus, the wise king joined his palms together. With his eyes dimmed with tears of joy, he bowed down and said to the goddess:

9. "O goddess, if you are pleased with me and if I deserve boons, may all the ailments in my body be destroyed and expelled."

10. On being told thus the goddess said to the king again: "O great king, all will happen as mentioned now."

11. As soon as it was uttered by the goddess, all the ailments came out severally from the body of the king in the form of goats.

12. These were definitely five thousand fifty of them. When this happened, the king was again addressed by the goddess:

13. "O king, take full care of these ailments in the forms of goats. They will be your servants carrying out your behests.

14. Your name will become well-known in the world as Ajāpāla and after your name, my name Ajāpāleśvarī shall spread over the earth till the *Caturyuga* is complete.

15. When pleased, I shall undoubtedly grant eightfold *Aiśvarya* (prosperity and power) to the person who adores me here on the eighth and fourteenth lunar days.

16. On the eighth lunar day in the bright half of the month of Aśvayuj, the devotee should circumambulate Someśa three times. He should keep me in the centre, bathe me and adore me separately. No fear or sorrow shall befall him, O king, for three years.

17. A barren woman, a sick one and an unlucky one should perform worship in front of me on the ninth lunar day of the half and month mentioned before. It shall enhance her pleasure.

Īśvara said:

18-19. After saying this, the goddess vanished there itself. Staying in the middle of the holy spot of Prabhāsa Kṣetra, that king of unequalled valour righteously reared those transformations of ailments into goats. He fed them with various kinds of medicinal herbs causing their nourishment.

20. The goats were nourished thus for more than a hundred years. A big place for storage was built by Ajāpāla.

21. Then due to her (the deity's) favour the king became extremely valorous. An ornament unto the solar race, he became the Lord of all the seven continents.

The Devī said:

22-23. O Lord, this origin of the goddess Ajā is wonderful. I wish to know further the great, miraculous story of that king. O Lord of Devas, how did that king rule the earth consisting of seven continents by himself alone? How were those Ailments kept?

Īśvara said:

24. Formerly there was a saintly king well-known as Dilīpa. His son was Dīrgha (?) and Raghu was born of him[1].

25. Aja was the son of Raghu. He excelled him in valour. By propitiating Bhairavī, he transformed the ailments into groups of goats.

26. With great delight he reared them. Therefore, he became Ajāpāla. Rāvaṇa was the king of Rākṣasas at that time.

27. Residing in Laṅkā, he employed groups of Suras in his own service. He made the Moon of complete disc, his own umbrella.

28. He made Indra the chief of his army, Vāyu, the sweeper of dust particles, Varuṇa, one engaged in carrying messages, and Dhanada cashier in-charge of monetary affairs.

29. He employed Yama for curbing and controlling his enemies, and Manu as counsellor. Clouds vomited (showered) and smeared (?). The trees scattered flowers.

30. The Saptarṣis (seven sages) of quiescent disposition were appointed as the Brāhmaṇas, speaking pleasing things. *Nāgas* (Serpents) were put in the guardroom and Gandharvas were made to attend musical performance.

31. The group of celestial damsels was engaged in dramatic performance. Vidyādharas were assigned musical instruments. Gaṅgā and other rivers were made in-charge of preparation of beverages. Hutāśana (Fire-god) was given the charge of *Gārhapatya* (culinary duties).

32. The divine architect Viśvakarman was engaged by him in Aṅgasaṁskāra (the duties of a barber for massage etc.). All the kings stood before him ready to serve him.

---

1. Dilīpa was the father of Raghu according to VR and Mbh. "Dīrgha" is a new name not traceable (as Dilīpa's son) both in VR and Mbh.

33-34. They faltered in their steps due to their dazzling jewels. On seeing them, Rāvaṇa said to Prahasta, his door-keeper: "Tell me, who have all come to my place in order to render service?".

The demon-attendant armed with his staff bowed before him and said:

35[1]-36. "This is Kākutstha, this is Māndhātā, this Dhundhumāra, this Nala, this Arjuna, Yayāti, Nahuṣa, Bhīma, Vidūratha the scion of the family of Raghu—these and many other kings have come here to your place for rendering services. But Ajāpāla has not come here."

37. The furious Rāvaṇa said: "Send a messenger quickly." After being told thus, the Rākṣasa named Dhūmrākṣa was sent as messenger:

38-40. "O Dhūmrākṣa, go. Tell Ajāpāla at my behest: O king, either come to render service or pay tribute. If not I will make you headless by means of my sword Candrahāsa."

On being told thus by Rāvaṇa, Dhūmrākṣa flew like Garuḍa, reached that beautiful city and entered the royal abode. There he saw Ajāpāla coming alone but surrounded by his goats.

41. His hairs were dishevelled. His robes were loose. He was having a golden blanket round his body. There was a staff on his shoulder. He was dust-covered and surrounded by the ailments.

42. He was like a murderous (ferocious) tiger ready to destroy and resist all onslaughts. He was killing the groups of enemies simply by writing down their names on the earth.

43. He appeared to have had his bath and food. He was seated in his place blessed and contented like Manu. On seeing him, Dhūmrākṣa was delighted in his mind. He spoke out what was spoken by Rāvaṇa.

44. After a defiant reproach and a suitable reply Ajāpāla dismissed Dhūmrākṣa back and attended to his duties.

45. The king summoned *Jvara* (fever) and spoke thus, "Go to the abode of the king of Laṅkā and do as you are ordered."

46. Directed by Ajāpāla, *Jvara* went through space. After going (to Laṅkā) he made the Rākṣasa king Rāvaṇa tremble.

---

1. Fictitious big names. None of them was a contemporary of Rāvaṇa.

47. Rāvaṇa realized that it was the highly terrible *Jvara* and said: "Let the king stay away. I don't have anything to do with him."

48. Then the younger brother of Dhanada, the king (Rāvaṇa), became free from fever. Thus there are millions of his other activities.

49. O goddess of Devas, there are innumerable such acts of Ajāpāla having a crown resplendent like the sun. This goddess was propitiated by such an intelligent king Ajāpāla. The deity suppresses all ailments. She destroys all torments.

50. If a man is desirous of enjoyment of pleasure, he should worship her in accordance with the injunctions, devoutly offering scents, incense, ornaments, garments and other things.

51. Thus the origin of Ajādevī has been fully narrated to you. It suppresses all miseries and destroys all sins.

CHAPTER FIFTYNINE

Greatness of Ajādevī

Īśvara said:

1-2. Henceforth, I shall describe unto you the third deity *Jñānaśakti* (power of knowledge), identical with Śiva. She resides in the holy Prabhāsa Kṣetra and is destructive of poverty in abundance.

The goddess is named Ajā. She is stationed to the south of Rāhvīśa. She has issued forth from my sixth mouth/face adored by Viṣṇu.

The Devī said:

3. O my Lord, O Lord of Devas! Five faces of yours are well-known. What may be the name of the sixth face, O Lord? How did the deity well-known as Ajādevī issue forth therefrom?

Īśvara said:

4. O goddess, what has been asked by you is pertinent. I

shall describe unto you what should be kept as a secret even from one's own sons. It was (originally) narrated in an *Āgama* (scriptural text) which is not (so) well-known.

5. Earlier, even at the outset, O goddess of Devas, I had seven faces. Five are *Sadyojāta*[1] etc. The sixth one is remembered as *Aja* (Unborn).

6. The seventh one was named *Picu*. Thus I had seven faces. Of them *Aja* was given to Brahmā and *Picu* to Viṣṇu.

7. Hence, O great goddess, I now become five-faced. *Aja* became Brahmā and *Picu* became Viṣṇu.

8. From the face *Aja,* O great goddess, (the Deity) *Ajā* of great lustre was born. O beautiful lady, it was at the time of the terrible fight with Andhāsura and that too due to my anger.

9. The goddess held a sword and a shield. Riding on a lion, she had a splendid form. She was accompanied by crores of other goddesses. She crushed the great Daityas.

10. A few Daityas fled to the southern sea out of fear of her. The lion-riding goddess chased them closely behind.

11. Running here and there, they were slain by her Gaṇas. In the course of their destruction, they proceeded towards the great sea and reached Prabhāsa.

12-13. Some of the Daityas were slain there. Some went to Pātāla (nether worlds). On seeing that they were all killed, the goddess riding a lion realized the sanctity of the place. The splendid deity haltred at that place, stationing herself to the north-east of Someśa and to the north of Saurīśa.

14. Whoever, whether a man or a woman, views her stationed there, shall become endowed with Sattva quality and conjugal felicity for the duration of seven births.

15. If a man arranges for vocal music, instrumental music and dance there, there shall be no wretchedness in his family, due to her favour.

16. O great goddess, if any woman offers a lamp with ghee (clarified butter) with a red wick there, she will attain conjugal felicity in the course of as many births as there are threads there in the wick.

---

1. This is the *Pratīka* (first word) of the first of the five Mantras from *Taittirīya Āraṇyaka* XVII. 1-5. There five Mantras constitute the five heads of Śiva.

17. He who reads this daily, especially on the third lunar day, or listens to this devoutly, shall obtain all cherished desires.

18-19. Thus it has been described succinctly how, in what order, the three *Śaktis* of Rudra are to be worshipped.

After adoring these *Śaktis* the devotee should worship Someśa, if he is desirous of the full benefit of the pilgrimage. Or he may worship one *Śakti* who is the bestower of boons.

CHAPTER SIXTY

Greatness of Maṅgalā

Īśvara said:

1-3. O my beloved, one of excellent complexion, I shall describe the three *Dūtīs* (lady-messengers) of the holy spot of Prabhāsa. Listen with an attentive mind.

The first one is goddess Maṅgalā. The second one is Viśālākṣī and goddess Catvaradevī is glorified as the third one.

O lady of excellent countenance, those *Śaktis* are to be worshipped in this order, if a man is desirous of attaining the benefit of the pilgrimage to Prabhāsa.

The Devī said:

4. O Lord, at what spot did those *Dūtīs,* the guardians of the holy spot, halt and stationed themselves. Of whom are they the *Śaktis*? How are they to be propitiated? O Lord of the universe, how are they to be adored?

Īśvara said:

5. Maṅgalā is said to be of Brahmā; Viśālākṣi is of Viṣṇu. The deity Catvarapriyā is the *Śakti* of Rudra.

6. O lady of excellent countenance, Maṅgalā who is stationed to the north of Ajādevī and to the south of Rāhvīśa, not very far, should be worshipped first.

7. When Someśvara was installed and the rite of *Yajña* was started, she had come there along with Soma (the Moon) with a desire to see the Devas.

8. O Umā, since she gave auspiciousness unto Brahmā and others, she is called Maṅgalā. She is the bestower of all auspiciousness.

9. Inauspiciousness and miseries due to it, shall entirely perish in regard to that person, be it a man or a woman, who adores her on the third lunar day.

10. Feeding a couple and offering them fruits along with a bodice at that site is laudable. Feeding of *Pṛṣadājya* (ghee mixed with curds) is destructive of sins.

11. Thus the greatness of Maṅgalā has been succinctly spoken. It is conducive to great fortune and great benefit as a result and it is destructive of all sins.

CHAPTER SIXTYONE

Greatness of Lalitomāviśālākṣī

Īśvara said:

1-4. Then a pilgrim should go to the great goddess *Kṣetradevī* of Viṣṇu, O goddess. She is stationed to the east of Śrīdaityasūdana and within a distance of seven bows *(Dhanus)* to the north-east of Yogeśvarī.

She has established herself as the medicine (balm) unto those who are burned (by the fire) of great wretchedness.

In the Cākṣuṣa Manvantara, O goddess, when the excessively powerful Daityas proceeded towards the southern quarter on being slain by Viṣṇu, they fought for more than a hundred years in a great battle there with Viṣṇu. O goddess of Devas, they fought with wonderful missiles of various kinds.

5. Knowing that they could not be killed easily, the lotus-eyed Viṣṇu remembered Bhairavī *Śakti*, the Mahāmāyā of great lustre.

6. On being remembered by Viṣṇu, the all-powerful one, the great goddess came there within a moment with her eyes shining with great delight.

7. At the sight of Viṣṇu, the eyes became large and wide *(Viśāla)*. Hence the goddess stationed there who is the destroyer of Daityas, became (known as) Viśālākṣī.

8. In this Kalpa, O lady of excellent countenance, she is called Lalitomā. Thus there are two Umās mentioned, one in Someśa and the other in Daityasūdana (Viṣṇu).

9. The pilgrim should view (Umā) at the outset in Someśvara and then in *Daityasūdana* thereafter. By worshipping the two Umās, one will derive the full benefit of the pilgrimage.

10. If a devotee duly worships her on the third lunar day in the month of Māgha, he shall never be devoid of progeny. His line will extend to ten millions.

11. He who is endowed with great devotion and visits her everyday, shall be always blessed with health, happiness and conjugal felicity for a long time.

12. Thus the greatness of Lalitā has been succinctly spoken. If listened to, it becomes conducive to the destruction of sins and increase of piety.

CHAPTER SIXTYTWO

Greatness of Catvarādevī

Īśvara said:

1-4. Thereafter, a pilgrim should go to the third goddess Catvarapriyā. O great goddess, she is stationed on the eastern side of Lalitā within a distance of ten *Dhanus*.

She is the great and terrible Kṣetradūtī, the *Śakti* of Rudra possessing great lustre. She was left there in the centre for the job of guarding the holy spot by me.

She is accompanied by a crore of *Bhūtas* (goblins). She is huge-bodied and highly lustrous. Surrounded by crores of *Bhūtas*, the goddess wanders at night in dilapidated houses, gardens, palaces, attics, paths, courtyards—everywhere within the holy spot.

5-6. If a man or a woman duly adores her on the great Navamī day, with all types of service-offerings, the splendid goddess becomes pleased with him or her and grants all cherished desires. Feeding of couples must be performed by those who wish for the benefit of the pilgrimage.

7. Thus the greatness of the third Kṣetradūtī has been succinctly spoken. On being listened to it she bestows prosperity and destroys sins.

CHAPTER SIXTYTHREE

Greatness of Bhairaveśvara

Īśvara said:

1-3. Thereafter, O great goddess, a pilgrim should go to the excellent Bhairaveśvara. It is stationed not very far from Yogeśvarī to the south.

It is destructive of sins. It bestows supernatural prosperity and glory. Formerly when the goddess made effort for the destruction of Daityas, she summoned Bhairava and employed him as a messenger. Then she became well-known as Śivadūtī and thereafter as Yogeśvarī.

4-5. The place where Bhairava was employed as a messenger by the goddess, has the Liṅga called by the name Bhairaveśvara.

It is installed by Bhairava and is adored by Devas and Daityas. A man who devoutly adores it duly on the Kārttikī day or continuously for six months, obtains the desired benefit.

CHAPTER SIXTYFOUR

Greatness of Lakṣmīśvara

Īśvara said:

1-3. To the eastern side of the same is the shrine well-known as Lakṣmīśvara stationed within a distance of ten *Dhanus*. It is destructive of series of impoverished states.

At the place where Lakṣmī was brought by the Supreme Devī after killing the Daityas, is the idol named Lakṣmīśvara installed by the supreme goddess herself.

He who devoutly worships that Lord in accordance with the

injunctions on Śrīpañcamī day (i.e. the fifth lunar day in the bright half of Māgha) is never separated from Lakṣmī (fortune) till the end of the Manvantara, O my beloved!

CHAPTER SIXTYFIVE

Greatness of Vāḍaveśvara

Īśvara said:

1-4. Thereafter, a pilgrim should go to the shrine of Vāḍaveśvara Liṅga to the northern side of Lakṣmīśa and to south of Viśālākṣī.

It is stationed there. It has great efficacy. It was installed by Vāḍava at the time when the mountain Kṛtasmara was burnt by the Vāḍava fire.

The Liṅga was installed by him after levelling the entire spot. After bathing Lord Śaṅkara with curds, the pilgrim should worship him in accordance with the injunctions.

The pilgrim should offer curds there to a Brāhmaṇa who has mastered the Vedas. Thereby he attains the Agniloka and obtains the full benefit of a perfect pilgrimage.

CHAPTER SIXTYSIX

Greatness of Arghyeśvara

Īśvara said:

1-4. Thereafter, a pilgrim should go to the great Liṅga well- known as Arghyeśvara. It is situated to the north of Viśālākṣī not very far from there.

Worshipped by Suras and Gandharvas, this Liṅga is highly powerful. The goddess (river) reached Prabhāsa Kṣetra holding the Vāḍava fire and when she saw the great ocean there, she offered *Arghya* in accordance with the injunctions to the great ocean.

After installing the great Liṅga and worshipping it in accordance with the injunctions, O goddess of Devas, she entered the great ocean for the sake of holy ablution.

5-6. Since the *Arghya* was offered earlier and the Lord is installed later, the Liṅga is well-known as Arghyeśa.

It is destructive of sins. O goddess of Devas, one who bathes the Lord with Pañcāmṛta in accordance with the injunctions and worships him, acquires learning in seven births. He will be a perfect expounder of the scriptures. He will have perfect knowledge, enabling him to clarify all doubts.

CHAPTER SIXTYSEVEN

Greatness of Kāmeśvara

Īśvara said:

1-4. Thereafter, a pilgrim should go to the shrine of the great Liṅga well-known as Kāmeśvara. It is to the west of Daityasūdana and was worshipped by Kāma. O goddess, it is stationed within a distance of seven *Dhanus* and is highly refulgent.

When Kāma was reduced to ashes by my third (eye) of fire, he propitiated Maheśvara. The disembodied one propitiated Maheśvara for a thousand years and attained a creative form as he desired.

Therefore, the Liṅga became well-known all over the earth by the name Kāmeśvara. O goddess, it is destructive of all sins and it bestows all the desired benefits.

5. One who worships the Liṅga according to injunctions on the thirteenth lunar day in the bright half of the month of Vaiśākha, shall become one like Kāma unto women.

CHAPTER SIXTYEIGHT

Greatness of Gaurī-Tapovana

Īśvara said:

1-3. Thus, O goddess, the five Vaktra-Liṅgas (or Liṅgas corresponding to the five faces) have been described to you. Henceforth, I shall describe the holy spot where there is the penance grove of Gaurī. It is highly powerful and is resorted to by Suras and Siddhas.

It is situated within a distance of sixty *Dhanus* on the eastern side of Someśa. It is the place where penance was performed by goddess Satī in her earlier birth.

Due to offended love, she was angry with me, O lady of excellent countenance, and she came to Prabhāsa Kṣetra and remained here performing penance.

The Devī said:

4. Why did Satī forsake you and resort to penance? At what place did the goddess establish herself? Do tell me all this in detail.

Īśvara said:

5. O great goddess, formerly you were a lady of exalted mind but of dark complexion. While (we were in a splendid spot) you were called Kālī by me simply for fun (Read: *narmārtham* for *nāmārtham*).

6. On hearing the surprising statment, she (you) became highly furious. Knitting her (your) eyebrows crookedly in the face, she (you) spoke harsh words:

7. "Since I was called "blackie" (Kālī), O Śaṁbhu, with great malice, I shall go away to a place where I will become *Gaurī* (fair-complexioned)."

8. After saying thus, the highly esteemed lady surrounded by groups of companions went to Prabhāsa Kṣetra. She installed Maheśvara, later famous as Gaurīśvara, and adored in accordance with the injunctions.

9. Closely standing near the Liṅga on a single foot, the chaste lady propitiated the Liṅga and performed a very great penance.

10. Engaging herself in *Japa,* the goddess practised penance in the midst of five fires in summer. During rainy season, she remained lying down under the open sky. During *Hemanta* (early winter) she stood under water.

11. As her penance advanced, the excessive refulgence of her body assumed whitishness (fair complexion).

12. After a great deal of time she became *Gaurī* (fair-complexioned) in all her limbs. Thereupon, the Moon-crested Lord laughed and said:

13. He uttered the epithet (Gaurī) many times—"O Gaurī, get up. Come on to the mansion. O auspicious lady, choose your boon, whatever may be in your mind."

Gaurī said:

14. A person whether a man or a woman, who may view me stationed here, shall become endowed with sons and good fortunes for seven births (in succession).

15. Due to your favour, let there be no wretchedness in the family of a person who makes arrangement for vocal and instrumental music as well as dance in front of me.

16. He who adores the Liṅga installed by me at the outset and then devoutly adores me, shall attain the highest region.

17. O Lord, let the name of the Lord be Gaurīśvara and be well-known.

I promised, "So it shall be" and stationed myself at that holy spot.

18-19. O great goddess, I stationed myself there in the company of the goddess with a delighted mind. Even today, during the transit of the Sun in the northern as well as the southern direction I go to the holy spot of Gaurī accompanied by groups of Devas. He who offers excellent fruits to Brāhmaṇas on that day, will have sons.

20. A woman without a son, who offers a coconut fruit there, shall soon obtain a strong son endowed with all good features.

21-22. If, O great goddess, a woman offers a light with ghee and red wicks, she shall attain conjugal felicity in as many successive births as there are threads in the wick.

23. One who performs a dance there full of great devotion, shall become blessed with freedom from ailments, happiness, and conjugal felicity for a long time.

24. There, at the boundary, there is a great pond. It is a holy *Tīrtha* filled with clear water. One who takes his holy bath there becomes rid of all sins.

25. He who performs Śrāddha there with the Pitṛs in view

devoutly attains the highest region along with the Pitṛs. He will be a meritorious person.

26. Hence by all means a devotee should perform Śrāddha there. He should keep vigil at night amidst songs, instrumental music and dances at night.

27. Garments should be given to couples there along with Dakṣiṇā. He who reads this everyday, particularly on the third lunar day, O goddess, in front of Pārvatī shall obtain good fortune and conjugal felicity.

28. Or one who listens to this fully endowed with devotion shall also undoubtedly attain conjugal felicity as long as he lives.

CHAPTER SIXTYNINE

Greatness of Gaurīśvara

Devī said:

1. The Liṅga of great renown that has been mentioned by you as Gaurīśvara is very excellent. Where is that Liṅga situated, which when adored bestows great benefit?

Īśvara said:

2-3. Listen, O goddess, I shall explain the sin-destroying greatness of Lord Gaurīśvara, the bestower of all cherished desires.

This penance-grove of Gaurī is well-known, O goddess, and is highly lustrous. On the whole, it extends to an area of fifty-five *Dhanus*.

4-5. There, in the middle, is stationed the goddess standing on a single foot as she is engaged in penance. To the north thereof and within four *Dhanus* distance is stationed the Liṅga that dispels fear from sin.

A man who adores, with devotion, the Liṅga especially on the eighth lunar day of the dark half, shall become rid of sins.

6. Gifting cows to a eminent Brāhmaṇa here is highly commended. So also is gifting gold. Especially, gifting of cooked food (is recommended) for quelling all sins.

7. By visiting that Liṅga, one is rid of all sins whether one

is a slayer of cows, murderer of a Brāhmaṇa or perpetrator of evil crimes.

CHAPTER SEVENTY

Greatness of Varuṇeśvara

Īśvara said:

1. Thereafter, O great goddess, a pilgrim should go to the excellent shrine of Varuṇeśvara. It is situated within a distance of twenty *Dhanus* to the south-east of Gaurī's penance-grove. The Liṅga that was installed by Varuṇa possesses great power.

2-3. Formerly, O goddess, when the ocean was quaffed off by Agasti (the Pot-born One), Varuṇa, the Lord of rivers, became furious.

After realizing that the Prabhāsika Kṣetra is a bestower of desires, O goddess, he performed a severely difficult penance.

4. He installed a great Liṅga and worshipped it devoutly. The Bull-emblemed Lord was worshipped for more than ten thousand years.

5. Pleased thereby, O goddess of Devas, the Lord filled the empty ocean,the lord of aquatic animals,with the waters of his own Gaṅgā.

6. He gratified him by means of diverse kinds of boons granted through the Liṅga. Ever since then all the oceans became full.

7. Ever since then, that Liṅga came to be known by the name Varuṇeśvara.

8. O beautiful lady of Suras, what is the use of visiting many Liṅgas, when one obtains the merit of all the Tīrthas on visiting Varuṇeśa.

9. That Brāhmaṇa who bathes that Liṅga with curds on the eighth and fourteenth lunar days, becomes a master of all the four Vedas. There is no doubt about this.

10-11. O lady of excellent countenance, all the Brāhmaṇas, Kṣatriyas, Vaiśyas, Śūdras and others, dumb, blind and deaf people, children, women and even eunuchs go to heaven after visiting the deity. O goddess, they shall be abiding by piety.

If holy ablution, *Japa,* oblation, adoration, eulogy and dance are performed there, all those activities shall give everlasting benefits.

12. A man who keenly desires for the benefit of a perfect pilgrimage and also for the heavenly pleasures should make there gift of golden lotus, pearls etc.

CHAPTER SEVENTYONE

Greatness of Uṣeśvara

Īśvara said:

1-3. Thereafter, O great goddess, a pilgrim should go to the shrine of the Liṅga situated there itself to the south of Varuṇeśa within a distance of three *Dhanus.*

O Lady of excellent countenance, the wife of Varuṇa named Uṣā, performed a terrible penance when she was sad over her husband and installed that great Liṅga, the bestower of all *Siddhis* (supernatural powers). It is well-known as Uṣeśvara and is adored by all the Siddhas.

4. He who worships that sin-destroying Liṅga with devotion shall attain the highest goal even if he be contaminated by a series of great sins.

5. It accords the benefit of conjugal felicity to women. It is destructive of miseries and bad luck.

CHAPTER SEVENTYTWO

Greatness of Jalavāsagaṇapati

Īśvara said:

1-3. For the sake of destroying all obstacles and for the accomplishment of all tasks, one should visit Vighneśa called *Jalavāsas* (Having water as robes) stationed there itself.

O great goddess, he was adored by means of lotuses with devotion by Varuṇa for averting obstacles to his penance. Therefore, he is remembered as *Jalavāsas*.

A devotee should propitiate him devoutly with scents and flowers along with sweetmeats on the *Caturthī* day (fourth lunar day) as much as the devotion allows. Gaṇādhipa becomes pleased with him.

CHAPTER SEVENTYTHREE

Greatness of Kumāreśvara

Īśvara said:

1-3. Thereafter, a pilgrim should go to the excellent shrine of Kumāreśvara. The Liṅga is highly powerful and is destructive of great sins.

O goddess, it is stationed within thirty *Dhanus* to the southwest of Varuṇeśvara. O goddess, it is stationed on the southern side of Gaurī's penance-grove. O great goddess, after performing a great penance there, the great Liṅga was installed by the Six-faced Lord. Therefore, it became Kumāreśa.

4-5. If a devotee worships (the Liṅga) duly, he gets much merit in a single day by adoring Kumāreśa once. He gets the entire merit of six months of adoration by worshipping for a month continuously.

6. If a person eschews lust, anger, avariciousness, passion and rivalry, it is enough if the devotee worships him once. He should be celibate and shall conquer the sense-organs.

7. If he is worshipped thus, O goddess, a pilgrim gets the entire benefit of a perfect pilgrimage.

CHAPTER SEVENTYFOUR

Greatness of Śākalyeśvara

Īśvara said:

1-3. Thereafter, O great goddess, a pilgrim should go to

the excellent shrine of Śākalyeśvara. It is situated within a distance of thirty *Dhanus* to the north-west of Daityasūdana.

It is the bestower of all desires, O great goddess. It was worshipped by Śākalya. It is the spot where the saintly king named Śākalya performed great penance. By propitiating the great Lord Bhava, he made him manifest to himself. He made the delighted Maheśvara descend into the Liṅga.

4. O beautiful lady of elegence, when the Lord is visited sins committed in the course of seven births get dissolved quickly like darkness at sunrise.

5. A pilgrim should bathe god Śiva there with milk on the eighth and fourteenth lunar days. He should duly adore with scents, flowers etc. in the proper order.

6. Gold should be offered there by those who wish the benefit of a perfect pilgrimage. Listen, as I enumerate the four names (of the deity).

7. At the outset, in the Kṛta Age, O goddess, the Lord was glorified as Bhairaveśvara. Then, O my beloved, he was perfectly propitiated by Manu named Sāvarṇi.

8. The name of that Lord in Tretā was Sāvarṇikeśvara. Then in Dvāpara, O goddess, the Bull-emblemed Lord in the form of a Liṅga was perfectly propitiated by the noble-souled Gālava.

9-10. The third appellation of the Lord was Gālaveśvara. When Kali Yuga set in, the sage named Śākalya attained Siddhi there and acquired the great powers of *Aṇimā* (minuteness) etc. Therefore, the fourth name is well-known as Śākalyeśvara.

11. Thus the names of that Liṅga in all the four Yugas have been glorified. They are destructive of sins. They confer merit on men. They have been glorified as the bestowers of all cherished desires.

12. O my beloved, listen from me the origin of the holy spot of the same Lord of Devas.

13. The area all round, O goddess, extends to eighteen *Dhanus*. It is destructive of all great sins of the residents of the holy spot, O goddess.

14. There the water in the wells etc. is remembered as *Śārasvata* (belonging to river Sarasvatī). It accords salvation unto even worms, insects, locusts—unto all lower creatures.

15-18. A man may take his bath anywhere. He is honoured

in the heavenly world. By visiting that Liṅga, one attains the entire benefit of a thousand horse-sacrifices and a hundred Vājapeya sacrifices.

During lunar *Parva* (i.e. New-Moon and Full-Moon) a devotee should remain pure and self-controlled and perform the *Japa* of *Aghora Mantra* along with the perfect *Ājyahoma* (consigning ghee to fire). He should remain all the while in the vicinity of the Liṅga. O my beloved of excellent complexion, he attains all excellent *Siddhis* even if he has been defiled by major sins or minor ones.

19. That Liṅga is remembered as *Kāmika,* that is the bestower of all the desired benefits. The face of the Lord there is (called) *Aghora* (benign). It is highly terrible (Bhairava).

20. It was well-known formerly by the name Bhairaveśvara on the earth. After the advent of this Yuga, it has been named Śākalyeśvara.

CHAPTER SEVENTYFIVE

Greatness of Kalakaleśvara

Īśvara said:

1-3. Thereafter, O great goddess, a pilgrim should go to the Liṅga called Śākalakaleśvara. It is situated within a distance of sixty *Dhanus* to the south-west of Śākalyeśvara.

It is also remembered as having different names in the four Yugas. It is destructive of sins. Formerly (in Kṛtayuga) its name was Kāmeśvara. In Tretā, it was Pulaheśvara. In Dvāpara it was Siddhinātha and it is remembered as Nāradeśa in Kali age. It is also known by the name Kalakaleśa.

4. At the time when the highly esteemed river Sarasvatī entered the extremely meritorious ocean, the most excellent one of the rivers became delighted, and satisfied by the sound of the waters (waves) of the big ocean.

5. Thereupon, Devas sages, Siddhas and Cāraṇas along with Gandharvas raised a melodious, tumultuous sound that was exciting and thrilling.

6. Due to that loud sound, my idol (Liṅga) rose up. Therefore, the Liṅga was named Kalakaleśvara.

7. Thus a former incident which caused its name has been stated to you. Now recently it again became Kalakaleśvara. How it was brought about, I shall explain, O my beloved. Listen attentively.

8. Formerly at the junction of Kali Yuga and Dvāpara, Nārada came to the splendid Prābhāsika Kṣetra and performed a severe penance there near the Liṅga.

9. Then for a hundred years, he propitiated the Bull-emblemed Lord, O goddess of Devas. He obtained *Gāndharva* (proficiency in music) embellished with the seven *Svaras* (Notes).

10. Thereupon, he became delighted in his mind and performed a great Yajña well-known as Pauṇḍarīka in the vicinity of that Liṅga.

11. With his soul always kept pure, he performed the Yajña for pleasing the Lord of Devas. He invited thousands of sages from Brahmaloka.

12. Equipped with all the requisite (for the Yajña) he gathered together various provisions. Having prepared the Kuṇḍas etc. he began the *Kratu* (sacrifice).

13-14. O lady of excellent countenance, as the *Kratu* concluded, the Brāhmaṇas residing in the Kṣetra came there, O great goddess, in hundreds and thousands for the sake of Dakṣiṇā.

15. In a sporting way, to make them fight among themselves, he scattered pieces of gold and jewels on the ground.

16. With the intention of seizing maximum of the valuable things, those Brāhmaṇas noisily fought with one another.

17. O goddess, some of them were denuded of their garments. Some lost their sacred threads. Some were seen deprived of hair. Others were bleeding profusely.

18. A few others hit one another with kicks and fists for securing the valuables scattered by Nārada in this manner.

19-22. Nothing of value remained there. Some of the poor Brāhmaṇas, very learned and humble to the utmost, got wounded and disabled by other Brāhmaṇas. Yet they remained quiescent. They saw (Nārada) laughing incessantly. They said to him: "O Sage, you had excluded the learned ones. The gift that you made brought about only quarrel. Thereby you have flouted the conventions of Yajñas, O excellent Brāhmaṇa and sage. The name of this deity shall be Kalakaleśvara. This Liṅga will become well-known by this name."

O goddess, that was why the deity became (known as) Kalakaleśvara.

23. A man who bathes the Liṅga devoutly and circumambulates thrice, shall with your favour, go to Rudraloka undoubtedly.

24. He who adores it with devotion by means of sweet scents, flowers and unguents and offers gold to Brāhmaṇas shall attain the highest status.

CHAPTER SEVENTYSIX

Importance of the Pair of Lakulīśa Liṅgas

Īśvara said:

1-5. In the vicinity of the very same Lord of Devas, shines a pair of Liṅgas of excessive merit, installed by Lakulīśa.[1]

The name of both the Liṅgas is Lakulīśvara. By visiting this most excellent pair of Liṅgas, one is rid of all the sins committed between birth and death.

O my beloved, a pilgrim should observe fast there on the fourteenth lunar day in the bright half of the month of Bhādrapada, and keep awake during the night. At the outset the highly resplendent Lakulīśa present in the idol[2] should be worshipped. Then the pair of Liṅgas should be separately worshipped in accordance with the perfect injunctions regarding adoration with the recitation of eulogies and Mantras in the proper order. He goes to the great region where Lord Maheśvara is present.

1. Lakulīśa is a historical person. He was born at Karwan (Baroda Dist., Gujarat) in the 2nd Century AD. He is the founder of Pāśupatism. The *Pāśupata-Sūtra* is attributed to him. Purāṇas regard him as the 28th incarnation of Śiva in Kali Yuga.
2. Icons of Lakulīśa armed with a heavy stick *(Lakuta, Lakuṭa)* are found in many parts of India. *'Lakula'* (a big stick) being his characteristic, he is called 'Lakulīśa'.

CHAPTER SEVENTYSEVEN

Greatness of Uttaṅkeśvara

Īśvara said:

1-2. Thereafter, a pilgrim should go to the excellent Uttaṅkeśvara shrine, O great goddess. It is situated not very far from the same deity (i.e. Kalakaleśvara) on the southern side.

It was devoutly installed by the noble-souled Uttaṅka[1] himself. O great goddess, by visiting it, and touching it with great mental purity and concentration and by worshipping it devoutly and duly, one is rid of all sins.

CHAPTER SEVENTYEIGHT

Greatness of Vaiśvānareśvara

Īśvara said:

1-4. Thereafter, a devotee should go to the shrine of Lord Vaiśvānareśvara, O great goddess. It is stationed within a distance of five *Dhanus* of the same deity (i.e. Uttaṅkeśvara) in the south-east corner. Through visiting and touching it destroys the sins of all creatures.

O goddess, formerly a parrot had built its nest there. He stayed for a long time in the mansion (of the temple) along with his wife. The couple circumambulated it everyday not at all due to any special devotion but because their nest happened to be there, O goddess. After a long time, they met with their death.

5. It is mentioned that they were born on the earth with the power to remember previous births. They became famous by the names Lopāmudrā and Agastya.

---

1. An ideal disciple of Veda, the disciple of Āpoda-dhaumya (Mbh, *Ādi.* 3.83-184.)

6. There is a couplet (a verse) formerly sung by the noble-souled Agastya who recollected the previous birth with the wonder arising from his own experience.

7. "After circumambulating perfectly if anyone visits Vahnīśa, he shall certainly attain renown thereby like me formerly."

8. Thus, O goddess, the greatness of the deity of Fire has been stated to you. On being listened to, it dispels the sins of men and bestows all desired benefits.

9. An eminent Brāhmaṇa should bathe the deity with ghee and adore him duly. With perfect faith he should offer gold too.

10. After doing this in accordance with the injunctions one shall attain full benefit of the pilgrimage. He attains Vahniloka and rejoices there for an endless time.

CHAPTER SEVENTYNINE

Greatness of Lakulīśvara

Īśvara said:

1-5. Then, a pilgrim should go to the shrine of Lakulīśa of great lustre, O great goddess. It is situated within a distance of seven *Dhanus* on the western side thereof (i.e. of Vaiśvānareśvara).

It had arrived there in the great Kṣetra from Kāyāvarohaṇa[1]. It is destructive of the sins of all creatures. The Lord is stationed in the *Mūrti* (idol). Lakulīśa (the sage) performed a severe penance there. He initiated his four disciples Kuśaka etc., and taught them many *Śāstras* (Scriptures) such as Nyāya, Vaiśeṣika etc. Thereafter, he attained the greatest Siddhi.

A man (devotee) should realize this and worship the Lord perfectly, particularly in the Uttarāyaṇa (northern transit of the Sun) and on the Kārttikī day. The gift of learning should be offered to a Brāhmaṇa of good habit.

6. He will be repeatedly born as highly intelligent with exalted mind and prosperity of wealth, in the excellent family of rich Brāhmaṇas in the course of seven successive births.

---

1. Karwah in Dabhor Tehsil of Baroda Dist. It was the birth place of Lakulīśa. (For details, Supra Ch. 76. 1-5.)

CHAPTER EIGHTY

Greatness of Gautameśvara

Īśvara said:

1-5. To the east thereof (i.e. Lakulīśa) and to the west of Daityasūdana, there is a sin-destroying Liṅga Gautameśvara by name. O goddess, it is stationed within a distance of five *Dhanus*. It bestows all desires. O beautiful lady, it was propitiated by Śalya, the king of Madra[1]. After propitiating Maheśvara, a severe penance was performed by him.

Any other man who propitiates that deity thus will attain the greatest Siddhi like Śalya, a king of exalted mind.

He who bathes the deity with milk on the fourteenth lunar day in the bright half of Citrā and with scented water too, attains the benefit of a horse-sacrifice. Further, he must worship the deity duly with excellent flowers with great devotion.

6. O goddess, by visiting that Liṅga all the sins committed mentally, verbally and physically perish.

CHAPTER EIGHTYONE

Greatness of Śrī Daityasūdana

Īśvara said:

1-6. Thereafter, a pilgrim should go to the shrine of Daityasūdana, the Lord of Devas, O great goddess. The deity destroys the sins of all the creatures residing in Prabhāsa Kṣetra.

It has been there for ages and is beginningless. It is splendid and it bestows all desires. For the sake of crossing the terrible ocean of worldly existence, it is stationed like a boat.

At the end of a Kalpa, i.e. a day of Brahmā, O goddess of Devas, all other things perish excepting these. They are: *Nyagrodha* (holy fig tree) that lives for seven Kalpas, *Kalpa Vṛkṣa* (Wish-yielding Kalpa tree), the *Agāra* (Mine) of Vaiḍūrya (gem) and the excellent mountain of Vaiḍūrya, Lord Śrīdaityasūdana and the great sage Mārkaṇḍeya.

---

1. Maternal uncle of Nakula and Sahadeva (Paṇḍavas).

O beautiful lady, these are everlasting and immutable for seven Kalpas. O goddess, of what avail is saying too much and describing repeatedly?

There is no other deity on the earth, O goddess, superior to Śrīdaityasūdana. His holy spot is of the shape of a *Yava* (barley) and it is sin-destroying.

7. It is resorted to by Sages *(Ṛṣis)*, Siddhas, Yakṣas, Vidyādharas and *Uragas,* O beautiful lady. I shall tell you the borders of that holy spot of Viṣṇu.

8. In east the holy spot extends upto Yameśvara; in west upto Śrīsomeśa, In the north, the limit is Viśālākṣī and in south it is the Lord of rivers (Sea).

9. This holy spot of Viṣṇu, of the shape of a barley grain, is destructive of sins.

10. Even sinning men who die here in the holy spot all go to heaven like good men of meritorious deeds.

11. O my beloved, donations as charity, *Homa* or *Japa* and penance performed here, and whatever is done is said to be everlasting, for a period of seven Kalpas.

12. O goddess, if a devotee feeds even one Brāhmaṇa with Viṣṇu in view there in accordance with the injunctions, it is as good as feeding ten millions.

13-14. A devout man should observe fast with great devotion. Even from a single *Upavāsa* (fast) the benefit of ten thousand *Upavāsas* is obtained. The man shall take his holy bath in the Cakra Tīrtha and observe fast fully controlling all the sense-organs. On the twelfth lunar day in the month of Kārttika, he should offer gold to Brāhmaṇas after duly adoring Viṣṇu. He is rid of all sins.

The Devī said:

15. O Lord of Devas, why does he have the name Daityasūdana? And at what time? Tell it to me in detailṣ

Īśvara said:

16. Listen, O goddess, I shall describe his demon-destroying (Daityasūdana's) greatness. The previous activities of Lord Daityasūdana are conducive to great prosperity.

17. His names are different in the different Kalpas, O goddess. Though beginningless and deathless, they appear repeatedly.

18. In the earlier Kalpa it was Śriyāvṛtta. In the second Kalpa it is Vāmana. In the third it is Vajrāṅga and in the fourth it is Kamalāpriya.

19. He is remembered as Duḥkhahartā (Destroyer of Miseries) in the fifth Kalpa and in the sixth it is Puruṣottama. The Lord is remembered as Śrī Daityasūdana in the seventh Kalpa.

20. I shall correctly tell his name and its origin.

21. Formerly in battle, all the Devas were conquered by the Dānavas, the thorns unto Devas. They sought refuge in Hari, the resident of the Milk Ocean. They eulogized him and stood by bowing down.

The Devas said:

22. Hail unto you, O Lord, O Lord of the worlds! O suppressor of the Daityas, be victorious. After assuming the form of Boar, the earth was raised up by you.

23-24. Adopting the form of Fish, the Vedas were lifted up by you from within the ocean. You became one in the form of Tortoise and churned the Milk Ocean. O Lord of the worlds, Śrī (Lakṣmī) was then lifted up. Obeisance to you, O Lord, O consort of Śrī. O supporter of Śrī, you are the destroyer of the distress of distressed ones.

25. Bali was kept bound by you in the form of a dwarf; by you, the enemy of Asuras, the great Daitya Hiraṇyākṣa and Hiraṇyakaśipu were killed.

26. He was held in the space by you in the form of a Man-lion. O great Lord, O origin of the Devas, the universe is raised up by you.

27. Without you, O Lord of the worlds, the Cosmos is rendered lustreless. When the universe is over-run by Dānavas as though by darkness, you showed your exploit like the Sun.

28. On hearing this prayer, O goddess, the lotus-eyed Viṣṇu spoke to the Devas beginning with Brahmā when he was wakened up from the Milk Ocean.

29. "Give up your fear, O Devas, of Dānavas in every respect. Ere long I shall slay the Dānavas."

30. After saying thus, Janārdana came down along with them. With his discus, he slew the Dānavas one by one.

31. All the Dānavas began to flee in their distress due to

fear. They reached the holy spot of Prabhāsa and stood face to face with the Sea.

32. The destroyer of the *Daityas* (Viṣṇu) saw them ready to perish. With his discus he killed all the Dānavas without leaving anyone behind.

33. When all the Daityas had been killed, the whole universe along with the Devas, Brāhmaṇas, and ascetics came to normalcy without agitation.

34. Ever since then, the deity came to be known by the name *Daityasūdana*. O beautiful lady, his greatness has been spoken to you entirely. The greatness of Lord Daityasūdana is conducive to great fortune and prosperity.

35. On seeing him no one is ever born dullard, blind, poor or miserable for seven successive generations. O lady of excellent countenance, this is the truth. I repeat, this is the truth.

36-37. Men should assiduously observe fast in the presence of Daityasūdana on the twelfth lunar day in the month of Śrāvaṇa, the meritoriously splendid *Aṣṭamī* (eighth lunar day) coinciding with Rohiṇī and on the eleventh days of Āṣāḍha and Kārttika (Śayana and Utthāpana). By means of a single fast, the merit of ten thousand fasts is obtained. There is no doubt.

38. Even a dog-cooking Cāṇḍāla, a creature of the low status and strata attains the world of Acyuta on the cessation of life therein.

39. Persons in the holy spot of Daityasūdana should have perfect faith. They should observe fast for the whole months of Kārttika and Vaiśākha.

40. By the power of the holy spot of Viṣṇu, they obtain the merit of crores and crores of fasts for each of the fasts.

41. If anyone offers a lamp there for a month or even a fortnight, he shall get the fruit of a crore of lamps on account of the offer for everyone of the lamps.

42. The devotee abstaining from food on the eleventh lunar day shall bathe the Four-armed Lord of Devas with Pañcāmṛta and worship him. He shall become Acyuta himself.

43. Keśava becomes pleased with one who regularly spends *Cāturmāsya* (the period of the four months of rainy season) in the presence of Daityasūdana in accordance with the injunctions.

44. By visiting Daityasūdana, one obtains that fruit entirely which one obtains by performing crores of *Cāturmāsyas* in the other holy spots.

45. By visiting Daityasūdana one gets that meritorious fruit which one may obtain by offering the entire Cosmic Egg (as a charitable gift).

46. A man who performs the rite of *Jāgara* (keeping awake at night) there on the eleventh lunar day along with songs, instrumental music, dances and dramatic presentations of various kinds goes to the world of Viṣṇu. He does not return after going there.

47. *Bhadrā* (the twelfth lunar day), by means of *Jāgara* during the night, dispels all the sins committed by anyone formerly and held pending such as ten thousand crimes of murder and innumerable thefts of gold.

48. If the night of *Bhadrā* is spent in *Jāgara* men do not see evil dreams of the pathways of death, City of Death, Yama's messengers and the forest of *Khaḍgapatra* (sword-leaved trees) hanging from the sky.

49. One may duly offer a thousand virgins after adorning them with jewels considering that it is his pious duty; another may offer a thousand cows in Kurujāṅgala. But the benefits of all these are obtained by means of *Jāgara* of Viṣṇu.

50. After observing fast one should eat the *Naivedya* (food offered to the deity) mixed with Tulasī leaves. This destroys the sin of crores of murders.

51. Thus, O goddess, the sin-destroying greatness of Lord Daityasūdana has been described to you. What else do you ask?

52. One shall offer yellow garments, cows and gold to the deity after taking holy bath in the excellent Cakra Tīrtha. One is thus rid of all sins.

CHAPTER EIGHTYTWO

Origin of Cakratīrtha

The Devī said:

1. O Bull-emblemed One, what is that Tīrtha mentioned

by you by the name Cakratīrtha? Where is that Tīrtha situated? What is its power? Do tell me.

Īśvara said:

2. Formerly, in the battle between Devas and Asuras, Janārdana killed the Daityas and thereafter washed his blood-stained discus there.

3. Hari brought there himself, eight crores of excellent Tīrthas and set them up in this Tīrtha. After cleansing Sudarśana, he gave the name Cakratīrtha unto it whereby it became well-known.

4. There is no doubt, O great goddess, that in Cakratīrtha, there are altogether eight crore eight hundred thousand Tīrthas.

5. An excellent man who takes his holy bath there with single-minded attention, attains the full benefit of ablution in all the Tīrthas.

6. O lady of excellent countenance, eight crores of (extra) Tīrthas remain there particularly on the Ekādaśī day as well as during solar and lunar eclipses.

7-8. O great goddess, by taking the holy bath there, one obtains the benefit of a crore of Yajñas. Listen to its own names in different Kalpas. I shall enumerate them to you. It was Koṭitīrtha in the earliest Kalpa, Śrīnidhāna in the second, Śatadhāra in the third, and Cakratīrtha in the fourth Kalpa.

9. Thus all the previous Kalpa names have been told to you. In a similar manner, other names should be understood by learned men in the proper order.

10. There is no limit unto the *Dāna* that is offered there. Viṣṇukṣetra is said as extending to half a *Krośa* (3 Kms.).

11-14. It is the truth that has been mentioned by me. The Sin (Demon) of Brāhmaṇa-slaughter does not approach him.

A person can perform all these rites there: monthly fasts, *Agnihotra,* observance of holy vows with self-control, self-study of the Vedas, performance of Yajñas, *Tapas,* Cāndrāyaṇa etc., offering libations to the Pitṛs, performing Śrāddha unto them with due observance of regulations, single-night rites, three-night rites of Kṛcchra and Sāntapana and other holy rites. Whatever a man does after coming to the Daityārikṣetra shall yield merit a crore times more than in the other holy Kṣetras.

15. One who desires the benefit of perfect pilgrimage should

perform Godāna (gifting cows) in the excellent Sudarśana Kṣetra for the eradication of all sins.

16-17. A dog-cooking Cāṇḍāla or a creature of the lower strata, meeting with death in that holy spot shall attain the world of Acyuta. Thus the greatness of Cakratīrtha has been briefly told. It is destructive of all sins. It yields all desired benefits.

CHAPTER EIGHTYTHREE

Greatness of Yogeśvarī

Īśvara said:

1-3. Thereafter, O great goddess, a pilgrim should go to the shrine of the great goddess Yogeśvarī stationed to the east thereof (Daityasūdana).

The deity bestows the fruit in the form of Yogic powers. I shall describe its origin. Listen to it with faith.

Once, there was a mighty demon named Mahiṣa, a tiger among Dānavas. O goddess, he was the chief among them and highly terrible and frightening unto all the Devas. He could assume any form he pleased. Subjecting all the three worlds under his control, he remained happy.

4. On a certain occasion, a charming girl unparalleled in beauty in heaven was created by Brahmā, the creator of the worlds.

5. She performed a very severe penance. O lady of excellent countenance, once that chaste girl of excellent beauty was seen by Nārada.

6. He was struck with great wonder, O goddess, at once when he thought: 'Oh, what an excellent beauty! Oh, what an excellent fortitude! Oh, what a great splendour! Oh, what a youthful age!'

7. Thinking thus, he spoke to the lady these words: "O fair lady, offer yourself to me. I have not yet taken a wife unto me. I have been afflicted by the arrows of Kāma on seeing you."

She said:

8-9a. O venerable one,I have nothing to do with the dallying of love. I have taken up the vow of celibacy. I shall accomplish what I desire. Do not be offended in this matter nor be sorry for it.

9b-10. On hearing her words, O my beloved, Sage Nārada went to the wonderful city ruled by Mahiṣa within the ocean. Indeed the sage was honoured by that noble-souled Mahiṣa.

11. O goddess, after offering the excellent *Arghya* and enquiring after his health, he stood with palms joined in reverence. He spoke: "O Nārada, what may be the reason for your visit? What are your intentions? I shall do everything (necessary for them)."

12-13. Thereupon the sage said to Mahiṣa, the Lord of Dānavas: "O great Asura, a jewel of a girl has been born in Jaṁbūdvīpa. Neither in heaven nor in the mortal world nor also in the nether worlds, a beauty such as she, has been seen or heard about by me. I have now been victimised by the darts of the god of Love due to her."

14. On hearing his words which generated a great deal of lust in him too, the demon went to the Prābhāsika Kṣetra where that chaste lady was staying.

15. He was accompanied by a great army. The demon pleaded before her: "O timid lady, be my wife. Enjoy charming pleasures. O highly esteemed lady, the penance that you are engaged in is antagonistic to your youthful charms."

16-17. On hearing those words of that demon, the lady of excellent complexion laughed. O goddess of Devas, hundreds and thousands of terrible women holding weapons in their hands issued forth from the exhaled breath of the goddess, as she laughed. The army of the evil-souled Mahiṣa was destroyed by them.

18. When the army was being destroyed, the most excellent one among Dānavas became furious and rushed quickly towards her.

19-20. The great Asura shook vigorously and frequently his terrible, sharp-pointed horns and fought a great battle with her. He caught hold of the goddess with his horns. Standing above him, she trampled on the demon under her feet. Then the leading Daitya was killed by means of her trident.

21. When his head was cut off with a sword, a person of the same form as his, issued forth from it. Thus though the

Daitya was terrible, he went to Svarga on being slain by the weapons of the goddess.

22. On seeing Mahiṣa defeated all the groups of the Devas beginning with Mahendra, eulogized the goddess with delighted minds.

The Devas said:

23. O highly esteemed goddess, O majestic one of terrible appearance, O three-eyed goddess, abiding by good means for achieving the ends, O goddess with faces all round, obeisance to you!

24. O subduer of Mahiṣa the Asura, O omnipresent goddess identical with Vidyā and Avidyā, O victorious one worthy of being meditated upon by Japa, O controlling deity of all lores, O goddess with universe as your form!

25. O eternal goddess devoid of sorrow, O goddess with long eyes like the petals of lotus, O goddess of pure *Sattva* quality, O goddess observing *Vratas,* O goddess of terrific form like the night!

26. O goddess, O bestower of prosperity and superior powers, O goddess engaged in *Kālanṛtya* (dance of destruction), O goddess fond of fortitude, O Śakti of Śaṅkara, O Brāhmaṇical power, O Śakti of Brahmā bowed down to by all the Devas!

27. O subduer of big Mahiṣa, O goddess armed with *Ghaṇṭā* (bell) and *Śūla* (trident), O goddess of frightful form, O goddess Śivā with hideous eyes, O great Māyā, O nectarine goddess!

28. O omnipresent goddess, O bestower of everything, O origin of all living beings and one identical with them, O mother of *Vidyās* (lores), Purāṇas and *Śalyas* (darts), O supporter of *Bhūtas* (living beings)!

29. O splendid one among all the esoteric doctrines of the Devas and all those who possess Sattva quality, O goddess, you alone are our refuge. O Vidyā, O Avidyā, O Śrī, O Aśrī (non-Śrī)!

30. On being thus eulogized by the Devas and the Sages after due obeisance, the goddess spoke laughingly: "Choose an excellent boon."

The Devas said:

31. O goddess, may those excellent men who eulogize you

by means of this prayer have all their desires fulfilled and continuously get showers of boons.

32. O goddess of pure smiles, you shall stay in this holy spot for ever.

33. O lady of excellent countenance, that goddess said to the Devas, "This will be so." She sent away the groups of sages too and remained engaged there.

34. O lady of excellent countenance, a devotee should observe fast on the ninth lunar day in the bright half of the month of *Aśvayuj* and devoutly visit the deity. His sins get dissolved like darkness at sunrise.

35. If a man gets up early in morning and recites this prayer he will never be assailed by any fear all through his life.

36-37. The eighth lunar day in the bright half of the month of *Aśvayuj* in conjunction with the constellation *Mūla* is called *Mahānāmikā* (of great name). O splendid lady, those who give up their life on that day, shall certainly stay in Svarga. Those heroic ones become the favourites of celestial damsels.

38. In all the Manvantaras and beginnings of Kalpas, O goddess of Suras, it is said that the sequence is the same. Now listen to the special features.

39. The fifth lunar day in the bright half of the month of *Aśvayuj* is called *Pāpanāśinī* (the destroyer of sins). During the night on that day, one should worship (her) adorned by means of Khaḍga Mantra.

40. In a place sloping towards the north-east a Brāhmaṇa should duly make a beautiful pavilion of sixteen pillars in the vicinity of Yogeśvarī. It should be embellished with banners.

41. The priest should make a very splendid Kuṇḍa (sacrificial pit) of the length of a hand with three *Mekhalās* (slopes) and the *Yonī* (pit) shall have the semblance of a leaf of Aśvattha.

42. Pāyasa (milk pudding) is to be used for Homa as mentioned in the scriptures with due utterance of Mantras. The sword is bathed in Pañcāmṛta. Excellent Brāhmaṇas should worship it with various kinds of flowers uttering the following Mantra:

The Mantra for the Khaḍga worship:

43-44. The following are the eight names uttered by *Vedhas* (god Brahmā) himself: *Abhī* (fearless), *Viśasana* (cutting), *Khaḍga* (sword), *Prāṇabhūta* (that which is the very vital life), *Durāsada* (difficult of approach), *Agamya* (impossible to reach), *Vijaya* (victory) and *Dharmādhāra* (the basis of piety). Thy constellation is Kṛttikā; the preceptor is Lord Maheśvara. Gold is thy body; the *Dhātā* (Creator) is Lord Janārdana; the father Lord Pitāmaha (Brahmā). Do protect (us) always with everything belonging to you.

45. After duly worshipping it thus, the Sword is taken round in the city at night by excellent Brāhmaṇas along with Nāndīghoṣa (loudly proclaiming the praise of the deity).

46. The king who performs thus shall be accompanied by all the armies and excellent Brāhmaṇas. After proceeding thus in accordance with the injunctions, it should be taken to Yogeśvarī. The Mantra is uttered and the *Khaḍga* is dedicated to the deity.

47. It should be splashed with collyrium (application) and smeared with sandalpaste. A garland made of Bilva leaves is offered to the goddess.

The Arghya Mantra:

48. O goddess Durgā, O destroyer of intractable distresses, O goddess destroying all evil ends (disasters), save me in all difficult situations. O Durgā, I have sought refuge in you.

49. O goddess of Devas, after offering the *Arghya* thus, the *Khaḍga* is kept there with vigilant guards (attending it). Till the Aṣṭamī (eighth day) it shall be adored everyday.

50. After keeping awake that night, when the day has dawned, at the rise of Aruṇa, buffaloes and sheep should be beheaded in front.

51. The animals may number a hundred, half of it (fifty) or half of half (twenty-five) as the devotee pleases. With potful of *Surā* and *Āsava* (liquor) the great goddess should be propitiated.

52-53. The meat thereof should be given to Kāpālikas as well as to servants and maid servants. In the afternoon of the *Navamī* day, Yogeśī should be placed on a chariot and taken round the whole realm by the king himself along with his army. Conchs and *Paṭaha* drums should be sounded. Baṭus and Cāraṇas should recite, sing and chant.

The Bali Mantra:

54-56. May these Devas, Ādityas, Vasus, Maruts, Aśvins, Rudras, Suparṇas, Pannagas etc. accept this oblation. Let all the spirits and ghosts become mild and conducive to happiness.

O beautiful woman, the king should offer Bali (oblation) to the spirits with this Mantra. The oblation shall consist of water, blood, cooked rice, sweet scents, raw rice grains and flowers. The king should scatter this *Bali* three times in all the quarters and inner spaces by means of the trident.

57. The Brāhmaṇas residing in the holy spot should perform the *Yātrā* thus. O goddess of Devas, due to the favour of Yogeśvarī, they will have no enemies. Neither fire nor thieves, nor Vināyakas (Trouble-making gods) will impede their progress.

58. They shall be happy enjoying all pleasures. They shall be devoid of all *Ātaṅkas* (anguish, agony). The men shall become permanent devotees of Yogeśvarī.

59. Thus the great festival of Yogeśvarī has been narrated to you. It destroys all inauspiciousness of those who read and listen to it.

60. Men who worship Durgā on the *Navamī* day do cross the forests of impassable difficulties—the goddess who has pierced with the tip of the trident, the back of demon Mahiṣa and with her drawn sword, has cut up the staff-like arms (of the demon) adorned with armlets, and who is followed by Pañcavadana (Lord Śiva).

CHAPTER EIGHTYFOUR

Greatness of Ādinārāyaṇa

Īśvara said:

1-3. Thereafter, O great goddess, a pilgrim should go to Lord Viṣṇu called Ādinārāyaṇa. The deity is destructive of all sins. He is stationed on the eastern side of Yogeśvarī.

The Lord is the destroyer of all Daityas. He has sandals and a seat.

At the beginning (of the creation) in Kṛtayuga, O fair lady, there was a Daitya named Meghavāhana. He had a huge body extending to ten thousand Yojanas. He was very mighty. He could not be conquered by all the Devas joined together. He caused the destruction of all the three worlds. O lady of excellent countenance, Brahmā, pleased by his penance, had granted him a boon.

4. "Your death will take place only when in a battle Viṣṇu strikes you with Pādukā (sandal), not otherwise."

5. The Daitya who got this boon, began to oppress the whole of the earth along with Devas and Asuras and human beings. This continued for a period of a crore of Yugas.

6. After tormenting (all) in various ways, O goddess, he came to the southern sea. There he destroyed the hermitages of sages.

7. Then all those sages whose hermitages and surroundings had been destroyed sought refuge in Keśava, the Lord of Devas. Knowing fully well that he is invincible, they eulogized the Garuḍa-emblemed Lord.

The Sages said:

8. Obeisance to the *Ātmayogin* (the Supreme Soul as a Yogin) highly auspicious and cause of auspiciousness. Obeisance to Janārdana, to Lord Śrīdhara, to Vedhas.

9. Obeisance to Keśava with the golden coronet resembling the filaments of a lotus. Obeisance, obeisance to the extremely subtle in form, to one having a huge form.

10. Obeisance to the lotus-navelled one, to the most preeminent one, to the most desirable one, to the great Ātman. Obeisance to Hari in the form of Man-lion (Narasiṁha), to the creator of Indra.

11. Obeisance to the Ātman, to the cause of the universe, Obeisance to the Absolute having Hiraṇyagarbha (Brahmā) in his womb. Obeisance to Acyuta always. Obeisance, obeisance to the infinite one.

12. Obeisance to the great Ātman whose refulgence is concealed by the veil of Māyā, to the abode of the universe. Obeisance to the bestower of the raft of knowledge enabling one to cross the ocean of worldly existence. Obeisance to the *Dhātṛ* (Creator) of unobstructed intelligence, to the Dhātṛ performing the duties of creation, maintenance and annihilation.

13. Just as a sin gets destroyed when the name 'Vāsudeva'

is uttered once, so also let this Daitya Meghavāhana undergo destruction.

14. Just as Viṣṇu takes away a sin that is settled upon his devotees, so also may this Daitya, the perpetrator of sinful activities, meet with destruction.

15. Even as Viṣṇu dispels all sins as soon as he is remembered,so also may this Daitya Meghavāhana attain annihilation.

16. When the Supreme Lord of great Lords, Vāsudeva, the creator of the universe is remembered with impregnable (very firm) devotion, let there be auspicious results; may all the defects of the entire universe meet with destruction.

17. May excellent men, all those who are on the earth, those who are in heaven, those who are in the intervening space, all those living beings that live in Rasātala, become endowed with *Siddhi* (spiritual perfection) when Vāsudeva, the creator of the universe, is remembered.

18. May those living beings that live anywhere in this Cosmic Egg and beings living beyond that too, attain the greatest *Siddhi* when Vāsudeva, the creator of the universe, is eulogized.

Īśvara said:

19-21. O fair lady, on being thus eulogized, Hari Ādinārāyaṇa (the primordial Nārāyaṇa) visualized the future task, stepped on the (Vehicle-like?) Sandals and became perceptible to those sages. The Lord, the destroyer of sins, spoke to them as they bowed down: "What is there in your heart that you wish to be done by me? May that be mentioned. Propitiated by the eulogy of you all, I shall duly accomplish it."

22. On being told thus, all those sages stood with palms joined in reverence. With the heads bowed down, they spoke to Hari, the primordial Lord.

The Sages said:

23. O Lord, you know everything. Nothing is unknown to you. O great Lord, slay this highly powerful Daitya, O Lord, so that this entire universe maybe free from dread.

24. O splendid lady, on being told thus then by all of them, Viṣṇu challenged the Daitya for a combat. He hit him on his chest with his sandal.

25. On being struck down, the Daitya fell dead into the great ocean. After killing the notorious Daitya, the Lord stationed himself there. O lady of excellent countenance, even today, he is stationed there on the sandal-shaped seat.

26. Any excellent man who devoutly worships him gets the benefit of a horse-sacrifice and rejoices in heaven like a Deva.

27. When Govinda, the primordial Lord, is visited devoutly the man gets the same benefit which is attained by giving away a hundred thousand cows to a Brāhmaṇa.

28. The suffering of those who have Lord Ādinārāyaṇa in their heart is less than happiness. It is as though they are having Kṛtayuga in Kali itself.

29-30. By worshipping Ādinārāyaṇa after bathing in the waters of Sannihitā (a river)on a Sunday coinciding with the eleventh lunar day, one is rid of the bondage of worldly existence. Thus, O goddess, the greatness of Viṣṇu, the deity, has been spoken to you. If it is listened to by men, it destroys sins and a series of states of poverty.

CHAPTER EIGHTYFIVE

Greatness of Sannihitā[1]

The Devī said:

1-5. O Bull-emblemed One, you have said that there is (the river) Sannihitā. How did that great river come there from Kurukṣetra? Of what special efficacy is she reputed? What is the benefit derived by holy ablution etc.?

Īśvara said:

Listen, O goddess, I shall tell you where the splendid Sannihitā which destroys sins of all creatures through viewing and touching is flowing.

That great goddess, in the form of a great river, is situated within a distance of three *Dhanus* to the west of Ādinārāyaṇa. O my beloved, I shall succinctly describe its origin. Listen.

Due to the fear of Jarāsandha, O goddess, Viṣṇu (Kṛṣṇa)

1. Sannihitī in Mbh (Vana 83) is a lake and not a river. This is an ancient Tīrtha (lake) in Kurudeśa. By bath in it at the time of solar eclipse one derives the fruit of Aśvamedha.

took all the Yādavas including children, old people and merchant folk and his relatives and attendants. Having deserted Mathurā he came to Prabhāsa.

6-7. He requested the Ocean for some space for the sake of residence.

At that festival time *Divākara* (Sun-god), the Lord of Devas, was swallowed by Rāhu. On seeing this, all the Yādavas experienced great grief.

8-9. They were sorry because they could not reach Sannihitā (-tyā) (at Kurukṣetra). Janārdana spoke to them: "O excellent Yādavas, when I am here you need not experience any grief. May my power be witnessed. In order to boost up piety on the earth, I will bring here the sacred lake of Sannihitā."

10-11. After saying thus, the Lord got absorbed in deep meditation. While Viṣṇu of immeasurable refulgence was engaged in meditation thus, a splendid stream of water appeared in front of him. It had pierced the surface of the earth and presented itself for the holy ablution of the enemy of Asuras (i.e. Kṛṣṇa).

12. Thereupon, O great goddess, all the Yādavas with Balarāma and Sāmba as their leaders, performed their holy ablution while the Sun was being swallowed by Rāhu (i.e. Solar eclipse).

13. They obtained the excellent fruit of the pilgrimage to Kurukṣetra, the merit arising from (ablution in) Sannihityā.

14. Thus the holy lake Sannihitā came to be there. While the Sun is in the grasp of Rāhu, O great goddess, one should take one's holy ablution there. He will get the entire benefit of Agniṣṭoma Yajña.

15. The devotee should feed a Brāhmaṇa with foodstuffs of all six tastes in accordance with the injunctions. Even if one is fed, the person (s) (so feeding) gets the benefit of feeding ten million people.

16. If *Homa* is performed in the vicinity of Sannihityā, the fruit of ten million Homas is derived at each *Āhuti*.

17. If Mantras are uttered there, the fruit of ten million *Japas* is derived from the *Japa* of every Mantra.

18-19. Gold is to be gifted by those who wish to get the benefit of the pilgrimage. After the holy ablution Janārdana, the primordial Lord, should be worshipped. Thus the perfect benefit derived from Sannihitā has been spoken to you. O my beloved, if it is listened to it destroys the sins of those who have great faith.

CHAPTER EIGHTYSIX

Greatness of Pāṇḍaveśvara

Īśvara said:

1. To the south thereof is situated a Liṅga of great lustre named Pāṇḍaveśvara. It has been installed by the five (Pāṇḍavas) in due order.

2. When the Pāṇḍavas were obliged to remain incognito they were roaming in forests. They came to Prabhāsa Kṣetra with a view to perform their holy pilgrimage.

3. O great goddess, when the Somaparvan occurred, at that time all of them installed the Liṅga on the banks of Sannihitā.

4. Making the excellent Brāhmaṇas beginning with Mārkaṇḍeya their Ṛtviks, they performed the *Abhiṣeka* (Ablution) with the Mantras from the Vedas and gifted bulls (one each).

5. O my beloved of excellent complexion, when the Liṅga was installed, the sages beginning with Mārkaṇḍa became pleased.

The sages said:

6. Those who will worship this Liṅga adored by Pāṇḍavas will be worthy of adoration by Devas, Dānavas and Rākṣasas.

7. There is no doubt. By our statement they will get the fruit of Aśvamedha due to their faith and worship.

8. If, after taking bath in Sannihitā Kuṇḍa any person adores Pāṇḍaveśvara during the whole of the month of Māgha, he becomes Puruṣottama himself.

9. By simply visiting him, sin gets rent into a thousand bits. He is said to be Viṣṇu himself incarnate. There is no need to think over it.

CHAPTER EIGHTYSEVEN

Greatness of Bhūteśvara

Īśvara said:

1-4. Thus after performing the *Yātrā* (of Pāṇḍaveśvara), a

pilgrim, endowed with perfect faith, should, O great goddess, go to the eleven Rudras in due course.

They are stationed in the centre of Prabhāsa Kṣetra and are the destroyers of great sins. Sins are acquired severally by men in eleven ways (through the ten *Indriyas* and *Manas*). Those sins are eradicated through the worship of the eleven Rudras.

Becoming sanctified by good emotional feelings, a pilgrim should worship the eleven Rudras in due order during *Saṁkrānti* (transit of the Sun), *Ayana* (on days when the Sun moves northwards and southwards), during solar and lunar eclipses or during other holy festival days.

5. I shall tell their previous names as they were in Kṛtayuga. O goddess, listen to them correctly.

6. (They are) Ajaikapāt, Ahirbudhnya, Virūpākṣa, Raivata, Hara, Bahurūpa, Tryaṁbaka, Sureśvara, Vṛṣākapi, Śaṁbhu and Kapardin the undefeated.

7. O goddess, these were the names first in Kṛtayuga. They continued in Tretā and Dvāpara also. (But) After the advent of the Kali Age, other names came into vogue.

8-9.[1] The names of Rudras were eleven. I shall, tell them to you now. They are: Bhūteśa, Nīlarudra, Kapālin, Vṛṣavāhana, Tryaṁbaka, Aghoranāman (named as Aghora), Mahākāla, Bhairava, Mṛtyuñjaya, Kāmeśa and Yogeśa. O my beloved, the eleven Rudras have been enumerated to you.

10. O goddess, they have neither beginning nor end. They are differentiated into eleven forms conforming to the names:

The Devī said:

11. O Lord, tell me in detail, the due order of the eleven Liṅgas, as based on the extension of their places, their greatness and origin.

12. O Lord, how are they to be worshipped? What are the Mantras? What is the mode of procedure of worship? On which festival day? Occasion? Do mention everything in detail.

Īśvara said:

13. Listen, O goddess. I shall tell you the secret that is destructive of sins. Somanātha is at the beginning and Siddhinātha is the cause.

1. From this chapter to the end of Chapter 97, the eleven Liṅgas enumerated in vv 8-9 are described.

14-15. On listening to this, a creature is rid of the sins accumulated previously. O my beloved, the eleven Rudras mentioned to you by me are said to be the ten *Vāyus* (vital airs) and the *Ātman* is remembered as the eleventh one. I shall tell the names of those ten *Vāyus* in due order. Listen.

16-17. The Lords, the Rudras, should be known in order thus: Prāṇa, Apāna, Samāna, Udāna, Vyāna, Nāga, Kūrma, Kṛkala, Devadatta, Dhanañjaya and Ātman. For the sake of the welfare of all living beings, I shall explain the Yātrā (pilgrimage, religious procession) pertaining to them, in due order.

18. O my beloved, formerly the first Lord of the Rudras was Someśvara. He should be worshipped in accordance with the injunctions under the name Bhūteśvara.

19. The services rendered should be those pertaining to and befitting kings. The mind should be sanctified by means of faith. The deity should be bathed in Pañcāmṛta and worshipped uttering the Mantra *Sadyojāta* etc.(*Taitt. Āraṇyaka.*XVII.1)

20. The pilgrim should meditate on Lord Sadāśiva and worship with charming flowers with great devotion. He should then circumambulate thrice and prostrate before the deity with the eight limbs touching the ground (*Sāṣṭāṅga*).

21. One desirous of performing the Yātrā of the eleven Rudras should proceed therefrom for the sake of averting obstacles. I shall explain the name Bhūteśvara mentioned to you.

22-23. The twenty-five Principles beginning with *Mahat* and ending with *Viśeṣa* are called *Bhūtas*. Since the Lord is remembered as their Lord, he was called Bhūteśvara formerly. After knowing the twenty-five Tattvas one shall attain salvation.

24. After worshipping Bhūteśa Rudra, one shall attain the imperishable salvation.

Thus the glorification of Ādirudra is briefly told. It is worthy of glorification by the twice-born. When glorified, it enhances merit.

CHAPTER EIGHTYEIGHT

Greatness of Nīlarudra

Īśvara said:

1-2. Thereafter, O great goddess, a pilgrim should go to

the second shrine of Nīlarudra situated within sixteen *Dhanus* to the north of Bhūteśa.

It is a great Liṅga, O great goddess, worshipped by the Gaṇas and Gandharvas. After bathing the Liṅga in accordance with injunctions, the pilgrim should worship it uttering the Mantra of Īśa.

3. By means of blue and white water lilies in abundance as well as other requisites for adoration, he should worship the deity after sanctifying his soul perfectly. After circumambulation, he should prostrate before the deity and worship (it).

4. By performing the rites thus, O goddess, he shall obtain the fruit of a Rājasūya Sacrifice. A bull should be gifted by those who wish to obtain the benefit of a perfect pilgrimage.

5. A Daitya who resembled blue collyrium and whose name was Antaka was killed formerly. The Lord caused the wives of that demon to lament and cry. Hence he is remembered as Nīlarudra.

6. The sin-destroying greatness of that deity has been succinctly spoken. It should be attained by those endowed with perfect faith. The story of the deity should be listened to by those who are eager to visit it.

CHAPTER EIGHTYNINE

Greatness of Kapālīśvara

Īśvara said:

1-3. Thereafter, O beautiful lady, a devotee should go to the excellent shrine of Kapālīśvara. This is the third Rudra shrine. It is destructive of sins. It is stationed to the east of Nīlarudra and within a distance of seven bows to the west of Budheśvara.

You know, O goddess, that the fifth head of Brahmā was formerly cut off by me and the skull got struck up to my hand. I then came to the holy place of Prabhāsa and remained within the Kṣetra for a thousand years.

4. Nude as I was, I went on holding the skull and am hence remembered as Kapālin. O my beloved, for ten thousand years, the Liṅga was worshipped by me.

5. I had assumed the form of a Kapālin (holder of a skull). Therefore, I am remembered as Kapālīśa. By seeing and touching (me), all the sins of men are dispelled (by me).

6. O goddess, thousands of Gaṇas armed with tridents were engaged there by me to save people from evil-minded sinners.

7-10. Hence by making all efforts, a pilgrim should worship the great Lord Kapālin, devoid of ailments. After worshipping the Lord with the Mantra *"tatpuruṣāya vidmahe"* (*Taitt. Āraṇyaka* XVII, 4) etc., gold should be given to a Brāhmaṇa well-versed in the Vedas. All the sins acquired by the creature, ever since the nativity are dispelled by that Liṅga on being visited in the morning of the Ṣaḍaśīti holy hour.

Thus the sin-destroying greatness of Kapālī Rudra Deva, the third deity, has been succinctly spoken (to you), O lady of excellent countenance.

CHAPTER NINETY

Greatness of Vṛṣavāhaneśvara

Īśvara said:

1-3. Thereafter, O great goddess, a pilgrim should go to the excellent shrine of the fourth Rudra. The Liṅga named Vṛṣabheśvara is a *Kalpaliṅga,* a favourite of Suras.

There, O great goddess, Brahmā himself is stationed in the form of a boy. This shrine is situated within a distance of three *Dhanus* on the northern side.

A man devoid of merits does not comprehend this primordial Liṅga of great efficacy. I shall now enumerate to you the names of the Liṅga in different Kalpas.

4-5. O great goddess, the deity was remembered as Brahmeśvara in the earlier Kalpa. O my beloved, it was propitiated for ten thousand years by Brahmā, the Lord who was desirous of creating the world. Maheśvara was pleased thereby. Thereafter, Pitāmaha carried out the creation of the four types of *Bhūtas* (living beings).

6. The name Brahmeśvara was formerly applied to the Liṅga since Hara was pleased with the status of being the Lord unto Brahmā.

7. Then, O lady of excellent complexion, when the second Kalpa arrived, the shrine became well-known on the earth by the name Raivateśvara.

8. There was a king named Raivata in the Cosmic Egg consisting of mobile and immobile beings. As a result of the power of that Liṅga, he conquered this world.

9-10. Therefore, the Liṅga of great lustre came to be known by the name Raivateśvara.

Again, O lady of excellent complexion, at the advent of the third Kalpa the name of that Liṅga was Vṛṣabheśvara. Vṛṣa (Bull) is my vehicle and it is Dharma (Virtue, Piety) who has taken the form of a bull.

11. That Liṅga was worshipped by him for a thousand years as per celestial reckoning. The bull attained *Sāyujya* (merging into the divinity), a type of salvation, when the Lord was pleased, O goddess of Devas.

12-13. Hence that Liṅga became known as Vṛṣabha on the earth.

At the advent of the fourth Kalpa named Vārāha, at the beginning of the twenty-eighth Tretāyuga there was a king named Ikṣvāku. He was an ornament unto the Solar race.

14. Excessively sanctified through devotion, he worshipped the Liṅga thrice a day. He took food only once a day. He conquered the craving for food and all the sense-organs. He slept on bare ground.

15. Thus, much time elapsed. Then Maheśvara became pleased. He granted highly prosperous kingdom and progeny in the form of sons and grandsons.

16-17. Therefore, this excellent Liṅga became known by the name Ikṣvākvīśvara. He who devoutly worship the Bull-vehicled Lord gets rid of sins incurred in the course of seven births. There is no doubt about it. That holy spot extends upto thirty *Dhanus* on the four sides.

18. Whatever is performed in that Tīrtha such as bath, *Jāpya*, oblation, *Homa*, adoration, eulogy and chanting of Vedic Mantra, shall be everlasting.

19-23. By measurement and magnitude, the holy spot is rectangular. One who spends a night in the vicinity of that Liṅga, observes celibacy, and keeps awake at night doing dance, (amidst) vocal and instrumental music gets rid of all sins.

A man may be a cow-slayer or a Brāhmaṇa murderer, yet he is rid of all evil deeds if he performs *Homa* and *Japa* and meditates. The pilgrim should delight Brāhmaṇas by means of different kinds of edible things. Feeding only one Brāhmaṇa here is as good as feeding ten million.

O goddess, the following eight Tīrthas are well settled in that Liṅga: Bhairava, Kedāra, Puṣkara, Drutijaṅgama, Vārāṇasī, Kurukṣetra, Mahākāla and Naimiṣa.

24-26. He who keeps awake at night on the fourteenth lunar day in the dark half of Māgha and worships the Lord duly, shall get the fruit of (visiting) the (above) eight Tīrthas.

If a pilgrim offers rice-balls in the vicinity of Śiva, on the day when the Moon is not visible (New-Moon day) the Pitṛs become pleased with him till the close of the day of Brahmā.

A devotee should adore that Liṅga at night with curds, ghee, milk, the five products from a cow, water from Kuśa grass, saffron, agallochum and camphor.

27. If the devotee utters the Aghora Mantra and meditates on Lord Sadāśiva, O great goddess, he is rid of the five sins.

28. If a Brāhmaṇa bathes the deity with curds on the eighth and fourteenth lunar days, he shall undoubtedly become well-versed in all the four Vedas.

29. O goddess, if he bathes the deity Vṛṣabheśvara with milk, he obtains the great fruit of offering seven thousand cows as gift.

30. O beautiful woman, the sins committed in the previous births and also committed now are destroyed, O my beloved, through the ablution (of the Liṅga) with curds.

31. O goddess, he who bathes Vṛṣabheśvara with the five products from a cow burns all sins and obtains the fruit of all Yajñas.

32-33. On seeing him, if a person endeavours to propitiate that Liṅga, the following sinners are rid of all their sins: a Brāhmaṇa-slayer, a cow-slayer, a thief, a defiler of preceptor's bed, a murderer of one seeking refuge, one who betrays friends, all evil-minded sinners, slayers of mother and father.

34. He who worships the great Liṅga Brahmeśvara during the whole of Kārttika month along with Brahmā shall be rid of sins.

35. If anyone worships Vṛṣabheśvara, the Lord of all the

Devas, he is as good as one who gives away everything, who pleases all the preceptors, who performs Śrāddha in Gayā Tīrtha.

36. Thus the greatness honoured by the Devas has been wholly told to you, O goddess. O beautiful woman, the greatness of Lord Vṛṣabheśvara, the *Kalpaliṅga,* has been told.

37. He who listens to the greatness of the Lord of Devas, O great goddess, attains the greatest goal even if he be a fool or a scholar.

CHAPTER NINETYONE

Greatness of Tryaṁbakeśvara

Īśvara said:

1-2. Thereafter, O goddess, a pilgrim should go to the immutable Tryaṁbakeśvara. It has been proclaimed as the fifth of the Rudras, the primordial deity.

O my beloved, it was named in the earlier Tretā yuga as Śikhaṇḍīśvara. I shall describe it now in the manner known to people.

3-4. O goddess Parameśvarī, there is the city of Sāṁbapura situated there. The holy spot remembered as Kāpālika is established to the north thereof. The Lord named Kapāleśvara is stationed there in the form of a Liṅga for the sake of dispelling sins of men by seeing and touching it.

5. Within a distance of sixteen *Dhanus* from that deity (i.e. Kapāleśvara) in the north-eastern direction, the deity Rudra called Tryaṁbakeśvara is stationed.

6. The deity blesses all and bestows all cherished desires. It was at this holy spot that the excellent sage named Guru performed a very severe and difficult penance unbearable even to Devas and Dānavas.

7. He worshipped Śaṅkara thrice a day in an excellent manner. He performed the Japa of the great Tryaṁbaka Mantra[1] three crore times.

8. Thereby he propitiated the Lord of Devas and obtained

1. The Mantra is - *tryaṁbakaṁ yajāmahe* etc. RV VII.59.12.

divine powers and prosperity. He himself designated the immutable deity as Tryaṁbakeśvara.

9. It was by repeating the Tryaṁbaka Mantra that he obtained supernatural power and eightfold divine *Aiśvarya* (Mastery). Therefore, the deity is called Tryaṁbakeśvara.

10. Even by viewing or touching the deity it destroys sins. A Brāhmaṇa who performs *Japa* in the vicinity of Tryaṁbakeśvara attains the great Siddhi. He becomes the veritable Rudra himself.

11. By merely viewing it, sin is broken into a thousand bits. He who devoutly worships it with sanctity and in the prescribed manner uttering *Vāmadeva Mantra*[1] will be rid of sins.

12. He who keeps awake at night on the fourteenth lunar day in the bright half of the month of Caitra doing adoration, singing eulogy and hearing/telling devotional stories gets the desired fruit.

13. A cow should be gifted there itself by those who desire to get the fruit of the perfect pilgrimage.

14. Thus, O goddess, the sin-destroying greatness of Tryaṁbakeśvara Rudra has been spoken to you. It bestows meritorious fruits on men.

CHAPTER NINETYTWO

Greatness of Aghoreśvara

Īśvara said:

1-3. Thereafter, O great goddess, a devotee should proceed to the excellent Aghoreśvara. It is the sixth Liṅga and its face is remembered as Bhairava (terrible). Its shrine is situated to the north-west of Tryaṁbakeśvara within a distance of five *Dhanus*. It is meritorious. It bestows all desires. It is destructive of the sins of Kali Age. A man who adores it devoutly by means of ablution, eulogy etc, in due order, shall get the entire fruit of the gift of Meru.

---

1. Probably *vāmadevāya namaḥ* in *Taitt. Āraṇyaka* XVII. 2.

4. Depending on Dakṣiṇāmūrti everything that is offered there to Lord Aghoreśvara shall be everlasting.

5-7. If a devotee performs Śrāddha to the south of Aghoreśvara, the Pitṛs so propitiated remain happy for a Kalpa. Of what avail is *Śrāddha* at Gayā Tīrtha, O my beloved? Of what avail is a horse-sacrifice? By performing Śrāddha there, all these benefits and even more are obtained. He who offers even a bit of gold during the pilgrimage, obtains abundant fruit of a great act of charity.

8-9. He who performs Brahmakūrca in accordance with the injunctions on the eighth lunar day on a Monday in the vicinity of Aghoreśvara uttering *Aghora Mantra*[1] gets the fruit of performing *Prāyaścitta* (expiation) for six years. Thus the great glory of Aghoreśa has been briefly spoken. The greatness is destructive of all sins. If listened to it accomplishes all objectives.

CHAPTER NINETYTHREE

Greatness of Mahākāleśvara

Īśvara said:

1-2. Thereafter, O beautiful lady, a pilgrim should go to the shrine of Hara called Mahākāleśvara situated slightly to the north rather to the north-west of Aghoreśa within a distance of thirty *Dhanus.* O goddess, on being listened to, it destroys sins. O fair lady, formerly in Kṛtayuga it was remembered as Citrāṅgadeśvara.

3. O goddess, in Kali age, its name is proclaimed as Mahākālveśvara. The great Rudra in the form of Kāla is stationed in that Liṅga.

4-5. O my beloved, he is the preceptor of the mobile and immobile beings. The Lord destroys the arrogance of Devas and Dānavas. O my beloved, in the form of the Sun-god, he swallows the whole of the Cosmic Egg. O goddess, that Lord

1. Probably *aghorebhyo' tha ghorebhyo* etc.-*Taitt. Āraṇyaka* XVII.3.

of great lustre is stationed in that Liṅga. One who devoutly worships the Liṅga of mine early in the morning uttering the six syllabled Mantra conquers death in a moment. I am fond of that Liṅga.

6-7. Especially on the eighth day in the dark half, the devotee should perform the adoration at nightfall and burn Guggula along with ghee duly. Bhairava exonerates a hundred crimes of his. Great sages praise gifting cows at that holy spot.

8-9. Certainly a person who gifts cows here redeems ten generations before and ten generations after him.

A man who mutters *Śatarudriya* hymn in the spot to the south of the Lord, will uplift all the members of his father's and mother's family. By visiting Hara named Kāleśvara, one dispels all the sins committed in childhood, youth or old age.

10. If a person performs the rite of *Ghṛtakaṁbala* (covering the Liṅga with ghee) at the time of the northern transit of the Sun, he never again takes another birth in the world.

11. By visiting Mahākāleśvara, one can avert the eventuality of becoming poor, miserable and unlucky in the course of seven subsequent births.

12. He is reborn in a dignified well-to-do family. He will have even more devotion to the adoration of Mahākāleśvara.

13-14. Thus, O my beloved, the description of Mahākāleśvara has been given by me briefly. O goddess, there is a Gaṇa named Citrāṅgada. The deity Mahākāleśvara was formerly propitiated by him for a period of a thousand years according to the reckoning of Devas. Hence it became well-known as Citrāṅgadeśvara.

CHAPTER NINETYFOUR

Greatness of Bhairaveśvara

Īśvara said:

1-3. Thereafter, a pilgrim should go to the excellent Bhairaveśvara stationed within a distance of ten *Dhanus* in the south-east corner of the same (i.e. Mahākāleśvara). O fair lady, it fulfills all cherished desires and destroys a series of states of poverty.

O my beloved, formerly in Kṛtayuga it was well-known by the name Caṇḍeśvara. There was a Gaṇa named Caṇḍa, O goddess, and the deity was propitiated by him for a thousand divine years. Hence it is remembered as Caṇḍeśvara.

4-5. By visiting the Lord of the chiefs of Devas and by touching him with concentration and mental purity, one is rid of all sins committed between birth and death. He who keeps awake at night after fasting on the fourteenth day in the dark half of the month of Bhādrapada, goes to the great region where Lord Maheśvara dwells.

6-8. All sins incurred verbally, mentally and physically are destroyed by visiting that Liṅga. Gingelly seeds, gold and garments should be gifted there to an enlightened scholar for destroying all sins by one who desires to get the fruit of a well performed pilgrimage. At the end of a Kalpa the Lord assumes a Bhairava (terrible) form and annihilates the entire universe. O goddess of gods, he is then remembered as Bhairava.

9-10. O great goddess, in this Kalpa, Rudra named Bhairava resorted to Prabhāsa Kṣetra and had the form of a Liṅga till the end of the Kalpa. Thus the greatness of Bhairaveśvara has been briefly spoken. By listening to this, the creature is rid of highly terrible sins.

CHAPTER NINETYFIVE

Greatness of Mṛtyuñjaya

Īśvara said:

1-3. Thereafter, O beautiful lady, a pilgrim should go to the Liṅga named Mṛtyuñjayeśvara situated within a distance of ten *Dhanus* in the south-east corner thereof.

In the western direction, it is situated within a distance of four *Dhanus* from the shrine of Sagarāditya. It destroys the sins of all creatures who visit and touch it. In the earlier Yuga, it was called Nandīśvara, because it is the place where a severe penance was performed by my Gaṇa named Nandin.

4. After installing the great Liṅga, he became engaged in its worship always and performed the Japa of the great Mantra well-known as *Mṛtyuñjaya.*

5. O goddess, he muttered the Mantra millions and crores of times. Thereby Lord Maheśvara became pleased. The Lord gave him chieftainship of Gaṇas and salvation called *Sāmīpya* (nearness to the Lord).

6. Since Hara became pleased with him due to (the *Japa* of) Mṛtyuñjaya Mantra, the Liṅga therefore, became famous all over the earth as Mṛtyuñjayeśa.

7. If anyone worships it devoutly or visits it with sanctified soul, he will destroy all the sins acquired even in the course of seven births.

8. The devotee should bathe the Liṅga with milk, curds, honey mixed with ghee, or sugarcane juice. He should apply Kuṁkuma (saffron) to it.

9. The juice of (liquid) musk mixed with camphor and Uśīra, or scented sandalwood also should be applied. Then he should worship it with flowers.

10-11. O goddess, incense and Aguru should be fumigated before the Lord. Then he (the devotee) should honour the Lord (or priest) with different kinds of garments in accordance with his capacity. He shall then offer milk pudding as *Naivedya* along with lamps. Thereafter, *Aṣṭāṅga* prostration should be devoutly performed touching the ground with eight parts of the body.

12-14. Gold should be offered to a Brāhmaṇa who has mastered the Vedas. In this manner his pilgrimage shall become one conforming to the scriptural texts. There is no doubt about it. By doing this, O goddess, the man gets the fruit of his birth.

Thus the great glory (of the worship) of Mṛtyuñjaya has been succinctly stated. It is destructive of the sins of all creatures. It causes the fulfilment of all cherished desires.

CHAPTER NINETYSIX

Greatness of Kāmeśvara

Īśvara said:

1-2. Thereafter, O goddess, a pilgrim should go to the

shrine proclaimed as Kāmeśvara. It is stationed within a distance of three *Dhanus* to the north thereof. O goddess of Suras, in Tretā, it was famous by the name Ratīśvara. O lady of excellent countenance, if it is visited and worshipped, the sins of men committed during the period of seven births get destroyed. There shall be no break-up of households.

The Devī said:

3. O Lord, by whom was this installed? Why is it called Ratīśvara? What fruit is obtained by visiting it? Mention everything in detail.

Īśvara said:

4-6. Listen, O fair lady, I shall narrate to you a sin-destroying story. There was a chaste lady named Rati. She was the well-known wife of Kāma.

Formerly when *Manasija* (i.e. Kāma) was burnt by Lord Tripurāri, it is said that Rati performed a penance at that spot for the sake of getting him (Kāma) back.

For a period of four Yugas, she stood on the tip of her toes, O my beloved, and with a tranquil mind Mahādeva was propitiated (by her).

7-9. At a certain time, O my beloved, the Maheśvara Liṅga pierced through the ground and came up before her.

At the same time, an unembodied voice spoke as follows, O lady of excellent countenance, and delighted her. "Since, O highly esteemed lady, the Maheśvara Liṅga suddenly rose up as a result of your devotion, you should worship it. You will get back your husband."

10. On hearing these words of the divine messenger, that chaste lady worshipped the Liṅga with great devotion.

11. Then, O my beloved one, Kāma rose up as though he was getting up from sleep. Ever since then that Liṅga is known as Kāmeśvara.

12. Delighted due to the return of Kāmadeva the wife of Kāma spoke these words to the Flower-weaponed One:

13-14. "Those others who concentrate their minds with purity and worship this Liṅga thus, acquire their desired supernatural powers and attain the excellent goal. By the favour of this Liṅga, they will get everything mentally desired even if it happens to be very difficult to get. There is no doubt."

15. After saying thus, the chaste lady Rati went away accompanied by Kāma. With the innermost soul delighted and with desires fulfilled, she went to her abode.

16. He who perfectly worships this (Liṅga) on the thirteenth lunar day in the bright half of Caitra, shall become one like Kāma. If listened to, this story accords conjugal felicity.

CHAPTER NINETYSEVEN

Greatness of Yogeśvara

Īśvara said:

1-3. Thereafter, a pilgrim should go to the shrine well-known as Yogeśvara, O great goddess. It is situated within a distance of seven *Dhanus* from Kāmeśa in the north-western direction.

The Liṅga is of great power. It destroys sins through viewing (it). In the earlier Yuga, it was well-known as Gaṇeśvara.

O goddess, formerly the highly powerful innumerable Gaṇas of mine came to Prabhāsa after knowing that it is a holy spot of Maheśvara.

4. Staying there they resorted to Yoga practice and performed a great penance for a thousand years according to the divine reckoning. Maheśvara was pleased thereby.

5. The Lord granted them salvation called Sālokya (Residence in the world of the Lord) as a result of their Yogic power. Since the Bull-bannered Lord was pleased with their Yogic practice consisting of six ancillaries, the Liṅga was given the name Yogeśvara. It bestows the fruit in the form of Yogic power.

6. He who devoutly worships it in accordance with the injunctions of a perfect adoration, attains Yogic Siddhi and rejoices in heaven like Devas.

7. A man may gift away the golden Meru or the entire earth. But he who worships Yogeśa is remembered as superior to both of them.

8. For the sake of the full benefit, a bull should be given as a charitable gift there.

Thus the eleven Rudras stationed in Prabhāsa Kṣetra have been described. They are to be worshipped and honoured everyday by those who desire to attain the fruit of (visiting) the holy spot.

9. He who listens to the *Saṁhitā* (Scriptural Text) pertaining to the eleven Rudras attains the entire fruit of (visiting) the holy spot like the residents of Prabhāsa.

10. He who resides within this holy place yet does not know these Rudras stationed in Prabhāsa is no better than non-existent (despite his residence therein). He is remembered as a beast.

11. After worshipping all these eleven Rudras or one only, and visiting the deity Someśvara, a devotee should perform the *Japa* of *Śatarudriya*. There is no doubt about this that he acquires the fruit (of the worship) of all the Rudras.

12. O beautiful woman, this secret of the greatness of the Rudras has been fully spoken to you. When listened to, it destroys sins and increases merit.

CHAPTER NINETYEIGHT

Greatness of Pṛthvīśvara

Īśvara said:

1-3. Thereafter, O great goddess, a pilgrim should go to the shrine well-known as Caṇḍeśvara. It is situated to the northwest of Someśa within a distance of sixty *Dhanus*. It is a divine Liṅga, O great goddess, and destroys all sins.

In an earlier Yuga, in the Svāyaṁbhuva Manvantara, at the beginning of Tretāyuga, it was installed by Pṛthivī (goddess Earth). In this previous Manvantara, O my beloved, the Liṅga was called Pṛthvīśvara.

4. Further, O my beloved, it was acquired by Candra. The Liṅga (came to be called) Candreśvara. It destroys sins like Brāhmaṇa-slaughter etc. It is conducive to the increase of merit.

5. On visiting the deity, O goddess, a man is rid of all the

sins originating (committed) in the course of seven births. He becomes contented and blessed.

The Devī said:

6. How did that sin-destroying Liṅga come to be well-known as Pṛthvīśvara? How did it further become famous as Candreśvara, O my Lord. Do narrate this in detail. I am desirous of listening to it respectfully.

Īśvara said:

7. Listen, O goddess, I shall narrate the sin-annihilating story. On listening to this, a creature is rid of the three types of Karma-bondages.

8. O great goddess, the Earth became afflicted formerly by the burden of the Daityas. Slipping and going down suddenly, she became transformed into a cow.

9-10. Running about here and there, she could not get relief anywhere. She went on wandering from place to place for a hundred years. When a hundred years were completed, she reached the great holy spot well-known as Prabhāsa which destroys sins. It has been resorted to by Devas, Dānavas and Gandharvas.

11. Endowed with great devotion, she stayed in that great holy place and resolving in her mind she eventually installed the Liṅga.

12. When an extremely difficult penance was performed for a period of more than a hundred years, Lord Rudra became pleased and spoke to Dharitrī (Earth) these words:

13. "O fair lady Viśvaṁbharā (Earth), all the austerities have been performed quite well by you. O auspicious one, do not be grief-stricken. Your wish will become fulfilled.

14. Daityas will meet with destruction after being slain by Viṣṇu on the Earth. O extremely great lady, you will be relieved of the burden of Daityas.

15. This highly excellent Liṅga installed by you will be very famous after your name Dharitrī, all over the world.

16. I shall stay here, the great Lord, in the form of a Liṅga in every Kalpa dispelling sins of men.

17. Endowed with my eightfold Cosmic form I shall be present in this Liṅga for ever. I shall destroy all sins of mankind incurred during hundreds of previous births.

18. He who adores this Liṅga on the third lunar day in the dark half of the month of Bhādrapada, shall undoubtedly acquire the fruit of a thousand horse-sacrifices.

19. By worshipping this Liṅga alone, the fruit acquired shall be that of ablution in all the Tīrthas and giving all kinds of charitable gifts.

20. An area of about sixteen *Dhanus* all round is the extent of this holy place which grants salvation unto all living beings.

21-22. Living beings like even worms and insects that die within this range attain the highest goal. A person may gift away the golden Meru or the entire earth but he who adores Pṛthvīśa Liṅga is proclaimed as superior to both of them."

Īśvara said:

23-26. After saying thus and granting the boons, the Lord vanished there itself. Ever since then, Śaṅkara became a deity with the name Pṛthvīśvara. Again in this Kalpa, well-known as Vārāhakalpa, Candra become debilitated once due to Dakṣa's curse, O goddess. Śaśin fell on to the ground afflicted by phthysis. He came to the Prabhāsa Kṣetra on the shore of the ocean. On seeing the powerful Liṅga of great lustre named Pṛthvīśvara, he became engaged in worshipping it for a thousand years.

27-30. He performed a very terrible penance with only fallen leaves and water constituting his diet. Due to the greatness of that Liṅga, Śaśin became a delighter of everyone with his refulgence.

Therefore, the deity became Candreśvara. Due to the greatness of that Liṅga, Candra was rid of all sins. He obtained a very powerful Siddhi revealing a Sparśaliṅga. That deity in the form of a Liṅga they call Somanātha, the well-known deity.

Thus the greatness of the deity Candra has been briefly mentioned. If listened to, it destroys sins and grants health.

CHAPTER NINETYNINE

Greatness of Daṇḍapāṇi-Cakradhara

Īśvara said:

1-3. Thereafter, O goddess, a pilgrim should go to the holy

place where Cakradhara (Discus-bearing Lord) and the staff-bearing deities are present, O goddess of Devas. They are stationed in the same spot.

They are situated within a distance of five *Dhanus* to the north of Someśa and to the east of Candreśa. They are very near Gandharveśa.

It is also on the south-western side of Umā. It is honoured by Brāhmaṇical and celestial sages. I shall narrate its origin which destroys all sins.

4-5. Formerly there was Pauṇḍraka[1] (King of the country Puṇḍra) Vāsudeva in Vārāṇasī. While the Purāṇas were being read by Brāhmaṇas, he heard that at the beginning of the Kalpa, towards the close of the Dvāpara Yuga, the mighty Vāsudeva would be taking his incarnation in the household of Kṣatriyas.

6. The foolish fellow considered himself Vāsudeva, O my beloved of excellent countenance, and bore (his) marks such as holding a discus.

7-10. He sent a messenger (called) Mahodara to Dvārakā. He went there and said to Viṣṇu: "Give up your discus etc. King Pauṇḍraka says so. If you do not, you will meet with death." Thereupon, Lord Viṣṇu told him these charming words: "That king Pauṇḍraka should be told these words of mine: 'I will come to your city Kāśī holding my discus. I will then leave (hurl) the discus as well as this club. Undoubtedly you should accept (receive) the discus or the other thing as you wish.'"

11. On being told thus the messenger went away. Hari remembered Garuḍa and when he came, he rode on it and immediately went to that City (Vārāṇasī).

12. Due to his friendship, the king of Kāśī approached (joined) Pauṇḍraka along with all his attendants, armies and followers.

13. Thereupon. accompanied by his own big army and that of the king of Kāśī, Pauṇḍraka Vāsudeva marched against Keśava.

14. Hari saw him from a distance. He was seated in his irresistible chariot. He held a discus, a club and the Śārṅga bow. He had the emblem of Garuḍa.

15. On seeing him, Kṛṣṇa with the real Garuḍa as his emblem

1. Pauṇḍraka was not the king of Vārāṇasī. He was the king of Kuruṣa (Mod. Shahabad, District Bihar). Kṛṣṇa killed him when challenged. (Bh.P.X.65)

laughed meaningfully. He then spoke to the foolish Pauṇḍraka characterised with his (Hari's) own marks:

16-17. "O Pauṇḍraka, through your messenger's oral message, you told me thus: 'Leave (hurl) the marks', I shall leave (discharge) everything. This discus has been discharged. So also this club. Let this Garuḍa go and climb on to your banner."

18. After saying thus, the discus was discharged and the (enemy) was caused to fall down. The chariot was broken by the club. The elephants and the horses were smashed into smithereens.

19. Thereat a loud cry of lamentation spread in the world. The highly powerful king of Kāśī, who grieved at the misery (death) of his friend, fought with Vāsudeva.

20. By means of arrows discharged from his Śārṅga bow his head was cut off (by Vāsudeva) and hurled into the city of Kāśī. This caused great wonder in the minds of the people.

21. After killing Pauṇḍraka and the King of Kāśī along with his followers, Śauri came back to Dvārakā like one who had gone ahunting.

22. Thereafter, the son of the king of Kāśī, miserable due to his father's mishap, propitiated Śaṅkara. He (Śaṅkara) granted him a boon.

23. He wooed: "O Lord, O Lord of Suras, with your favour let a Kṛtyā (Ogress of destruction) appear before me for killing Kṛṣṇa, the slayer of my father."

24. "It will happen so". When this was uttered (by the Lord) a great *Kṛtyā* rose up from the centre of the Dakṣiṇāgni (Sacrificial Fire) and started towards Dvārakā.

25. On seeing the terrible *Kṛtyā* emitting wreaths of flames, all the frightened Yādavas approached Janārdana seeking refuge.

26. Then the Garuḍa-emblemed Lord discharged Sudarśana for the destruction of the *Kṛtyā* which was shattered (fled) on being afflicted by the brilliance of the discus.

27. The discus of Viṣṇu, Sudarśana, pursued the *Kṛtyā* immediately. The *Kṛtyā* reached Vārāṇasī and the discus followed closely.

28. Then excessively frightened, the *Kṛtyā* sought refuge in Śaṅkara, Somanātha, the Lord of the universe. No one else was competent to save it.

29. Then Śaṅkara hit the discus with his excellent arrows. Getting entangled with the arrows of Śiva it returned to Dvārāvatī.

30. On seeing his discus hit with the arrows marked by Śiva's name, Lord Hari became furious. He seized it with his hand and went to the place where Kālabhairava Someśa was present.

31. His eyes became red like copper. He stood there raising the discus with his hand. He determined to destroy the *Kṛtyā* created by Kālabhairava.

32. He was seen thus by all the Devas and the Gaṇa of the Staff-bearing Lord (Daṇḍapāṇi). Even as the Devas were looking, the great Gaṇa Daṇḍapāṇi looked at the Lotus-eyed Viṣṇu with the discus in his raised hand and requested him:

Daṇḍapāṇi said:

33. O Lord of Devas, O Lord of the universe, do not be angry with the *Kṛtyā*.

34. Your discus is infallible in battle. Śaṅkara's *Kṛtyā* too is so. When the discus is hurled and if Hara becomes furious, a great calamity will befall or the destruction of the worlds will follow.

35. Hence the discus should not be released. Listen once again to our words. O Hari, I have been appointed in this holy spot by Śaṅkara formerly.

36. It is for the sake of protection the sinners[1] and to obstruct the evil-minded ones. Hence, O Hari, do stand beside me holding the discus.

37. Men will worship Lord Cakradhara here by means of incense, garlands, offerings and various kinds of *Naivedyas* (foodstuffs).

Viṣṇu said:

38. Here I am restrained by your words as though with a goad. I shall stay here by your side with my hand holding the Cakra raised up.

39. It was thus, O my beloved, that Lord Cakradhara

1. The reading should have been *prāṇinām* instead of *pāpinām*.

stationed himself there. So also Lord Daṇḍapāṇi, the Lord of Gaṇas, my own form.

40. A man who devoutly worships Daṇḍapāṇi and Hari duly will be rid of sins. He shall go to the city of Śiva.

41. If anyone worships Daṇḍanāyaka with scents, incense and offerings especially on the fourteenth lunar day as well as eighth lunar day in the dark half of the month of Māgha, he will have no obstacle anywhere while he stays in the holy spot.

42-43. He who abstains from food on the eleventh day and worships Cakrapāṇi shall be rid of all sins. He will attain *Salokatā* (residing in the same world) of Viṣṇu.

Thus the greatness of Cakrapāṇi has been briefly stated. So also that of Daṇḍapāṇi Gaṇa. If listened to it destroys sins.

CHAPTER ONE HUNDRED

Durvāsas Curses Sāṁba

Īśvara said:

1-3. Thereafter, O great goddess, a pilgrim should go to the shrine of Sāṁbāditya situated to the north of those two (Daṇḍapāṇi and Cakradhara) and to the north-west of Brahmā in the form of a boy.

O most excellent lady among Suras, the deity was installed by Sāṁba. In this Dvīpa, there are three holy places of Lord Bhāskara (the Sun-god). The first one is Mitravana by name. Then the next is called Muṇḍīra and the third one in Prabhāsa Kṣetra is Sāṁbāditya.

4. O great goddess, the city called Sāṁba in that holy spot is the second permanent abode of the Sun-god there.

5-6. Due to his affection for Sāṁba and in order to bless the people, Arka (the Sun-god) stays there with a twelfth part of his self for the purpose of general welfare. He views all the worlds always with a friendly eye. The Lord himself (directly) accepts the adoration duly performed.

The Devī said:

7. Who is this Sāṁba? Whose son is he? Wherefore is the

city of Ravi (Sun-god) named after him? Wherefore does this person of meritorious activities get the boon granted by the Thousand-rayed Lord?

Īśvara said:

8-9. There are highly powerful twelve Ādityas (Suns) shining. Among them the Lord named Viṣṇu is well-known in all the worlds. This omnipresent Lord attained the status of being the son of Vasudeva.

10. Sāṁba was born as his powerful son of Jāṁbavatī. Vehemently cursed by his father, he contracted the fell disease of leprosy. The Sun-god was installed by him and a city was built after his own name.

The Devī said:

11. For what reason was the son cursed by the father himself? O Lord, the reason cannot be insignificant because he cursed his own son.

Īśvara said:

12. Listen with attention to the reason for the curse given to him. There is a holy sage named Durvāsas, born of my own part.

13. That holy sage was moving about wandering in the three worlds. Then he came to Dvārāvatī and the people gathered before him.

14-15. Sāṁba who was arrogant due to his handsome features, saw the sage who arrived. The sage was tawny-eyed with matted hairs. He was emaciated, rough and very ugly. By looking at him and touching him, he insulted the sage. The stupid fellow saw his face and made his face appear similar. The most excellent one among the members of Yadu's family did thus because he was proud of his youthful features.

16. Thereat, the highly refulgent Durvāsas, the most excellent one among sages, became furious. Shaking his face (head) the holy sage spoke to Sāṁba:

17. "After looking at me and finding me ugly you became all the more proud of your handsome features. You showed your haughtiness by imitating my appearance and manner of

walking. Therefore, you will be overpowered by the fell disease of leprosy ere long."

CHAPTER ONE HUNDRED ONE

Greatness of Sāṁbāditya

Īśvara said:

1-3. At this very juncture (came) venerable sage Nārada, the mental son of Brahmā, who was proud that he could wander all over the three worlds. Though young, he was bowed to by all Devas. In the course of his wandering at will, he always used to come to Dvārāvatī to pay a visit to Vāsudeva. That excellent sage came furiously along with other sages.

4. As he came on quickly all the Yādava youths beginning with Pradyumna remained with their heads (politely) bent down.

5-6. Only there was neither *Arghya* nor *Pādya*, but they honoured him all round, but Sāṁba due to the inevitability of the curse, slighted the noble-souled Nārada as usual.

Being very proud of his youth and handsome features he was forever indulgent in sexual dalliance and liquor.

7. On seeing him impolite and rude, Nārada thought thus: 'Today I shall try to curb this impolite one and make him adopt auspicious (behaviour of) humility.'

8-10a. After thinking thus, he spoke to Vāsudeva: "O most excellent one among Devas, here there are sixteen thousand women. O my Lord,their emotional fondness for Sāṁba is much. No doubt, Sāṁba is unrivalled in all the worlds consisting of mobile and immobile beings. Further, those good women do deservingly need to see him always."

10b. On hearing these words from Nārada, Keśava began to think.

11. 'What has thus been mentioned by Nārada may have some truth in it. Moreover this is often heard (as being) said that there is fickleness in women. These two verses have been recited formerly by Brāhmaṇas well aware of the workings of the minds of women:

12-13. Though guarded vigilantly, they act unfaithfully to their husbands and betray their husbands due to their innate ignorance, fickleness and womanly incontinence. They never care to examine handsomeness. Nor do they resort to youthful charms alone. A man may be handsome or ugly, they enjoy him merely because he is a man.'

Īśvara said:

14. After thinking thus in his mind, Kṛṣṇa spoke to Nārada: "I do not believe in this ancient saying."

15. When the Lord said thus, Nārada replied "I shall so manage everything as to convince you."

16. After saying thus, Nārada went away as he came. A few days thereafter, he returned to Dvārakā.

17. On that day the Lord was engaged in drinking liquor after enjoying aquatic sports along with all the members of his Antaḥpura (inner apartment). They were in a secluded place.

18-21. It was in the beautiful Raivataka park embellished with different kinds of trees and rendered fragrant and charming to all by means of the flowers of all the seasons.

Large lakes abounding in different kinds of lotuses in full bloom added to its beauty. Warbling swans and *Sārasa* (ducks) birds and ruddy geese increased its splendour. The Lord was sporting about there surrounded by women fully bedecked in necklaces, anklets, armlets, girdles and other ornaments. The excellent maidens had some jewels on every limb. Staying there the Lord drank the liquor of great auspicious flavour.

22-24. In the meantime, fully aware that the women were inebriated due to liquor, Nārada spoke to Sāṁba: " O princely youth, do come and stand here.The Lord calls you. It is not proper on my part to stay on there."

Urged by Nārada but not realizing the implication of Nārada's utterance, Śāṁba entered quickly and bowed down to his father. He took the seat pointed out by Viṣṇu with natural feeling.

25. In the meantime those women there who were deficient in self-control became highly agitated as soon as they saw Sāṁba.

26-27. As they were staying within the Antaḥpura so long, they had not seen him before. The liquor had its own effect in making them forget everything. Further they were naturally devoid of self-control. Hence their loins became moistened. Moreover this verse is heard everywhere on the earth as proclaimed in the Purāṇas:

28.[1] "On seeing an excellent man, the excellent organ of generation of women becomes moistened and dump even if they are observing celibacy or are Yoginīs".

29. Such things are seen in the world: By taking in liquor even bashful women discard shame and become unsuspecting.

30. Kāma (passion) becomes clearly manifest in women due to tasty, delicious foodstuffs containing meat as well as beverages of *Sīdhu, Surā* and *Āsava* (different varieties of liquor) and fascinating scents and garments.

31. Too much of liquor should not be given to them by a sensible man, because women are naturally already inebriated with wantonly sexual desires.

32. After sending Sāṁba in, Nārada also came hurriedly closely on the heels of Sāṁba.

33. On seeing the sage coming with pleasant manners, all those women suddenly got up; they were tipsy.

34-35. Even as Vāsudeva was watching, when they got up suddenly their valuable garments got torn and fell down into the pots (of liquor). The clothes clinging to their loins (underwear) also fell separately. On seeing it Hari became angry. He cursed those women:

36-37. "O women, since your minds strayed elsewhere unmindful of me, you will not get into the regions occupied by your husband at the close of your life.

Slipping down from the world of your husband as well as from the path of heaven, you will have no refuge and will fall into the clutches of robbers."

38. As a result of this defect and curse, those women, at the time of Kṛṣṇa's heavenward departure, were abducted by robbers belonging to Pañcanada even as Arjuna was looking on.

39-40. Those women who were deficient in inherent moral strength and grit became defiled, O my beloved, But Rukmiṇī,

1. In the text, the number wrongly printed as 27.

Satyavatī and Jāmbavatī did not fall into the hands of the robbers[1].
They were protected by their own intrinsic power.
After cursing the women Kṛṣṇa cursed Sāṁba too:

41. "Since, on perceiving your extremely attractive features all these women became agitated, you do be afflicted by the disease of leprosy."

42. On hearing his words Sāṁba became ashamed. Remembering the earlier words of the excellent sage he said with a subdued smile:

43. "O my father, I was devoid of impure emotion yet I have been cursed (by you) without any reason. How could the angry Durvāsas have said otherwise?"

44-45. After having said thus to the lotus-eyed Kṛṣṇa Sāṁba was overcome with anxiety and grief. He was disgusted with everything. He then went to the Prabhāsa Kṣetra that destroys all sins. After reaching that holy place, he practised a very severe penance.

46. He installed Lord Sun, the thousand-rayed deity, who destroys sins. Then he propitiated it fully conforming to the (prescribed) rules and restrictions.

47. He worshipped the Lord thrice a day during the three junctions (morning, midday and dusk) by means of divine scents and unguents. He used to eulogize the Lord of day everyday by means of this prayer:

Sāṁba said:

48. Obeisance to the light of the three worlds. O destroyer of darkness, obeisance to you. Obeisance to the Lord of lotuses: obeisance to the enemy of Kumuda (lily, night-lotus)

49. Obeisance to the firm base of the universe, Obeisance to thee, the creator of the universe. O Lord of Devas, I bow down to Sūrya, the illuminator of the three worlds.

50. "Having the complexion of Āditya, he is the protector of the universe. He is unprecedented, the foremost one of

1. According to Mbh *Mausala* 7.73-74; Satyavatī (Bhāmā) performed penance and Rukmiṇī and Jāṁbavatī entered fire after Kṛṣṇa's death.

all Suras. He is the being with the golden womb. He is spoken as being the noble-souled one beyond all darkness."

51. On being eulogized thus, Sūrya became manifest to him and said to Sāṁba, the son of Jāṁbavatī, with a highly delighted heart:

52. "O Sāṁba, O mighty-armed Sāṁba, O son of Govinda, listen. I am delighted with this prayer. Tell me the boon desired by you (to be granted).

Sāṁba said:

53. O most excellent one among Suras, I have been cursed by Kṛṣṇa. I am a sinner with a defiled mind; O Lord, if you are pleased with me, heal completely the fell disease of leprosy.

Śrī Bhānu said:

54. O highly fortunate one, you shall be free from ailments, once again, with my favour you will be in the same form as you were in before.

55. From now onwards, those wives of Viṣṇu should not at all be looked at by you, O scion of the family of Yadu. You should never stay within the range of their vision.

56. O excellent Yādava, you had to contract leprosy transmitted to you by the noble-souled, all powerful Viṣṇu who was overpowered by jealous feelings for them.

57. If anyone comes here and eulogizes me with this prayer, no one born of his family will be a leper.

58. Understand perfectly the twelve names of Āditya. I shall tell you another set of twelve names fully.

59-61. They are: Āditya, Savitṛ, Sūrya, Mihira, Arka, Pratapana, Mārtaṇḍa, Bhāskara, Bhānu, Citrabhānu, Divākara and Ravi. These twelve names should be known along with the general names which are: Viṣṇu, Dhātṛ, Bhaga, Pūṣan, Mitra, Aṁśu, Varuṇa, Aryaman, Indra, Vivasvat, Tvaṣṭṛ and Parjanya remembered as the twelfth. Thus the twelve Ādityas have been enumerated severally.

62. They rise up always along with the twelve months in

due order. Viṣṇu blazes in Caitra, Aryaman in Vaiśākha always.

63-65. Vivasvat (blazes) in the month of Jyeṣṭha, and Aṁśvmat in Āṣāḍha, Parjanya in the month of Śrāvaṇa and Varuṇa in the month called Proṣṭhapada (Bhādrapada). Indra in the month of Aśvayuja and Dhātṛ blazes in Kārttika. Mitra blazes in Mārgaśīrṣa; the Āditya Pūṣan in the month of Pauṣa. Bhaga should be known (blazing) in the month of Māgha. Tvaṣṭṛ blazes in Phālguna. Viṣṇu blazes always with twelve hundreds of rays.

66. Aryaman blazes with one thousand three hundred rays; Vivasvat with twice seven hundred rays; Aṁśumān with eight hundred rays.

67. Parjanya is like Vivasvat. Varuṇa is like Aryaman. Indra shines with twice six and eleven hundred.

68. Bhaga and Tvaṣṭṛ with a thousand and one hundred (rays). During the northern transit, the rays of the Sun increase always. During the southern transit, the rays of the Sun decrease.

69-73. Thus I take up twelve *Mūrtis* at the centre of Prabhāsa Kṣetra. I am well-known as Sāṁbāditya and will stay thus in another Manvantara. O most excellent one among the descendants of Yadu, on the fifth lunar day in the bright half of Māgha, taking *Ekabhakta* (a single meal) is recommended; taking food at night is cited for the sixth lunar day. On the seventh lunar day a devotee fasts in the presence of Sāṁbārka. The devotee of great vows offers Karavīra flowers mixed with red sandal.

A sensible man should offer *Kuṇḍaraka* incense and worship Bhāskara. He should feed Brāhmaṇas with divine foods in accordance with his financial capacity. He who performs duly the adoration of Sāṁbāditya with great faith, obtains the entire benefit.

Īśvara said:

74-75. After saying thus, the Thousand-rayed One vanished there itself. Sāṁba became rid of his ailments and returned to Dvārakā. Thus, O goddess, the great deliverance of Sāṁbāditya has been narrated. On being listened to it dispels sins and accords health.

CHAPTER ONE HUNDRED TWO

Greatness of Kaṇṭakaśodhinī

Īśvara said:

1-3. Thereafter, a pilgrim should go to the shrine of Goddess Kaṇṭakaśodhinī situated within a distance of two bows to the north thereof.

O great goddess, she is the destroyer of Mahiṣa. She is hugebodies and adored by Brahmā, Devas and sages.

Sinful Dānavas were Devakaṇṭakas (Thorns unto the Devas) and the goddess purged the worlds of those demons in every Yuga. Hence she is Kaṇṭakaśodhinī. A devotee should worship her on the ninth day in the bright half of the month of Aśvayuj.

4. If a devotee worships her with the offerings of animals, flowers, excellent lights and incense, O lady of excellent countenance, he will have no enemies in the course of a full year.

5. It anyonc visits her with excellent devotion on the fourteenth lunar day (in dark half) or everyday the benefactress guards him like her own son. There is no doubt about it.

6. Thus, O goddess, the sin-destroying greatness of Kaṇṭakaśodhinī has been spoken succinctly. If it is listened to it is a great succour.

CHAPTER ONE HUNDRED THREE

Greatness of Kapāleśvara

Īśvara said:

1-3. Thereafter, O beautiful lady, a pilgrim should go to the excellent Kapāleśvara shrine situated to the north thereof. It is worshipped by Suras and Gandharvas.

Formerly when the Yajña of the intelligent Dakṣarāja was going on, while Homa was being performed in the holy fire, when all the Brāhmaṇas were seated there, Śaṅkara came there in the form of a Jālma (wretched rogue). O goddess, he was clad in old tattered rags. He was covered with dust and dirt.

He appeared grey in colour due to the dust particles.

4. On seeing him in the form of a ruffian holding a skull, those Brāhmaṇas became angry and all of them rebuked him with shouts of "Fie upon you!"

5. They called him many times, "O you sinner! O sinner!" and told him, "O base one, go away. The sacrificial altar is no place for you, as you are holding a human bone."

6. Then, O goddess of Suras, the Lord laughed loudly and hurled the skull on the sacrificial altar. He vanished somewhere and could not be found out by those learned ones.

7. When he vanished thus, they threw the skull out of the pavilion. But, O lady of excellent countenance, another skull of the same form cropped up there.

8. As and when one skull was thrown out another one sprang up from the ground. Thus there were hundreds of thousands, millions and trillions of skulls.

9. The skulls were cast out and they sprang up again. They were struck with wonder. Getting frustrated thus, the sages commented on his activities:

10. "Who else other than Mahādeva whose head is washed by the waters of Gaṅgā is capable to do something like this, particularly in this Yajña?"

11. They eulogized the Bull-emblemed Lord. They performed Homas in the sacred fire uttering the Śatarudriya Mantras.

12. Thereupon Lord Maheśvara became manifest unto them. Then they eulogized the Trident-bearing Lord by means of various hymns of the Vedas and the diverse Mantras mentioned in the Purāṇas.

[Sages' prayer (13-16):]

The Sages said:

13. Om. Obeisance to the primordial Prakṛti, Obeisance to the unvanquished and the noble-souled one. Obeisance, obeisance to the unconcealed, desireless Lord.

14. Obeisance to the original seed, to the promoter of saintly activities. Obeisance to the one without a parallel, to the only one. Obeisance, obeisance to the unmanifest one.

15. Obeisance to the Lord having serpents of different kinds and variegated colours for his armlets, to the Lord of all,

to the one without the Rajas element. Obeisance to the excellent one. Obeisance to the soul of the universe, to the cause of the ultimate causes. Obeisance to the Lord with eyes resembling lotus in full bloom.

16. I seek refuge in that primordial Lord, on seeing whom one is redeemed from the jaws of death, the Lord whom they call the invisible Brahman (Absolute), the omnipresent one, the immutable, the unmanifest, the beginningless and the unchanging one.

17. On being eulogized then in this manner by all those sages devoid of sins, the great Lord became pleased. Becoming manifest to them the Lord spoke to those sages: "Choose your boons."

The Brāhmaṇas said:

18-19. O Lord, if you are pleased with us, do be staying in this holy spot with the name Kapāleśvara, because, O Lord, innumerable skulls *(Kapālas)* cropped up here though they were removed. O Lord of Suras, undoubtedly this holy spot deserves it.

20. O Lord of Devas, the Liṅga by itself shall stay for another Manvantara. You do stay here in this holy spot by the name Kapāleśvara.

21. In the case of those who worship you with incense, garlands and unguents, let them attain the highest region inaccessible to even Devas.

22. After saying "So be it" Lord Maheśvara stationed himself there. O beautiful lady, the Yajña of the Lord of the night was resumed again.

23. On seeing the shrine, O my beloved, a man shall attain the fruit of a horse-sacrifice. He shall be rid of all sins incurred in the course of all the births.

24. This incident happened in the Svāyaṁbhuva Manvantara. But in the Vaivasvata Manvantara, another event occurred ending with the destruction of Dakṣa's Yajña.

25. Formerly the great Lord Hara was called Kapālī by Dakṣa. Therefore, Kapālī caused the destruction of that Yajña. In this Manvantara, he stationed himself as Kapāleśvara by name.

26. Further, in the Sūrya Sāvarṇika Manvantara, O beautiful woman, the name of this Lord shall be Tattveśvara.

27. Thus the greatness of the deity, Rudra, has been succinctly spoken. It causes destruction of the sins of all creatures. It causes the bonds of the *Paśu* (individual soul) to be snapped.

CHAPTER ONE HUNDRED FOUR

Greatness of Koṭīśvara

Īśvara said:

1-5. Thereafter, O great goddess, a pilgrim should go to the excellent Koṭīśvara shrine situated to the north thereof. It is well-known as Koṭīśa.

It destroys all sins of all creatures. It gives liberation from bondage to the *Paśus* (individual souls).

Formerly, O goddess, Pāśupata sages used to perform penance in the vicinity of Kapāleśvara. With bodies smeared with holy ash, they used to perform elaborate penance. They had matted hairs like coronets. They wore girdles of the Muñja grass. All of them were quiescent. They were Śivayogīs, Brāhmaṇas who had subdued their anger. They spread all over the holy spot in all directions.

O great goddess, they numbered a crore and they were eagerly devoted to the *Japa* of Mantras and they had installed the Liṅga very near Kapāleśa.

6. Then, with great devotion, they worshipped the Liṅga. Then Hara, the great Lord, was pleased with them and granted them salvation.

7. O my beloved, a crore *(Koṭi)* of sages became Siddhas there. Hence the Liṅga became famous by the name Koṭīśvara.

8. A man who devoutly worships the *Anāmaya* (one who dispels internal sufferings) Koṭīśvara obtains the fruit of the *Japa* of a crore of Mantras.

9. Gold should be gifted there to a Brāhmaṇa who has mastered the Vedas. He shall get the fruit of a crore of *Homas* and the merit of a perfect pilgrimage.

CHAPTER ONE HUNDRED FIVE

Greatness of Brahmā

Īśvara said:

1-4. Henceforth, I shall describe another secret and excellent holy place. It destroys all the sins of men. I shall describe it in detail to you the greatness of the principal deity, the greatness of the residents throughout the Kalpa.

Someśa, Daitya-Hantā (destroyer of demons i.e. Viṣṇu), Pitāmaha in the form of a boy, Āditya belonging to Arkasthala, Prabhāsa and Śaśibhūṣaṇa (Moon-adorned One i.e. Śiva)—these six leading deities are stationed in the holy place Prābhāsika.

Merely by viewing them, a devotee becomes contented and one who has fulfilled his duties. Certainly he is redeemed from terrible sins incurred throughout the life.

The Devī said:

5. The greatness of the deities who were mentioned earlier (in the above list) has been described by you. What about that which you refer to as the deity in the form of a boy?

6. In all other holy places Pitāmaha is in the form of an old one. How did he happen to be a boy ? What is the greatness thereof?

7. O Lord, if you are pleased with me, do tell me this in detail. O Lord of Devas, how is he to be worshipped? How is the pilgrimage (religious procession, *Yātrā*) to be performed by men?

Īśvara said:

8. O goddess, listen. I shall describe the greatness pertaining to Brahmā. Merely by listening to this one is liberated from all sins.

9. There is no other deity equal to Brahmā. There is no elderly preceptor equal to Brahmā. There is no knowledge like that of Brahmā. There is no penance like that pertaining to Brahmā.

10. People wander in the course of mundane existence, utterly overwhelmed by misery, grief and terror as long as they do not become devoted to Pitāmaha, the eldest of all the Suras.

11. Who will not become liberated from bondage, if the mind of a creature is directed towards and placed steadily in god Brahmā just as it is directed to worldly topics.

The Devī said:

12-13. If Brahmā is the preceptor of the universe and possesses such greatness, why has he come to the holy place of Prābhāsika? Where is he stationed in that great Tīrtha? At what time did the most excellent one of Suras come there? How is he to be worshipped by leading Brāhmaṇas and on what lunar day? Do mention all these in due order.

Īśvara said:

14. The great holy spot of Brahmā is on the north-east side of Somanātha and on the south-east of Sāṁbāditya. It is like another world of Brahmā.

15. There in his holy spot where Pitāmaha is stationed in the form of a boy, O goddess, these residents of the whole Kalpa are also present.

16. The creator of the universe, the Lord of the universe is highly refulgent and this is his Sattva form. In the splendid holy spot of Prābhāsika, he happened to arrive when he was eight years old.

17. Desirous of creating different kinds of subjects, he installed the great Liṅga there and performed penance for a thousand years according to the divine reckoning.

18. After the lapse of some time, the Lord was requested by Soma. He had been rid of his phthisis and had sound faith.

19. It was for the purpose of installing the Liṅga in the splendid Prābhāsika Kṣetra. Accompanied by Viśvakarman and a crore of the Brāhmaṇa-sages, he carried out the installation of the excellent Liṅga.

20. Then, O lady of excellent countenance, after the installation of Somanātha Liṅga, he caused plenty of Yajña-Dakṣiṇās to be given to Brāhmaṇas.

21-22. The Liṅga was installed by Brahmā, the creator of the worlds, in this manner. Many years passed by even as he was in the form of a boy in the holy spot Prabhāsa. As he stayed in the centre of the holy spot forty-two *(catvāriṁśad dvayam ca)* years passed by. Thus Parārdha - the earlier half of 100 years of Brahmā's life[1]—passed by while he was staying at the holy spot of Prabhāsa.

The Devī said:

23. Do mention to me the measure (or extent) of a day, a month or a thousand years of Brahmā in detail. What is the span of the life of Brahmā as proclaimed (by sages)?

Īśvara said:

24. Brahmā is remembered as having the greatest span of life. A Parārdha has passed by even as he stayed in the holy spot of *Prabhāsa.* The second half will start now.

25. When Brahmā, the grandfather of the worlds, came to the holy spot of Prabhāsa, it is said that, he was eight years old.

26. O goddess fond of Devas, excepting the holy spot of Prabhāsa, in all other Tīrthas, the grandfather (Brahmā) is in the form of an old person.

27. There are many Tīrthas in the whole Brahmāṇḍa. Among all where Brahmā is remembered as present there, the first and the foremost one of great splendour is he (that Brahmā) who is stationed in Prabhāsa.

28. O my beloved, listen to the names (of Brahmā) in the different Kalpas. It is *Svayaṁbhū* in the first Kalpa, in the second it was *Padmabhū* who was stationed there.

29. In the third (Kalpa), he is (was) called *Viśvakartā* and in the fourth, *Bālarūpin* (one in the form of a boy). These are mentioned as the principal names of Svayaṁbhū, the self-born god Brahmā.

30. He who remembers these names every day shall be a long-lived man.

31. At the advent of the night of Brahmā, all the Planets, Moon, Sun, along with Devas, Asuras, and human beings, the entire range of the three worlds, perish.

32. Again, when the day dawns, Pitāmaha wakes up and resumes creation as it was before,O my beloved.

---

1. Brahmā came to Prabhāsa when he was eight years old. He stayed for forty-two years at Prabhāsa. He was then fifty years old (8+42). Half of his life (of 100 years) was spent at Prabhāsa.

33. I shall mention the measure of the day of Brahmā, the creator of the worlds. That time unit is called *Truṭi* which is a fourth of the *Netra Bhaṅga* (? wink of the eye)

34. O lady of excellent countenance, twice that time unit should be known as a *Nimiṣa.* Fifteen such *Nimiṣas* are termed *Kāṣṭhā* by learned men. Thirty such *Kāṣṭhās* make a *Kalā* as mentioned by learned men.

35. A *Muhūrta* is made up of thirty Kalās. A day is made up of fifteen *Muhūrtas.* A night should be known as having the same duration as that of the day. The two together make an *Ahorātra* (complete day).

36. Fifteen *Ahorātras* make one *Pakṣa* (fortnight). The time unit formed by two *Pakṣas* is called a *Māsa* (month). Six months constitute an *Ayana.* An *Abda* (year) is formed by two *Ayanas.*

37. Four million three hundred twenty thousand years should be known as a *Caturyuga* according to solar reckoning.

38. Seventy-one *Catruyugas* make one *Manvantara.* This shall be the span of life of an Indra. This has thus been succinctly mentioned to you.

39. The first Manu is *Svāyaṁbhuva.* Then the next Manu was *Svārociṣa.* Then follow *Auttama, Tāmasa, Raivata* and *Cākṣuṣa.*

40. Thereafter come *Vaivasvata, Arkasāvarṇi, Brahmasāvarṇi, Dharmasāvarṇi, Raucya* and *Bhūtya* (along with *Indrasāvarṇi* and *Dakṣasāvarṇi* to be added to the lists).

41. These are the fourteen Manus enumerated in due order. I shall now enumerate all the Indras of the past and future in order.

42-43. They are: *Viśvabhuk, Vipaścit, Sukīrti, Śibi, Vibhu, Manobhuva, Ojasvin,* the powerful *Bali. Adbhuta, Śānti, Ramya, Devavara, Vṛṣā Ṛtadhāman, Divassvāmin* and *Śuci.* These are the fourteen *Śakras* (Indras).[1]

44. O my beloved, all these die in the course of one day of Brahmā. His night is as long (as the day). This is remembered as the measure of a *Kalpa* (Their list follows).

45. The first Kalpa is *Śvetakalpa.* The second is *Nīlalohita.* The third one is *Vāmadeva,* then *Rathantara.*

46. *Raurava* is mentioned as the fifth; the sixth one is

1. The list of Indras is different in *Devī Purāṇa* (in chapter on *Kāla-vyavasthā*)

remembered as *Prāṇa;* the seventh one is *Bṛhatkalpa. Kandarpa* is mentioned as the eighth.

47-48. *Śadya* is mentioned as the ninth, *Īśāna* is remembered as the tenth, *Dhyāna* is mentioned as the eleventh. Then *Sārasvata* is the next. *Udāna* is the thirteenth. *Garuḍa* is the fourteenth. *Kaurma* should be known as the fifteenth. This is the *Paurṇamāsī* (Full-Moon day) of Prajāpati (Brahmā).

49. The sixteenth is *Narasiṁha. Samādhi* is the next one. *Āgneya* is the eighteenth; then the next one is *Somakalpa.*

50. *Bhāvana* is mentioned as the twentieth. *Suptamālin* is another. Then *Vaikuṇṭha, Arciṣa, Rudra* and *Lakṣmī Kalpa.*

51. The twenty-seventh is *Vairāja.* Then *Gaurīkalpa* i.e. *Andhaka* (i.e. when Andhaka was subdued). Then *Māheśvara* when Tripuras were killed.

52. In the end came *Pitṛkalpa* which is remembered as the New-Moon day of Brahmā. Thus, O my beloved, the thirty Kalpas in a month of Brahmā have been mentioned.

53. All the past days of Brahmā have been mentioned. It is *Vārāha* Kalpa now, the first lunar day of Brahmā when the Earth was lifted up by the Divine Boar.

54. These thirty Kalpas make one time unit remembered as *Māsa.* Such twelve units make one year. Under this reckoing of a year, Brahmā was eight years old when he was brought by Somarāja and then Somanātha was installed.

55. Thus even as Brahmā was residing in the Prabhāsa Kṣetra in the form of a boy, a Parārdha elapsed. The second one is running now.

56. Thus Brahmā, the Self-born Lord, residing in the centre of Prabhāsa Kṣetra has a great power. The Lord resorted to the Kṣetra in the form of a boy.

57. He should be worshipped, should be saluted by learned men. At the outset, he alone should be worshipped by those who wish to get the fruit of the perfect pilgrimage.

58. He who devoutly worships him, certainly worships me. He who hates him, hates me. One who is venerable to him is so to me also.

59. Viṣṇu and I are worshipped by one who is venerated by Brahmā. Brahmā and I are worshipped by one who is venerated by Viṣṇu.

60. Brahmā and Viṣṇu are worshipped when worship was

performed by me. Brahmā is Sattva quality (?), Viṣṇu is Rajas quality (?) and I am Tamas quality, so it has been proclaimed.

61. Brahmā is glorified as *Vāyu,* Rudra as *Anala* (Fire) and Viṣṇu as *AP* (Water). Viṣṇu is *Rātri* (night); Rudra is *Ahan* (day); Pitāmaha is what is termed as *Sandhyā* (dusk).

62. O goddess, I am Sāma Veda. Brahmā is called Ṛg Veda. Viṣṇu shall be Yajur Veda and *Kulādhāra* (basis of the family) is Atharvaṇa.

63. O goddess, I am summer (season of heat). Pitāmaha is the season of rains. Viṣṇu shall be winter (cold season). Thus he constitutes the three units of time.

64. I should be known as the sacred fire called *Dakṣiṇāgnī.* Hari is remembered as *Gārhapatya* fire and Brahmā is *Āhavanīya* fire. Thus everything has the three divinities.

65. I am stationed in the form of Liṅga; Viṣṇu is glorified as *Bhaga* (the base of Liṅga). Brahmā shall be set up in the seed. Viṣṇu is glorified as *AP* (water).

66. I abide in the form of Ākāśa (Ether). Thus the Lord is identical with the *Tattvas* (Elements). The *Bīja* (seed) that drops down from the ether is set up in Brahmā. Resorting to the form of Brahmā, he is the one who makes the seed grow.

67. Brahmā is stationed in the middle of the navel; Viṣṇu in the middle of the heart. O goddess, I am in the middle of the face as the support of all embodied beings.

68. That which I am is Brahmā himself; that which Brahmā is, is Hutāśana (fire). That which the goddess is, is Viṣṇu and that which is Viṣṇu is the Moon.

69. That which Kāla (Time) is, is Brahmā himself; that who is Rudra, is Bhāskara (the Sun god). Thus, O my beloved, the highest Brahman is stationed with a special Śakti (power).

70. Oṁkāra is the Supreme Brahman (Absolute). Gāyatrī is the ultimate Prakṛti (source of origin). Knowing these two, a man becomes liberated. He does not fall.

71. He who knows the ultimate, imperishable, non-dual principle, O goddess of Devas, shall know everything. Not the other one, the base man who causes differences.

72. The Supreme Brahman is in the form of one entire whole. It is stationed separately in the form of the effect. He who hates it, O beautiful woman, is called a hater of Brahman.

73. Brahmā is stationed on my right limb (part of the body). Keśava is stationed on my left limb (Part). He who entertains hatred towards them both, O beautiful woman is a hater of mine.

74. Thus, O beautiful woman, knowing (the reality) by the non-different inner Ātman, one should worship Brahmā, Keśava and Rudra in the same form.

CHAPTER ONE HUNDRED SIX

Glorification of Brāhmaṇas

The Devī said:

1-5. Tell me exactly the procedure of the worship of Brahman which has been glorified thus in non-dualistic terms.

That Pitāmaha is in the form of a boy in the holy spot of Prabhāsa. O Lord, how is he whose form is that of the ultimate Absolute, worshipped by people?

What are the Mantras? What is the procedure? Of what nature are the Brāhmaṇas thereof? How do the Brāhmaṇas staying there, derive the benefit of the holy spot?

Of how many classes are the Brāhmaṇas residing in the holy place? O great Lord, of what nature are their manners and customs? What are their habits? What do they resort to? Do explain in detail the great prosperity of these Brāhmaṇas.

Īśvara said:

6. Very well! Very well! O great goddess proficient in asking questions! Be attentive and listen to the greatness of the deities in the form of Brāhmaṇas.

7-10. On listening to it, O goddess, a man is rid of all sins.

O goddess of Devas, all those Brāhmaṇas glorified on the earth surrounded by seas, constitute my form. This form is visible on the earth. Brāhmaṇas are Devas perceptible on the earth while Devas in heaven are imperceptible. Brāhmaṇas are always dear to me. Brāhmaṇas constitute my body. He who devoutly worships them, worships me always. He who devoutly propitiates them shall propitiate me.

11. O my beloved, undoubtedly I am identical with those who are Brāhmaṇas, if they are worshipped, I shall become worshipped. Only when they are pleased, do I become pleased. He who entertains enmity to them, is inimical to me also.

12. If anyone worships my replica in the form of a stone icon with sandalpaste along with a agallochum, sweet scents and garlands he does not (really) worship me. If one venerates Brāhmaṇas and adores them, I am really worshipped.

13. O my beloved, all the Brāhmaṇas within this world are worthy of veneration, whether they have performed the Vratas mentioned in the Vedas or not.

14. At the time of Śrāddha,one should not subject Brāhmaṇas to a close test, if they are residents of the holy spot. In the case of testing Brāhmaṇas, there is a great deal of abuse.

15. One-eyed, lame, hump-backed, poor and sick—all these should be engaged in a Śrāddha mixed (along) with Brāhmaṇas who have mastered the Vedas.

16. Brāhmaṇas are worthy of veneration merely because of their birth. So if they are well-versed much more in the Vedas and the practice thereof. Therefore, Brāhmaṇas should not be censured in any respect in the cases of Havya and Kavya offerings.

17. One-eyed persons, bulky ones, hump-backed ones, poor and sick ones should not be insulted. A sensible man should not insult such Brāhmaṇas because their forms are remembered as my form.

18. Many men do not know as they are beyond the ken of wisdom. They are not aware that I wander on the earth in the form of a Brāhmaṇa.

19-20. If people strike or kill Brāhmaṇas of my form, if they make them perform impious jobs, if they send them on an errand to places where they should not be sent, if they compel them to be slaves, then the powerful messengers of Yama cut them with a saw after their death, even as artisans cut off a piece of wood with a string.

21-24. If base men threaten them with harsh speech, if they utter cruel words due to anger, if they kick with their foot, then the people in Yama's world strike them and make them fall down on the ground. With the eyes turned red due to anger, they kick them with their feet. Yama plucks out their tongue by means of hot and fiery tongs.

Those men who hate Brāhmaṇas, the sinners who look at Brāhmaṇas with an evil eye are enemies of Brāhmaṇas. Crows with huge bodies and adamantine beaks pluck their eyes out in a trice at the behest of Yama.

25-27. If anyone beats or wounds a Brāhmaṇa, if anyone sheds his blood, breaks his bone or slays him out, he should be known as *Brahmaghna* (Brāhmaṇa-slayer). There is no expiation at all in his case. There are fifty crores of Narakas. A fellow who slays Brāhmaṇas is thoroughly cooked in them successively for many thousand years. Hence, O beautiful woman, a Brāhmaṇa shall always be saluted by men.

28. Brāhmaṇas should be honoured always by offerings of food and drink. All Brāhmaṇas are persons deserving to receive all kinds of gifts.

29-30. O goddess of Devas, no one else deserves the same. If (another one) receives a gift, he attains downfall (low position). O goddess, a Brāhmaṇa sanctified by penance is one who has shaken off all sins. He does not incur anything adverse, if he accepts as gift the whole world surrounded by oceans. O goddess, there is nothing sinful in the case of a Brāhmaṇa.

31. A Brāhmaṇa who abides always by spiritual principles, who is sanctified by good emotional fervour, is by birth a great holy spirit.

32. All the Guardians of the Quarters in the world are worshippers of Brāhmaṇas. Hence one should not insult them if one wishes for a long life.

33. If Brāhmaṇas are infuriated, they will reduce everything to ashes by means of their own refulgence. They may even create other worlds and other guardians of the quarters.

34-35. They are the leaders of the heaven, the eternal Lords of Devas. By those noble-souled ones, the ocean was rendered impotable when they became infuriated. Even today their fiery anger does not cool down in the Daṇḍaka forest. The path made by them is called *Devayāna* (a path of Devas).

36. They are worthy of veneration. They should be bowed down to. Everything is well-established in them. It is they who make the worlds hold one another together.

37. Their penance and self-study of the Vedas is well-guarded and kept secret. Brāhmaṇas have their own esteemed Vratas.

They are perfect in all lores and Vratas well-concluded. They lead life without resorting to anyone else.

38. When infuriated, Brāhmaṇas become like serpents. They should be well attended to and served. Blazing by means of their power of penance, they may burn even oceans.

39. When Brāhmaṇas are pleased, all the deities become pleased. They are the ultimate goal of all living beings. They ponder over the spiritual pursuit.

40. They have all their doubts perfectly resolved in the pursuit of all types of knowledge in the beginning, middle or end. They are conversant with the higher and lower features (of everything). They lead others to the ultimate goal. Hence, even if Brāhmaṇas be always engaged in sinful deeds, they should not be killed.

41. He who destroys all this world may destroy Brāhmaṇa also in the same manner. If infuriated a Brāhmaṇa becomes like fire, the highly blazing *Arka* (Sun)and poison.

42. A Brāhmaṇa has precedence in the matter of taking food, among all living beings. He is the most excellent among all castes. He is the father, the preceptor. He does not perish. He does not incur pain or loss. He is not afflicted at all.

43. What is consigned to the mouth of a Brāhmaṇa is more excellent than (oblation in fire) even in *Agnihotra*. All Devas stay resorting to the bodies of Brāhmaṇas.

44. Hence Brāhmaṇas are worthy of being worshipped. If they be not available, idols and images are to be adored.

45. Whether he is equipped with learning or not, a Brāhmaṇa is my deity, just as the fire is a great divinity whether consecrated with prayers or not.

46. A fire does not become impure even in cremation grounds. A Brāhmaṇa even bereft of *Havya* and *Kavya* does not become impure.

47. Barring the case where a *Mahāpātaka* (great sin) is involved, O lady of excellent countenance, a Brāhmaṇa is worthy of veneration. By all means Brāhmaṇas are to be worshipped. He is a great divinity by all means. Hence, by all efforts, a Brāhmaṇa in danger should be protected.

48. Thus, O great goddess, Brāhmaṇas are to be worshipped everywhere by men. Those who have subdued their selves and especially those who reside in a Kṣetra (holy place) are still more venerable.

49. Henceforth I shall describe the difference among the Brāhmaṇa residents of a holy spot of all the four stages in life in due order as based on their avocation.

50. Those Brāhmaṇas who know the procedure of *Sannyāsa* (perfect placement) of the Kṣetra and also the difference in avocation in due order are the partakers of the benefit of the holy spot.

51. O lady of excellent countenance, listen to the details of how a Brāhmaṇa-resident of a Kṣetra is to conduct himself in the different avocations of *Prājāpatya* etc.

52-54. O lady of excellent countenance, the following are the pursuits of the residents under the different names (titles) such as *Prājāpatyas, Mahīpālas, Kapotas, Granthikas, Kuṭikas, Vaitalas, Padmahaṁsas, Dhṛtarāṣṭras, Bakas, Kaṅkas, Gopālas, Truṭikas, Maṭharas* and *Guṭikas*. O beautiful woman, the others are *Daṇḍikas*. Listen to their special activities for maintaining themselves.

55. These are remembered as constituting the Vrata called prājāpatya: non-violence, service to preceptors and elders, self-study of the Vedas, cleanliness of the body, restraint of the sense-organs, truthfulness and abstention from theft.

56. The second category of people is remembered as *Mahīpāla* because they sustain the earth by means of the rites such as *Śāntika* (conducive to tranquality) etc. with destruction, nourishment and enmity as the objective.

57. Those *Sādhakas* (persons in pursuit of perfection in spirituality) whose sustenance is affected by means of gleaning grains that are scattered on the ground as in the case of pigeons *(Kapotas)* are also called *Kapotas*.

58. Those who get houses built and stay in them are called *Sadgranthas* (or *Granthikas*).

Those *Sādhakas* who suddenly forsake houses after building them are called *Kuṭikas* (dwellers of huts). They are devoted to the propitiation of Śiva.

59. The Sādhakas called *Vaitālas* are attached to Tīrthas. With great daring, they live there with their wives and sustain themselves with what they casually get.

60. Those who have self-restraint though they are attracted by desires, and who pursue the desire for kingdom and wealth are known as *Padmas*. They are always engaged in seeking alms.

61. Those *Sādhakas* who adopt Jñānayoga (pursuit of the

path of *Jñāna*—spiritual knowledge) and are engaged in the practice of dualism are well-known as *Haṁsas*. Knowledge dawns on them automatically.

62. Those who sustain the universe won over by means of celibacy, Sattva quality and absence of greed, are known as *Dhṛtarāṣṭras*.

63. Those *Sādhakas* are known as *Bakas* who secretly pursue knowledge *(Jñāna), Vrata* and *Dharma* but whose *Niṣṭhā* (established faith) is in their own selfish interest.

64. Those who for the purpose of achieving the noblest objectives resort to ponds and water reservoirs and subsist on lotus stalks and Śṛṅgāṭaka plants, are remembered as the *Sādhakas* of the *Kaṅka* type.

65. Those Sādhakas who wander along with cows and stay in cowpen, and subsist on *Pañcagavya* (five cow products) are (known as) *Gopālas*.

66. Those who let their bodies become emaciated by the practice of *Kṛcchra* and *Cāndrāyaṇa* vows and eat only very small quantity (Cardamom size) (Truṭi) of food are known as the Sādhakas of the *Truṭika* type.

67. The *Sādhakas* called *Maṭharas* consider themselves householders in a *Maṭha* (monastery) with the replica of a woman made of Kuśa Grass representing their wives. They are very pure and simple. They sustain themselves by seeking alms.

68. Those Brāhmaṇas who regularly eat eight morsel like pills made of bulbous roots, roots and fruits are called *Guṭikas*.

69. They keep their bodies well-disciplined and subjected to restraints. During nights they remain in *Vīrāsana* (hero-like posture). They are called *Daṇḍins (Daṇḍikas)*. Now everything has been explained to you.

70. The general and particular avocations of the householders and others among the residents of holy spots along with their diverse varieties have been fully narrated to you.

71. The residents of the Prabhāsa Kṣetra have the *Dharmas* (rites and customs) in this manner and Lord Pitāmaha in the form of a boy is worthy of their adoration.

72. Those who are guilty of Mahāpātakas, those who have been excommunicated by Brāhmaṇas, should never touch Brahmā in the form of a boy.

73. They are always celibate. They are self-controlled. They

subdue their anger. They control all the sense-organs. Thus the Brāhmaṇas residing in a Kṣetra are known.

74. The holy Lord Pitāmaha in the form of a boy is worthy of their veneration. Pitāmaha is to be perfectly worshipped by those who regularly study (and recite) the Vedas.

CHAPTER ONE HUNDRED SEVEN

Procedure of the Worship of Brahmā

Īśvara said:

1. Henceforth I shall succinctly describe to you the procedure for the worship of Brahmā as a boy. I shall mention different types of adoration.

2. I shall tell you the procedure of chariot procession, the (serial) order of eulogies, Mantras as well as different types of devotion, viz. physical, oral and mental.

3. Further, it may be *Laukikī* (Mundane), *Vaidikī* (Vedic) and *Ādhyātmikī* (spiritual).

That which causes delight to Brahmā by means of *Dhyāna* (meditation) and *Dhāraṇā* (steady absorption of the mind) as well as recollecting Vedic *Mantras* is called *Mānasī* (mental) *Bhakti.*

4. Recitation of Vedic Mantras, prostrating oneself while bowing, performance of rites in the sacred fire, *Śrāddha* ceremonies, *Japa* and repetition of *Āraṇyaka* passages—This is called *Vācikī* (verbal) Bhakti.

5-6. The *Kāyikī* (physical) *Bhakti* includes the following: Restraints of the mind and the sense-organs through the regulations of *Vratas,* fasts etc., observance of *Kṛcchra, Sāntapana, Cāndrāyaṇa* and other expiatory rites, and of auspicious *Vratas* as explained in the Scriptural Texts and similar fasts. Thus Bhakti in the case of Brāhmaṇas is of three kinds.

7-10. The worship of Brahmā of the worldly kind is called *Laukikī Bhakti.* The following articles are made use of therein: cow's ghee, milk, curds, honey, sugarcane juice, water from excellent Kuśa grass, sweet scents, garlands, various subsidiary articles of worship, incense from Guggala and ghee, black Aguru of sweet scent, gold ornaments, jewels, wreaths of various sorts, *Nyāsa* (ritualistic touching of the limbs), *Parisara* (circumambulation), flags, banners, prayers in chorus, dances, songs, musical instruments, offerings of all kinds of articles, foodstuffs, cooked rice, beverages etc.

11. The sacred rite performed with Vedic Mantras, *Havis* etc. is remembered as *Vaidikī* (Vedic type) *Bhakti.*

12-13. Various sacred rites are performed with Brahmā in view. Those rites constitute what is called *Vaidikā Bhakti: Agnihotra* rite is performed on New-Moon day and Full-Moon day. The holy *Havis* is consumed. Monetary gifts are offered. *Puroḍāśa* is offered in sacrificial rites such as *Iṣṭi* and *Dhṛti.* Soma juice is drunk as a sacrificial rite. Rk., Yajus and Sāma Mantras are used in *Japa.* The *Saṁhitā* texts are studied and recited.

14-16. A person who is called *Brahmabhakta* (devotee of Brahmā) is like this: He is always engaged in *Prāṇāyāma* (restraint of breath). He meditates with full control over the sense-organs. He eats what is obtained by way of alms. He observes Vratas. He withdraws his sense-organs from everything (with the aim of sublimating his desires). *Prajeśvara* (i.e. Lord of the Subjects, Brahmā) is retained by him in his heart. Brahmā is meditated upon as seated in the pericarp of the lotus of the heart, red in colour and having excellent eyes. The devotee visualizes Brahmā with excellent waist and seat and beaming face. The Lord has four arms granting boons and fearlessness (freedom from fear). Such is the devotee of Brahmā.

17. O goddess, listen to the procedure and injunction regarding the residents of the holy spot.

18. They are free from the sense of *Mamatva* (my-ness, possession). They are not egoistic. They have no close attachments (with anything). They do not accept gifts. They have no love for the usual four aims of life *(Puruṣārthas).* They view (regard) equally a lump of clay, a stone and a piece of gold.

19. By means of their three-fold activity (verbal, mental and physical) they grant freedom from fear to all living beings. They perform *Prāṇāyāma* always. They are devoted to the meditation of the Supreme Absolute.

20. They are engaged in the performance of *Japa* always. They remain always pure. They are engaged in the pious activities of ascetics. They are conversant with the procedures of Sāṁkhya

and Yoga. They get all their doubts cleared by persons well-versed in the Dharma Śāstras.

21-22. Those Brāhmaṇas residing in holy spots are always engaged in the worship of Brahmā. I shall explain how Pitāmaha in the form of a boy, should be worshipped by them. O my beloved, listen attentively. After taking holy bath in the Tīrtha free from impurities, he should wear white clothes and remain pure and clean. Fully equipping himself with the requisites for adoration and offerings he should worship Brahmā.

23. At the outset, he has to bathe the deity in accordance with the injunctions, by means of Pañcāmṛtarasa (may be *Pañca Gavya*) and water. He has to take cow's urine, dung, milk, curds and ghee. Then water with Kuśa blades.

24. He takes *Gomūtra* (cow's urine) uttering the Gāyatrī Mantra. He takes cowdung uttering the Vedic text beginning with *gandhadvārā*. He takes cow's milk uttering the Mantra beginning with *apyāvasva*. He takes up curds with the Mantra beginning with *dadhikrāvṇa*.

25. He takes *Ājya* (ghee) uttering the Mantra beginning with *tejośi śukram* He takes the Kuśa water uttering the Mantra beginning with *devasya tvā*. He should then bathe the deity uttering the Mantra beginning with *āpo hiṣṭhā*.

26. The devotee thus bathes the deity with the five milk products from a Kapilā (tawny-coloured) cow further sanctified by the Mantras. This is remembered as *Brahmasnāna*.

27. By bathing *Surajyeṣṭha* (the seniormost god i.e. Brahmā) one undoubtedly reduces to ash all the sins incurred in the course of thousands of crores of years.

28. After duly bathing thus, the deity Brahmā in the form of a boy, the Brāhmaṇa then bathes the deity further with water mixed with camphor and agallochum.

29. After doing this the devotee should worship the Lord through the *Gāyatrī Nyāsa* (ritualistic touching of the limbs while uttering the syllables of the Gāyatrī Mantra[1]). A wise man should perform the Nyāsa with *Praṇava* (all over the body) beginning with the head and ending with the sole of the foot.

1. VV 29-36 express belief in the protective power of every syllable of the *Gāyatrī Mantra*.

30. The *Nyāsa* of *Takāra* (the syllable *tat*) is on the head, that of *'sa'* syllable is in the region of the face, that of *'vi'* is in the region of the throat and that of *'tu'* (that is *tur*) is in the joints of the limbs.

31. The *Nyāsa* of syllable *'va'* is in the centre of the heart and of the syllable *'re'* at the two sides. The Nyāsa of syllable *'ni'* is in the right side of belly and that of *'ya'* in the left one (*'nya'* split into *'ni'* and *'ya'*).

32. The Nyāsa of syllable *'bha'* (i.e. *bhar*) should be in the navel of the waist and of *'go'* in the two sides (in the Jaṅghā-calf muscles). After the *Nyāsa* of *'de'* on the two knees that of the syllable *'va'* is to be on the lotus-like feet.

33. After the ritualistic touch of the two thumbs with the syllable *'sye'* that of the chest shall be made with syllable *'dhi'*. The *Nyāsa* of syllable *'ma'* is at the root of the knee and of the syllable *'hi'* is on the private parts.

34. The *Nyāsa* of syllable *'dhi'* is on the heart and that of *'yo'* is in the lower lips. A wise devotee should perform the *Nyāśa* of the other syllable *'yo'* on the upper lip.

35. The *Nyāsa* of the syllable *'na'* (i.e. *naḥ*) is at the tip of the nose and that of *'pra'* is on the eye. The *Nyāsa* of syllable *'co'* is in the middle of the eyebrows and of the syllable *'da'* is on *Prāṇa* (life breath).

36. O goddess of Suras, the *Nyāsa* of the syllable *'ya'* is on the forehead. O beloved, after the *Nyāsa* on his own body, the devotee shall make the *Nyāsa* on the deity too.

37-38. After making the deity full with all the offerings, the devotee reviews it completely. After supplementing the holy articles mixed with saffron, Agaru, camphor and sandal by means of scented water, the devotee sprinkles all those articles uttering *Gāyatrī* (beginning with Oṁ) and *Praṇava*. Thereafter he should begin the adoration.

39. He should worship in due order with divine flowers of sweet scents such as Mālatī, Kamala, Aśoka, Śatapatra and Bakula.

40. Fumigation should be done with excellent incense of black Agaru as well as excellent lamps with ghee. Thereafter the devotee should offer the *Naivedya* of different kinds in due order.

41. The Naivedya should consist of *Khaṇḍa, Laḍḍuka, Śrīveṣṭa, Kāṁsāra, Aśoka Pallava* (sprouts and shoots of Aśoka), *Svastika*

(Marathi—Saṅkarapāli), *Ullipikā,Dugdhā, Tila-veṣṭa* as well as *Kilāṭikā*[1].

42. Ripe fruits should be offered uttering the *Mūla* Mantra. The devotee should worship Ṛgveda, Yajurveda and Sāmaveda.

43. A wise man should worship *Jñāna* (knowledge), *Vairāgya* (disinterestedness), *Aiśvarya* (or authority) and *Dharma* (piety), O goddess, in the quarters and the intervening spaces between them beginning with north-east and proceeding in due order.

44. The devotee should worship the places of the fourteen *Vidyās*[2](Lores) before Brahmā. Then *Nyāsa* on *Hṛdaya* (heart) etc. should be performed in front of the Lord in the proper order.

45-46. The Mantra for the *Nyāsa* on the heart is the Ṛk beginning with *āpo hi ṣṭhā* . The Mantra beginning with *ṛtam satyam* is said to be the Mantra for the *Nyāsa* of *Śikhā* (tuft of hair). The Mantra for the Nyāsa on the eyes is that beginning with *udutyam.* The Mantra beginning with *citram devānām* is well-known in all the worlds. It is pointed out that the *Kavaca* (protective Mantra) is uttering the Mantra *brahmaṁs te chādayāmi.*

47. The worship of *Īśa* is proclaimed with the utterance of *bhūḥ bhuvaḥ svaḥ* After consecrating with *Oṁkāra* the devotee should worship the Lord by means of Gāyatrī Mantra.

48. The devotee should worship all the others beginning with Ṛgveda by means of Praṇava. Gāyatrī is the greatest Mantra, it is the mother of the Vedas. It is *Vibhāvarī* (excellent due to its splendour).

49. He who observes fast on the *Pañcadaśī* (fifteenth day, Full-Moon or New-Moon day) and worships Brahmā by means of the principles underlying the syllables of the Gāyatrī attains the greatest position *(Mokṣa).*

50. If a Brāhmaṇa is desirous of crossing the terrible ocean of mundane existence, he should always worship Brahmā in the Prabhāsa Kṣetra in the month of Kārttika.

51. As a mere sight of Brahmā in the form of a boy gives the fruit of a horse-sacrifice, a sensible learned man will not worship him.

---

1. These are varieties of sweet dishes.
2. According to *Viṣṇu P.* the Vidyās are as follows: Six Aṅgas, four Vedas, Mīmāṁsā, Nyāya, Dharma Śāstra and Purāṇas.

52. O goddess of Devas, who will not eagerly worship Brahmā within whose unit of time reckoned as one day, all the Devas, Asuras and human beings become annihilated?

53. It is he who is the father of all the Devas. He is the grandfather of all the living beings. Hence he should be worshipped by all the Brāhmaṇas residing in the holy spot.

54. He alone is the Lord of the *Bhuvana* (universe). He is in the form of Rudra. He is multiformed. He who observes fast on the Full-Moon day and duly worships Brahmā, the Lord of the worlds, shall get the fruit of a horse sacrifice.

55. The *Rathayātrā* (religious procession or a Car festival) of the Lord in the month of Kārttika is glorified. A man who devoutly performs it, attains *Sālokya Mukti* i.e. residence in the same world as that of Brahmā.

56-57. O goddess of Devas, a king who wishes to be a *Parantapa* (destroyer of enemies) should take the Four-faced Lord clad in deerhide and accompanied by Sāvitrī all through the city. It shall be on the Full-Moon day. Many kinds of musical instruments should be played. After taking the deity round the entire city, he shall be installed.

58. At the outset a Brāhmaṇa belonging to the Śāṇḍilya Gotra should be honoured. Then the Brāhmaṇas should be fed. Then the Lord is to be placed on a chariot (car) to the accompaniment of music played on different musical instruments.

59. In front of the *Ratha* (chariot) the son of Śāṇḍilī should be worshipped in accordance with the injunctions. The Brāhmaṇas should be made to recite the Mantras and the auspicious ceremony of *Puṇyāha* (*-vācana*) is to be performed.

60. The Lord (deity) is to be placed on the chariot. The devotees then keep awake by seeing various kinds of visual scenes of dramatic performance and listening to profound sounds of the Vedic chant.

61. A Śūdra who wishes for welfare should not ride the chariot. O my beloved wife and goddess, particularly a man of no pious nature abstains from riding it. In fact excepting a Bhojaka (Brāhmaṇa of Bhoja clan—MW) no one gets into the chariot.

62. O my beloved, the devotee should place Sāvitrī on the right side of Brahmā. The *Bhojaka* should be seated on the left side. A lotus is to be placed in front.

63. Thus, a wise devotee makes the chariot go round the city to the accompaniment of sounds of conchs and musical instruments, O goddess. After performing the *Nīrājana* rite (waving lights before an idol) the deity is placed on its own original place.

64. He who devoutly conducts this religious procession, he who views it and he who pulls the car, shall go to the region of Brahmā.

65. He who holds a lamp there at the back of the car of Brahmā, obtains the great fruit of a horse-sacrifice at every step.

66. O great goddess, a king who does not make arrangements for the car festival of Brahmā is cooked in Raurava hell for an endless period of time.

67. Hence by all means, with a keen desire for the welfare of the nation, a king himself should make special arrangements for the chariot festival.

68. A wise king should duly feed Brāhmaṇas on the first lunar day and honour them with unwashed clothes (fresh from the loom), sweet scents, garlands and unguents.

69. He who lights lamps in the sacred chamber of Brahmā on the New-Moon day in the month of Kārttika, shall go to the highest region.

70. During all festivals, especially on all occasions, Brāhmaṇas should worship Brahmā, the preceptor of all the worlds.

71. Those Brāhmaṇas should possess perfect faith and celebrations should be befitting their duties. The deity should be honoured with divine offerings and services according to one's means and affluence.

72. Thus, O goddess, the excellent greatness of the worship of Brahmā in the form of a boy, along with the greatness of Prabhāsa Kṣetra has been narrated to you.

73. I shall now mention his (Brahmā's) one hundred eight names by reciting and handing over of which to others, one will derive the fruit of ten thousand Yajñas.

74. By reciting this prayer, one obtains that fruit which accrues by perfect articulation of a hundred thousand *Gāyatrī Japas*.

75. This is the most excellent of all eulogies. It has divine esoteric significance. It is destructive of all sins. It should not

be imparted to evil-minded persons indulging in censuring others.

76. It should be given to a noble-souled Brāhmaṇa having perfect acquaintance with the Vedic texts.

Formerly this excellent eulogy of Brahmā was enquired about by Viṣṇu:

77. "O Pitāmaha, O Lord of Devas, how are you to be meditated upon and in which holy spot? Do tell this to me. You are indeed the most excellent one of the omniscient ones."

Brahmā said:

78. I am *Suraśreṣṭha* in Puṣkara. *Prapitāmaha* (Great-grandfather) in Gayā, *Vedagarbha* in Kānyakubja and *Caturmukha* (Four-faced) in Bhṛgu Kṣetra.

79. I am: *Sṛṣṭikartā* (Creator) in Kauberī (northern region), *Bṛhaspati* in Nandipurī. (I am one) in the form of a boy at Prabhāsa and *Surapriya* in Vārāṇasī.

80. (I am) *Cakradeva* in Dvārāvatī. *Bhuvanādhipa* in Vaidiśa (Vidiśa), *Puṇḍarīkākṣa* (Lotus-eyed) in *Pauṇḍraka* (N. Bengal?) and Pītākṣa in Hastināpura.

81. I am *Vijaya* in Jayantī (Jyntia in Assam). *Jayanta* in Puruṣottama (Jagannāthapurī), *Padmahasta* in Vāḍa, and *Tamonuda* in Tamolipta (Tāmralipti—mod. Tamluk).

82. (I am) *Janānanda* in Āhicchatrī[1], *Janapriya* (favourite of the people) in Kāñcīpurī[2], *Brahmā* in Karṇāṭa's city and *Muni* in Ṛṣikuṇḍa.

83. (I am called) *Śrīnivāsa* in Śrīkaṇṭha; *Śubhaṁkara* in Kāmarūpa (Assam), *Devakartā* in Ucchriyāṇa[3] (Orissa) and *Sraṣṭā* (Creator) in Jālandhara (Punjab);

84. *Viṣṇu* in the holy spot named Mallika[4]; *Bhārgava* in Mahendra; *Gonarda* in Sthavirākāra and *Pitāmaha* in Ujjayinī;

85. *Mahādeva* in Kauśāmbi[5]; *Rāghava* in Ayodhyā; *Virañci* in Citrakūṭa and *Vārāha* in Vindhyaparvata;

86. *Suraśreṣṭha* in Gaṅgā dvāra; *Śaṅkara* in Himavanta; *Srucāhasta* in Dehikā; *Padmahasta* in Arbuda (Mt. Abu);

1. Rāmnagar in Rohil Khanda (Uttar Pradesh)
2. Kānchī in Tamil Nadu
3. V.L. Uḍḍiyana (Orissa)
4. If Mallikārjuna, Mod. Śrīśaila.
5. Mod. Kosam, a village.

87. *Padmanetra* in Vṛndāvana, *Kuśahasta* in Naimiṣa; *Govinda* in Gopakṣetra and *Surendra* in Yamunātaṭa (the banks of Yamunā);

88. *Padmatanu* in Bhāgīrathi and *Janānanda* in Janasthala. *Madhvakṣa* in Kauṅkaṇa and *Kanakaprabha* in Kāmpilya (Farrukhabad in U.P.);

89. *Annadātā* (one who provides with food) in Kheṭaka (Kaira-Gujarat); *Śaṁbhu* in Kratusthala; *Paulastya* in Laṅkā and *Haṁsavāhana* (Swan-vehicled) in Kaśmīra;

90. *Vasiṣṭha* too in Arbuda (See 86); *Nārada* in Utpalavana; *Śrutidātā* in Medhaka; and *Yajuṣāmpati* (Lord of *Yajus Mantras*) in Prayāga.

91. *Sāmaveda* in Śivaliṅga; *Madhupriya* in Markaṭa; *Nārāyaṇa* in Gomanta (Goa) and *Dvijapriya* (favourite of Brāhmaṇas) in Vidarbha (Maharashtra);

92. *Brahmagarbha* in Aṅkulaka (Aṅkola in Gujarat); *Sutapriya* in Brahmavāha; *Durādharṣa* in Indraprastha (Delhi); and *Suramardana* in Campā (Bhagalpur) (Orissa, around Jaypur on the river Vaitaraṇī);

93. *Mahārūpa* in Virajā; *Surūpa* in Rāṣṭravardhana; *Janādhyakṣa* in Kadambaka; and *Devādhyakṣa* in Samasthala;

94. *Gaṅgādhara* in Rudrapīṭha; remembered as *Jalada* in Supīṭha; *Tripurāri* in Tryaṁbaka (Nasik, Maharashtra); and *Trilocana* in Śriśaila (Karnul, Andhra);

95. *Mahādeva* in Plakṣapura; *Vedhanāśana* in Kapāla; Śauri in Śṛṅgaverapura (Singraur on Gaṅgā; Allahabad Dist.), and *Cakradharaka* in Nimiṣa;

96. *Virūpākṣa* in Nandipurī (See 79); *Gautama* in Plakṣapādapa, *Mālyavān* in Hastinātha and *Dvijendra* in Vācika (Vaṭika?);

97. *Divānātha* in Indrapurī; and *Purandara* in Bhūtikā; *Haṁsabāhu* in Candrā and *Garuḍapriya* in Caṁpā (see v 92);

98. *Mahāyakṣa* in Mahodaya (Kanoj); *Suyajña* in Pūtakavana; *Śuklavarṇa* in Siddheśvara and *Padmabodhaka* in Vibhā;

99. *Liṅgin* in Devadāruvana, *Umāpati* in Udaka; *Vināyaka* in Mātṛsthāna and *Dhanādhipa* in Alakā;

100. *Govinda* in Trikūṭa (a mountain in Laṅkā), Vāsuki in Pātāla, *Yugādhyakṣa* in Kovidāra and *Surapriya* in Strīrājya (kingdom of women—Kāmarūpa, Assam);

101. *Subhoga* in Pūrṇagiri; *Takṣaka* in Śālmalī; *Pāpahā* in Amara; and *Sudarśana* in Aṁbikā;

102. *Mahāvīra* in Naravāpī; *Durganāśana* in Kāntāra; *Padmagṛha* in Padmāvatī and *Mṛgalāñchana* in Gagana (Sky).

103. O Madhusūdana, my presence all through the three twilights is only in that place where these one hundred eight names are recited.

104. He who views anyone of these in the form of the boy-Brahmā, obtains the merit of all the *Vedhas* (gods—Brahmās) mentioned before.

105. O Kṛṣṇa, he who always eulogizes me at Prabhāsa by means of these names, goes to my region called Vijaya and rejoices there for endless years.

106. By reciting my prayer, all the sins, mental, verbal and physical, get destroyed.

107. By reciting my prayer one obtains that fruit which is attained by men through offerings of flowers and incense, propitiation of Brāhmaṇas and by steady meditation.

108. The sins of Brāhmaṇa-slaughter etc. committed in this world knowingly or unknowingly, do perish in a moment.

109. This eulogy of mine is liked by me. He who listens to it or recites it shall be rid of all sins. He will obtain intensely desired things.

110. O Kṛṣṇa, I shall tell you another secret thing. Listen to it with attention.

111. In the month of Kārttika, if the constellation Kṛttikā coincides with the Kārttikī day, that lunar day is to be considered very great. It is my favourite in Prabhāsa.

112. If the constellation Rohiṇī coincides with that lunar day, that is the meritorious Mahākārttika day inaccessible even to Devas.

113. If the constellation Kṛttikā coincides with the Kārttikī lunar day or Saturday, Sunday or Thursday and the devotee views Brahmā in the form of a boy, he attains the fruit of a horse-sacrifice.

114. When the Sun is in the constellation Viśākhā and the Moon in Kṛttikā, that *Yoga* is called *Padmaka.* O Hari, it is very rare in Prabhāsa.

115. During that Yoga a man must view Brahmā in the form of a boy at Prabhāsa. Even if he is defiled by crores of sins he does not see the world of Yama.

Īśvara said:

116. In this manner, the prayer was recounted to Hari by Brahmā. The greatness of Brahmā as a deity has been explained by me to you.

117. If it is listened to, it destroys all sins of men. It facilitates the acquisition of all objectives. Gift of a plot of land should be made there by those who desire the fruit of the (complete) pilgrimage.

118. O goddess, there itself a water-pot, a white cloth and sixteen great gifts should be made to Brahmā in the form of a boy.

119. When great *Parvan* days (festival days) come all the Brāhmaṇas residing in the holy place should perform *Pārāyaṇa* (reading and reciting the scriptures), O goddess.

CHAPTER ONE HUNDRED EIGHT

Greatness of Pratyūṣeśvara

Īśvara said:

1-3. Thereafter, O great goddess, a devotee should go to the excellent Liṅga of Vasus. It is within a distance of fifty *Dhanus* from Someśa, in the north-eastern direction.

The Liṅga installed there, O great goddess, has four faces and is a favourite of Suras. Its name is Pratyūṣeśvara and it destroys great sins.

By visiting that deity, sins incurred in the course of seven births get destroyed, O lady of excellent countenance. It is truth, it is the truth.

The Devī said:

4. Who is this person named Pratyūṣa? Whose son was he? How was the Liṅga installed? How is he famous? O Śaṅkara do tell me all this.

Īśvara said:

5. O goddess, Dakṣa, a son of Brahmā, is remembered as

Prajāpati.He had sixty daughters. He gave ten of them to Dharma.

6. Among them, O great goddess, one was well-known as Viśvā. She begot of Dharma eight sons.

7. They are glorified as the eight Vasus. They are Apa, Dhruva, Soma, Dhara, Anala, Anila, Pratyūṣa and Prabhāsa.

8. The seventh among them (the Vasus) is well-known as Pratyūṣa. O goddess of Devas, desirous of begetting a son, he came to the holy spot of Prabhāsa.

9. He came to know that the holy spot is *Kāmika* (wish-yielding) and installed Maheśvara. O my beloved, he performed an elaborate penance for a hundred years according to divine reckoning. Tranquil and concentrating his mind within himself, he meditated on Mahādeva.

10. O goddess, the unsullied great Lord became pleased with his devotion and granted him a son *Devala,* a most excellent one among Yogins.

11. Ever since then, by the power of that Liṅga, Devala, the son of Pratyūṣa, became a divine Yogin.

12. For this same reason, the deity is designated Pratyūṣeśvara.

13. If any person without a child propitiates that Lord, O goddess of Devas, the line of progeny in his race never gets broken.

14. O great goddess, if anyone worships the excellent deity Pratyūṣeśvara, early at dawn with excellent devotion and perpetual restraint of himself, his sin gets destroyed even if it is incurred by the slaughter of a Brāhmaṇa.

15. A bull should be given away there by those who wish to get the perfect fruit of the pilgrimage.

16. The devotee should keep awake at night on the fourteenth lunar day in the dark half of the month of Māgha. By keeping awake one shall attain the fruit of all Dānas and Yajñas.

CHAPTER ONE HUNDRED NINE

Greatness of Anileśvara

Īśvara said:

1-3. Thereafter, O great goddess, a pilgrim should go to

the excellent shrine of Anileśvara. O my beloved, it is situated within a distance of three *Dhanus* to the north-east thereof (i.e. of Pratyūṣeśvara).

The Liṅga is highly powerful. By merely viewing, it destroys sins. The fifth among Vasus who is known as Anila (Wind god) propitiated Mahādeva and made him manifest to him. Equipped with perfect faith, he installed the Liṅga.

4. Thus, by the power of Īśa, his son became very strong. He became well-known as Manojava (having speed of the mind) and his movement could not be comprehended fully.

5. By visiting him, a man ceases to be afflicted with sickness. He will never again be sick. If he is viewed, neither a blind one, nor a deaf one, neither a dumb person nor a sickly and impoverished one is born in the family.

6. He who offers a single flower on the Liṅga becomes richly endowed with happiness and good fortune. He will always be handsome.

7. Thus, O goddess, the greatness that destroys sins, has been narrated. By listening to this and approving this with emotional fervour, one becomes rich by realizing all his desires.

CHAPTER ONE HUNDRED TEN

Greatness of Prabhāseśvara

Īśvara said:

1-3. Thereafter, O beautiful woman, a pilgrim should go to the excellent shrine of Prabhāseśvara. O goddess, it is stated to be situated within a distance of seven *Dhanus* to the west of Gaurītapovana (penance grove of Gaurī). It is not very far away. That great Liṅga was installed by the eighth of the Vasus named Prabhāsa, who was engaged in the adoration of Śiva. O goddess of Devas, he had come to the holy spot of Prabhāsa with a keen desire for a son.

4. After installing the great Liṅga well-known as Āgneya (fiery), he performed an elaborate penance for a hundred years according to divine reckoning, O my beloved.

5. Thereafter, O great goddess, Lord Rudra became pleased with him as he had great faith. The Lord granted him what he had desired in his mind.

6. Bhuvanā, the sister of Bṛhaspati, was an expounder of Brahman. She was the wife of Prabhāsa, the eighth one among Vasus.

7. Her son was Viśvakarman, creator of the universe and a patriarch. He is remembered as the maternal grandfather of Manu. He was an expert architect.

8. He became the fashioner of the Solar disc, the great hewer of the refulgence. The son of the eighth one among the Vasus was like this.

9. O goddess of Devas, the son of the Vasu named Prabhāsa was also engaged in the propitiation of that Liṅga. Thus, O goddess, the greatness pertaining to Prabhāseśvara has been spoken to you.

10. The greatness is destroyer of all sins. It is splendid and it fulfills all desires. A devotee should worship him with devotion and should possess perfect faith.

11. He should observe fast and recite the *Śatarudriya* Mantra. He should lie down on the bare ground. On the fourteenth lunar day in the month of Māgha, he should take a holy dip at the confluence with the ocean (of a river).

12. He should bathe the deity with Pañcāmṛta and worship it in accordance with the injunctions.

13. O goddess, he who performs the great festival of the chariot and concludes the pilgrimage shall be rid of all sins. He becomes prosperous with the realization of all desires. A bull should be offered as a gift there by those who wish to get the fruit of a perfect pilgrimage.

CHAPTER ONE HUNDRED ELEVEN

Greatness of Rāmeśvara Kṣetra

Īśvara said:

1-4. Thereafter, a pilgrim should go to the excellent Puṣkarāraṇya, O great goddess, situated within sixty *Dhanus* in the north-eastern corner thereof.

O great goddess, there is a *Kuṇḍa* there named Aṣṭapuṣkara. It is a destroyer of all sins. O goddess, it is inaccessible to those who have not controlled their selves.

Near the Kuṇḍa is the great Liṅga named Rāmeśvara installed by the intelligent Rāmeśa (Rama). Merely through its worship, one is rid of the sin of Brāhmaṇa-slaughter.

Śrī Devī said:

5. O great Lord, do tell me in detail everything pertaining to Rāmeśvara. How did Rāma come there accompanied by Sītā and Lakṣmaṇa?

6. How was the Liṅga installed in Puṣkara that removes all sins? Describe this in detail as well as the benefit along with its greatness.

Īśvara said:

7. In the twenty-fourth Yuga, formerly Rāma was born as the son of Daśaratha with Vasiṣṭha as his family priest. He was born for the purpose of slaying Rāvaṇa.

8. Then, O goddess, due to the curse of a sage (?) Rāma, the son of Daśaratha, went (to the forest) after some time along with Sītā and Lakṣmaṇa and performed a great penance.

9. He set out surrounded by divine Brāhmaṇa-sages, for a stay in the forest. In the course of his wanderings he came to Prabhāsa Kṣetra.

10. After reaching that spot, he sat there because he was extremely tired. When the Sun set he prepared a bed of leaves on the ground.

11. He went to sleep. O goddess, at the close of the night, he saw his father Daśaratha in a dream. He was highly brilliant yet gentle in appearance.

12. After getting up in the morning, he related to the Brāhmaṇas how Daśaratha was seen in dream by that noble-souled one.

The Brāhmaṇas said:

13. Pitṛs desirous of the prosperity of the persons born in their family appear before them in dreams. O Rāghava, your ancestors do bestow boons on you.

14. This Tīrtha of Śārṅgadhanvan (Viṣṇu, the bearer of Śārṅga bow) is highly meritorious and well-guarded. It is called Puṣkara. May the Śrāddha be offered here.

15. Indeed King Daśaratha desires that an auspicious ball of rice should be offered by you in this Tīrtha. Therefore, he has appeared to you.

Īśvara said:

16. On hearing their words, the lotus-eyed Rāma invited splendid Brāhmaṇas worthy of the invitation to Śrāddha.

17. He told Lakṣmaṇa who was standing humbly at his side: "O son of Sumitrā, go to fetch fruits for the Śrāddha. Do go quickly."

18-20. After saying "So it shall be", the scion of the family of Raghu went out and quickly brought different kinds of fruits like *Bilva, Kapittha,* plenty of *Tinduka, Badara, Karīra* and *Karamarda,* O my beloved. There were also *Cirbhaṭa, Parūṣa, Mātuliṅga* (citron), *Nālikera* (coconut) and white *Iṅgudi* fruits.

21-24. Sītā, the daughter of Janaka, cooked them immediately. Then at the auspicious hour of *Kutapa* Rāma had his bath and wore a clean bark garment and invited excellent Brāhmaṇas worthy of the Śrāddha honour. They were: Gālava, Devala, Raibhya, Yavakrīta, Parvata, Bharadvāja, Vasiṣṭha, Jābāli, Gautama, Bhṛgu etc. These and many other Brāhmaṇas who had mastered the Vedas (came there). They came there for the Śrāddha to be performed by Rāma of energetic actions. At that time Rāma spoke to Sītā:

25. "Do come, O Vaidehī, for the holy rite of washing the feet of the Brāhmaṇas." On hearing this, Sītā entered a place in the midst of the trees.

26. She got hidden among the bushes. She was out of Rāmā's sight, despite the fact that Rāma repeatedly called "Sītā ! Sītā!"

27. Seeing Rāma very angry and Sītā out of view, Lakṣmaṇa himself performed the duty of honouring the Brāhmaṇas.

28. After the Brāhmaṇas had taken their food and the ball of rice was also offered, Sītā, the daughter of Janaka, came to the place where Rāma was present.

29. On seeing her, Rāghava rebuked her with harsh words: "Fie upon you, O sinful woman! Where had you been leaving me as well as the Brāhmaṇas when the time for *Śrāddha* had

arrived? This was the holy rite of Pitṛs which brings about great prosperity."

Īśvara said:

30. On hearing his words Jānakī became extremely frightened.

31-36. With palms joined in veneration and trembling much she spoke: "O noble one, do not be angry. O Lord, do not rebuke me. Listen, O my Lord, why I went elsewhere leaving your side. Your father was seen by me. So also your grandfather. The one earlier than he and the maternal grandfather and others were seen separately in the bodies of the leading Brāhmaṇas. They had separately occupied those bodies. So, O scion of the family of Raghu, bashfulness overwhelmed me. O mighty one, your father was accustomed to eat charmingly delicious food-stuffs of good qualities. O great king, how will he eat this saltish, astringent and bitter stuff? So I became miserable. O leader of the descendants of Raghu, for this reason, on seeing the kinsmen of the father-in-law I disappeared through bashfulness. Hence eschew your anger."

37. On hearing her words Rāghava became surprised. He offered a special Śrāddha in the holy Puṣkara Tīrtha.

38. There in the vicinity of Puṣkara itself, within a distance of three *Dhanus* to the south, he installed the Liṅga well-known as Rāmeśvara.

39. He who devoutly worships him with sweet scents, flowers etc. in due order, attains the great region where Lord Janārdana is present.

40. Of what avail is profuse talk? If the *Śrāddha* is offered on Dvādaśī (twelfth lunar day) the merit thereof cannot be properly estimated in all the three worlds.

41. O beautiful lady, there is great merit in offering *Śrāddha* on any day when *Ṣaṣṭhī* (6th lunar day) or *Caturthī* (4th lunar day) coincides with Friday or Tuesday.

42. If propitiated in Puṣkara by one of their own family, the fathers and grandfathers become delighted for a period of twelve years. They never wish for anything else.

43. A man who offers the gift of a horse there with perfect devotion, attains the fruit of an Aśvamedha Yajña (horse-sacrifice).

44. Thus the sin-destroying greatness of Lord Rāmeśvara and Puṣkara has been perfectly spoken to you, O beautiful woman.

CHAPTER ONE HUNDRED TWELVE

Greatness of Lakṣmaṇeśvara

Īśvara said:

1-3. Thereafter, a pilgrim should go to the excellent Lakṣmaṇeśvara, O great goddess. It is situated within a distance of thirty Dhanus to the east of Rāmeśa.

It was installed by Lakṣmaṇa who had come there in the course of his pilgrimage. O goddess, that Liṅga is a destroyer of great sins. It is adored by Suras.

He who worships it devoutly and remains absorbed in meditation and also offers dance, instrumental music and songs along with *Homa* and *Japa* attains the greatest goal.

4. Cooked food, water and gold should be gifted there to a Brāhmaṇa after worshipping the Lord of the chiefs of Devas with sweet scents, flowers etc, in due order.

5. Worshipping there on the fourteenth day in the dark half of Māgha is particularly recommended. Holy ablution, donation and *Japa* there shall be of everlasting benefit.

CHAPTER ONE HUNDRED THIRTEEN

Greatness of Jānakīśvara

Īśvara said:

1-3. Thereafter, O great goddess, a pilgrim should go to the excellent shrine of Jānakīśvara situated within a distance of thirty *Dhanus* to the south-west of Rāmeśa.

Formerly it was worshipped by Jānakī. It destroys sins of all creatures. It was installed after propitiating Śaṅkara perfectly.

Earlier, the very same Liṅga was called Vasiṣṭheśa. Thereafter, it became famous on the earth in Tretā as Jānakīśa.

4. Thereafter, sixty thousand great sages named Vālakhilyas attained Siddhi there. So it is known as Siddheśvara also.

5. O great goddess, that Yugaliṅga of great refulgence became well-known as Siddheśvara in Kali Age. On seeing it one is rid of sins arising from misery and bad luck.

6. A pilgrim who worships it devoutly after bathing it duly, shall be rid of sins whether one is a man or a woman.

7-8. A pilgrim should bathe in the Puṣkara Tīrtha and worship the Liṅga regularly for a month continuously with restriction in his diet. Each day he will get more fruit than that of a horse-sacrifice. If a woman worships it on the third lunar day in the month of Māgha, there shall be no ill-luck, misery or grief in that family.

9. Thus, O goddess, the sin-destroying greatness has been related to you. If listened to, it eradicates sins and accords conjugal felicity.

CHAPTER ONE HUNDRED FOURTEEN

Greatness of Vāmanasvāmī

Īśvara said:

1-3. Thereafter, O great goddess, a pilgrim should go to the shrine of sin-destroying Viṣṇu named Vāmanasvāmin. He is the destroyer of all sins.

It is remembered that the deity is stationed within a distance of twenty Dhanus on the south-western side of Puṣkara.

When, O goddess, Bali was bound by the powerful Viṣṇu, the right foot was placed there by the Viśvarūpin (Omniformed One). O beloved, the second step was placed on the peak of Meru and the third in the firmament.

4. When he lifted up the foot the Cosmic Egg received a long crack by the tip of the foot (of Viṣṇu) and water gushed forth therefrom.

5. It came up to his knees on the earth. Therefore, it became famous on the earth as Viṣṇupadī Gaṅgā (the Gaṅgā arising from Viṣṇu's foot).

6. At the outset that great river reached Puṣkara from the sky. The sky is called by the name Puṣkara. Water is also called Puṣkara. Hence the place of the presence of Prajāpati is famous as Puṣkara.

7. After taking holy bath there, the man who views the foot of Hari, attains the greatest region where Hari himself is present.

8. O beautiful lady, by offering balls of rice there to the Pitṛs, they become satisfied for a crore of years. Hari himself has said this.

9. In this context a couplet has been sung by the great sage Vasiṣṭha after viewing Vāmanasvāmin. Listen to it attentively.

10. "After bathing in Puṣkara and viewing Viṣṇu's foot thereafter, why should there be worry even after committing great sins?"

11. He who makes a gift of a pair of shoes to a Brāhmaṇa and observes Vratas, proceeds to Viṣṇu's world riding on a vehicle and is also honoured in Viṣṇuloka.

CHAPTER ONE HUNDRED FIFTEEN

Greatness of Puṣkareśvara

Īśvara said:

1-4. Thereafter, O great goddess, a pilgrim should go to the excellent shrine of Puṣkareśvara to the south of the excellent Jānakīśvara.

The Liṅga is of great power and has been worshipped by sage Sanatkumāra, a son of Brahmā. It has been worshipped with faith by means of golden lotuses in accordance with the injunctions. Hence it is well-known as Puṣkareśvara. O beautiful lady, it is a destroyer of all sins.

If anyone devoutly worships him with sweet scents, flowers etc, it is as good as a pilgrimage to Puṣkara performed by him. There is no doubt about it.

CHAPTER ONE HUNDRED SIXTEEN

Greatness of Śaṅkhodakakuṇḍeśvarī Gaurī

Īśvara said:

1-3. Thereafter, a pilgrim should go to the shrine of the goddess well-known as Kuṇḍeśvarī, O great goddess. She confers conjugal felicity. The shrine is situated within a distance of thirty Dhanus to the north-west of Puṣkara and south-west of Bhūtanātha. The goddess that supresses sins and destroys a series of impoverished states is stationed there. There is a *Kuṇḍa* (holy pit) named Śaṅkhodaka situated within a distance of fifteen *Dhanus* to the south-west of the shrine of the goddess. This holy pit destroys all sins.

4. Whether a man or a woman, the pilgrim should take the holy bath in the auspicious water, O great goddess and worship that goddess well-known as Śaṅkhāvartā.

5-6. The name of that goddess during Kali is Kuṇḍeśvarī. She bestows all happiness. O my beloved goddess, a (demon) named Śaṅkha was formerly killed by Viṣṇu. He took his huge body in the form of a conch shell, filled it with the waters of the Tīrtha and came to Prabhāsa Kṣetra.

7-8. After washing the conch he created the highly lustrous Tīrtha. Then he blew the conch shell producing a sound majestically rumbling like a cloud. Due to the loud sound, the goddess came there enquiring about the cause. She stayed near the Kuṇḍa. So she became famous as Kuṇḍeśvarī. The Kuṇḍa is remembered as Śaṅkhodaka.

9-10. Whether one is a man or a woman, one who worships her on the third lunar day of Māgha with great devotion shall attain the region of Gaurī. Couples should be fed there by those who wish for the fruit of the pilgrimage. Gifts of bodice, fruits and meal are to be made to virgins.

CHAPTER ONE HUNDRED SEVENTEEN

Greatness of Bhūtanātheśvara

Īśvara said:

1-4. Thereafter, O great goddess, a pilgrim should go to

the shrine of Hara known as Bhūtanātheśvara. It is situated within a distance of twenty *Dhanus* to the north-east of Kuṇḍeśvarī.

O great goddess, this Kalpaliṅga is without beginning and end. Formerly in Tretā Yuga, it was famous on the earth as Vīrabhadreśvara. O goddess of Devas, it is remembered as Bhūteśvara in Kali Age.

Formerly at the juncture of Dvāpara, crores of Bhūtas (spirits, goblins) attained great Siddhi there by the power of that Liṅga. Hence it became famous by the name Bhūteśvara on the earth.

5-6. The pilgrim should be fearless. With all sense-organs conquered, he must meditate on the Lord perfectly. On the fourteenth lunar day in the dark half of the month, he should worship Śaṅkara and then Aghora in the southern quarter. Only he will attain whatever Siddhi there is on the earth.

7. Homas, gifts of gingelly seeds and offerings of balls of rice with Pitṛs in view, should be made for realizing their release from the state of ghosthood.

8. Thus the greatness of Bhūtanātheśvara has been expounded. It destroys the extensive sins of the Kali Age. It is the cause of merit. A person who reads or listens to the greatness of the most excellent one among Suras with devotion, is rid of the multitude of sins.

CHAPTER ONE HUNDRED EIGHTEEN

Greatness of Gopyāditya

Īśvara said:

1-3. Thereafter, O great goddess, a pilgrim should go to the excellent shrine of Gopyāditya situated within thirty *Dhanus* on the north-west of Bhūteśa and within a distance of ten *Dhanus* on the south and south-east side of the goddess destroying *Balātibala* Daityas (powerful and super-powerful demons). O goddess, the shrine is a destroyer of sins.

I shall explain its origin that is auspicious and destroys great sins. A man who devoutly listens to it, is rid of misery and grief.

4-6. O my beloved, when the powerful Kṛṣṇa came to Prabhāsa

accompanied by all the fifty-six crores of Yādavas, sixteen thousand *Gopīs* (cowherdesses) as well as one hundred thousand sixty sons of Kṛṣṇa, they stayed in the sin-destroying holy spot of Prābhāsika occupying Yādavasthala (region of the Yādavas) extending up to the Raivataka mountain.

7. Those powerful ones stayed there for twelve years. After marking them with their names, they installed Śiva Liṅga in the holy spot.

8. Thus all those leading Yādavas made the entire holy spot extending to twelve Yojanas, marked with their banners as well as Śiva Liṅgas.

9. O goddess, the Liṅgas were at a distance of a *Hasta* from each other. Temples were built in the centre of the holy spot. They had golden pot-like domes. Banners and festoons fluttered. These shrines shone in different places like pillars of Hari's fame.

10. I shall mention the names of sixteen senior Gopīs. Listen to them with attention, O great goddess.

11-12. They are: Lambinī, Candrikā, Kāntā, Krūrā, Śāntā, Mahodayā, Nandinī, Bhīṣaṇā, Aśokā, Suparṇā, Vimalā, Akṣayā, Śubhadā, Śobhanā, and Puṇyā. These are remembered as the *Kalās* (digits) of *Haṁsa*. Kṛṣṇa, the Supreme Absolute, Janārdana, alone is considered as *Haṁsa*.

13. O goddess, these sixteen are glorified as his Śaktis. Kṛṣṇa is in the form of Candra (Moon). They are remembered to be in the form of *Kalās* (digits).

14. Mālinī, the sixteenth Kalā, has perfect and full disc. Candramas moves in these Kalās beginning with the first lunar day.

15. O lady of excellent countenance, the Kalās are only those sixteen in the form of the Gopīs. Each of them is separately involved with a thousand (Gopīs).

16. Thus, O goddess, the secret pertaining to knowledge (and wisdom) has been spoken to you. He who knows this in this manner, should be known as Vaiṣṇavapuruṣa (Viṣṇu's devotee) by wise persons.

17. Having come to know that the shrines (temples) were built separately by the Yādavas, all those sixteen thousand Gopīs informed (and received the permission of) Kṛṣṇa and installed Ravi (Sun-god) with feelings of devotion.

18. In accordance with the injunctions, they got (the idols of) Ravi installed through Nārada and other sages as well as those residing in the holy spot.

19. After the installation of Sun-god, they gave plenty of gifts such as plots of land, cows, gold and garments to the residents of the holy place.

20-21. After having finished thus, they became happy and contented. They earned great fame. Accompanied by Kṛṣṇa, they went back to Dvārakā by the way they came by. All the sages became satisfied and delighted in their minds. They named the idol of the Sun there as Gopyāditya. It became well-known as such. The deity is a destroyer of all sins and confers great conjugal felicity.

22. After some time again, O my beloved goddess, they arrived at the Yādavasthala in the sin-destroying Prabhāsa. (They went there) on account of the curse of Durvāsas.

23. Thus, O goddess, the greatness pertaining to Gopyāditya has been spoken to you. I shall now mention to you the details of adoration and obeisance thereof in due order.

24. Merely by visiting the deity that was installed by Gopīs a devotee gets rid of misery and grief, O goddess, in *Mitravana* (the park of Sun-god).

25. Men who seek refuge in *Gopīravi* (the deity Gopyāditya) attain that goal which is usually obtained through perfectly performed penance as well as *Yajñas* with plenty of monetary gifts.

26. O Maheśvarī, if a devotee places all his emotional and devout fervour in Gopyāditya with all his heart and soul, he has fulfilled his duty. He is really praiseworthy.

27. (Even Pitṛs wish like this) : 'Would that, a blessed son, a sanctifier of the family, were born in our family—a blessed fellow who will adore (perform *Upāsti* of) Bhānu with devout feelings.'

28. O my beloved, a man who worships the deity early in the morning on the seventh lunar day in the month of Māgha, shall redeem the members of his family of seven earlier generations and of seven succeeding generations.

29. The devotee of Gopyāditya dispels ailments and conquers invisible enemies of evil conduct.

30. One should not touch gingelly oil on the Saptamī day

nor should he wear a blue cloth, nor should one bathe with *Āmalaka* (Indian Gooseberry), nor should one quarrel at any cost.

31. If a Brāhmaṇa performs any sacred rite wearing blue or red cloth, such rites as holy ablution, donation, *Japa, Homa,* self-study of the Vedas and offering libations to the Pitṛs, performing great Yajñas, all that becomes futile.

32. If a Brāhmaṇa wears on his body a cloth dyed in Nīlī (blue) (the indigo plant) he regains purity by fasting for a day and a night and consuming *Pañcagavya* (five cow products such as milk, curds, ghee etc.)

33. If the juice of indigo plant gets into the hair pores of any Brāhmaṇa, he shall become a *Patita* (a fallen, sinful man). He can, however, expiate by means of three *Kṛcchras.*

34. If any Brāhmaṇa inadvertently gets into the midst of Nīla (indigo plants) he regains purity by fasting for a night and a day and consuming *Pañcagavya.*

35. If the indigo plant causes bruises in the body of Brāhmaṇas and blood comes out, the Brāhmaṇas should perform *Cāndrāyaṇa* expiation.

36. If any one inadvertently uses an indigo twig as tooth brush, it is said by learned men that he gets purity by performing two Kṛcchras.

37. Thus, O goddess, the great prosperity resulting from (the adoration of) Gopyāditya has been spoken to you. It destroys sins of all creatures. When listened to, it causes the acquisition of all objectives.

38. O goddess of Devas, by visiting Gopyāditya one gets that merit which is obtained by gifting hundreds and thousands of cows in Kurujāñgala country.

CHAPTER ONE HUNDRED NINETEEN

Greatness of Balātibaladaityaghnī

Īśvara said:

1. Then, O great goddess, a devotee should go to the shrine of the highly resplendent Mahādevī well-known all over the earth by the name Balātibaladaityaghnī.

2. The goddess has neither beginning nor death. She is stationed in the holy spot with a crore of Bhūtas as her attendants. She is the destroyer of all Daityas.

The Devī said:

3. O Lord, why has she been mentioned as Balātibala-daityaghnī? How were the Daityas named Bala and Atibala struck down (by her)?

4. O Maheśvara, where does that goddess reside? Of what power is she? Mention in detail the entire greatness of that goddess.

Īśvara said:

5. Listen, O goddess, I shall describe the sin-destroying story by listening to which devoutly a man is rid of all sins.

6. There was a powerful demon named Raktāsura. He was son of Mahiṣa. With a huge body and powerful arms, he was another Hiraṇyākṣa.

7-8. He had two sons named Bala and Atibala. They defeated all the Suras with Devendra and Agni as their leaders. In the entire region of the three worlds, they established their suzerainty without fear and apprehension. Thirty-three warriors were glorified as the leaders of their army.

9. Ferocious by nature, they were great warriors leading a thousand *Akṣauhiṇīs*. They had huge bodies and stout shoulders like lions. Those mighty ones were wicked by nature.

10-13. The following Daityas of very huge bodies were the officials in their army: Dhūmrākṣa, Bhīmadaṁṣṭra, Kālavaśya, Mahāhanu, Brahmaghna, Yajñakopa, Strīghna, Pāpaniketana, Vidyunmālin, Bandhūka, Śaṅkukarṇa, Vibhāvasu, Devāntaka, Vikarman, Durbhikṣa, Krūra, Hayagrīva, Aśvakarṇa, Ketumān, Vṛṣabha, Dvija, Śarabha, Śalabha, Vyāghra, Nikuṁbha, Maṇika, Baka, Śūrpaka, Vikṣara, Mālin, Kāla, Daṇḍaka and Kerala.

14. The earth extending to fifty crores of Yojanas in area was thus occupied by them. On coming to know of this, the Devas were distressed in mind due to fear.

15. They went to the Himālaya forest along with all the celestial sages. Remaining pure in mind, they eulogized the goddess with this prayer:

The Devas said:

16. O imperishable one, be victorious! O infinite one, be victorious! O unmanifest one free from ailments, be victorious! O goddess of great Māyā, be victorious! O goddess, saluted to by Devas and sages, be victorious!

17. Be victorious, O ruler of the universe! O Gaṅgā, be victorious! O bestower of all Siddhis, be victorious! O Brahmāṇī. O Kaumārī, O Nārāyaṇī, O Īśvarī, be victorious!

18. Be victorious, O Brahmāṇī, O Cāmuṇḍā ! Be victorious, O Indrāṇī, O Maheśvarī! Be victorious, O mother Mahālakṣmī, O omnipresent Pārvatī!

19. Be victorious, O refulgent goddess, O creator of the universe! Be victorious, O Airāvatī, O Bhāratī! Be victorious, O infinite one! Be victorious, O Jayā, the victorious one, be victorious, O goddess Jalāvilā (confusing to the confounded ones?)!

20. Be victorious, O Īśānī, O Śivā, O Śarvā! Be victorious always, O goddess adored with victory! Be victorious, O bestower of salvation; be victorious, O omniscient one; be victorious, O bestower of piety, wealth and desire!

21. O Gāyatrī, be victorious! O Kalyāṇī (bestower of welfare), be victorious! Be victorious, O Sahyā (the endurable one), O Vibhāvarī (the most excellent one due to brilliance)! Be victorious, O Durgā, O Mahākālī, O Śivadūtī (one with Śiva as messenger); be victorious, O invincible one!

22. Be victorious, O Caṇḍā (fierce one); be victorious, O Mahāmuṇḍa! Be victorious, O Nandā,the beloved of Śiva; be victorious, O Kṣemaṁkarī (One who causes welfare), O Śivā, be victorious, O Kalyāṇī, O Revatī!

23. Be victorious, O Umā, O Siddhi-Māṅgalyā (perfect achievement and auspicious one)! Obeisance to you, O Harasiddhā; be victorious, O Aparṇā; be victorious, O Anandā, O destroyer of the demon Mahiṣa!

24. Be victorious, O Medhā (intelligence), O Viśālākṣī (one with wide eyes), be victorious O Anaṅgā, O Sarasvatī, be victorious, O receptable of all good qualities! Be Victorious, O Āvartā, O destroyer of Asuras.

25. Be victorious, O goddess of perfect achievement by mere will. Be victorious, O sole beautiful lady of the three worlds !Be victorious, O destroyer of Śuṁbha and Niśuṁbha!

Be victorious, O Padmā, O Adrisaṁbhavā (born of the Mountain)!

26. O Kauśikī, be victorious! O Kaumārī! Be victorious, O Vāruṇī, O bestower of desires! Obeisance, obeisance to you, O Śarvāṇī; O Aṁbikā, be victorious, again and again!

27. Save us, save us, O goddess, save us who have sought refuge in you, O Śaraṇyā (One worthy of being a refuge)!

28. On being eulogized thus, O lady of excellent countenance, by all the Devas, the goddess manifested her own form that had illuminated the quarters.

29. After making obeisance to her, those Suras spoke to the goddess who dispelled their fear: "Kill the highly powerful Daityas named Bala and Atibala as well as their vast army. Save us from this great danger."

30. On hearing their words and after granting them freedom from fear, she assumed a wonderful form with three eyes and the Moon on the head.

31. The great goddess held different kinds of weapons and missiles and was riding a lion. She could be compared to a streak of a refulgent lightning. She had twenty arms and an excellent countenance.

32. Then Aṁbikā (the mother) roared loudly with repeated boisterous laughs.

33. On account of her terrible sound, the entire earth girdled by rivers and oceans quaked. The echoes filled the entire firmament.

34. Her breasts were protruding like mountains. She was like a beautiful woman. Like a woman she appeared to be distressed due to fear. The Asuras too with the four divisions of their army came there.

35. The Rākṣasas, Dānavas and Daityas who were dwelling in the nether worlds, who were well-known for their valour and resembled Kāla, Antaka and Yama (god of death) reached the place.

36. Crores of leading Daityas came there. Thereupon there started a great battle between the goddess and the Asuras.

37-39. The battle that enveloped the entire Cosmic Egg became the cause of sudden annihilation thereof. The goddess sportingly annihilated thousands of the Daityas. O goddess of Suras, thirty-three thousands of *Akṣauhiṇīs* (of foot soldiers) twenty-one thousand attendants and seven thousand eight hundred fast moving chariots were destroyed. The goddess thereby brought tremendous annihilation without the least agitation.

40. The entire battlefield was strewn with the bodies of the horses and elephants and the highly powerful Daityas killed by the goddess.

41. In the arena of the war, where headless bodies writhed and danced about recklessly, where the suet issuing from the bones caused a large slush, the energetic Niśācaras (Night-stalkers; ghosts etc.) wandered about.

42. In some places jackals, vultures and crows flew and fluttered and jumped about. The Niśācaras drank blood profusely and arrogantly ingratiated themselves. After propitiating their Pitṛs, they adored the sages too.

43. Many of them ruthlessly ate up elephants and men as well as the horses. They crossed the oceans of blood by means of chariots serving the function of rafts.

44 While the war was thus taking a more serious turn, with the groups of the Asuras agitating all round, the Mother Divine made her brilliant appearance there holding and wielding her bow, arrows, sword and trident.

45. She suppressed the arrogance of the huge tuskers; she thrashed the assemblage of the horses; she destroyed the armies of the demons and surveyed all round.

46[1]. On seeing the lady of exalted mind riding a great *Pretaka* (spirit, ghost) joined with eight lions, shining brightly and having refulgent splendour like a mountain, like a swan and resembling a bull, the Daitya warriors became furious. They rushed thereat roaring like rumbling clouds.

47. When they were killed, they shouted *"Hā! Hā!"* Some of the Asuras entered the sea. A few Dānavas went over the mountains.

48. Some of them had tonsured their heads and they stayed within forests as rogues. Some of them adopted the Vrata of the *Nirgranthas* (nude sages or Digambara Jainas) and preached sermons on the pious activities of merciful nature.

49. Some of them became afraid of (the goddess) for their

1. Seems to be a piece in prose and not a verse.

lives. They resorted to the life of heretics. They were fools engaged in arguments and disputations about basic or original causes. They had no cleanliness and they did not crave for anything.

50. They are indeed seen even today in the world of *Kṣapaṇakas* (Buddhist monks). Others are *Bhindakas* excluded from the scriptures of Śaiva cult.

51. Some of the *Kaulavratas* (persons practising the left-hand *Śākta* cult) are seen in this world by all the people. They are most addicted to *Surā* (liquor), *Strī* (women) and *Māṁsa* (meat). They follow the path of unfair activities. They are *Liṅgins* (Liṅga worshippers).

52. Many of them were sinful *Naiskṛtikas* (rogues, having no virtuous activities) too much addicted to tongue (gluttonous) and organs of generation (given to debauchery). Thus all connected with Bala and Atibala were killed by the goddess.

53. Then Aṁbikā (Mother Divine) came to Prabhāsa and settled there. The sin-destroying goddess was accompanied by sixty-four Yoginīs. In Prabhāsa she was well-known all over the world as *Balātibalanāśinī*.

The Devī said:

54. O Lord of Suras, do tell me the sin-destroying names of the Yoginīs mentioned by you as numbering sixty-four.

Īśvara said:

55. Listen, O goddess, I shall describe to you the great glory of the Yoginīs. It gives protection to everyone. It is divine and remover of great fear.

56-62. The first is Mahālakṣmī. Then come Nandā. Kṣemaṁkarī, Śivadūtī, Mahābhadrā, Bhrāmarī, Candramaṇḍalā, Revatī, Harasiddhi, Durgā, Viṣamalocanā, Sahajā, Kulajā, Kubjā, Māyāvī, Śāṁbhavī, Kriyā, Ādyā, Sarvagatā, Śuddhā, Bhāvagamyā, Manotigā, Vidyā, Avidyā, Mahāmāyā, Suṣumnā, Sarvamaṅgalā, Oṁkārātmā, Mahādevī, Vedarthā, jananī, Śivā, Purāṇānvīkṣikī, Dīkṣā, Cāmuṇḍā, Śaṅkarapriyā, Brāhmī, Śāntikarī, Gaurī, Brahmaṇyā, Brāhmaṇapriyā, Bhadrā, Bhagavatī, Kṛṣṇā, Grahanakṣatramālinī, Tripurā, Tvaritā, Nityā, Saṁkhyā, Kuṇḍalinī, Dhruvā, Kalyāṇī, Śobhanā, Nityā, Niṣkalā, Paramā, Kalā, Yoginī,

Yogasadbhāvā, Yogagamyā, Guhāśayā, Kātyāyanī, Umā, Śarvā and Aparṇā the glorified one.

63-69. O great goddess, thus I have enumerated to you all the sixty-four (Yoginīs).

Śarvāṇī will protect from all dangers like her own son, a devotee who devoutly eulogizes Caṇḍikā by means of this *Stotra* of divine features.

On the eighth, ninth and fourteenth lunar days, the devotees should observe fasts or take only a single meal, that too unsolicited. They should observe all restrictions and continue thus for one year or six months. They shall become Siddhas and Tattvacārins (observers of great principles).

For increase in welfare a devotee should worship the goddess by celebrating great festival during Aṣṭakā days, Manvādis (first day of Manvantaras) and in the bright half of Aśvayuk month.

A devotee of Durgā should hold the golden sandals of the goddess for the suppression of blunders and obstacles. He should also hold a dagger.

Those with Asura (Demoniac) tendencies who worship Aṁbikā by means of meat of beasts and liquor shall become Daityas enjoying prosperity and Lordship.

Those who adopt Sāttvika type of devotion attain *Devatva* (godhood).

70. Thus succinctly the sin-destroying greatness of goddess Balātibalanāśinī residing in the holy spot of Prabhāsa has been explained to you, O fair lady. It augments fame and facilitates the acquisition of all objectives.

CHAPTER ONE HUNDRED TWENTY

Greatness of Gopīśvara

Īśvara said:

1-4. Thereafter, a pilgrim should go to the excellent shrine of Gopīśvara, O great goddess. It is situated within a distance of three *Dhanus* to the north of Balātibaladaityaghnī.

It was installed by the Gopīs (cowherdesses) and it is destructive of sins. They had propitiated Maheśvara for the sake of sons. When adored, it bestows all the desires unto men. It bestows progeny also.

A man who worships the deity on the third lunar day in the bright half of Caitra by offerings of sweet scents and flowers, attains desired benefit.

Thus the sin-destroying greatness of Lord Gopīśvara stationed in Prabhāsa Kṣetra has been succinctly described.